**RACE
ON THE
LINE**

DUKE | Durham
UNIVERSITY | and London
PRESS | 2001

RACE ON THE LINE

Gender, Labor, and Technology
in the Bell System, 1880–1980

Venus Green

© 2001 Duke University Press
All rights reserved
Printed in the United States
of America on acid-free paper ∞
Designed by Rebecca M. Giménez
Typeset in Scala with Franklin Gothic
display by Keystone Typesetting, Inc.
Library of Congress Cataloging-in-
Publication Data appear on the
last printed page of this book.
Acknowledgments for the use
of copyrighted material appear
on page 371, which constitutes
an extension of the copyright page.

To my mother,

Dorothy Lee Jones

and to my dearest friend,

Mamadou Bathily

CONTENTS

Preface | ix

Acknowledgments | xiii

Introduction | 1

PART 1: THE BEGINNINGS OF TELEPHONY

1 "Hello Central": The Beginning of a New Industry | 11

2 "Hello Girls": The Making of the Voice with a Smile | 53

3 The "Ladies" Rebel: Unions and Resistance | 89

PART 2: THE DIAL ERA, 1920–1960

4 "Goodbye Central": Automating Telephone Service | 115

5 The Bell System Family: The Formation
of Employee Associations | 137

6 The Dial Era | 159

PART 3: THE COMPUTER ERA

7 Racial Integration and the Demise of the "White Lady" Image | 195

8 Black Operators in the Computer Age | 227

Epilogue | 258

Notes | 265

Selected Bibliography | 339

Index | 351

PREFACE

In the fall of 1973, I became disillusioned with a job in publishing that I had thought would provide an opportunity for me to express my creativity and advance my career. Instead, I found myself in a status-inflated, low-paying clerical job that brought little recognition and no respect. My decision to leave was sealed after my boss was insensitive enough to send me to cash her paycheck, which was more than twice the amount of mine. A few days after this incident, I visited my old school (Hunter College) where I discovered that a few days earlier one of my classmates also had visited—dressed in jeans, construction boots, and a toolbelt. She worked at the telephone company, repairing telephones. I thought that a job like hers would be a good one to have. I do not recall exactly what I told the New York Telephone Company personnel people, but I am sure that I said I wanted a job where I would not have to type. After a series of tests, I was offered a job as a "switchman." Although I had no idea of what "switchmen" did, I immediately accepted the offer based on the salary, which was significantly higher than what my publishing job paid. And typing was not required.

I had been a student/community activist, marched in countless demonstrations, participated in boycotts, strikes, and other job actions in different workplaces, and certainly considered myself a feminist. However, I was not making an overt political statement when I accepted this job offer. I did not realize that I was one of the first hundred or so women to enter the male-dominated field of telephone switching in New York City. At the time, I was conscious of my own resistance to "women's work," and I was vaguely aware of the AT&T case that had opened male-dominated work to women. But I certainly had not specifically connected my employment with the EEOC/AT&T litigation. Aside from women's general struggle for better jobs and pay equity, I made no historical interpretation of my individual search for challenging and higher-paid work. That would come much later—when I studied history.

After six months of training at a highly regimented telephone company school, I went to work at 140 West Street where I was one of four or five women among hundreds of men, mostly white. As crafts people (installation, repair, and maintenance technicians), we worked on the first ten floors of a 32-story building. Many top-level managers had offices in this building, but the vast majority of office workers and telephone operators were women with whom crafts people had hardly any contact. We did not even use the same elevators.[1]

On the job, men quickly made my women coworkers and me acutely aware that our presence was unwanted. In addition to the notion that this was a male job that women simply could not perform, men were extremely hostile over what they perceived as women taking jobs away from men with families, especially returning Vietnam veterans. Men expressed their anger verbally and in a division of labor based on sex. Experienced men rarely shared their knowledge with the women who had been schooled in theory but had no practical experience. As a result, women were assigned to the repetitive and less-demanding tasks. Generally, men were the troubleshooters who had opportunities to exercise their own initiative, judgment, and intellectual capabilities. Over time, a few women became "heavies" who could perform all aspects of the job, but most of us were lucky if we acquired competency in one.[2]

My personal history is typically and atypically a woman worker's experience. As with most post-World War II women workers, the best opportunities available to me were clerical. Even with a bachelor's degree, I ended up as a glorified clerk/typist. With the distinguished title of Assistant to the Managing Editor, I received very low pay in what was essentially a dead-end publishing job. On the other hand, when the telephone company hired me as a "switchman," I received credit for my degree (since this job required only a high school diploma), and my salary was more than 30 percent higher than what I earned in publishing. I had entered the world of white-male-dominated work where union protections provided a modicum of job security, higher salaries, a variety of benefits (medical, vacation, tuition assistance, savings plans), and a significant amount of control over the pace and methods of the work process.[3]

Over the course of sixteen years (1974–90), however, I witnessed many changes in what had been stereotypically either male- or female-dominated work. Men entered operating work, but there were significantly fewer operator jobs available. More women performed "craft" work, but they increasingly became ghettoized in the lower craft category of "frameman" (later frame attendant). In the higher crafts, men still dominated, but new technologies profoundly changed those jobs so that workers had few opportunities to use their intelligence in performing their duties. Modern supercomputers diagnosed troubles on their own and indicated to the "switchman" (now called switching equipment technician) where to change the circuit pack. Parts of the job had been chipped off and assigned to departments composed exclusively of women. These new clerical jobs paid 25–30 percent less than the switchman's job. They also mostly employed black women. Because of changes in duties, crafts people had far more contact with these women than they had with telephone operators.

This contact motivated me to study the history of women telephone workers. After a few years on the job, I had worked in several telephone buildings and noticed that many departments in the New York Telephone Company seemed to be segregated by sex and race. During the last twelve years of my tenure as a telephone worker, I also attended Columbia University as a graduate student. At Columbia, my training inspired me to search for historical explanations for what I witnessed as a worker. Why the low-level clerical departments at New York Telephone appeared to be dominated by black women intrigued me. Having observed massive technological changes in my own work process, I suspected that technological development greatly influenced the creation of these segregated departments. In my research I focused on telephone operators because the Bell System had employed hundreds of thousands of women as operators and invested enormously in the development of switchboards and other telephone-processing equipment that affected these women's work. And, after 1965, Bell companies in the largest American cities embraced a hiring policy that changed a white operating force into a mostly black one. Hence, this book explores the dynamics of race, class, and gender in a work environment that is constantly changing as a result of new technologies and broader social and economic forces.

ACKNOWLEDGMENTS

This book has come into existence as a result of enormous intellectual and emotional support. It evolved from my doctoral dissertation at Columbia University where James P. Shenton provided mentoring that was crucial to my continuation there. He, Elizabeth Blackmar, Eric Foner, and Joshua Freeman gave me critical guidance through the completion of the dissertation. I am immensely indebted to Elizabeth Blackmar, who has read countless manuscript revisions and never wavered in her belief that this book would come to fruition. Her support and criticism have been essential. Among the many friends and colleagues who have read either the entire manuscript or various chapters and given valuable suggestions, criticism, and ideas are Susan Porter Benson, anonymous Duke University Press reviewers, Ula Y. Taylor, David Montgomery, Bruce Sinclair, Joe W. Trotter, and Ilene Winkler. Before her unfortunate death, Sally L. Hacker gave me advice and encouragement to continue working on this subject. I want to express my unlimited gratitude to all of these scholars as well as to the numerous unnamed scholars and workers with whom I have discussed many of the ideas presented in these pages.

Distance and time constraints arising from my work schedules have made the cooperation of archivists and librarians pivotal to the completion of this work. I am particularly grateful to the ones I encountered during the course of my research. Mildred Daghli tirelessly assisted me in locating materials at the AT&T Archives when they were in New York City. Simultaneously, conversations with Alan Gardner helped me clarify the early history of telephony. More recently, AT&T Archivist Sheldon Hochheiser (at the Warren, New Jersey site) has made it possible for me to easily and comfortably review hundreds of photographs. Bruce Montgomery pointed me to important sources when the Communications Workers of America Archives were in Washington, D.C. Archivists at the Chicago Historical Society and the National Archives pointed me to sources I would otherwise have overlooked. Diana Lachataneré and André Elizeé at the Schomburg Center for Research in Black Culture also assisted me in finding sources that were not easily retrieved. At the New York University Tamiment Library/Wagner Labor Archives, Debra Bernhardt, Gail Malmgreen, Andrew Lee, and especially Jane Latour were extremely helpful in finding documents and giving me immediate access to newly acquired CWA materials.

At different stages of this project I have received invaluable research assistance from Fia Reavis, Phyllis Weeks, Anthony Fletcher, Jenny Radtke, William Cobb Jr., and Peter Hobbs. I want to acknowledge my appreciation for the many "favors" they responded to on very short notice.

I thank the Ford Foundation (Dissertation and Postdoctoral Fellowships), the National Endowment for the Humanities Schomburg Center for Research in Black Culture Scholars-in-Residence Fellowship, New York State/United University Professions Professional Development and Quality of Working Life Committee's New Faculty Development Award, the Professional Staff Congress of the City University of New York Research Award, and the City College Simon H. Rifkind Center Fellowship for the financial support they provided for the completion of the dissertation and the manuscript revisions.

I am ever grateful to members of my family, especially my siblings, Alonza and his wife Millie Brown, Oscar Green, and Wanda Brown for their help and encouragement throughout this process; and to Aunt Venus who in addition to having blind faith in her namesake, provided meals and house maintenance as long as her health allowed. My niece Samantha Green, nephews Oscar and Brian Green, and cousins Katherine Dunaway and Raycine Jones have all inspired me to be a good example when my own volition may have been otherwise. Of course, friends too numerous to name have also been essential to the completion of this project. Among them I owe special debts to Cleo, Jackie, Barbara, Laila, Darryl, Stephanie, Martia, Kathy, Sonali, Vaughn, Paulette, Bernadette, Rudy, and Shalaman.

I would also like to thank Rachel Toor for bringing my work to the attention of Duke University Press, where the editorial and production departments have worked tirelessly to get this book into print.

Despite these many debts, the contents of this book are my own, and therefore I am solely responsible for its strengths and weaknesses.

INTRODUCTION

This book is a history of Bell System telephone operators, their equipment, and their work processes.[1] It explores the convergence of gender, class, race, and technology in the workplace by analyzing Bell System research and development policies, investigating the way management organized work around new technologies, and identifying the personnel practices that shaped both the workforce and the application of new technologies. In this context, the study examines concepts relevant to the feminization of occupations, work and workplace organization, gender and racial segregation, skill definitions, the introduction of new technologies and their impact on the labor process, cultural factors influencing the dissemination of new technologies, and the ways in which workers' responses shape managerial goals.[2] Despite an extensive literature that describes even the most minute technological discoveries pertaining to the telephone, little has been written about how this technology affected women's work in the industry. This book aims to contribute to correcting this omission by analyzing the impact of technology on telephone women's work from the invention of the telephone in 1876 to the period immediately before the breakup (divestiture) of the American Telephone and Telegraph Company (AT&T) and its associated companies in 1984.

For this entire period, the Bell System was a leader in technological development and in hiring large numbers of women. Over time, telephone women's work process underwent a phenomenal transformation. The transition from electromechanical to computerized service continuously changed the telephone workplace, constantly creating new employment possibilities for women. From the time when women entered the telephone labor force in 1878, their numbers within the industry increased steadily. By World War I and up to the early 1970s, one-half of Bell System employees were women. Hence, the history of work particular to Bell System women offers an ideal case study into technological change and its effect on the nature of women's work. Although a case study, this book does not seek to separate the history of telephone operators from the history of all workers. Indeed, it illustrates how telephone operators' experiences exemplify and add to a number of theories relevant to the study of the entire American working class.

As it narrates the evolution of switchboard development, this book analyzes the history of telephone operators and, to a lesser degree, other clerical workers in the context of debates over the degradation of skills, job loss, worker's control, job segregation and segmentation, and race and labor/management relations. Race is highlighted among these issues, not to weigh or evaluate oppressions, but to show how race modifies the discussion of all workplace-related issues.[3] The argument is that race, class, gender, and technology do not simply converge in the workplace. Racial ideology actively shapes the interplay of these variables. For instance, this book reveals that during the first sixty years of telephony, skill was not defined only in terms of training and experience, but also as a matter of gender and race. Like waitresses, saleswomen, and a majority of clerical workers before World War II, white skin and an idealization of its meaning significantly determined skill for telephone operators.[4] In these occupations dominated by white women, the attributes associated with white skin implied innate characteristics that women of color could never possess. The importance of this point lies not only in the exclusion of African American women from the industry, but also in the impact of their exclusion on issues such as feminization and work segregation, worker's control, unionism, work segmentation, and the introduction and diffusion of new technologies.

The sexual division of labor and the job segregation that results from it are among the most significant issues for the study of women workers. Scholars attribute the origins of work segregation, unequal pay, and a lack of career opportunities to several factors. Among the important historical explanations for the sexual division of labor are the concept of women's work (work that flowed from women's domestic roles, required exceptional patience and nimble fingers, or was monotonous and/or repetitive), capitalism (profitability of low wages), and patriarchy (male domination).[5] The feminization of formerly male-dominated work includes more complicated explanations such as labor market changes (i.e., the availability of large numbers of educated women with few other opportunities); notions of women's passivity (that women were more easily controlled by managers and therefore less likely to organize into unions and participate in job actions); industrial structure (managerial insistence on a sex-segregated workplace); and technological degradation of male skills (craft work fragmented into small tasks easily accomplished by "unskilled" women).[6]

For most of their history, telephone operators fit the model that finds historical continuity in the sexual division of labor and the sexually segregated workplace. However, telephone managers initially hired native-born, young white girls as operators in the belief that girls were more patient and civil, not necessarily more docile. In this sense, the invention of the telephone opened work opportunities for women. In contrast to other industries, where managers replaced men with women as a method of suppressing wages, most of nineteenth-century men and women operators received the same meager wages. After the feminization of the job, the pay for women remained low compared to that of male telephone workers who had access to career ladders leading to higher pay. Hence, sex segregation among telephone operators had economic origins (to win customers), but the reduction of wages was not the most important one of them.

Race segregation complicates the study of sex segregation among telephone operators. The telephone industry constructed an image of white womanhood that excluded black women and simultaneously inhibited the development of a feminist working-class consciousness among white women. This book argues that white women's acceptance of a white identity in effect contributed to Bell System management's ability to control the work and the workplace. It demonstrates how executives used a paternalistic racial ideology as the most salient form of repressive control and how they introduced new technologies as a means of both repressive and nonrepressive control.[7]

Each major development in switchboard technology is analyzed with regard to whether it divided operators' skills into smaller tasks that required less skill, or whether the new switchboards augmented, broadened, and upgraded older skills.[8] The issue of workers' control is addressed by examining how the new switchboards changed pacing and methods in the labor process.[9] This study evaluates how each switchboard affected the operators' ability to use their own judgment and initiative in completing telephone calls.[10] Simultaneously, it assesses whether these technological innovations created new jobs and opportunities or simply displaced workers.

The wide array of telephone operators' responses to their segregated work environments, working conditions, and the impact of new technologies also form important parts of this analysis. Telephone operators, despite conforming to a management-imposed racial identity, refused to adhere to a model of passivity. Very early in their history, women operators overtly and covertly resisted Bell System attempts to mold them into obedience. As they worked, they found ways to subvert the innumerable rules and regulations designed to pace them. At different times they organized themselves and male workers into unions. In unions, these women fought against unfair company practices, and they battled to obtain representation in the union leadership, even when male-dominated unions resisted female participation and failed to represent women adequately. Although racial and gendered identities often modified their reactions, white and black operators challenged the repressive and patriarchal environments in which they worked.

In these environments, engineers developed new equipment and procedures for telephone service that were disseminated both to the larger society and within the workplace. Race and gender influenced these technological developments, not only in the sense that mostly white males had the opportunity to create these new machines and receive the major benefits, but because race and gender shaped the process of diffusion. For example, Bell executives had to disassemble the nineteenth-century servant image of the female operator that they had used to sell the telephone before they could automate telephone service in the 1920s.[11] Later, when computerized switching systems were developed, the racial composition of the workforce helped to determine whether these machines would be kept in larger urban areas or moved to the suburbs. Ironically, unlike the situation in some manufacturing industries, the availability of large groups of inexpensive labor (black or white women) did not inhibit the Bell System's enthusiasm for adopting new technologies.[12] Until very recently, engineers developed switching systems that tended to replace women operators, as the machines opened opportunities for men in supervision, installation, repair, and maintenance. Race and gender significantly differentiated the impact of technological development and diffusion on women and men workers in the telephone workplace.

Accordingly, this book traces technological innovations in telephone switchboards and switching systems that transformed operators' work in three distinct and sometimes overlapping stages. Improvements in mechanical and electrical devices characterized the first stage—mechanization (1878–1920). It simplified or eliminated physical tasks, making it possible to increase worker productivity and efficiency. During the second stage—automation (1920–60)—machines replaced operators for calls that could be dialed without operator assistance. Computerization (1960–80) completely transformed the operator's work process by eliminating the switchboards and the operating methods they required. While these stages occurred unevenly across the nation, they represent developments in the largest American cities.

This book is divided into three parts that illustrate these stages of development. Part 1, "The Beginnings of Telephony," opens by relating early corporate history and showing the importance of technological advances for Bell System's eventual domination of the industry (chapter 1). The history of switchboard development and the solutions to various service problems are discussed. Chapter 1 also describes the different operating methods used on the early switchboards and illustrates how technology reduced the amount of physical labor required to operate the more advanced switchboards. The elimination of operators or a reduction in the operating force during this period was not a primary objective. Faulty and unreliable equipment required the operators to appease customers by giving them "personal" attention. A distinction between the physical and the social skills of operating is thus made in this chapter. During the first twenty years of telephony, when the Bell System had to persuade the public to accept the telephone and when it experienced fierce competition from the Independents (non-Bell companies), managers recognized the operators' importance. In that period, executives acknowledged that they needed women operators to attract and to keep their customers.

Chapter 2 describes the feminization of the operating room, the creation of the "white lady" identity for operators, and early working conditions. The significance of race and gender to the definition of operating skill is analyzed in the context of company hiring, training, and discipline policies. Before the turn of the century, operators worked in a lenient and flexible work environment in which they had ample opportunities to use their initiative and judgment. Many former operators held positions of authority and responsibility at this time. By 1900, however, technical advances had standardized equipment and made it possible for the Bell System to provide a reliable service to its local customers.

A transformation in management objectives occurred. Nineteenth-century engineers designed new switchboards that often increased the number of operators or enhanced their skills, whereas in the twentieth century the Bell System waged a deliberate campaign to reduce their operating force and to gain greater control over the work process. From that time and throughout World War I, operators resisted Bell System attempts to control them. They spontaneously formulated demands that sought to correct the abuses of their work environment. However, their allies (male unionists and female reformers) misunderstood these demands and replaced them with more traditional trade union goals. Racial homogeneity, youth, women's work culture, and other characteristics contributed to the ease with which the first operators formed and joined unions, but their militancy and focus were misdirected by their acceptance of union structure and craft ideology. Chapter 3 analyzes the operators' resistance to management's attempt to standardize work methods and practices. During the World War I era, with the assistance provided under government control, management defeated independent unionism among operators but not without an intense and protracted struggle.

Part 2, "The Dial Era, 1920–1960," outlines the Bell System's suppression of operator militancy and the eventual rebirth of that militancy in the form of independent unions. Managers chose automation and representative associations (company unions) as tools to stifle independent unionism and thereby solidify control over the workplace. Gradually, over the long term, automation (chapter 4) would reduce the operating force. In the short term, employee representation (chapter 5) would dissipate militancy and restructure the workforce. Of course, operators cooperated, resisted, or quit as their circumstances allowed. The overthrow of employee representation and the rebirth of independent unionism within the context of the Great Depression, World War II, and its aftermath are charted in chapter 6.

Part 3, "The Computer Era," analyzes the disintegration of the "white lady" image and the entry of African American and other "minority" women into the Bell System at the time when computerization severely reduced the numbers of operators and degraded the work of other men and women. Chapter 7 depicts African American women's successful struggle to integrate telephone operating in 1944. The Equal Employment Opportunity Commission/American Telephone and Telegraph Company Consent Decrees and the unions' objections to them are detailed in chapter 8. Attention is given to the proposition that the Bell System administered both the EEOC Consent Decrees and the union contract clauses to the disadvantage of women and nonwhites.

In sum, this book contributes to the historical literature which argues that work degradation and deskilling are not inherent in new technologies. It asserts that management deliberately chose to develop and use technologies that would increase their control over workers. Yet when worker autonomy and initiative were needed to facilitate service and therefore increase profits, the Bell System showed flexibility in its work organization and in its application of new technologies. The more prevalent trend, however, has been toward the use of computers to monitor, measure, supervise, and replace workers where possible. Technological innovation has meant higher profits for the Bell System, but at the same time it has resulted in degraded and unrewarding work for the majority of Bell System workers—particularly women.[13]

PART ONE | The Beginnings of Telephony

The mammoth American Telephone and Telegraph Company
(AT&T) and its associated companies, formerly known as the Bell
System, evolved from a small, unincorporated patent association
formed in 1875 into a national monopoly that amassed huge profits and
dominated virtually the entire telephone service and equipment manufacturing industry by the eve of World War I.[1] From March 7, 1876,
when the U.S. Patent Office issued Alexander Graham Bell U.S. Patent
No. 174,465 for an "improvement in telegraphy" (the electric speaking
telephone) to the divestiture of AT&T in 1984, Bell interests focused on
technological development as the most important tool for achieving domination over the industry as well as over the workers. Consequently, the
history of the various company formations that eventually became the
Bell System is characterized by the tireless pursuit of new technologies
and machine innovations.

The first Bell companies faced a multitude of financial, technical, organizational, personnel, and industrial competition problems that needed
solutions before the companies could control the industry and provide
the kind of service that Bell and his colleagues envisioned. Technical
difficulties threatened to completely repel an already skeptical public, and
a constant shortage of capital to finance equipment development and
expansion plagued the new investors. Other inventors and even large
corporations ceaselessly encroached on the Bell patents, while trying either to take over the Bell companies or to steal the industry outright. From
Bell's point of view, government officials and regulations not only limited
Bell expansion but inhibited Bell defenses against its predatory competitors. Added to these external pressures, the Bell companies' own internal
structure lacked coherent organization and a consistent personnel policy.

From the beginning, managers faced these challenges by using technology to attract and direct investment capital, to defeat competitors, to organize production of telephones, telephone equipment, and service, and to reorganize internal corporate and personnel structure.

Bell Corporate Evolution and Development of Long Distance

After several successful experiments, the receipt of another patent (U.S. Patent No. 178,399 granted in June 1876), and the formation of the Bell Patent Association on September 1, 1876 (to obtain future patents), Alexander Graham Bell signed over his patent rights to the Bell Telephone Company on July 9, 1877.[2] This company established the important and fundamental Bell policy of leasing (not selling) telephones and telephone service, but the advancement of the industry required a more intense financial investment and a more complex organization.[3] After two years of experimenting with different corporate and licensing arrangements, in 1879 the first Bell trustees established the National Bell Telephone Company. Capitalized at $850,000 and incorporated in Massachusetts, this company absorbed the stock and rights of all other Bell companies, making it the most significant telephone company in the United States and Canada.[4]

The potential for high profits in telephone technology triggered fierce competition and patent litigation. Alexander Graham Bell had not been the only contender for a telephone patent.[5] Elisha Gray, who had received a patent on the very same day as Bell, signed his over to Western Union Telegraph Company. Western Union entered the telephone business in 1878. Armed with telephone patents, Thomas Edison transmitters (the best at that time), an established wire system, and huge capital resources, Western Union presented a formidable opposition to the National Bell Telephone Company.[6] Fortuitously, the invention of an even better (the Blake) transmitter in 1879 shifted the advantage back to the Bell company.[7] The Blake transmitter, along with other factors, persuaded Western Union to sell its telephones and patent royalties to the Bell interests, thereby giving Bell the patent monopoly for nearly fifteen years. After this agreement, Bell interests aggressively defended their technological superiority.[8]

They also quickly recognized their exalted position and their need to expand through greater capitalization. Under the provisions of a special legislative act, the American Bell Telephone Company (ABT) filed for its Certificate of Incorporation, on April 17, 1880, which empowered it to own stock in its licensed companies, including 30 percent of another corporation in Massachusetts.[9] By licensing small local investors, the Bell System induced them to use their money to finance the companies necessary for the proliferation of telephone use. And more importantly, ownership of significant percentages of the licensees' stock, as with leasing, gave the parent company control over the industry. In order to strengthen this control and to achieve equipment uniformity over telephone technology, American Bell Telephone Company purchased a majority interest in the Western Electric Manufacturing Company, transferred other manufacturing resources to it, and changed its name to the Western Electric Company (WECO) in 1881. The next year WECO became the sole authorized manufacturer of all Bell System equipment.[10]

The incorporation of the American Bell Telephone Company, the licensing of associated companies, and the acquisition of the Western Electric Company were cornerstones for a completely universal system, but long distance service, the most profitable part of the business and the most effective means of suppressing competition, required greater development. American Bell Telephone Company, under the capitalization permitted at that time by the Massachusetts legislature, could not afford the construction costs of the long distance lines to interconnect each licensee. When the legislature refused to raise the limits on ABT capital stock, the directors formed and incorporated the American Telephone and Telegraph Company in New York state as an ABT licensee in 1885. Free to construct and maintain long distance lines throughout the United States, Canada, and Mexico, the new company rapidly developed the technology that eventually resulted in communication between New York and San Francisco in 1915.[11]

Defeat of Independent Competition

Independent telephone companies had always existed, but Bell System patent infringement suits had limited their operations. After the original Bell patents expired in 1894–95, the entire industry experienced a period of intense competition. Independents had avoided direct conflict by opening exchanges in small Midwestern and Southern towns and in rural and farming areas. Using this strategy, they captured nearly 50 percent of the national telephone business by 1902 and maintained that position until 1907.[12]

Determined to conquer the entire field, the Bell System fought back. In many places, Bell companies changed a flat-rate charge to a measured one, expanded into suburban and outlying areas, and used their influence to bar bank financing and municipal franchises to Independents. AT&T refused to interconnect with them, refused to sell Bell equipment to them, consolidated their licensees into larger operating units, and resisted government intervention.[13] The most effective oppositional policy isolated the Independents by not allowing them to connect to Bell long distance lines. Thus, by manipulating technology, AT&T kept the Independents from making further inroads into the industry. To protect this advantage and to escape an attempt by the state of Massachusetts to regulate its stock prices, ABT transferred its stock to AT&T in New York City in 1899, making AT&T the holding company for the licensees, long distance carrier, WECO, and other Bell interests.[14] The Bell System had emerged.

Theodore N. Vail brought to this corporate entity the management "vision that finally ended the competitive era and created the unified organization capable of controlling and directing the whole industry."[15] Instead of refusing interconnection, he extended the policy, begun in 1902, of interconnecting with Independents not in direct competition with the system. Vail bought competing Independents wherever he could, and AT&T in 1909 gained a controlling interest in Western Union Telegraph Company.

Bell's rapid acquisition of Independents and its control of Western Union created a public uproar, which prompted complaints against AT&T to the Interstate Commerce Commission (ICC).[16] Agitation also was widespread for government ownership of the industry. In 1912, the ICC considered allegations that AT&T was in violation of the Sherman Anti-Trust law, and in 1913 U.S. Postmaster General Albert S. Burleson instructed post office officials to investigate the feasibility of administering telephones under his supervision.[17] To avoid the possibility of government ownership, Vail accepted regulation in the belief that he could direct its outcome.[18] In 1913, AT&T agreed to sell its Western Union stock, to stop buying controlling interests in competing companies, and to interconnect locally and for long distance with Independent systems that were compatible with Bell System equipment.[19] This public relations victory, known as the Kingsbury Commitment, made the Bell System appear highly conciliatory, while not restricting it from buying up noncompeting Independents.

AT&T's ascendancy resulted not only from owning the most advanced technology but from building the corporate structure that created the technology and organized the workers around it. As they defeated the competition, Bell executives took measures to reorganize the companies on a functional basis rather than a territorial one. In order to achieve national standardization of departments and technology, AT&T and each associated company formed three separate departments. The Plant Department carried out construction, installation, and maintenance of line and switchboard equipment. The Commercial Department's duties included billing, customer services, advertising, accounting, etc. The Traffic Department handled telephone service, operator discipline, and training. AT&T, in addition, established standards and procedures for the operating companies to provide uniform telephone service nationally.

The Bell System also adopted a more elaborate managerial hierarchy to enforce its standards and methods and to nurture experts in each field of work. The new policies redefined engineering work along plant, traffic, and commercial lines with an emphasis on advancing telephony through scientific research and development. A reorganized Western Electric handled equipment standardization and quality testing, whereas the new engineering departments concentrated on areas such as long distance development and switchboard equipment installation and maintenance.[20] The Engineering Department rapidly increased in size and importance.[21] Before this time, in order to sustain technological superiority, the Bell System had placed a priority on the acquisition of all new patents pertinent to telephony. Competition, however, induced the desire for independent internal research.[22]

Technological and organizational changes within the Bell System affected its major group of employees—telephone operators. Between the 1880s and the end of World War I, these forces transformed telephone operators' work and working conditions in major ways. Technological improvements in switchboards and transmission required different skills and tasks. In the midst of the competition, operators had to learn new operating methods at the same time that the pressure fell on them to deliver the quick service each consumer requested. Competition compelled the Bell System to tighten its discipline and seek methods to increase the number of calls an operator could handle. As with equipment, Bell engineers standardized operating methods and procedures subsequent to corporate reorganization. Hence, the labor process of operators evolved in concert with these developments.

The Labor Process

During the first two years of telephone service (1876–78), subscribers made connections simply by picking up the phone and talking directly to the person called (usually signified by the number of times a bell would be rung).[23] One wire connected each subscriber to the other (so there were as many wires as each subscriber had access to other people). Of course, this method of providing telephone service was chaotic, expensive, and unreliable because the subscribers were responsible for their own wires. Technical experts invented exchange systems and switchboards so that all lines would be wired into a central office, where they could be connected to other lines through the switchboard, thereby eliminating all except one wire (or later, a pair of wires) to the subscriber. Using a variety of skills, telephone operators, sometimes with the assistance of other technicians, made the connections.

In September 1878, Emma M. Nutt began working on an experimental basis as the Bell System's first woman operator at 342 Washington Street in Boston. Some forty-seven years later and nearly fourteen years after her retirement, she wrote an enduring sketch of an early switchboard and the major components of telephone operating skill:

> The switchboard extended nearly the length of the room, a space between that and the operator's tables for the switchman who answered the calls; he stood in front of the switchboard with several long cords hanging around his neck, on each end of which was a plug and another cord in his hand with a plug on one end and a telephone on the other. When a subscriber rang the switchman would plug in and, using the telephone as both receiver and transmitter, ascertain the name of party wanted (numbers were not used at that time). He would then take two of the cords from around his neck and connect the party calling and

the party called with the operator's table. There were seven tables arranged in a line in front of the switchboard one after the other A.B. C.D.E.F. and G. a chair at each table.

The tables were similar to an old style sewing machine. On each there were two black walnut stands or standards on one of which was a Blake transmitter in a walnut box, on the other . . . telephones. Along the front of the table there were I think three pairs of nickel strips and a cord to which was attached a jack with a push button on it. Directly in front of the operator resting on the back of her table was placed a "list board" on which was tacked a sheet of paper nearly the size of the board on which was written the names of the subscribers, they were written in red and blue pencil. The bells corresponded with the colors. Numbers were not in use then, the switchman called out the names of the party called and calling also on which strips he had put them. The operator after she had called the subscriber was supposed to listen to the conversation as much as possible to make sure the message went through correctly. If they could not hear distinctly or get the message correctly, the operator was supposed to transmit. When they had finished she notified the switchman and he disconnected the lines.[24]

Nutt emphasized both the "physical" and the "personal" components of skill used "to transmit" or to insure that each party communicated with the other.[25] Even though she worked on a switchboard that quickly passed out of existence, Nutt's recollections describe the core of telephone operators' labor process.

As switchboard technology developed, operators' tasks constantly changed to accommodate new switchboards and methods of operating.[26] However, certain fundamental mechanical manipulations and physical motions required to make these connections persisted. Like Emma Nutt, every switchboard operator recognized that a caller desired attention, answered, and received the request. On learning the called party's identity (numbers came later), the operator located the called party on the board (assuming this was a local call), performed a busy test, rang (even with automatic ringing she had to insert a plug), and connected the two parties. After making sure they were speaking, the operators continued to make calls for other subscribers while listening in (or, later, observing a lamp signal) to determine if the subscribers had finished talking or wanted further assistance. Finally, the operator disconnected the call by pulling down the cords, restoring the line to normal.

Aside from the mechanical manipulations involved in call completions, the operators' mental tasks became even more challenging as customers increased and switchboards became more complex. For instance, operators knew the prescribed methods for handling local, long distance, emergency, collect, and other types of calls. With the aid of black, white, red, and blue color-coded plugs, they learned how to recognize whether a line was permanently or temporarily disconnected, changed, or transferred. While the operators made that assessment, they also determined the type of service by the color of the subscriber lamp. They knew the rates for the various types of service: flat rate, measured rate, message rate, party lines, pay stations (nickel, toll, or long distance), and private branch exchange.

Routing procedures required the operator to master another large body of knowledge, especially in the bigger cities. In New York City, for example, one could not simply connect a call from Wall Street to Harlem. The call involved the assistance of one or two additional operators, either in the distant exchange or in a tandem office that interconnected exchanges. An experienced operator knew the various routes, including city districts and exchanges that could be used to complete such a call. Operators were aware of the number of rings for each situation, and they read cord and lamp signals to determine further rings, disconnects, new calls, busies, or "don't answers." This was basic operating; twenty-one other types of operators learned additional specialized tasks.

The operator's skillful physical manipulation of equipment connected two parties, but the operator's intelligence and personality transmitted the conversation and encouraged the subscribers to continue despite technically unreliable equipment. Bell telephone officials made a distinction between "getting people talking" and simply connecting two wires. In their infancy, telephones competed with the telegraph, the prevalent method of communication at the time, and telephone companies competed for hegemony over the entire business. Bell managers introduced a wide variety of conveniences called "personalized service" to capture the market and to simultaneously increase the number of subscribers.[27] Although available technology and market forces constantly revised its definition of personalized service, for most managers it meant "a service that

[was] not only as nearly perfect technically as possible, but that [was] as pleasing as possible to the telephone user."[28] Similar to department store managers and restaurant owners, telephone management needed skilled workers to sell their products.

In the early years imperfect equipment foiled connections and required "social abilities" and "emotional labor" to preserve subscriber loyalty.[29] Personality and intelligence, in this era, constituted the primary components of telephone operating skill. These characteristics were so important that managers replaced boy operators with young women within two years of the telephone's invention. Indeed, gender significantly influenced Bell management's and the operators' definition of skill (see chapter 2). Here it is important to make a distinction between skill defined as a craft and operating skill defined as the ability to perform a job. Crafts, usually associated with male-dominated work and therefore male-defined, were acquired through stages of training that may have included some schooling and an apprenticeship before the full title was bestowed. In contrast, as grammar school and high school graduates who had been socialized to "please" others, female operators achieved literacy and social skills before employment. Afterward, they learned how to use these skills in combination with mechanical switchboard operations on the job.[30] Gender defined both sets of skills and determined their social and economic value.[31]

Despite the job's classification as unskilled or low-skilled by male craft workers and other outsiders, pioneer women telephone operators were very proud of their abilities. Ellen Considine explained how she and the repairman replaced each other at their tasks when the need arose.[32] Mary Kennedy, the first New York City "girl" operator hired in 1878, claimed that when she was transferred to Jersey City as a chief operator she "had plenty of training in every kind of telephone work except climbing a pole." "Every Sunday morning," she said, "I had to test trunk lines, and report them for repair. Going up into a cupola to splice a cable or adjust a lightning arrester was part of the day's work." She spent more than thirty-six years in the telephone company.[33]

Margaret J. Lynch, who worked more than forty-six years in New York City, was promoted to chief operator in 1896 after ten years of service. She was "just tickled to death . . . because there wasn't any extra job there that I couldn't take care of." She recounted that she "used to sweep up, put coal on the fire, keep the records and do practically all the work on the switchboard . . . and the job of cutting in lines, testing, and pulling the heat coils and replacing them in the storms all fell to me. . . . I could cut off a wire, clean it and solder it up like a regular plant man. I cut in all the lines of that office for five years, and I never got one call for doing a poor job."[34] Although these exceptional examples of female competence disappeared as telephone service proliferated and male maintenance crafts grew, switchboard operating on the most basic level continued to comprise a multitude of methods and procedures that were truly baffling.[35]

Switchboard Evolution and Methods of Operation

Each major technological breakthrough in switchboard development involved an adjustment in how the operator made connections. The absence of a single large telephone manufacturer, and the consequent lack of uniformity in switchboards, immensely complicated these tasks.[36] The licensees had full authority to adopt whatever system met their specific service and regional needs.[37] According to Thomas D. Lockwood, each engineer brought equipment from his personal background to the switchboard he favored.[38] Consequently, early switchboards were littered with devices from the telegraph, burglar alarm systems, and law offices, all requiring distinct skills to operate.[39] An examination of the earliest boards and their operations demonstrates that intelligence, physical dexterity, clarity of thought, and some mechanical aptitude were required of the switchboard operator.

Commercial telephony began in New Haven, Connecticut, when George W. Coy, a Bell licensee, opened an exchange of eight party lines (each with a capacity for twelve subscribers) on January 28, 1878, for twenty-one customers. A subscriber placed a call on this equipment by rotating switches. First, he pushed a button that caused an annunciator at the switchboard to drop, informing the operator that a call was desired. In order to speak with the calling party, the operator moved a switch from its metal stud and rotated it "into contact with the metal strip beneath, which connected the operator's telephone." After learning the identity of the called party, the operator moved the original switch to its "off" position and then operated two more switches in order to make a connection with the signaling apparatus. To actually buzz the called party, the operator moved a lever from side to side and pressed a plunger the number of

1. This model of the first Commercial Telephone Switchboard was operated in New Haven, Connecticut, in 1878. Notice the levers and brass plate. This board had eight lines and twenty-one subscribers. (Property of AT&T Archives; reprinted with permission of AT&T)

times required by that party's signaling code. The operator then moved the signaling switches to their "off" position and connected herself with the listening strip to wait for the called person's response.

When the subscriber answered, the operator disconnected the listening switch and completed the call by rotating the switch arm contacts with the metal studs for each line. To determine the completion of a call, the operator connected the listening switch of either line and listened. If the call was completed, he moved the switch arms to their "off" position and connected the listening switches to their metal studs. At this point, the operator could restore the annunciators for each line by hand. Whew!!!!![40] For the operator's sake, it was a good thing that only two conversations could occur simultaneously on this board. Obviously, the Coy board presaged major switchboard development. Intensely active attempts to invent a board with a larger calling capacity resulted in countless designs.

With the introduction of brass bar switchboards in the 1880s, operators manipulated switches and metal plugs along brass cross-strips, which were sometimes the length of a room.[41] As many as three operators and a switchman made calls on these boards by yelling back and forth across the room to indicate the locations for connections and disconnections. This type of connection was often inadequate and required the operator to remain on the line to "coax along" the conversation.[42] For the subscriber, too, call completion required the manipulation of various

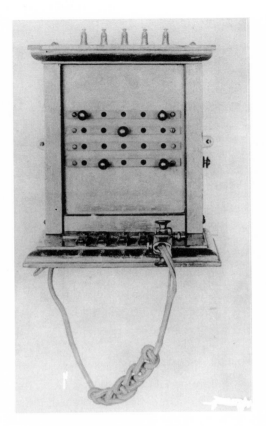

2. Another early switchboard made in 1879 by Charles Williams of Boston, the first Bell System telephone manufacturer. It has five lines with metal strips with holes indicating subscribers' lines. (Property of AT&T Archives; reprinted with permission of AT&T)

pieces of apparatus. At the customer's premises, for example, equipment included "a wall set containing a Blake transmitter, a toothed lightning arrester, a receiver hung on an automatic hook-switch, a pair of exposed call bells, a small magneto, operated by a crank, for calling the central office, and a battery, usually set on the floor, to supply talking current."[43] Despite the bulky equipment and the poor service it provided, these boards remained in use because they were inexpensive.

The Universal switchboard, first developed in 1879, improved on brass boards by rearranging the annunciators and the connecting and ringing strips. More significantly, each line ended in a "jackknife" switch that not only replaced the rotary arm switches of the Coy era, but simultaneously performed two other important functions: connecting and signaling. This innovation is believed to be "the first of many steps taken to reduce the number of motions made by the operator."[44]

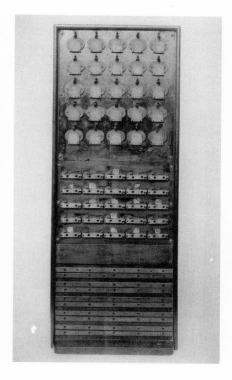

3. The Western Electric Universal Switchboard held twenty-five annunciators/drops on the top third, "jackknife" switches in the middle, and connecting holes along a brass plate on the bottom third. When the metal flap "dropped," it indicated to the operator which subscriber required service. (Property of AT&T Archives; reprinted with permission of AT&T)

Mechanization advanced rapidly after 1880 when the Western Electric Manufacturing Company introduced the board on which all future boards would be modeled. Appropriately named Standard, this board featured innovative new methods for organizing the work and new devices for accomplishing the connective tasks. The Standard board design included a key shelf, on which were mounted weighted, self-restoring cords; associated keys for answering and ringing; and "clearing-out" drops for the cords. A transmitter suspended above the switchboard (adjustable to reach the operators' lips), and a "receiving" telephone attached to an adjustable headband freed the operators' hands for switchboard operation.

These improvements enabled the operator to handle many more calls. The addition of a key shelf to the board furnished a better-organized workspace on which the operator could instantaneously ascertain the status of all lines and other equipment. Simply manipulating a key obviated all motions needed to plug and unplug cords. By a similar key manip-

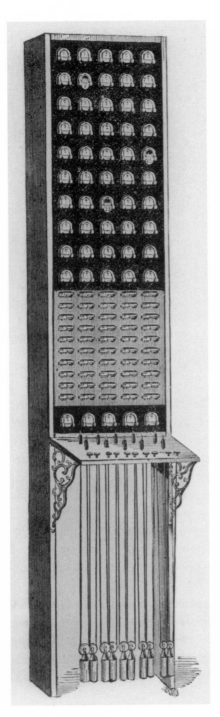

4. In 1880, the Western Electric introduced the Standard Switchboard, which had a fifty-line capacity with a newly added keyshelf on which were mounted weighted, self-restoring cords, associated keys for answering and ringing, and "clearing-out" drops for the cords. (Property of AT&T Archives; reprinted with permission of AT&T)

ulation, the operator could speak with a subscriber while another call was in progress.

No time was wasted untangling cords, since the weights pulled the cords back into their proper places. Clearing-out drops shifted some of the responsibility for disconnects to the subscriber, who had to depress the call key, which notified the operator by causing a shutter to be released. In sum, the operator learned to use new types of apparatus with the Standard, which significantly diminished physical exertion.

While switchboard operations became simpler, call completion and operator tasks became more complex. A single two-foot-wide Standard board panel had a fifty-line capacity that could be increased by installing more panels. For each operator, a typical arrangement consisted of three contiguous panels six feet wide and not more than three feet high.[45] Completion of some calls required only one operator situated at the midpoint of three panels. When both parties could not be reached by the same operator, the answering operator would connect the line to a trunk circuit and then communicate the need for assistance either by shouting to the distant end or by using another type of trunk designed for interoperator communication.[46] Eventually, managers introduced tickets to reduce the noise created by this procedure. Messengers picked up tickets placed by operators in special holders and delivered them to the appropriate board. A call going outside immediately local areas could require the cooperation of as many as seven operators, depending on the necessary trunking.[47]

Telephone managers called this system of relaying a call through a series of operators the "division-of-labor" method. Unlike some other industries where the division of labor often meant a specialization of tasks that reduced the workforce and the workers' knowledge of the job, the division of labor in nineteenth-century telephone operation increased the number of operators and their skills. This method required large numbers of operators because it divided the tasks and because switchboards expanded and developed in response to rapidly growing demand.

To meet the demand for telephone service during this early period of mechanization, the telephone industry introduced new technology with little regard for labor costs, control, or, to some extent, productivity. Management's emphasis on personal service lowered productivity by requiring operators to remain on the line rather than allowing the subscriber to call back if he encountered any difficulties. The work organization manifested in the division-of-labor method wasted operating time and equipment and did not give managers the control over the operators. At the 1887 Switchboard Conference, one executive argued against the division-of-labor method: "We were never able . . . to fix the responsibility for disconnections or to find why connections were not made, or why there were delays. One operator would blame it upon another."[48] In large exchanges where it took more operators and more time to complete calls and where operators generally received the highest salaries, Bell managers did not achieve any significant operating economy.[49]

The drive to capture the market had led the Bell companies to adopt new equipment with little emphasis on work organization. When it became clear that the telephone would be a permanent feature in American life, Bell System management focused on solving the problems of scale and expense associated with the switchboard. In 1887, Thomas D. Lockwood called on managers to determine which method of organization "is the most efficient; . . . the most prompt, and the more certain mode."[50] Thereafter, management began to correct its past neglect of work organization by using technological developments to change the process.

The Standard board only temporarily had solved the problems inherent in telephone expansion. As the number of subscribers increased and more Standard panels were added, call completion became slower and more prone to error. Operators made panel-to-panel transfers orally, by call circuit or by ticket. Elapsed time increased to as much as five minutes for a local call. Errors often caused the whole process to begin anew. For such mediocre service, call connections in the larger cities used more time and two to four times as many operators, who manipulated more equipment with less efficiency than those in smaller towns who handled comparable numbers of subscribers.[51]

This problem was even more complicated because the number of wires required to provide possible connections between all subscribers exceeded the number of subscribers in a central office. Some 250 subscribers, for example, could make a possible 32,640 connections for which wiring had to be made available on five panels through the office.[52] For the larger exchanges in the major cities, the "plant" costs rapidly became prohibitive. Low rates established during the era of competition with the telegraph also exacerbated the industry's economic problems.[53] These diseconomies of scale were known as the "big city" problem.

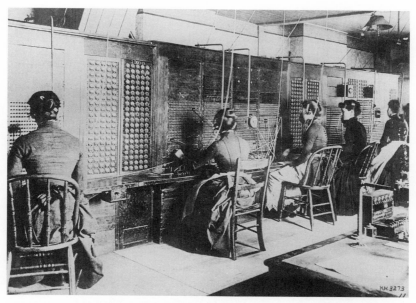

5. Women operators, Milwaukee, 1883. United-type switchboard with the annunciators on side panels between the boards. (Property of AT&T Archives; reprinted with permission of AT&T)

6. This 450-line board (with an additional twenty-five lines to the extreme left) serviced Charleston, West Virginia, from 1887 to 1896. Notice the operators' transmitters suspended from the boards and the magneto hand crank under the keyshelf. (Property of AT&T Archives; reprinted with permission of AT&T)

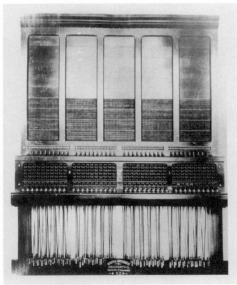

7. Law Board, St. Louis, 1888. Note the position of the plugs, cords, and transmitters. (Property of AT&T Archives; reprinted with permission of AT&T)

8. Multiple Switchboard, Cincinnati, 1885. The new, smaller "jacks" on the top portion of the board increased the capacity of the switchboard and put each subscriber within the reach of each operator. However, the operator was responsible only for connecting her fifty to one hundred subscribers on the lower part of the board to any of the others. (Property of AT&T Archives; reprinted with permission of AT&T)

Managers chose the obvious solution to low rates: they raised them. Companies, according to the specific conditions in their particular territories, based charges either on time, distance, or quantity of calls. Managers then sought to decrease the number of operators by changing work organization and methods. Finally, they pursued economy in equipment costs by developing more efficient switchboards. Eliminating the excessive transfers from operator to operator required with the Standard, managers adopted the Multiple board.[54]

Multiple switchboards placed every line in the exchange within each operator's reach, thereby eliminating most intraoffice trunking and lessening the excessive transfers required for call completion on a Standard. An operator answered only the subscribers on the answering part of her board, which usually consisted of fifty to a hundred unique to that board. One operator could now complete a call to anyone in the exchange without transfers. When smaller jacks, two-wire metallic circuits, and other improvements were applied to the Multiple, the Standard's 500 to 600 size limitation was extended to as many as 10,000 subscribers, and it occupied less space.[55]

The Multiple switchboard was important for two reasons. It alleviated many of the technical difficulties presented by the Standard. And it gave management greater control over the operators by facilitating reorganization of the work process. The method of organizing the work around the Multiple principle (one operator to complete a local call) also brought about more efficient and reliable service.[56] Statistics showed that fewer operators made more connections and handled more subscribers per board at an increased speed (see table 1).[57] John J. Carty, ABT manager, confidently assured his colleagues that he considered "the switch-board problem solved."[58]

Management's confidence in the Multiple was based on technical efficiency and work centralization, not a decrease in skills. Initially, Multiples expanded and enhanced both kinds of skills. Operators continued to physically manipulate the equipment and to give each subscriber personal attention by meeting individual needs. A new feature, the busy test (to determine if the line was in use) and the concentration of all subscribers within the reach of each operator were the two most significant changes in the physical operation of the Multiple.[59] Performing the busy test enskilled the operator by making it necessary for him or her to

Table 1. Number of Connections and Number of Subscribers
Per Operator

	1885	1886	1887
Average number of connections per operator			
Multiple	387	623	645
	8 Offices	8 Offices	18 Offices
Standard	268	309	350
	9 Offices	14 Offices	16 Offices
Average number of subscribers per operator			
Multiple	73	81	71
Standard	50	65	55

Source: Table 1 was created from reports made at the NTEA, 1885, p. 83, NTEA, 1886, pp. 58–59, and NTEA, 1887, pp. 42–43.

touch the plug to the ring of the socket (a motion not previously made) and to distinguish the busy click from other switching sounds. The Multiple also differed from the Standard in that the operator answered and connected all calls between the fifty to one hundred subscribers on her board and the rest of the exchange. In this arrangement, the operator needed to be familiar with the numbering patterns to immediately locate the called subscriber.

C. H. Wilson, assistant general superintendent of the Central Union Telephone Company, emphasized the personal aspect of the operating job in his arguments for the "centralization of labor" on a multiple board.

> one . . . ; the service has been made more efficient, more economical by dispensing with the extra operators employed for each connection; second, we are enabled to locate responsibility when there are complaints; and third, an operator becomes familiar with her subscribers, with the peculiarities of subscribers, and the subscribers become acquainted with the operator, and that goes a long way towards satisfactory service. Of course, our operators have all kinds of people to deal with, and when they learn the peculiarities of a certain subscriber they are enabled to treat that subscriber in a way which will satisfy him.[60]

The special ability to comprehend and appease the customer could not be mechanized.

Operators gained skills with the introduction of the Multiple, but in the process they lost some control over their work. They were more vulnerable to speedups and other forms of supervision because of the improved methods of monitoring created by the Multiple's reorganization of their work. At National Telephone Exchange Association and Switchboard Committee meetings, Wilson, Metzger, and other managers favorably mentioned the ability to ascertain responsibility for negligence or any other complaint.[61]

Despite making operators more accountable, the same problems of efficiency, economy, and reliability reemerged with the widespread use of Multiples. Even at the 1887 Switchboard Conference, managers feared that the Multiple could reach a size that extended beyond the operator's reach. Such a board would require wiring that exceeded the available conduits into company buildings, force a return to transferring calls from one section to another, and increase the risk of fire.[62] As the number of subscribers and wires increased, false busies, dirty jacks, and maintenance problems also increased.[63] Electrical complications caused individual lines to go out of service on every board and made it impossible to apply new inventions such as self-restoring drops to the Multiple.[64]

In 1891, the Bell System introduced the Branch Terminal Switchboard, which incorporated technical solutions that limited electrical problems to a single board.[65] In the essential tasks, operation of the Branch Terminal remained the same as that of other Multiples, with the exception that self-restoring drops eliminated the necessity for the operator to restore calling and clearing-out drops. They also provided certainty that the correct jack had been answered.[66] Yet even with new types of keys, drops, and jacks, the Branch Terminal Switchboard remained essentially a modified Multiple switchboard with many other electrical restraints.

The Common Battery Switchboard corrected the Multiple's electrical difficulties and facilitated the implementation of other major improvements.[67] Unlike all previous switchboards, these boards obtained their power from a central power source in a telephone building.[68] The Common Battery thus eliminated the messy batteries from the customers' premises, made the physical exertion of cranking up the generator unnecessary, and proved to be more reliable and less expensive.[69] Engineers first installed this system, using a non-Multiple board, at Lexington, Massachusetts, in 1893. Later, centralized energy and more reliable relays

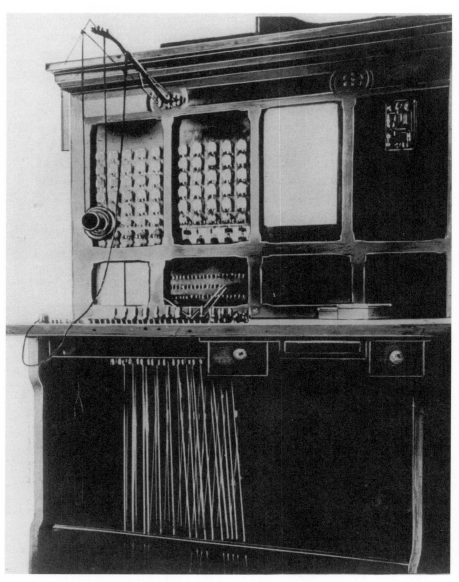

9. The first Common Battery Switchboard, a non-Multiple board, installed at Lexington, Massachusetts, in 1893. Note that the magneto crank is missing. (Property of AT&T Archives; reprinted with permission of AT&T)

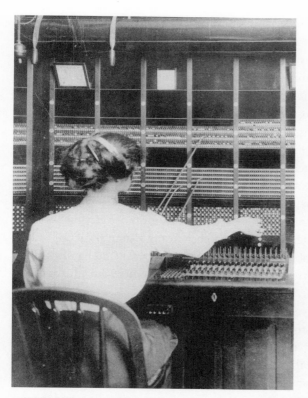

10. The Relay Switchboard with incandescent lamps that indicated to the operator when services were required. (Property of AT&T Archives; reprinted with permission of AT&T)

11. The Cortland Exchange in New York City, 1906, shows the size of a fully equipped Common Battery office. (Property of AT&T Archives; reprinted with permission of AT&T)

made possible the incorporation of small incandescent lamps on the switchboard for signaling purposes.[70]

These lamps alleviated several physical tasks because they completely replaced drops/annunciators, thereby opening more space on the switchboard and eliminating the "noise and confusion" created by "the falling and restoring of drops."[71] The operator no longer reached to restore the drops. She merely glanced at the lamps to determine if a subscriber wanted to place or disconnect a call, or needed further assistance. The automatic hookswitch, invented in 1877, in conjunction with the lamps enabled subscribers to signal their requests simply by lifting or resting the receiver. Thus, subscribers did not have to operate switches at their stations, and operators were relieved of the annoyance of trying to service subscribers who often left their switches in the wrong position.[72] Common Battery Switchboards transformed the awkward and haphazard operator's work performed on earlier boards into a more graceful and predictable set of tasks.

Common Battery Switchboards represent the era's single most important technical improvement and facilitated the introduction of labor-saving devices that reduced costs. Hammond V. Hayes, the electrical engineer, reported that Common Battery switchboards with automatic signaling had shown the "possibility of increasing the average speed of operating by at least forty per cent due to automatic signaling, and the use of a centralized battery for subscribers' instruments reduces the cost of battery maintenance by about seventy-five per cent, thus reducing the cost of service by a considerable amount."[73]

Nevertheless, ongoing electrical problems, excessive interoffice trunking, and increasing switchboard size and cost continued to plague the industry. In response, technicians designed the two-part No. 1 Relay Switchboard. They supplied one part (A) with answering jacks (to answer any subscriber) and trunks to transfer a call to another board either at that exchange or to a distant exchange. The second part (B) consisted of a Multiple board that housed the subscribers in that particular exchange. The No. 1 Relay Switchboard consisted of a common battery-powered board equipped with relay-operated incandescent lamps. Relay accuracy gave the board the reliability that the Branch Terminal Board lacked.[74]

While centralized power represented the era's single most important technical development, the No. 1 Relay Switchboard (the divided board) and its operation exemplified the era's most important development in work organization. The "A" operator answered all requests for calls and decided whether they should be trunked internally or externally. She communicated this information over a call circuit to the appropriate "B" operator, who indicated on which trunk the call for connection should be placed.[75] She answered any call within an exchange of more than 8,000 subscribers. By 1900, the larger cities like New York had generally adopted "A" and "B" board division, whereas smaller cities chose an "A" board that included the subscribers' Multiple, on which an operator could receive and connect calls internal to her central office.[76] With these developments, management initiated a work division and operating procedures that lasted into the early 1960s, when local service was completely automated.

Long Distance Switchboard Development

Long distance or toll service provided connections between large cities and their surrounding areas or between cities in different states. Subscribers paid an additional fee based on the distance and time of day involved.[77] This service lagged significantly behind the rapid progress made in local service. Consequently, long distance operators continued to work with faulty, unreliable equipment long after local systems had been perfected. Like local exchange development, long distance expansion depended on technological solutions to various problems in switchboard design, transmission, and operating methods.[78] Perhaps the most difficult problem faced by early long distance service involved transmission over significant distances. For example, in 1885, when local exchanges had become nationally dispersed, one hundred miles represented "the limit of distance" over which a "practical and profitable" business could be conducted.[79] Poor transmission because of noise unavoidable with the use of iron wires, and delays of up to forty-five minutes for completing a call, prevented the expansion of the service.[80] Toll service expansion, unlike local expansion, hinged on technical developments in transmission rather than switchboard designs.[81]

The technology to meet these demands was both more expensive and different from that used for local service. For the most part, subscriber station equipment, trunking, and switching apparatus and other equipment needed to provide local service did not work for long distance service. Until the mid-1890s, "high efficiency terminal equipment" required for long distances compelled the subscriber to use a "special telephone" to make a toll call.[82] Compatibility of equipment for both types of service had to be accomplished before a genuinely convenient long distance service could be offered.

Toll switchboards, tandems, and long distance offices did not exist before the late 1880s. The first toll service consisted of single lines or trunks connected through a special apparatus to a local switchboard. These systems had "disadvantages in delay, inductions, poor results, and limited facilities."[83] When increased traffic necessitated specific toll switchboards, technicians adapted local boards with long distance signaling and transmission apparatus for a single office. Apparently, the first office exclusively for toll and long distance service opened in New York City in 1889 with eighteen switchboard positions, on which the plugs "were said to have resembled clothespins and the drops as big as half dollars."[84] Though still a transformed local board, this equipment, located at 18 Cortlandt Street, marked the separation of long distance from local operating in large cities. Information gathered from the operation of these early toll boards led to standardization.

The Bell System developed the No. 1 Toll Switchboard, the very first standardized toll board, shortly after 1900.[85] With the exception of trunking, signaling, and transmission modifications made to accommodate changes in operating methods, the No. 1 board remained the equipment of choice until the mid-1920s when AT&T introduced the No. 3 Toll Switchboard. It, in turn, became the model for toll boards used during the remainder of the manual toll era.[86] Toll board development closely paralleled local development and progressively incorporated all advanced local switchboard technology (including Multiple and Common Battery boards, lamp signals, and various automatic devices) and methodology adaptable to toll service.[87] The expansion of long distance service occurred after local switchboards had been perfected; hence, toll boards did not change drastically during the manual period.[88] For this reason, toll switchboard development does not offer explanations for changing operating methods in the same way that local switchboard development does for its operation. Real transformations in the long distance operators' work resulted from changes in operating practices, not from switchboard design.[89] Like local switchboard design, long distance boards in many instances accom-

12. New York Long Distance switchboard, circa 1892. The recording board, the official board, and the local board are shown. (Property of AT&T Archives; reprinted with permission of AT&T)

modated the physical person as well as innovations made in operating techniques.

Long Distance Operating Methods

In contrast to local operators, long distance operators experienced a consistent increase in their skills during the manual era. Long distance operators facilitated speech over inadequate and unreliable equipment long after the major problems in local service had been solved. Under these irregular conditions, operating practices could not be standardized. Consequently, long distance operating retained more opportunities to exercise initiative and judgment than local operating because of special situations that could arise on long distance calls. A. S. Hibbard, Superintendent of the Wisconsin Telephone Company, noted that in the earliest years of long distance telephony "one of the most important features is the attention and cooperation of an intelligent operator . . . particularly necessary in making prompt connections and disconnections, and also in what is called 'getting the parties together.' "[90] Furthermore, in this period of noisy wires on which subscribers heard "the croaking of bull-frogs and the singing of the birds," Hibbard claimed that "it has fallen to the lot of the toll-line operators to educate the public in the use of long lines, and it is only after very many admonitions to 'stand closer to the instrument,' 'talk a little louder,' and 'go ahead,' that the present proficiency(?) has been reached."[91]

Toll development, like that for local telephone exchanges, initially emphasized savings in equipment rather than an elimination of operators. Undoubtedly, from the point of view of service and economy, managers wanted to reduce the number of operators; and they did so whenever it could be done without seriously disrupting service. However, savings from the elimination of operators only partially motivated the drive to reduce the number of operators involved in long distance call processing. Indeed, some methods introduced more operators into the process, and most increased operators' skills.[92]

Distance and "time of usage" usually determined long distance operating methods, which varied with the transmission quality of long distance circuits. Ordinary traffic operators or special toll operators completed most toll and short haul calls, depending on the distance and arrangement of circuits between the two points. Operators for AT&T Long Lines completed calls between associated companies and distances greater than a hundred miles.[93] Efficient operators knew the peculiarities of various routes and were familiar with both "personal" and technical methods of overcoming any difficulties that would prevent "getting the parties together." They knew how to coax the subscribers into conversation as well as how to change circuits when transmission problems arose.

Long distance operators not only followed the prescribed procedures for call completion, but they decided what set of procedures to follow in each situation. The complexity of long distance operating and the opportunities for the operator to use her own judgment were so numerous that standardized routines served as guidelines rather than as inflexible rules.[94] Of course, the operators did not ignore the procedures designated for specific situations. The Bell System aimed for standardization at all times, implementing an enforcement apparatus to insure that company routines were closely followed.[95] However, because of the diversity of locations and subscriber demands, the long distance operator continued to give "personal" attention to each call throughout the manual toll era.[96] Unlike the local operator, who was reduced to simply answering "number, please," the long distance operator had more freedom of expression and conversation with the subscriber, even when she had to use some prescribed phraseology.

Before she connected a call, an operator had to decide how to dispose of it "upon finding that the telephone of a party called for [was] not equipped for Long Distance service, or if she ha[d] reason to believe that the service from it [would] not be satisfactory."[97] An outward operator also had the responsibility of deciding to exceed the time allowance (two minutes for a direct circuit or five minutes for a circuit switched through tandems) for holding a toll circuit if a delay occurred. The manual instructed her "not to exceed the time allowance without authorization, except when she is reasonably sure the completion of a call-attempt can be hastened, and waste prevented, by holding the circuit slightly over the time allowance."[98] Appointment calls, delayed calls, messenger calls, busy circuits, particular party calls, and others allowed inward, outward, and tandem operators some flexibility under the rules.

However, management, when possible, severely limited operator discretion in other types of operating. Job descriptions confined recording, information, directory, and rate and route operators to set procedures.[99] Each operator learned an "authorized code" of abbreviations so that every ticket would be filled out in the same way and therefore understood by any operator who had to use it to complete a call.[100] Instructions ordered the information operator to "familiarize herself with, and be governed by, the instructions regarding rates and charges and the use of franks, coupons, and card passes in payment of charges as contained in the Tariff and Route Book, so as to be able to answer requests from patrons for information concerning their use." No deviation on rates was allowed, even though an outward operator could reduce the time for which a subscriber paid.[101] All long distance operators had limited time to answer signals and preset time allowances for each step in the operating procedure. Though more lenient than the 3.5 seconds required for local answers, standardization had narrowed long distance answers to fifteen seconds by 1910. Enforcement varied according to the workload.[102]

Unlike local service, which strove to meet demand, long distance circuits cost too much to provide enough circuits for peak use. When these circuits were unused, too much idle time would elapse.[103] The Bell System solved this problem in two ways: by offering a delayed service on a first-come basis, and by offering long distance service at a lower rate during off-peak hours.[104] Throughout the manual toll era, Bell System engineers searched for operating procedures that would decrease the delay for the subscriber and the amount of unpaid time a long distance circuit would be held.[105] To this end, routine procedures for person-to-person, station-to-station, messenger, appointment, pay station, collect, and other kinds of calls developed to standardize rates. Specific routines for tandem connections, busy numbers, unanswered numbers, numbers not provided, unavailable called parties, unavailable circuits, and many other situations helped to achieve maximized circuit use.[106]

The first formalized long distance operating methods specifically addressed charging, timing, and routing procedures necessary to all types of toll calls. When management installed the first toll board at Cortlandt Street in 1893, J. J. Carty devised a "recording system" that diverted the timing, charging, and routing of the call away from the "A" operator toward several other operators, each of whom performed special functions. In addition to the "A" operator at the local caller's end, and the local "B" operator at the called party's end, recording, distributing, information, appointment, messenger, Morse down, inward and outward toll line operators could be involved in a single call depending on the distance, method of operation, or status of the called party's line.[107] The two-ticket procedure required that both recording and distributing operators make tickets while establishing a connection. On disconnection, the outward operator, if she had no calculagraph (automatic timing device), wrote the completed time on the ticket and calculated the cost of the call based on rates she either held in the bulletin at her position or that she received from the rate and route operator.[108] This division of labor freed the toll line operator of all responsibilities except for making connections, which "enable[d] her to work with more certainty and very much more expeditiously, thus increasing her load and rendering her trunk line plant more efficient." The recording method minimized errors that resulted from passing numbers to each other, and the call back procedure prevented thieves from charging calls to another subscriber's number.[109]

The two-ticket method exemplified only one solution for handling different calls and situations that confronted long distance operators. Many versions of the two-ticket method dominated the early years of standardization because tickets at both ends effectively confirmed the accuracy of charges. By the turn of the century, however, it had become clear that this method "resulted in a duplication of work and an unnecessary use of circuits" and therefore required modification.[110] In 1905, management introduced the single-ticket method ("Method 103"), which could increase "the number of messages handled per circuit per day . . . about 25 per cent. and the operator cost reduced 25 per cent. to 33⅓ per cent."[111] Between 1900 and the early 1920s, experimentation led to the adoption or abandonment of several other operating methods. A reduction in the number of operators to complete a call and a reduction in the unpaid use of toll lines remained the aim of all Bell System experiments in toll service.[112]

In the 1920s, AT&T successfully tried and adopted two methods that would be used until the automation of long distance—Straightforward trunking and Combined Line and Recording. Straightforward trunking eliminated call circuit congestion among "A" operators, who competed for the same call wire by providing individual trunks to the distant "B" position over which the "A" connected the calling subscriber to the "B" operator and passed to her the called party's information at the same time. To accelerate the service even more, management introduced a "restricted repetition" practice, whereby the "A" operator no longer repeated the number back to the calling subscriber but repeated to the "B" operator within the hearing of the subscriber who could correct an error. Straightforward trunking drastically reduced the errors that occurred when outward operators passed numbers through tandem operators. Despite increased equipment costs, management estimated that the Bell System accrued an annual $5 million savings as a result of the increase in operators' loads from Straightforward trunking and "restricted repetition."[113]

By 1925, toll service had become profitable and efficient, with operators completing 70 percent of suburban and short haul calls within 1.25 minutes.[114] However, each long distance call continued to take from seven to fifteen minutes to complete. Eight operators, and sometimes a messenger, were needed to complete indirect calls through two separate tandems (see table 2). In order to overcome this deficiency, managers

Table 2. Classification of Toll Traffic (1926)

Method	Yearly Calls	Approximate Revenue	Average Speed
A-B Direct Trunk	410,000,000	$ 50,000,000	35 seconds
A-B Tandem	100,000,000		55 seconds
Two-number Toll Board	40,000,000	10,000,000	75 seconds
Regular Toll Board	235,000,000	140,000,000	7 minutes
Longer Haul (more than 250 miles)	5,000,000		12 minutes
	790,000,000	$200,000,000	2.6 minutes

Sources: K. W. Waterson, " The Functions and Management Problems of the Traffic Department," paper presented at the Bell System Educational Conference, June 1926, p. 59, fig. 6; Waterson, "Brief Review of Traffic Results since Last Conference and Outline of Present Problems," paper presented at the Bell System General Traffic Conference, June 1925, p. 6.

introduced the Combined Line and Recording (CLR) method, "a radical change from previous methods."[115] Using this approach on a call for which the subscriber provided the distant number, local operators connected subscribers directly to the CLR operator, and the subscriber, not the "A" operator, gave the information to the CLR operator, who recorded it and processed the call as the subscriber waited on the line. Operating positions using this method were arranged so that any CLR operator could connect a call to any place. CLR operators were not specified by location, as in other methods.[116] CLR eliminated the recording operator along with directory and other time-consuming distribution procedures that halved the average time needed to complete a call on toll boards.[117] More than 80 percent of the calls handled using CLR were completed within two minutes, compared to 20 percent for other methods.[118]

From the company point of view, CLR met "traffic rushes," efficiently used circuits, and had "some potential economy and the possibility of speeding up and toning up toll board operation in a manner approaching local operating."[119] Managers expected an operating savings of $1 million annually. By the spring of 1927, "195 out of the 267 largest toll offices" had been converted, and work had begun on all of the remaining ones.[120]

According to the Chief Engineer at the time, "no change of the magnitude of this one has been made as rapidly as the introduction of the CLR method."[121]

This rapid national toll transformation involved significant technological developments, but it was the revision in work organization and methods, not the technology, that revolutionized long distance operators' work. CLR concentrated a variety of operating jobs into a few highly skilled operating jobs. The magnitude of the task of retraining operators is indicated by AT&T's first issue of the "Combined Line and Recording Text Book" in which forty-one lessons detailed every aspect of the work.[122] CLR training made both recording and outward operating interchangeable. Additionally, all CLR operators learned how to use bulletins and booklets to obtain route and directory information. Where automatic exchanges existed, operators also studied special procedures for calls that originated in those offices.[123] CLR perfected operators' skills to the point where efforts to automate became stronger because the time limitations imposed upon the process by making a ticket, and speaking to another person could not be reduced any further. When long distance service became automated, the Combined Line and Recording method, in a modified form, had become the only method for handling long distance calls.

Operator and Switchboard Compatibility

In the first decades of telephone industry evolution, managerial decisions about switchboard development and operating methods were influenced not only by efficiency, reliability, and cost of equipment, but by how well the operator could provide service using the available equipment and methods. Operators' productivity, comfort, and body size influenced engineering designs and executive choices in telephone equipment. Managers frequently discussed human and machine compatibility in the context of the operators' workload.[124]

At a Switchboard Committee meeting in New York City during July 1891, Thomas D. Lockwood remarked that "it is not easy to separate the operator from the switchboard . . . , as whatever it may be the duty of the operator to do, it will be the duty of the switchboard to provide means for."[125] Later that year, Edward J. Hall, concerned about unnecessarily complex equipment, argued against making a two-point "busy" test for the reason "that you are charging an operator with some additional duty . . . , and that means additional strain on the operator."[126] Lockwood agreed.[127] The debate concluded with the committee's rejection of the two-point test.

The significance and, to some extent, the sincerity of managers' concern about operators' reach, back strain, and other pressures is palpable in the outcome of a project designed specifically "to facilitate the operator in making her connections and reading the numbers opposite her."[128] At the October 1891 Switchboard Committee meeting, executives decided to construct and install an experimental horizontal board. They wanted to determine how the operators' knees would be affected, whether this change in construction would affect operator clothing, whether two, three, or four operators could be placed at the board, and, if so, at what point they would interfere with each other's work.[129] Managers rejected the horizontal board after Boston operators complained that they could not see or reach the drops without difficulty in standing or sitting, for their cords became entangled and disrupted the work.[130]

Operators' reach, size, and comfort affected the design of successive switchboards and other apparatus. By 1880, an operator's reach had been established as two feet wide at varying heights to a maximum of three feet.[131] One manager argued against any board that would cause the operators to "reach further than half way in front of the operator on either side" or "rise from her chair," as the "side reach is more of a strain to the operator than the vertical reach."[132]

Even after switchboard development had stabilized, AT&T Chief Engineer J. J. Carty found it necessary to remind the associated companies that "it is upon the method of working which must be followed by the operating force that, in the last analysis, the design of the switchboard so largely depends." "In planning switchboards and their method of operation," he continued, "it is our constant endeavor to design and organize the system so as to simplify and make more easy and effective the work of the operator, always having in mind the requirement of the service which must be rendered to the public."[133]

Although switchboard design occupied the greater part of engineering attention, extensive research into such items as switchboard platforms, operators' chairs, foot rails, and transmitters also busied engineers.[134] Indeed, operators' complaints compelled engineers to make major ergonomic changes in their work space. Engineers studied women's heights so they could design chairs that provided "the proper reach for opera-tors."[135] They also considered building platforms so that operators would not have to stand to reach the highest point on an adjacent board and "in order to provide ample space for the supervisors when patrolling their sections." Uncomfortable chairs created only one source of complaints for operators, who wore heavy headbands (receivers) and/or breastplates (transmitters) until the early 1940s.[136]

Before 1900, much "time and money" had "been expended . . . to devise a transmitter which could be worn upon the operator's person." Several licensees tried a lightweight breastplate used in London, but "found that the operators became weary by even this light weight."[137] Observing that a new brass transmitter caused moisture problems, soiled operators' clothes, and reflected into the operators' eyes, causing head-aches, McBride recommended that a dull surface be substituted and some form of antiseptic be administered to keep mouthpieces clean.[138] Whether it was to make the operator comfortable for humane reasons or to get more work out of her, the person of the operator had to be consid-ered in developing new equipment.

Origins of Traffic Engineering and Work Distribution

Switchboard improvements represented the major focus of Bell Sys-tem engineers and managers, but they also searched for other ways to profitably provide efficient and reliable service. Proper administration and utilization of equipment sometimes brought results as favorable as tech-nological breakthroughs. Experts systematically gathered and analyzed statistics to maximize switchboard capacity by a more equitable redistribu-tion of work.[139] For instance, the "peg" count, introduced in 1892, com-piled "traffic" statistics. This study required each operator to count and record every call regardless of destination on a specified day each month. Engineers analyzed summaries of these records from each associated company to determine the size of the operating force, the size and dis-tribution of the operating load, and the need for additional equipment.[140]

At the Switchboard Conference in 1887, managers proposed that "if in any central station a certain number of lines are peculiarly and exceed-ingly busy, they should not be grouped together and assigned to one operator."[141] In 1891, A. S. Hibbard developed a Main Distributing Frame (MDF), which redistributed the most active wires evenly throughout the exchange as they entered the central office. E. M. Barton later designed the Intermediate Distributing Frame (IDF) to evenly disperse high-volume subscribers among operator positions.[142] By October 1891, the largest exchanges, especially the new ones, were equipped with IDF's, which management praised as a mechanical means to divide operators' work equally and simultaneously to provide subscribers with better service.[143] Officials claimed that these methods accurately measured equipment performance and were important in predicting future business needs. For the operators, however, the IDF and the "peg" count were harbingers of technological speedups, increased monitoring, and the opportunity to otherwise degrade operators' work.[144]

Technological Surveillance and Other Enforcement Methods

As the 1890s waned, Bell System managers expanded their focus to embrace methods for controlling and monitoring operators. Effectively, the major switchboard problems had been solved, and the public demand for telephone service was still growing. Competition was at its peak. To prevail, the Bell System needed to establish discipline and control in the switchroom. The "peg" count and other statistical data set performance standards by which operators could be disciplined, while technical and other means provided enforcement.

New technology not only enabled fewer operators to handle more calls quickly, but it provided the means of surveillance for insuring that operators worked to the full capacity of the various switchboards.[145] The installation of a "pilot" light at the top of each switchboard that would activate in conjunction with the subscribers' connect or disconnect signals exemplifies one of the earliest technological methods of control. The pilot light glowed as long as the signal remained unanswered, indicating to the monitor a "neglected or disregarded" subscriber.[146] Engineers further increased the operator's productivity by using the rewiring capabilities of the intermediate distributing frame and the secret monitoring devices it facilitated.

Operators experienced several types of surveillance simultaneously. From the Monitor Operator's desk, usually situated directly behind the line operators, monitors "listened in" to insure that operators followed correct operating procedures. In "special tests," monitors randomly called operators to time their speed of answer. Sometimes companies even used subscribers to initiate calls to test for operator courtesy and speed of answer.[147] Companies also employed "service testers" to call operators from public phones and subscriber lines to assess the quality of the service.

Service Inspectors with stopwatches timed "speed of answer" and "speed of handling calls," which included the time elapsed before an operator gave a "busy" or "don't answer" report. They also noted on a detail sheet such irregularities as improper answers and repeats, cutoffs, calling errors, and failure to perform "busy" tests. Under the "remarks" column, the inspectors would note "impolite or unnecessary remarks made by operator," "words used before disconnecting," "operator listens in on conversation," etc. Management rationalized their extreme measures by stating: "Service can be maintained at a high standard of efficiency only by means of a continuous system of inspection. . . . In fact, to maintain good service, it is advisable to have some portion of the traffic under observation at practically all times."[148]

Codification of Procedures and Loss of Autonomy

If operators were going to be observed at all times, they would have to know their responsibilities. By the early 1890s, associated companies began to print rule and instruction booklets to insure company-wide methods of operations. These new codes aimed to create a national operating force capable of communicating in common language and practice with any other operator in the system. Managers wanted firmer control over a workforce that could be moved around without retraining. Surveillance and codification of operating rules facilitated the standardization of work practices required by a company set on monopolizing telephone service. Before they concentrated on the operators, executives standardized managerial responsibilities.

The Central Union Telephone Company of Chicago codified its "rules and instructions" in 1888 when it printed a rule booklet that said little about employee discipline but outlined each manager's job.[149] The Delaware and Atlantic Telegraph and Telephone Company expanded and detailed this description in its 1890 "Rules and Regulations":

A good manager of a Telephone Exchange has business tact, is of industrious, sober habits and courteous in his manners. A proper fulfillment of his duties calls for the exercise of all a man's faculties. The conduct of the business in its various relations, in the proper management of employees; the courteous and judicious dealing with the public in obtaining subscribers, meeting complaints and collecting bills; the thorough and workmanlike construction of new lines; the watchful keeping [of] the plant in good condition; the careful maintenance of perfect service, orderly book keeping, and prompt and correct reports, . . . A prompt compliance with all rules and orders is expected of every manager.[150]

To enforce the desired behavior, the pamphlet stated that the managers' "books must be always in readiness for inspection at any time" without prior notice.[151] Executives used this model to cultivate, monitor, and control lower-level managers. At the same time, upper management instituted a more distinct hierarchy to enhance the image of authority and to distance the managers from the operators.

This goal necessitated differentiation between the blurred responsibilities of Chief Operator and Manager. A new hierarchy placed a Monitor Operator (who listened in directly on operators' work) and the Chief Operator between the regular operator and the Office Manager. Kansas City operators, as early as 1887, were supervised not only by monitors and chief operators but by "floor walkers" who paced up and down the room "watching operators in their conduct of the service." Already, these operators had been instructed to respond to specific situations with the "same language" or predetermined phrases.[152] In the mid-1890s, Bell managers revised the Chief Operators' job so that she (manuals after 1900 almost always referred to the chief operator as "she") was no longer directly responsible for supervising the operators.

Management created a special supervisor title expressly for the purpose of operator discipline.[153] The supervisor usually watched a group of nine operators. She stood directly in back of her group to insure that they delivered prompt, courteous, and accurate service without holding any conversations with their coworkers or the subscribers. Male managers retained authority and responsibility for running the exchange.[154]

As executives established and clarified the hierarchy, they also incrementally standardized operating practices. Chicago's Central Union Telephone Company's "Rules and Instructions" (1888) made no reference to operators except in the general rule "to be uniformly courteous and obliging."[155] In 1890, the Delaware and Atlantic Telephone & Telegraph Company's "Rules and Regulations" contained only two specific instructions regarding operators: operators needed a manager's permission to be absent from the office, and, equally important, operators were forbidden to converse with subscribers.[156]

However, the New York and New Jersey Telephone Company's "Instructions for the Guidance of Employes" dated January 1, 1893, included among dozens of other rules twelve specific "Duties of Operators." A significant shift is evident in this set of rules. One new rule instructed operators to use "only the words 'What number?'" when they answered a call.[157] In essence, this rule forbade all amenities formerly exchanged between the operators and their subscribers.[158] The era of the friendly operator who gave information, exchanged gossip, and worked at her own pace was in decline.

Rule No. 53 stated that "employes are forbidden to disclose any communication between patrons of the telephone."[159] Since earlier operators had informed customers of the whereabouts and other activities of their friends and colleagues, this rule resulted in a further distancing of the subscriber from the operator. These stringent rules simply augmented Rule No. 49 that forbade all but "the few short words necessary to receive a call, complete the connection and start the conversation."[160] All problems with subscribers or other operators were to be immediately referred to a superior. The end to all operator discretion and control over their work loomed. These twelve "Duties of Operators" presaged what would later become books of hundreds of pages that prescribed operators' work in the most minute detail.

Effective September 1, 1895, AT&T issued its 25-page "Rules for the Government and Information of the Employes" composed of ninety-five rules, forty-five of which directly pertained to operators. Except for the duties of the chief operator, still referred to as "he," the manual described few managerial duties but imposed a more rigorous discipline on operators.

"Permission from the Chief Operator or the Monitor, before leaving the switchboard" for temporary relief became necessary. In addition to speaking in clear tones, the operator had to retain the receiver at the ear "continuously while . . . at the switchboard."[161] Rule No. 21 forbade operators to use the lines for any personal business. And if they found it necessary to talk among themselves, then Rule No. 22 ordered them to speak in "a low tone of voice . . . for the proper conduct of the business."[162] Visitors could enter the operating room only by "special permission from the District Superintendent" (an official higher than the office manager). With such directives, AT&T modified the conduct of its operators and segregated them from the public and from their fellow workers. The indication that management had not yet been completely successful is Rule No. 17, which warned: "Reading letters, books, papers, eating lunch, etc., will not be permitted at the switchboard, except in special cases by permission of the Chief Operator."[163] Later versions of these rules prohibited these activities completely and deleted the exception.

As the Bell System standardized office behavior, it also routinized operating methods. Twenty of the forty-five rules affecting operators in the above mentioned document related to actual operating procedures. Detailed instructions outlined the proper response to various situations, the amount of time that must elapse before disconnecting a call or inquiring if the customer had finished and the handling of long distance calls of all types—collect, pay station, etc., routing knowledge, charging procedures, timing practices, handling toll tickets, and other service provisions. If any exceptions or special problems, requests, or information arose, regular operators referred them to the Chief Operator or Monitor. The new rules of call completion and operator conduct signaled the elimination of operator discretion. Sterilized, regimented, and synthetic pleasantries continually displaced genuine spontaneous discourse between the operator and subscriber.

After 1895, this trend toward codification of rules escalated into a national proliferation of operating manuals that left little for the operator to think about or decide. The New York Telephone Company's "Rules for the Government and Information of the Employes in the Traffic Department, 1897" described the hours of duty, the daily tests, how to file trouble reports, procedures governing visitors to the exchange, what to do in case of damage to the equipment, the various procedures for toll calls (including stamping of message rate checks), timing and stamping of pay station and suburban checks, various exchange records and reports, methods of completing the various types of calls, and many other items affecting the operator's job.

Central New York Telephone and Telegraph Company also issued a set of rules to take effect June 1, 1897. This booklet expressly prohibited "reading letters, books, papers, eating lunch, etc.," at the switchboard, tardiness, exchanging hours without the consent of the chief operators, accepting presents or fees of any nature (except for Christmas) from the subscribers, and receiving unauthorized visitors. Courtesy to the subscribers and among operators was mandated, but at this time the company felt a further proscription was necessary. "Impertinent language to a subscriber . . ." according to Rule No. 74, would not be tolerated and "a violation of this rule will be sufficient cause for dismissal." These instructions also mandated that a chief operator or some other operator must be in charge at all times and would be "held responsible for the strict enforcement" of the rules. Operators were to "carefully preserve and frequently read these rules."[164]

The Bell System insisted on formal discipline to control the workplace and for other business reasons. Charles Cutler, president of the Metropolitan Telephone and Telegraph Company of New York, wrote to ABT President Hudson, "the necessity of some very stringent rules and regulations as to the divulging of information obtained by operators or persons in the employ of the companies, becomes more apparent." Alarmed that breaches of confidentiality would "seriously retard the increase of the toll business," Cutler implored Hudson to take up the matter with the other Bell companies.[165] By 1897, operating manuals across the country emphasized secrecy. The Bell System needed system-wide discipline to insure larger profits and to avoid legal entanglements resulting from breaches of state privacy laws. The informal, flexible, and challenging working conditions typical of the operating room of the 1880s progressively changed into a rationalized and scientifically managed workplace.

Rapid telephone expansion, financial crises caused by the depressions of the 1890s, increased competition in the business, and a more sophisticated technology eliminated the casual atmosphere of the early 1880s and created the need for a more highly organized and regimented workforce. The "peg count," the IDF, and the divided board required a reorganization of work around machinery. If managers could reduce the number of operators through these methods, they did so. But equally as important, the introduction of the No. 1 Relay board and its division-of-labor method of operation demonstrated that managers readily increased the number of operators when it would improve service.

Although nineteenth-century executives codified rules and operating practices, solidified organizational hierarchy, developed statistical load measurements, and recognized the surveillance potential of the new technological innovations, neither the equipment nor the personnel policies had matured to the point where managers could fully implement a standardization program before the turn of the century.

After 1900, the struggle for workplace control intensified as the company aggressively pursued its standardization program. The trend toward consolidation of Bell companies into larger units and the trend toward standardization and functional organization within the entire Bell System accelerated. Measured by an increase in the total number of employees, the number of subscribers, profits, and the rise and entrenchment of a well-defined hierarchy, the Bell System experienced incredible growth and transformation between the late 1890s and the start of World War I. Management instituted policies that extended their control over the worker and the workplace by decreasing operator autonomy and by dividing jobs into smaller tasks that required less knowledge. The new technologies and associated changes in work organization transformed telephone operating from a complex but unstructured combination of personal and mechanical skills into a regimented and simple set of tasks.

The introduction of new technologies and changes in work organization have been significant forces in the transformation of telephone operators' work. These forces have shaped skill definitions, job content, and the levels of workers' control. Race and gender, in addition to technological and organizational improvements helped to define skill, especially because the nascent telephone industry faced a skeptical public with unreliable equipment. As a part of a strategy to attract and keep customers, telephone executives replaced boys with young, single, native-born white women, who were expected to deliver helpful, efficient, confidential, and, above all, courteous service.[1] These women needed more than the mechanical skills necessary to make switchboard connections.

The kind of service that Bell System managers envisioned required operators with social skills that emanated from high moral values and the ability to gracefully defer. Drawing on contemporary racial ideology, managers constructed an image of the ideal telephone operator as a woman who conformed to nineteenth-century notions of virtue and piety: a "lady." Only white women could be "ladies," and the telephone company hired only "ladies" as telephone operators. Skill for the first telephone operators was thus intrinsic to being a "respectable" white female with a middle-class background or aspirations. Managers used race and gender exclusion to create an operator identity that in the nineteenth century appeased disgruntled white male telephone customers and in the twentieth century contributed to workplace control.

To obscure the fact that telephone operators resembled nineteenth-century servants or factory workers more than upper-class "ladies," managers fostered notions of white privilege by excluding African American

13. This woman has been described as "one of the first black operators on the job" in Pittsburgh, 1891. This author has been unable to find an explanation for such a rarity if this operator is indeed African American. (Property of AT&T Archives; reprinted with permission of AT&T)

14. Chinese operators in the "China Exchange," San Francisco, circa 1930. These women represent one of the rare exceptions to the "white lady" image, albeit a segregated one. Of course, in dress and deportment, they conform to the Bell System model. (Property of AT&T Archives; reprinted with permission of AT&T)

and select groups of immigrant women from the occupation. Indeed, racial exclusivity became the foundation upon which Bell executives constructed and perfected other systems of control during the twentieth century. Management institutionalized superficial and fragmented job hierarchies, intensive training, and strictly enforced rules and penalties within the context of a racist hiring policy.

Gradually, the introduction of new machines and changes in work organization degraded the job and the skills that had been so essential to the early development of the telephone industry. The degradation of operating involved the complete feminization of the occupation, the entrenchment of a clearly defined male-dominated hierarchy, the codification of all operating methods, training, and practices, the dissolution of operators' control over their work pace, and a general erosion of relaxed working conditions and opportunities for advancement. In essence, the telephone operator's skills and control dissolved in proportion to the improved technology and the consequent decline in personal service. Ironically, the idealized image of the "lady operator" solidified as their contact with subscribers lessened. This chapter analyzes the process by which a new technology at first enskilled and offered opportunity to women in the nineteenth century but deskilled and limited that opportunity in the twentieth.

The First "Hello" Girls

Like other ideas borrowed from the telegraph industry, the telephone managers at first hired young boys as operators.[2] Some of these boys used their telegraph experience while they performed switchboard work and miscellaneous duties.[3] Even with these technical attributes, boys soon proved unsuitable because, as R. T. Barrett, a former boy operator, stated, "when one gets down to essentials, it was a job for which they were not fitted by temperament or training."[4]

Swearing, beer drinking, and fistfighting with customers reflected the temperamental defects for which boy operators achieved infamy. Impatient with the unreliable equipment, they often disconnected subscribers when they could not hear or were uncertain about the status of the call. Frequently, they would fail to disconnect completed calls, causing lines to be out of order for indefinite periods of time, or at least until the subscriber came to the exchange demanding service. When the boys were not yelling and scrambling around to plug and unplug lines, they were busy

15. Boy operator J. R. Haley, 1885, Marietta, Georgia, office. (Property of AT&T Archives; reprinted with permission of AT&T)

projecting volts of electricity at each others' "corns" or otherwise rough-housing.[5] Many other kinds of pranks, along with impudent and profane language, led to physical altercations with the subscribers.[6]

Dismissal seems to have been the only form of discipline exercised by the managers of these early exchanges. Male and later even female managers accepted the idea that it was natural for boys to behave in this way. After describing the "lurid" language used between boy operators and subscribers, one former manager proudly stated "there were no sissy-boys and no girls among the pioneer operators."[7] R. T. Barrett proclaimed them "a virile lot, those boy operators."[8] This lot, according to J. J. Carty, a boy operator who rose to Chief Engineer of AT&T, "were not old enough to be talked to like men and . . . not young enough to be spanked like children," and were "but a little lower than the wild Indian!"[9] Katherine M. Schmitt concurred: "As I listened to them I used to think that all

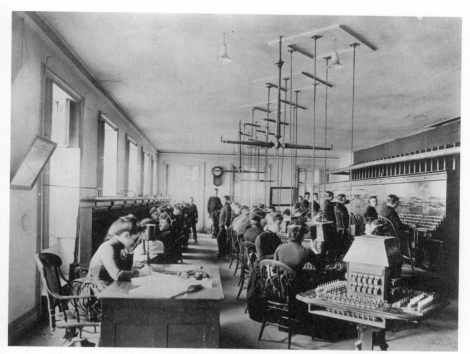

16. Young women operators and boy "switchmen," 1885. A pyramid-type board. (Property of AT&T Archives; reprinted with permission of AT&T)

the Indians had not yet left Manhattan. In short, nothing could be done with those boys, until, by common consent, they were abolished."[10]

In an effort to counter the unruly boys' negative effect on business, management consciously created a "white lady" identity for the telephone operator. In that era, executives believed that girls, socialized to defer on the basis of class, gender, and age, were best qualified to give the kind of service Bell envisioned. Although men dominated the profession for more than a decade afterward, especially as chief operators, management added women to the operating forces in 1878. Managers hired young women to create decorum in the switching room and to provide "congenial" service. The feminization of telephone operating during this period is an example of management exercising control over the workplace to provide a better service rather than an attempt to reduce wages and curtail militancy.[11]

Managers created a social and cultural relationship with the customers by employing young, single, native-born white women to cater to bourgeois concepts about servitude. Employers used this "civilized" female image as a way of seducing customers away from the telegraph, soothing customers frustrated by the still unreliable equipment, and keeping customers away from their competitors.[12] Neither boys nor girls possessed characteristics that would make one or the other inherently better telephone operators.

The contemporaneous social ideas that promoted boyish "virility" also promoted girlish "civility," which made female operators preferable. N. W. Lillie, manager of the Boston exchange in 1879, hired Emma M. Nutt ("a nice girl" who lived across the street from him) "to reduce the shouting" and confusion in the switchroom.[13] Henry W. Pope, a New York manager, stated in 1880 that he preferred boys' voices over girls,' but he found girls "generally polite and obliging, while boys are inclined to be impudent and boyish."[14]

Frank Rozzelle remembered "cussing" out boy operators when he became angry over "busy" lines, but with the girls "we simply hang up the receiver and pick[ed] on our office partners or whoever happen[ed] to be handy . . . because we cannot swear at a girl."[15] Many white women, regardless of class, accepted this idealization and sought to behave in conformity with it, as Miss Schmitt's racist characterization of Indians demonstrates. Women of all races and ethnic groups in this era aspired to the advantages and privileges of this identity, but not all women were acceptable to the economically and racially dominant classes. The men of these classes were socialized to "respect" and "protect" young white women as one of the responsibilities of their own exalted position. B. E. Sunny, general superintendent at Chicago Telephone Company, thought it especially important "to get girls of the right character" and "to keep the standard of intelligence and morality high."[16]

Young, native-born white women were chosen for telephone operating not because they could be paid less, could be worked harder, or could be exploited more in other ways but because they were literate and, more important, possessed the social characteristics and skills that the Bell System required to monopolize the business. Female gentility, not female docility, accounts for their introduction into the telephone exchange. Certainly blacks and immigrants, for economic as well as social reasons, would have been better candidates than native-born white women if malleability and low pay had been the market priorities.

Indeed, during the first years of telephony, both men and women received low salaries, and sometimes women earned more than men. Cecil MacKenzie made it perfectly clear that "titles were cheap and plentiful; but not so with salary."[17] Emma M. Nutt earned a weekly $6.00 starting salary in 1878, while the following year MacKenzie began with only $12.00 per month, subject to the collection of subscriber payments.[18] Women also held managerial titles and often supervised men during the early years.[19]

Before the mid-1880s, telephone use was uneven and distributed mostly among male business customers who had not yet become constant telephone users. During this period, the company had established no rules of behavior, no set phrases to be spoken, and no training in tone of voice or methods of handling calls. In fact, no buildings used exclusively for telephone exchanges existed before the 1890s. Decorum was impossible while the exchanges shared spaces in offices, stores, basements, attics, and railroad stations. These informal surroundings, combined with the operation of the awkward and defective equipment, produced a relaxed atmosphere in which boys could be up to their antics and girls could sew, crochet, knit, talk, read, or even engage in their own "electrifying" pranks at times.[20]

Despite the boy operators' misconduct among themselves and with subscribers, no evidence has been found that they combined or unionized against the companies to win higher wages or better working conditions before the 1890s, or even before women telephone workers.[21] If docility had characterized the girls, certainly the boys were not any more antagonistic toward the managers. As service expanded and traffic became heavier, girls were just as likely as boys to "throw up" the annunciators without answering them.[22] Officials at the 1887 Switchboard Conference debated exactly how frequently this occurred among women operators.[23] The first women telephone operators held substantial control over the content of their jobs and the pace at which they worked. During the period of market uncertainty, managers could control women only within the confines of the identity imposed on them and consciously or sometimes unconsciously accepted by them.

Career Women: A New Technology Provides New Opportunities

The "white lady" identity attracted young white women for several reasons. Faced with limited career choices, the first female switchboard operators enthusiastically entered a new field for which they needed no prior training beyond grammar school or high school English and mathematics. The opportunity provided by the telephone's invention coincided with a greater societal shift in which women began to seek clerical work away from the household. For those women, it was exciting to be a part of something totally new, and used only by upper-class people. Like most department store workers, many operators assumed the class outlook of their employers and customers. In the early years, operating offered "respectable girls" steady year-round employment in a relatively clean environment. As women began to dominate the field and telephone use expanded, management sequestered operators from the public (and, in some places, even from male telephone workers). Though many women operators worked long hours—at least six days a week for modest salaries—they were happy to be selected for what had quickly become a job with elitist qualifications.[24]

In their recollections, pioneer telephone operators attest to the excitement of working in this new occupation. Many of them had long careers characterized by rapid advancement and promotions to positions of considerable responsibility and power.[25] The country's first female operator, Emma M. Nutt, retired after thirty-seven years of service in Boston, having had a career as a chief operator and later as a matron who carried out the company policy of "welfare" work among operators.

Katherine M. Schmitt held even more enviable and varied positions at New York Telephone Company, where she worked for nearly half a century. She joined the company in 1882 because she "wanted to try something new," and the work was "not monotonous" but "fascinating." One of her first operating jobs was as an information operator, a job she described as "a combination of personal-service bureau and general guide to the city of New York." On a typical day she would be asked: "Information, where is the fire?" "Did anyone call me while I was out?" "How do I get to Central Park? And is that where the animals are?" In addition, she received constant requests of "Time, please?" This free service was abused so much that Schmitt "often wondered if it didn't interfere with watchmakers' profits."

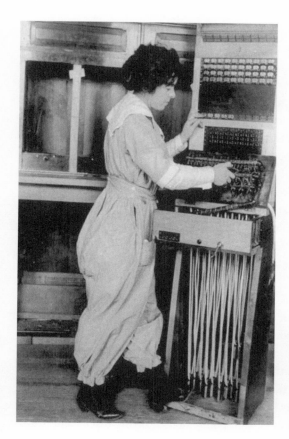

17. Young woman technician, constructing switchboard, Emeryville, California, circa 1890s. (Property of AT&T Archives; reprinted with permission of AT&T)

After fourteen years of service, Schmitt received a promotion to chief operator of the Cortlandt exchange, reported as the largest in the world at the time.[26] She had become office manager by the time she had opened the first telephone operator's school in 1902. Schmitt remained with the school until 1925, when she was promoted to supervisor of all the company's training schools. She retired in 1930.[27] Schmitt holds the somewhat ambiguous distinction of having originated the training method by which operators learned to enunciate their words distinctly and rapidly, regardless of what was said to them. Her advancement and enthusiasm about her job were not rare among early operators.

Pioneer operators advanced to positions that placed demands on their intelligence and judgment.[28] Before the turn of the century, the work brought these operators better pay, prestige, and real levels of advancement and responsibility. Women managers often supervised and trained new operators, including men.[29] Even when the positions were not clearly designated as supervisory, working as a toll operator, service observer, and information, weather, or time operator presented opportunities unavailable in other places. As late as 1895, Bell System managers explored the possibilities of using women in some high-paying, exclusively male occupations such as canvassing.[30]

These opportunities occurred within a flexible but paternalistic environment. By the end of the nineteenth century, however, technological development, industrial competition, and market expansion had created conditions that eliminated the variety and scope of women's careers. Managers established false job ladders and a more elaborate employee welfare program in the twentieth century. Nevertheless, telephone operating continued to provide a racially exclusive workplace for white women.

The Selection Criteria

Race was a significant attribute for the special class of girls chosen as telephone operators. Indeed, race defined the "lady" in the identity that telephone management created for them. This identity represented an idealization of white women that entailed demure and "ladylike" behavior, commanding only the highest reverence. Black women, of course, could never be revered as ladies. Except in extremely rare individual cases, companies maintained an explicit policy against hiring blacks and immigrants as operators.[31]

Managers most frequently rejected immigrants with strong accents. New England Telephone Company did not hire Jews, especially because of the company's objection to the observance of Jewish holidays, fear that Jews were labor agitators, and general anti-Semitism.[32] If their religious identity could not be immediately discerned, some Jews did slip through the discriminatory bars in New England. Bell System hiring practices did not exclude all immigrants, however. Some companies found women from English-speaking countries such as Canada, Ireland, and England acceptable. In the Midwest where pockets of immigrants lived, Norwegian or Scandinavian accents were heard on local lines.[33] However, African Americans were excluded from telephone operating on the basis of skin color.[34]

Since the Bell System trained all newly hired employees, neither spe-

"It's the *wrong* Hat!"

Simultaneously, Bell System publications reminded operators of their superior status and fortified the race and class dimensions of the "white lady" image by frequently portraying African American women in subservient positions. New York Telephone Company's magazine published two such covers within a six-month period.

18. Cover of the *Telephone Review*, 1911, depicting a black girl as a servant. (Image of a New York Telephone Company magazine that is now defunct)

19. Cover of the *Telephone Review*, 1911, depicting a black woman as a servant. (Image from a New York Telephone Company magazine that is now defunct)

cial training nor previous work experience outweighed race as a prerequisite to employment. A 1910 investigation of telephone companies showed that in one large city, 2,229 of 6,152 applicants were rejected for various reasons. Among them were eleven Jews who refused to work holidays, ninety women with unacceptable accents, and seven "colored" women.[35] This highly selective personnel policy reinforced the Bell System's carefully cultivated image of the telephone operator and insured the selection of white women as operators up to the World War II era.

Even though race was a defining characteristic, the "lady" operator had to possess other qualifications. For at least the first fifty years, the majority of telephone operators were usually young, single, native-born white women who lived with their parents. Census documents and internal AT&T records reveal that the Bell System placed a premium on youth for reasons of economy, discipline, and perceived physical stamina. In 1900, 93.7 percent of the 21,980 telegraph and telephone operators were native white women with native-born parents (54.6 percent) or foreign-born parents (39.1 percent).[36] More than two-thirds (71.7 percent) were between sixteen and twenty-four years old. Another 22.2 percent were between twenty-five and thirty-four.[37] Single women (92.7 percent) who lived with one or both parents or some other relative were most likely to find telegraph and telephone employment.[38] Managers believed inexperienced youths could be molded into model Bell employees.

Youth offered a significant guarantee that the applicant would be healthy and strong. "Experience," stated H. D. McBride, "justifies the placing of age limits . . . at 17 to 25 years" because people in this age group provided "more satisfactory" work and "their term of service is longer than with persons of more advanced age."[39] Managers believed that older people (i.e., twenty-five and older) could not perform certain jobs. This bias stigmatized both sexes and applied to telephone operating as well as to outside work.[40] The company disciplined this group by asserting a kind of parental responsibility and accountability. For instance, a prerequisite for employment often entailed home visits.[41] This practice continued into the 1940s as a method for insuring the "quality" of people hired and harnessing parental reinforcement of company practices.[42] Undesirable workers could not easily slip through this process.

Along with these demographic characteristics, the selection of a potential operator depended on a range of physical and attitudinal qualifications. H. D. McBride, superintendent of traffic, Boston, surmised that the necessary employment attributes included ordinary intelligence as reflected in at least a common school education or its equivalent and a good English-speaking voice and enunciation. High School graduates typified "the most desirable applicants." During the application process, the interviewer determined the applicant's desirability based on a "clear and agreeable tone of voice, distinct enunciation, abruptness or impertinence in manner of speaking [or] foreign accent."[43] Employment officials assessed the quality of the applicant's handwriting from the written application.

A potential operator's general appearance could show no sign of poor health: "uncleanliness of the hair, nervousness, skin diseases, nose, throat or lung troubles," or other chronic disorders.[44] By 1910, in many places, nurses or doctors conducted a complete physical examination. They tested the applicant's eyesight and hearing. Large cities usually required women to be at least five feet tall since shorter women probably would not have the reach for a large 4,900- or 9,600-line board. Medical officers screened applicants for these physical defects, but the personnel managers eliminated socially unacceptable job-seekers.

Bell System management organized recruitment through personal and social channels (white networks) that ensured the employment of workers with the desired "cultural attributes." Friends and relatives of employees constituted the majority of applicants.[45] All Bell companies requested references. Some companies solicited churches or schools, and, in emergencies, personnel officers tried "newspaper advertising, notices posted in women's clubs, lunch rooms and charitable organizations." The Bell System publicized its exclusivity and claimed to hire only a certain "class" of girls.[46]

One New England telephone exchange realized the efficacy of this publicity when a local chief operator "through a lack of knowledge of local conditions, . . . got into his force two or three operators whose reputations were not of the best." For "some years it was absolutely impossible to get a local girl to consent to work" for his exchange. Consequently, the exchange had to hire women "at a great expense . . . from outside sources." Under the authority of a new chief operator, the "undesirable element, though composed of skillful operators," was "weeded out." Once cleansed, there was "no difficulty whatever in obtaining local help."[47] The Bell System's standards and the local communities' agreement with them ensured that the exchanges and the telephone operators' image would be free of any "undesirable element."

Training

Competition with the Independents and poor service, precipitated by rapid expansion, forced Bell management to focus on operator training. Training and discipline became inseparable. In the opinion of one manager, the first and most serious effect of untrained operators was subscriber dissatisfaction, which, in turn increased supervisory work involved in appeasing subscribers. "The second effect would be in the increased operating expense which necessarily follows low operating loads, and, further, the additional expense of switchboard equipment which this condition requires."[48] The effort to standardize and anticipate every possible situation that an operator might encounter dominated the Bell System's goals in operators' training.

Like other aspects of operating, local conditions dictated training practices. Sometimes with pay but often without, the first operators learned their jobs by observing experienced operators. In some small exchanges, a prospective operator went in on a Saturday to learn the work before she started.[49] Sometimes the manager or chief operator would show the new hire the basics and let her work alone at a slow traffic board until her speed and skill improved. Standardized, industry-wide training in diction, enunciation, politeness, and conformity with company rules and policy did not become widespread until Katherine M. Schmitt opened the New York Operator's School on January 13, 1902.

At the school, Schmitt tried to produce the model operator who she believed "must now be made as nearly as possible a paragon of perfection, a kind of human machine, the exponent of speed and courtesy; a creature spirited enough to move like chain lightning, and with perfect accuracy; docile enough to deny herself the sweet privilege of the last word. She must assume that the subscriber is always right, and even when she knows he is not her only comeback must be: 'Excuse it please,' in the same smiling voice."[50]

Other large city exchanges soon copied the school's structure and methods. Formalized training indoctrinated new employees with company discipline in addition to teaching the mechanical manipulations required for switchboard operation.[51] All company literature (instruction manuals,

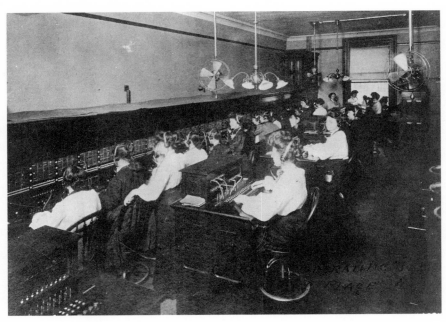

20. Original Operating Training School, New York City, 1902. Switchboard practice.
(Property of AT&T Archives; reprinted with permission of AT&T)

pamphlets, newspapers and magazines, circulars, etc.) addressed to operators emphasized the necessity of well-articulated courtesy. New York
Telephone Traffic Manager J. L. Turner of the Newark District explained
that "the words used by the operator are almost entirely prescribed in her
rules. It is the voice expression, therefore, that she must supply in order to
convey to the subscriber . . . the idea of pleasing and intelligent service as
well as the mere courtesy of the operator." According to him, the operator
should use the "tone quality, inflection and emphasis," to make the subscriber immediately respond "with a feeling of pleasure, whether expressed in so many words or not, 'Aha! There's my obliging operator. *She'll*
give me what I want.' "[52]

When the operator could not give the subscriber what he/she wanted,
then another emotion had to be communicated. For instance, to give a
busy report, the operator should emphasize the first syllable of "busy." So
that when she said "Cortlandt 5-9-8-0 is *busy*," it would be with a sympathetic tone to convey "I am *sorry,* Mr. Smith, but I cannot give you what
you want."[53] For the Bell System, the latter sentence had far too many

21. Operators' Training School, 1916. Operators hold their waists as they practice elocution to deliver the "Voice with a Smile." (Property of AT&T Archives; reprinted with permission of AT&T)

words and wasted time. It was the operator's responsibility to convey concern and sincerity without wasting valuable company time (and her own 3.5 seconds).[54]

In addition to a pleasing vocal expression, Bell System policies mandated "clear and distinct" enunciation of the set phrases in the prescribed manner.[55] Some telephone schools taught voice training, singing, and proper breathing.[56] At the practice switchboards (through simulated calls), supervisors further drilled and tested students' voice techniques and call completion methods and procedures. Yet the indoctrination process remained incomplete until the actual molding in the workplace occurred.

Working Conditions and Paternalistic Practices

Standardization of the workplace and working conditions only occurred gradually as the Bell System solved more pressing problems. Consequently, wages, hours of work, methods of operation, training, discipline, and other working conditions varied according to region, rural/or urban areas, size of exchanges/numbers of subscribers, and type of board.[57] Operators in smaller towns and outlying areas usually worked alone, whereas operators in the large cities worked in exchanges with dozens of other operators. Regional management policies affected opera-tor tours of duty, Sunday schedules, and vacations. In 1892, a day operator usually worked a minimum nine- or ten-hour tour six days a week, except in San Francisco, where they worked eight and one-half hours. Most operators remained on the job longer than their tours because lunch and rest periods were not included. Special operators or regular operators (paid and unpaid) worked on Sundays, depending on business needs and their own availability. In those places where operators received vacations, it was either paid or unpaid and extended from a week to ten days.[58] Night operators worked nine- to twelve-hour shifts.

Geographic location and type of switchboard also modified working conditions, the number of subscribers per operator, calls answered per day or per hour per operator, and the degree of supervision and disci-pline.[59] Operators in large cities handled fewer subscribers and connected fewer calls with more aggravation because of the large number of trunked calls necessary to make the majority of connections. Relaxed supervision continued in areas of less traffic, while it became more intense and rigid in big cities and other areas of heavy traffic.

The Bell System wage structure before the twentieth century also de-fies generalization. Labor shortages created by competition from other industries for the same "class" of women modified local pay scales. The National Telephone Exchange Association systematically gathered statis-tics relevant to all aspects of exchange operation from 1882 to the mid-1890s. By grouping exchanges according to city population, these reports show operator wages (including those of chief operators, which may tend to make the averages high) and other indications of working conditions that changed with size, switchboard type, and geographic location. Usu-ally, big city operators received higher wages than operators in small towns and rural areas.[60] Cities with populations of more than 150,000 had relatively higher wages but not always the highest. New York City, the largest city in the country, had a population greater than 1 million people, and its Metropolitan Telephone Company paid only a $2.50 weekly start-ing salary in 1882 to operators working on Bell System-recommended boards.[61] Those operators who operated Law boards in the same city were paid $6.00 to start, and they reached a maximum of $12.00 weekly, while others received $10.00. Exchanges in Brooklyn, with more than half a million people who were not residents of New York City at the time, paid their beginners $3.00 weekly with a maximum of $9.23. Philadelphia, next in size to New York City with a population of 847,170, paid salaries beginning at $4.03 and reaching $16.25. The highest salary reported for urban areas of roughly similar size was in St. Louis (population 350,518), where the top wage was $17.31 weekly with a beginning salary of $3.46. One explanation for the high wages in St. Louis may be that women operators still had not been hired in that city in 1881, and the company had to compete with other industries for young men.[62]

In cities with populations from 50,000 to 150,000, salaries ranged between $2.50 and $4.00 weekly for beginners. In Paterson, New Jersey (population 51,031 in 1880), operators were paid $2.50 on employment and received a $7.50 maximum wage. Detroit (population 116,340) employed operators at $3.75 and raised them to $16.25. Operators in areas with populations less than 50,000 rarely exceeded $10.00 weekly top salaries. Of fifty exchanges in cities of this size that reported wages to the Association, only seven paid wages of $10.00 or higher.

The exchange statistics reported by B. E. Sunny of Chicago at the seventh annual NTEA meeting in September 1885 included the first attempt to give a nationwide wage statement for male occupations. Many exchanges failed to send figures or they sent incomplete compilations, which makes the statement sketchy and incomplete.[63] However, the report does show that regardless of city size or geographic location, outside telephone men throughout the United States could reasonably expect to receive a dollar a day for their labor. In those rare instances where starting salaries were less than $1.00, the average salary was higher and the maximum wage was usually above $2.00. Maximum pay in cities with fewer than 10,000 people did not exceed $2.00 per day in any part of the country. Bell System companies in cities with populations between 10,000 and 50,000 frequently paid their men in excess of $2.00 per day, but in the majority of places the average salary was from $1.50 to $2.00. Average salaries in urban areas with populations above 50,000 but less than 150,000 were similar, but the highest wages for the most part exceeded $2.00, and in the case of Paterson the highest daily wage for a combination man was $3.84. Telephone men in cities of more than 150,000 people could expect starting salaries exceeding $1.50 in the overwhelming majority of cases, but, as in the rest of the country, wages above $3.00 a day were rare. These

1885 wages for all-male occupations in comparison with those for operators, an occupation in transition but still heavily male, shows that operating from the earliest years was segmented from other types of work and
that segmentation was reinforced by low wages. Even when operating was
all-male, it was low-paying.[64] In 1880, and as late as 1892, male and
female operators in New York City received the same wages. Women were
not paid less for the same operating work formerly dominated by men,
but women were deliberately excluded from other higher-paying occupations.[65] Consequently, by 1900, telephone operating was dominated by
women who received lower wages than male telephone workers.

Once telephone operating work had become fully associated with
women, operators suffered the same wage limitations as women in other
feminized occupations.[66] The assumption that women were temporary
workers who did not have to take care of themselves and therefore did not
qualify for a "family wage" suppressed operators' wages even more. Employers rationalized paying operators below the standard of living by assuming that these young women lived with their parents and would quit
as soon as they found husbands. Indeed, the Bell System sought to rein-
force this stereotype by establishing specific paternalistic practices from
the beginning.

Telephone managers tried to make the work environment an extension of the home hierarchy by assuming a parental role that became more
patriarchal and rigid as the industry stabilized. An employee's age and
later, as the occupation became feminized, her sex influenced the development of paternalistic methods of controlling workers. Before the advent of systematized company benefits, managerial concern for employee
welfare depended on the immediate supervisor's individual temperament or on regional policy. Workers could not receive wage increases,
time off, or company help in any emergencies without the beneficence of
their bosses. In 1891, Cincinnati's City and Suburban Bell Telephone
Association, for example, initiated a policy of giving each operator a $10
gold piece for Christmas, a practice continued for several years.[67] As
employees aged, pensions also became a matter of managerial discretion,
so that companies usually aided older people by carrying them on the
payroll for no-show or light-duty jobs.[68]

Licensees of the Bell System often adopted local policies to meet
emergency medical situations for their employees. In 1880, George C.

Maynard, general manager of the Chesapeake & Potomac Company in Washington, D.C., provided medical services for linemen and operators through doctor's home visits and employee office visits.[69] By an agreement with the Massachusetts General Hospital in 1882, President William H. Forbes made hospitalization possible for Boston employees. In exchange for the use of a hospital bed at an annual fee of $50, the company provided the hospital with telephone service at a reduced charge.[70] These unorganized paternalistic practices of the nineteenth century soon yielded to standardization.

Conforming to the twentieth-century trend in welfare programs, Bell companies provided operators with well-lit and ventilated "retiring" rooms supervised by matrons, free tea and coffee and in some places, lunches free or at cost. In big cities such as New York, special restrooms where women could see a nurse who would administer first aid in emergencies or give medications for "simple indispositions" became commonplace.[71] To show its appreciation for employees, the company established vacation camps, employee magazines and societies, company awards and prizes for good work and attendance, after-work educational programs, libraries, sports activities, and other gimmicks.[72]

Means for Control and Discipline
Within its carefully constructed paternalistic environment, management shifted its drive for increased productivity from switchboards to operators. The common battery-powered No. 1 Relay Switchboard and its supervisory capacities made uniform training, disciplinary measures, and operating methods possible. Katherine M. Schmitt recalled that when common battery switchboards were installed in every New York City exchange, "uniformity of operating practices was achieved," which "was very important, because it made possible uniform training of operators."[73] Speedups, load measurements, and other types of discipline and control were easily established.

Technology, in fact, facilitated the change in work organization, which in turn facilitated the division of operating. The Intermediate Distributing Frame and its various rewiring potentialities combined with the divided method of operating on a No. 1 Relay Switchboard to fragment operators' skills. A group of specialized operators who performed different tasks within the same job replaced the operator of the 1880s who

22. Telephone Operators' Lunch Room, Boston, 1916. (Courtesy of the Boston Public Library, Print Department)

23. Telephone Operators' Recreation Room, Boston, 1916. (Courtesy of the Boston Public Library, Print Department)

24. "Time of Day" service began in 1927. The operator made a "live" announcement. Later, these announcements were recorded. (Property of AT&T Archives; reprinted with permission of AT&T)

individually processed the entire call to completion. Within each department or division, highly stratified employee occupational classifications developed.[74] "Methods," "procedures," and "instruction" manuals or circulars, in addition to the duties described in company bulletins, further delineated each job classification. Accounting bulletin 108A lists five chief operator titles, eight supervisor titles, twenty-two operator titles, five public telephone attendant titles, five PBX titles, eight instructor including instructress titles, ten junior operator titles, and one student operator title.[75] These titles did not exist simultaneously in all places across the country, but they did represent AT&T's attempt to establish the same organization nationwide to the greatest extent possible.

As Bell System managers established functional organization, they also continued and expanded the system-wide standardization of rules and regulations begun in the 1890s.[76] Traffic engineers defined the standards and formulated operating rules, methods, and procedures according to these specifications. For long distance and local service, engineers wrote manuals, circulars, and additional leaflets that detailed the duties and responsibilities of every class and subclass of operators. Managers required that every type and every level of operator be familiar with a certain number of these manuals.[77]

These documents prescribed the Bell System response to nearly every conceivable telephone situation. Traffic engineers decided what an operator had to know and how she would use that knowledge quickly and efficiently in her work performance. If an operator received a call for which no prescribed response had been provided, the expected response was to transfer the call to the supervisor. A Bell System traffic manager explained:

> Would not general principles in accordance with which the operator could decide for herself, be sufficient? No. For in the first place, the operator must be able to proceed with any condition, or combination of conditions, *instantly* without losing so little as a few seconds time in deciding what to do; and in the second place, the service is so greatly affected by seemingly unimportant details of the work and the possible methods of procedure are so numerous, that it must all be worked out in advance with the idea of getting the best possible results. Hence the necessity not only for the rules themselves, but also for constant drilling of the operators in them.[78]

Twentieth-century operating rules and work reorganization thus deprived the operator of her decision-making opportunities. Worse still, engineers forced her to work like a machine.

For example, Bell System scientific management philosophy transformed a relatively general set of 1897 AT&T "Rules for the Government and Information of the Employes" into a rigidly specific "Traffic Department Operating Instructions" dated November 1, 1910. Five times larger than the former manual, the later document embodied engineers' efforts to mechanize human behavior. Unlike the 1897 booklet, the 1910 text describes *each* traffic employee's hierarchical tier, duties, responsibilities, and work procedures in detail. More significantly, it established rules of conduct. The very first one stated: "All employees shall keep fully informed regarding the letter and spirit of the rules. Ignorance of a rule will not be considered a sufficient excuse for failure to comply with it."[79]

Rules pertained to attendance, punctuality, resignations (two weeks' notice), health (report contagious diseases), dress (uniforms not required in most places, just sensible clothing that would not interfere with the work), sickness or accident, personal numbers (operators could not give their names), confidentiality, visitors, gifts and favors, verbal abuse, subscriber complaints and legal actions, and innumerable other details.

These rules forbade conversations between operators in the operating room, except to meet business needs. Witness the regimentation involved in the procedure for relieving an operator:

> The chairs of the operators to be relieved shall be pushed back from the switchboard and the operators shall rise and stand facing their positions. The relieving operators shall stand slightly back and to the left of the positions they are to occupy, and at offices provided with duplicate telephone jacks, shall insert their telephone plugs in the proper jacks. The operators to be relieved shall then inform the relief operators of the condition of any connections requiring special attention, withdraw their telephone plugs from the jacks, and surrender their positions by stepping back from the switchboard to the right. Chairs shall then be replaced and the relieving operators shall seat themselves. The change of operators must be made without a break in the service.[80]

Pacific Telephone and Telegraph Company saved time by utilizing a system of bells to signify when the operators should "march in single file" into the operating room to change the tour. Operators were instructed to hold a pair of plugs in each free hand in readiness to answer calls.[81] The engineers' attempts to "engineer" operators cannot be exaggerated.

Finding the Breaking Point: The Kalamazoo Experiment

A Kalamazoo, Michigan, experiment demonstrated the extreme to which management intended to regiment operators in the interest of "efficiency." On May 1, 1903, H. D. McBride began a study of the operating practices there. He wanted to determine the "number of calls an operator could handle and furnish a service which would meet the . . . requirements, without undue strain or effect on their physical condition."[82]

When the study began, McBride observed several inefficient work patterns and retrained the operators accordingly. Afterward, he successively increased operators' loads by rewiring the IDF. By the twentieth day of the study, the busy hour load had been increased from the starting point of 135 calls per hour to 260.

Of course, this speedup provoked operators' resistance. Absences and illnesses occurred. McBride discovered that all of the operators suffered from the same nervous headache condition because they "inaccurately" thought the object of the tests was "to determine the faults of the individual operators and to make a comparison of their merits." McBride posted a notice informing them that he was merely conducting a study. Naive about the consequences of such a study, the operators discontinued their resistance to the speedups.[83]

When the work resumed, operators achieved the "maximum load for the experiment of 358 calls per operator during the busy hour, with an average of 254 calls per position during the hours of test."[84] After Mc-Bride concluded the experiment, 260 calls per busy hour became the standard for all local companies. Chief Engineer Joseph P. Davis wrote to AT&T President Frederick Fish that as a result of this study, operating positions were reduced from fourteen to ten, which netted a 30 percent saving in operating, while a "decided *improvement* in character of service" had been achieved.[85] Scientifically, engineers had arrived at the "breakdown" point for operators. They issued Bulletin No. 10 in November 1903 to document the experiment and to show by example how to increase operator loads.

Penalties for "Irregularities"

Despite rigorous training and well-defined and codified work responsibilities, operators often could not work according to the engineers' specifications. When an operator performed poorly, the company did not immediately fire her. They trained her more. Bell System executives, always cognizant of expenses, did not want to lose their investment or to demoralize the other operators by firing an operator for trivial reasons. Instead, management in various localities enacted a system of penalties. Unlike the small fines of the 1880s and 1890s that helped purchase library books and furnishings for the operator lounges, these new penalties affected wages. Omaha instituted a system in 1899 that reduced operators' salaries according to the percentages of irregularities they received on the basis of a hundred calls. Operators lost their jobs if their performance fell below 70 percent.[86] Executives debated the fairness of this system in their correspondence and at the 1905 Traffic Conference. Nevertheless, Chicago and other cities adopted some form of wage penalty system during the early decades of the century.[87]

Punishment hours exemplified another Bell System method of penalization for "irregularities." The Los Angeles company forced operators to work the undesirable hours from 1 P.M. to 10 P.M. instead of the normal hours between 6 A.M. and 7:30 P.M. Day operators were forced to work evening tours at a daily rate (15 cents less) when they made too many mistakes.[88] Local exchanges also commonly used small fines and tour changes to enforce their speedup rules and regulations. By the 1910s, the Bell System had constructed a system of discipline with codified standards of technologically paced work regulated by a system of rewards and punishments. The glamour and high status that Bell managers associated with telephone operating could not mask the reality that operators had a great deal in common with factory girls. Long hours, low wages, tediously repetitive work, strict supervision, and speedups characterized both types of work by the turn of the twentieth century.[89] The job had been engineered to the point that operators had few of the freedoms taken for granted by nineteenth-century operators.

Operators Break Down, Governments Investigate

How did the combination of supervisors pacing up and down, flashing lights, long hours, few reliefs, the penalty system, and the pressure of having to perform numerous operating procedures subject to tests affect operators who answered calls within ten seconds? Not surprisingly, managers found that their requirements were not "detrimental." A field investigator, Nellie B. Curry, disagreed. According to her, "the operators themselves . . . tell different stories," which included "nervous, spasmodic movements of their bodies," frequent "nervous collapses at the switchboard," and "hysterical attacks, where the operator, after reaching the limit of nerve endurance, throws up her hands, screams and faints at her work."[90]

If these occurrences are difficult to imagine, one merely has to remember the numerous rules of conduct and procedures an operator observed while manipulating the switchboard at rapid speeds under continuous supervision for eight or nine hours daily. An operator stared at the board in front of her and could not speak to the person seated next to her. She dared not defend herself against irate subscribers who sometimes used abusive language and constantly clicked the receiver in her ear. Nor could she stand and take a break without permission. Above all, she could never question her "superiors."

An operator also suffered from physical constraints. On her head, she continuously wore a headset made of metal and rubber to which was appended a cord with a plug that connected her to the switchboard. She wore the transmitter suspended around her neck. An operator reached two feet to either side and thirty to forty-four inches above her head depending on the number of subscribers multiplied in the exchange. If an operator had to reach beyond her physical limits, she stood up momentarily to make the connection. In many places, an operator's reach to the sides exceeded the normally accepted thirty-six inches. Combined with an upward reach of thirty-nine inches, the "diagonal stretch for the operator at times . . . [was] 53 inches or more from the center of her position."[91] Under these conditions, operators often experienced loss of hearing and eye strain.

Concern, particularly on the part of Progressive reformers, for the nervous strain attendant to telephone operating led to agitation for government intervention. In January 1907, when operators struck in response to Bell Telephone Company of Canada, Ltd.'s attempt to increase the workday from five to eight hours, the Minister of Labor intervened and appointed a royal commission to investigate operators' wages and working conditions.[92] All of the twenty-six doctors who testified concurred that switchboard operating was one of the most strenuous of female occupations and that more than five hours of daily operating was too much.[93]

Operators testified that the strain caused them to suffer hysterical fits, to faint, and to have vision deterioration that required corrective glasses. Maud Orton said: "Well, I have gone home frequently exhausted, and I am always taking nerve medicines to keep me going. . . ."[94] Other operators reported electrical shocks and, in one case, loss of an arm's use as a result of overreaching.[95] When the strike ended, the operators received a seven-hour day spread over nine hours and a small increase in salary. The Royal Commission had recommended a six-hour day, with relief periods every two hours. Despite limited results for Toronto operators, the Royal Commission Report had a strong impact on investigations into the conditions of American operators.

The Canadians' findings incensed the Progressives, who were already sensitive to women's working conditions and always protective of women's reproductive health and moral fortitude. In her 1907–8 "Pittsburgh Survey," Elizabeth Beardsley Butler compared the findings of the Royal Commission with her own in Pittsburgh. She reported that Pittsburgh operators received less pay, worked longer hours (including unpaid overtime), with more supervision, shorter relief periods, and a heavier subscriber load. Butler concluded that "public opinion in a local community should demand a change. . . ."[96]

The 1910 U.S. Senate investigation of telephone companies studied 458 exchanges in twenty-four operating companies across the country. This investigation uncovered the same gruesome conditions as the others, but it made no recommendations for change.[97] However, Josephine Goldmark in her voluminous *Fatigue and Efficiency* used the weight of medical evidence to argue that telephone operators and other women workers needed legislation to protect them from the fatigue brought on by excessive work.[98]

Nelle B. Curry, a field investigator for the U.S. Commission on Industrial Relations, also recommended government intervention. Her findings in 1915 confirmed the conclusions of the other studies. Many operators told Curry that they had had more than one nervous breakdown and continued to suffer from "hysterical crying spells." Chicago Operator No. 71 said that "it is not so much the number of calls they handle that makes the operators nervous, but knowing they have to answer each call and make the connection within a certain time." Operator No. 140 of Los Angeles, who had crying spells without reason, said that what made the work so hard on the nerves was the constant driving. To be "poked in the back and told to hurry when you are working as fast as you possibly can," she complained, "is not very soothing to the nerves."[99] Curry recommended that the government establish a minimum $55 monthly as a living wage for operators, that the actual working time be set at six hours per day, and that a minimum age of eighteen be required for operators.[100] After unsuccessful attempts to suppress Curry's findings, Bell management refused to accept her recommendations.[101] And the government made no attempt to force them. By this time, the Bell System had firmly established technological and organizational control over the operators.

Transformation of Operating Leads to Depersonalized Service

As the twentieth century advanced, new switchboard technologies transformed the operators' work process, rendering the physical exertion less arduous and personal skills less prominent. Without explicitly deskilling telephone operators, technological development fostered a new managerial direction in personnel and operating policies with regard to operators. Depersonalizing telephone service was at the center of this direction. In the nineteenth century it occurred as a by-product of Bell managers' efforts to use new technologies to achieve greater economy and to defeat competition. New switchboards required different operating techniques that sometimes distanced the operator from the subscriber. In this sense, managers sought control over the workplace for service stability, not so much for higher operator productivity. With better switchboards, operators provided better service. In the twentieth century, however, managers deliberately used scientific management techniques and technology to depersonalize operators' work and thereby increase their productivity.

Although the twentieth-century operator still had to use her personality and intelligence to remember and apply the standardized procedures to "get" people talking, management's use of technology and new work practices robbed her of job satisfaction and many of her mental, personal, and mechanical tasks. When switchboards were small and subscribers few, operators knew each customer by name, business, and personal needs. Pioneer operator Jessie Mix remembered how businessmen "used to send us boxes of candy and flowers and drop in to see us from time to time, and on occasions some of the livery stables, like Barker and Ransom's, would put a horse and carriage or sleigh at our disposal, and take the girls on a picnic."[102] For Christmas, many operators received substantial gifts from subscribers. As they processed calls, operators observed social amenities and exchanged local gossip and news. In low traffic periods, nineteenth-century operators could knit, sew, crochet, watch passing parades, or play electrical pranks on each other.[103]

As Katherine M. Schmitt remarked, operators supervised themselves.[104] In many offices, if there was a manager, he or she supervised only two or three people. These circumstances called for a spirit of cooperation and sharing of responsibilities. Working at a slower pace, operators could provide businessmen with more personal services, such as calling them back when a busy line became idle. Or, when a subscriber returned to the city after a long absence, they would bring that subscriber up to date and inform others he had returned.[105]

In addition to the personal relationship provided by the individual operators, the Bell System, as a matter of policy, provided messenger service, news, racing results, time, weather, election results, football and baseball scores, and other auxiliary services at a minimum charge or for no charge at all. Slowly, however, both the operators' personal services and the company's public services declined. Each new technical advance eroded the company's commitment to personalized service, increased discipline, and otherwise degraded the operator's job. The Bell System managerial decision to give the subscriber less, or merely to connect calls, hastened this process.

One of the first noticeable changes concerned the amount of work each operator could do after the introduction of each new switchboard. Between 1880 and 1900, the number of calls that operators completed daily increased from 500 on the Standard to 1,400 on the common-battery No. 1 Relay Switchboard.[106] Managers used the pilot light, IDF, and other technical innovations to insure that operators worked the various switchboards' full capacity. Operators simply no longer had the time to indulge in social intercourse with subscribers. Between 1900 and 1920, operators not only lost the opportunity to use their initiative and independent judgment in their relations with subscribers, but they lost many of their mechanical tasks.[107]

Aside from speeding up the work pace and thereby increasing productivity, new technology caused other changes in operating. A typical operator in 1885 made her morning tests, called back on busy and don't-answer calls, knew everyone by name (even in New York City), performed innumerable special favors, listened in on conversations to ensure that people talked and to disconnect if they did not. The introduction of the Multiple and its enormous subscriber capacity removed the possibility that operators could know each subscriber by name, though they continued to be responsible for customers specific to their individual positions. This was the first step in distancing the operator from the subscriber. Common-battery displacement of the magneto system excluded the "morning test" contact between the operator and the subscriber.

With the introduction of the battery-powered No. 1 Relay Switchboard, subscribers could expect to be answered quickly but they could no longer expect the operator to know their identity or their personal habits. In the divided system, the operator who answered the subscriber did not connect the call. Instead, a completion operator, who never spoke with sub-

Photos 25–27 depict the transformation of the operators' workplace from a relaxed, "homey" environment to a scientifically managed and structured one.

25. Operator seated in a rocking chair at a switchboard in a room with bows hanging above, wallpaper, pictures on the wall, and a table with cloth. (Property of AT&T Archives; reprinted with permission of AT&T)

26. By 1913, things had changed into a highly standardized workplace. Madison Square Garden office, New York City. (Property of AT&T Archives; reprinted with permission of AT&T)

27. By 1922, the level of supervision (indicated by the women standing) had reached intense proportions. Charleston, West Virginia, 1922. (Property of AT&T Archives; reprinted with permission of AT&T)

scribers, connected the line to the called party. With the introduction of incandescent lamps, operators did not even have to "listen in" or ask if a call was finished; they simply observed a lamp and disconnected.

The application of several automatic features to the switchboard further reduced operators' interactions with subscribers. Recorded or automatic "busy backs" and automatic ringing, for example, eliminated the need for the operator to tell the subscriber the condition of the called line. The recorded message simply said that the "line was busy, try again." Automatic ringing allowed the caller to determine when to hang up. As these new devices proliferated, callers spoke with operators less frequently, and when they did, words were few. This transformation in operators' services to subscribers is indicative of the concomitant changes in their work spaces and their relations with management.

Though the first operators worked in telephone exchanges located above stores, in attics, and in other spaces, by the 1900s most exchanges were located in fireproof telephone buildings. Government investigations in 1910 and 1915 confirmed that most buildings were well-ventilated with adequate lighting and temperature controls. The company, of course, took credit for making operators comfortable, but in reality *the equipment* did not function well in hot dirty environments. An operator's actual work space was very small and uncomfortable, particularly when she had to reach over to another operator's board. In essence, the new and highly structured workplaces confined operators to smaller areas.

The turn of the twentieth century also marked a shift from haphazard local decision making on raises, promotions, and hiring to a nationwide, highly centralized policy that replaced personal managerial relationships with operators and substituted standardized procedures for hiring, training, promotions, punishments, and benefits. Every policy, no matter how beneficial, was ultimately paternalistic and aimed at keeping the operator under control. Hence, free lunches and comfortable "retiring" rooms became methods for keeping women inside the telephone building during their breaks. Through such strategies, managers ensured that the operators would return to their switchboards on time and it also prevented them from talking about improper subjects (i.e., unions) by keeping them under the matrons' constant watch. Management's dispensation of sickness and disability benefits made some operators feel obligated not to be absent or join a union. To further maintain and inspire company loyalty, the company organized choirs, clubs, theatrical groups, newspapers, magazines, vacation homes/camps, and other activities. Even though operators understood and often resisted management's efforts to control, they also knew that they worked in conditions far superior to those of factory operatives which gave them reason to believe that they occupied a higher social status.

Ironically, twentieth-century changes did not immediately alter the operators' image or chances for advancement. As late as the 1920s, vestiges of the early days could be found. The telephone industry was still a workplace where a young woman could better herself. Not only were positions in the grossly inflated hierarchy of operating available, but once a young woman entered the company she could transfer into the Accounting, Commercial, Personnel, or other departments that offered women slightly more pay. Young, native-born white women, single, living at home or with some other relative, and at least common school-educated, continued to dominate the occupation. Hence, operators maintained their "white lady" identity and the status associated with it.

Operators lived up to this self-perception in various ways. Many wore clothes more expensive than those of factory girls and others in their economic class. When New England Telephone and Telegraph Company in 1913 imported more than 1,200 strikebreaking operators from New York, Philadelphia, Pittsburgh, Chicago, and other places, the company housed them in the most luxurious hotels in Boston.[108] And the strikebreakers, according to the *Boston Post* "looked more like chorus girls from some high-class theatrical show than they did telephone operators."[109] The *Boston Globe* reported that the operators "showed no signs either in their faces or in their costumes of being in need of employment."[110] The strikers themselves wore "furs, hats of chic design, and smart-looking shoes."[111]

Elizabeth Beardsley Butler explained that women in Pittsburgh accepted lower wages and willingly worked for the Bell System because of the short training period and, more importantly, because "a telephone girl ranks higher socially than a factory operative."[112] Part of this social rank was derived from nativism and racism since many factories employed large numbers of immigrants and in some places African Americans. In addition to wearing fine clothes and seeking racial exclusion, operators reinforced their self-image by demanding better working con-

The Voice with a Smile | 87

ditions than those of domestic or factory workers. For example, class-conscious Chicago operators refused to pass through an alley to get to work "owing to the low character of the saloons in this alley way and to its dark and dirty condition. . . . When an effort was made to compel them . . . they struck and were successful after much notoriety for the telephone company in the newspapers."[113] Ladies did not walk through alleys of ill repute. In fact, some lady operators sought to accentuate their middle-class status by using their meager wages to hire African American domestic help on a part-time basis.[114]

When white women accepted these ideas, they unwittingly also accepted a wider ideology based on capitalist, racist, and sexist domination. Consequently, they internalized ideas about themselves that made them feel intellectually insecure and in need of male guidance and protection. Men—both unionists and capitalists—defined women in a way that crippled women in any struggle for control. By accepting others' definition of them, telephone women were never able to effectively fight the introduction of technology that degraded their work.

Rather than blame the victim, however, an attempt should be made to explain how psychological tradeoffs get translated into capital. Limited financial rewards came to women who accepted these conditions, but, more importantly, they also received immeasurable rewards attributable to elitist thinking. Objectively, these women worked to "the breaking point," and most accepted their condition in exchange for the intangible. Many women, of course, could do nothing else. Besides, it was true that they worked under slightly better conditions than other women and that a limited set of occupational opportunities were available to them. The women's quest for an elitist social standing and their wish to conform to ideas of "domesticity" contributed to their employer's ability to keep them under control while paying them low wages.

3 | The "Ladies" Rebel: Unions and Resistance

Depersonalization and deskilling provoked an intense struggle between telephone operators and their employers during the first twenty years of the twentieth century. New technologies, routinization, and standardization of operating rules and procedures continuously degraded every aspect of telephone operators' working conditions. With persistent loud outcries, operators resisted the company's campaign to "engineer" them into machinelike workers.

Like waitresses, saleswomen, and other women in female-dominated occupations, operators developed a vibrant work culture that reflected their self-definitions as well as different forms of resistance to managerial authority. They spoke a language specific to their work; formed social, charitable, and trade union organizations in which they organized events on and off the job; founded and disseminated their own newspapers; and even issued traveling cards for those who sought transfers to other places. At work, operators used a variety of terms to designate angry, profane, ignorant, and other subscriber behavior. Women shortened official Bell System work descriptions to interpret the work in their own words. They even manipulated technical terms to pun.[1] Evident from the very beginning of telephony, this language evolved with the work process and the technology.

In their own publications, or in "women's pages" of company magazines and mixed (men and women) union newspapers, operators expressed the values of their work culture.[2] Conforming to the "white lady" model, columns in company journals reported on company-sponsored social outings and advised on subjects as varied as "The Gentle Art of Man-Trapping," cosmetics and fashion, recipes, dressmaking, gardening, and weight loss.[3] In the pages of union newspapers, operators wrote about these topics and reported on sports events, dances, fashion shows, and beauty contests. These subjects illustrate a convergence of opinion among management and workers about how women should look and behave as ladies. On the other hand, union newspapers such as the *Union Telephone Operator* openly and frequently criticized wage rates, hours, supervision, automation, and other deficient working conditions.

In their writings and other activities, operators challenged company paternalism, cultivated themselves as leaders, asserted their independence, and educated themselves about unionism and their rights as workers. As a response to the Bell System's attempt to monitor operators' leisure time at company camps and vacation homes, the Boston Telephone Operators' Union purchased its own private 4.5-acre retreat where any operator in the country could go simply to stroll, bowl, dance, watch movies, or participate in other social activities.[4] Later in that same year (1921), eight telephone operators were among the first eighty-two women to attend the famous Bryn Mawr summer school for workers.[5] This was only one example of telephone operators' participation in training and leadership institutes (see chapter 6). These manifestations of telephone operators' work culture demonstrate how operators sought to create and preserve their identities as women and workers. However, the best expressions of their values are exemplified in their resistance to company practices.

Even as they clung to the "white lady" image of themselves, operators engaged in strikes, boycotts, and other militant union activities. In many instances they allied with male unionists and middle-class women reformers to challenge Bell System working conditions and antiunionism. Operators frequently set the pace and led other operators and sometimes plant men in their fights against management. However, this militancy, manifested in specific and appropriate demands, was often diluted as a result of their alliances. Not trusting themselves and accepting the "white lady" rhetoric of "protection," operators frequently yielded leadership to their allies, who then changed operators' spontaneous demands to conform with male craft union ideology that was not always useful for addressing operators' problems. Consequently, operators failed to develop a meaningful strategy against the introduction of new technologies that adversely affected their work.

However, without formal organization, nothing would have been gained. The operators' alliances provided the organizational framework in which operators sometimes won wage increases, shorter hours, and union recognition. Although significant, these occasional victories only partially relieved the most severe conditions. The solutions proposed by the operators' allies (and eventually absorbed by the operators themselves) did not strike at the core of operators' complaints—technological degradation of work. Higher wages, shorter hours, and union grievance procedures did not ameliorate the strictly supervised and relentless, machine-driven work pace from which operators suffered. Male craft union ideology provided, at best, indirect and generic solutions (shorter workweeks) for operators' highly specific needs and circumstances.

Even if operators had maintained their initial demands, it is unlikely that they would have been totally victorious. Despite occasional triumphs in their unionization efforts, the superior power commanded by the Bell System usually defeated their most courageous undertakings. Indeed, this chapter focuses more on the operators' resistance in the face of such overwhelming power than on their victories.

Operators revolted within the context of a complex, culturally imposed identity that allowed young women striking for higher wages and better working conditions to wear fur coats, fashionable shoes and hats, and gloves on picket lines. While picketing, these same "ladies" threw rotten eggs, hooted, shouted, and sometimes even physically attacked their adversaries. These young women saw no contradiction in their acceptance of a "white lady" image that required advice and protection from their allies and assertive behavior against the Bell System. Telephone operators accepted the status and the moral, pious, virtuous identity of the "white lady" image, but they helped to shape that image and did not allow it to turn them into docile workers.

Unorganized Resistance: "Civil" Ladies, "Unruly" Girls

Whether it was because of the boyish pranks and impertinence or the girlish tendency to "air their voices" (gossip), operators were difficult to control from the beginning of telephony. In the prescientifically managed switchroom, ABT electrician Thomas D. Lockwood believed "that good service need[ed] close watching" since "the best staff of operators require[d] discipline and constant supervision."[6] Katherine M. Schmitt remembered that the operators often verbally "harassed" the managers who occasionally read to the operators the "rules and regulations of service and the proper tone of voice to use" in an effort to restrain the operators. Schmitt said "the fight would go on the next minute" after he had finished.[7] When they felt abused or unfairly treated, nineteenth-century operators, without the benefit of union representation, overtly and covertly opposed company disciplinary methods.

Despite the tests, technological devices, and other supervisory tactics, operators resisted working at the pace set by management. Bell System corporate literature abounds with complaints against operators who "threw up the annunciators," plugged in without answering, failed to clear out lines after completing calls, and in general balked at the company's attempts to impose systematic discipline. Managers complained that operators did not follow procedures and in many cases deliberately disobeyed rules when their individual responsibility could not be established.[8] B. W. Trafford of Chicago reported that in the "Express" (divided) system, the operators had a "tendency" to work in a "slow and machine-like method."[9]

In 1899, W. R. Westcott found in Cleveland that poor supervision, excessive loads, and loose operating procedures caused "very slow" service, "with a large amount of 'plugging up' and almost no 'team work.'" "Plugging up" demonstrated an overt resistance to the "pilot" light, since operators would plug in when they saw a light or annunciator but would not answer immediately. Teamwork referred to the company's mandate for operators to help each other. Operators refused to work in this way under speedup conditions. After Westcott reorganized the switchboard sections of the office to more evenly distribute and lessen operators' loads, service improved.[10] Without any particular fanfare, operators slowed their work pace when they found the opportunity to do so.

When passive resistance and individual pleas to the managers failed, operators talked back and argued with their superiors over many issues. They became more assertive and organized themselves in loose temporary units as the work became more demanding and the discipline more strict. Seeking a wage increase, operators threatened to strike the City and Suburban Telegraph Association of Cincinnati in June 1891. George N. Stone "bridged" the crises for the moment, but he considered the situation serious enough to launch a nationwide survey of wages paid in thirteen of the largest cities.[11]

During the summer of 1894, thirty operators petitioned the Chesapeake & Potomac Telephone Company in Baltimore "in relation to an increase in pay," forcing the managers to seek a method for increasing and equalizing wages based on merit.[12] These were modest victories, which showed that the first operators challenged company policies and that the Bell System was forced at an early date to make some wage adjustments.

Operators organized themselves and exerted their power over issues other than wage increases. Eighteen Indianapolis women operators struck for ninety minutes on July 28, 1892, "because they had decided they would work no longer under Miss Jennie R. Condell, the chief operator," who they thought "was too officious and used more authority than was necessary." Thoroughly cognizant of their power and when to wield it, these operators struck when the exchange manager was out to "dinner" between 1:30 and 2:30 P.M.[13] This strike was no small matter, having been reported in the *New York Tribune*, which prompted the General Manager of American Bell Telephone Company to demand explanations from the managers at Central Union Telephone Company. General Superintendent Beach explained that "a prompt investigation brought to light information which satisfied our local management that the Chief Operator was not a fit person for the position; she was therefore removed, and harmony immediately restored."[14] This kind of victory could be obtained more readily while the Bell System had not yet fully matured as an organizational hierarchy with developed methods of handling strikes. After 1900, managers countered operator resistance intransigently and repressively.

Turnover

The operators' most common response to the Bell System's unfair treatment was to leave. Contrary to the management's publicity, marriage was not the primary reason for high operator turnover. For example, in Milwaukee exchanges, where the turnover rate approached 50 percent in 1907, only ten of 109 operators left to get married.[15] Government investigators, reformers, and unionists attributed the Bell System turnover rate to low wages, long hours, and stressful working conditions. The 1910 U.S. Senate investigation found that women on the lower levels of the pay scale were the ones most likely to leave the Milwaukee exchanges. At higher salaries, turnover declined significantly.[16] A 1915 Bell System study found an average turnover rate of 51 percent in all the associated companies. In individual companies like Southwestern Bell (Texas), the rate was as high as 125 percent. Boston had the lowest turnover rate (14 percent), possibly because of unionization or the fact that they had the highest average weekly wage ($10.02).[17] Referring to New York City in 1920, Teresa Sullivan, vice president of Boston Telephone Operators Department, stated unequivocally that "conditions force them [operators] to look for better jobs."[18] The Bell System managers knew from their own research that marriage was not the cause of high turnover, and they also knew that high turnover had positive aspects for their own goals of increasing profit and control.[19]

High turnover militated against stabilizing the operating forces, but it also had two important benefits for the Bell System. According to Nelle B. Curry, operators achieved their "full efficiency" within six months to a year, but they could only obtain the maximum wage by long service (five to seven years). Consequently, "the company profits enormously by withholding the difference between the wages paid the girls and the amount which they actually earn on the basis of efficiency."[20] High turnover further benefited the company because each operator began at the bottom of the wage scale. The majority of operators (more than 50,000 in 1915) earned the lowest wages. Turnover also helped the company maintain control by impeding unionism. New young employees fearful of losing their jobs were the least likely to organize or have the skills necessary to successfully confront the company.

That high turnover benefited the Bell System is suggested by the fact that it instituted few changes to keep operators from leaving. Bell System solutions included hiring women as young as possible at starting wages slightly higher than those paid by other local industries. In periods of labor strife or labor shortages and in regions with generally high wages, Bell managers temporarily offered bonuses and other tokens to stabilize their workforces until the crises had subsided. For these employers, the solution meant finding the right kind of women, not improving the job.

As late as the 1970s, Illinois Bell studied male force loss and found that men left for the same reasons as women. Recommendations included "speeding up promotion, increasing wages, and tailoring jobs to skills" for men.[21] In reference to women, however, consultants suggested that the companies "hire only those women who could be counted on not to complain. . . . stop recruiting ambitious, educated women and take older employees" who were "more realistic about [her] goals within the Company," or, "someone who isn't looking for a glamorous career."[22] As women's union activism shows, managers were not always successful in hiring women who would be easily placated. In spite of the company's numerous rules governing behavior and operating procedures, and its hostility toward unions, women did not always leave in protest; many stayed and fought.

Tactics: Unionism and Antiunionism

From 1900 to 1920, operators, alone or with plant men, readily formed unions and waged strikes, particularly during periods of national labor unrest. Operators and linemen, for example, from October to December 1900 struck Southwestern Telephone and Telegraph company in San Antonio, Houston, and Waco. In San Antonio and other places, the strikers held out until September 1901. When the company imported operators and linemen to replace the protesting workers, the strike spread. Sporadic sympathy strikes and strike threats plagued the company's offices in Galveston, Temple, Fort Worth, and Dallas.[23] In one case, linemen who discovered that they had been brought to San Antonio from Chicago to scab walked off to union headquarters.[24] Telephone service in each city was temporarily severed, either because most of the operators walked out or because subscribers refused to use the phones when scabs operated them.[25] Line-cutting hampered toll service, and other acts of sabotage continued throughout the strike.[26]

Union demands and tactics, as well as company responses to this strike, exemplify patterns that telephone strikes followed for the first twenty years of the century. The IBEW Local No. 66 demanded an eight-hour day, time and a half for overtime, double time for Sundays and legal holidays, wage increases, and the "closed shop" (employment of union members only).[27] The company responded to these demands with a ruthless "win at any cost policy." J. E. Farnsworth, general manager of Southwestern Telephone and Telegraph Company (ST&T), for example, wrote to the special agent:

If the company follows my advice we will win no matter at what cost. I realize fully that it may cost the company many thousands of dollars in the loss of revenue and loss of property, but what is the poor girl going to do? Are we going to allow these people who have never had sense enough to earn over $75 per month, to run our business? If we give in to them today they will want something more tomorrow, and another week after, something extra again. We are simply ruined if we do not win the fight as I see the situation.[28]

Determined to prevent unionization and wage demands in other cities, ST&T Vice President Pettingill used spies and strikebreakers to return the exchanges to service without recognizing the unions.[29]

This defeat neither discouraged telephone workers' enthusiasm for unionism nor limited their tactics in the struggle for union recognition. Telephone workers in one area not only called for sympathy strikes against the same company in other territories, but they received the help of workers in local non-Bell industries. Frequently, in the West and in rural areas, operators took advantage of the competition between the Bell System and the Independents by striking one, then the other. From 1900 through 1908, unions sometimes forced Independents to accept favorable contracts, which the unions then attempted to force on the Bell System.[30] Simultaneously, strikers enlisted subscribers, including local governments and small businesses, to remove their Bell System phones or to simply not use them during the strike. This tactic was particularly successful in Butte, Montana, and Des Moines, Iowa, during 1902 and 1903 strikes there.[31]

Unlike some managers who softened their antiunion stance and sought compromises with the unions, telephone officials in every situation except Boston, Butte (where all labor was "entirely under the control of the labor organizations"), and a few other towns in Montana refused to recognize unions, especially in the form of a written contract or "closed shop."[32] Between 1900 and 1907, President Fish wrote to each associated company experiencing labor difficulties to instruct them not to recognize unions and not to sign any written contracts under any circumstances, regardless of the cost.[33] For example, Fish cautioned Iowa Telephone Company General Manager E. B. Smith that he "ought not to recognize the Telephone Operators' Union" because "it is alarming to think what might happen in a hard fought fight with telephone operators."[34] About two months later, after operators had won a favorable contract from a non-Bell company, he wrote to Smith:

> I am firmly convinced that it will be far better for us to lose all our business in Des Moines, rather than to settle the strike upon the basis of such a contract as the Mutual Telephone Company has made, or upon any basis which will "recognize the Union" in the sense in which the strikers and their representatives use those words. . . .
>
> We must, however, fight to the last ditch for the maintenance of our right to hire and discharge operators in accordance with our best judgment as to the necessity of the situation, and to maintain our standard of discipline in the telephone business. . . .
>
> It seems to me perfectly clear that in every respect you and the Company are right, and the operators and their fellow conspirators absolutely wrong, and I am surprised that the people of Des Moines do not generally take the same view.[35]

Often Bell managers, including President Fish, voluntarily raised salaries but maintained the right to hire both union and nonunion workers.

Consistently, the company harassed union members, fired them, and, when it could, forced them to withdraw from the union by making them sign loyalty oaths. If the local government favored the company, officials called out the police, national guard, or other military troops to force an end to strikes. The Bell System hired spies and agents to infiltrate the unions to gather information and to foment dissension and dissatisfaction among union members.[36] Traffic Manager G. P. Robinson wrote to Assistant General Manager A. J. Steiss that the resolution of the 1904 Portland, Oregon, operator's strike had been "put into the hands of a committee of the Federated Trades and the Citizens' Alliance secret service man is on this committee so we are getting full reports of the conditions."[37] In Butte, Des Moines, and Wichita, where the mayor, local government, and police sided with the strikers, the company hired private detectives to protect its property and imported nonunion workers.[38]

When local governments did not cooperate, company officials also appealed to higher legislative and judicial bodies to grant and enforce injunctions. During the 1902–3 Butte strike, Rocky Mountain Bell President George Y. Wallace complained to AT&T President Fish that "the police are in perfect sympathy with the strikers, and will not render us one particle of service, neither will the Sheriff of the County." He suggested that U.S. marshals or U.S. troops should be called out against the strikers who if they had to face the U.S. Army, Wallace thought, would "hide and run to their holes like whipped curs."[39] If local newspapers showed hostility toward the unions, Bell companies enlisted their editorial support and advertised the company's point of view. Hence, Wallace was disappointed that Montana newspapers did not side with the company, even though it had given the newspapers a 50 percent rebate on toll calls and large amounts of advertising.[40] For the most part, however, Bell System management successfully used these strategies to limit the spread of unionism until the U.S. government took control of the Bell System in 1918 during World War I.

Bell Welfare Capitalism: Employee Benefit Plans

To soften the harshness of their antiunion stance and secure employee loyalty, the Bell System instituted a policy of welfare work that culminated in an Employee Benefit Plan. J. D. Ellsworth, an AT&T attorney, detailed the "business reasons" for establishing such a plan: "because some provision for employes [sic] is the logical concomitant of a functional organization and increasing specilization [sic]; because provision for employes makes it easier to maintain freedom from Labor Unions; because of the increased efficiency which may be expected, because it would help secure the right sort of advertising from our 100,000 employes."[41] To protect profits, Bell officials designed the plan so that the subscribers would have to pay for it through "sufficient rates."[42]

On January 1, 1913, the Bell System inaugurated its "Plan for Employees' Pensions, Disability Benefits and Insurance." The plan offered "payment of definite amounts to its employees when they [were] disabled by accident or sickness or when they [were] retired from service, or, in the event of death to their dependent relatives."[43] Only those who had served two years in the company received sickness benefits. The plan awarded pension benefits to women either after the age of fifty-five or at fifty with twenty-five or more years of service. Beneficiaries of employees who had served five years received life insurance benefits if death resulted from an illness or off the job. Beneficiaries of all employees who died as a result of an on-the-job accident received benefits. Obviously, women who, on the average, served between two and three years did not benefit much from these plans. For those women who did qualify, a rigorous set of restrictions based on managerial discretion had to be met before the benefits were dispensed (i.e., seeing the company doctor or reporting an illness within a certain time limit).[44]

Since few operators remained in the company long enough to receive pensions, in January 1915, the company established a Plan to Aid Employees of the Bell System to become stockholders of AT&T for the "purpose of [giving] employees . . . an opportunity to become part owners of the business" and thereby encourage them to remain with the company.[45] It was unlikely, however, that operators who averaged $30 monthly, would remain with the company just to be able to purchase a $110 share of stock at a contribution limited to $2 monthly.

In another attempt to appease women workers specifically, Bell System managers established a bonus system in some of the larger cities. Fearful that New England operators' militancy would spread, New York Telephone Company in 1912 instituted a bonus plan based on length of service. Aimed at retaining operators, the plan paid operators $25 for two years of continuous service. Operators with longer work histories received more. Suffering from a 40 percent turnover rate, New York managers determined that the cost of training new operators was more expensive than the cost of providing bonuses.[46] By February 1913, some form of the New York plan had been established in other large cities.[47] According to AT&T Vice President Thayer, the plan worked to the "satisfaction of the Company, the only drawback being some embarrassment in limiting it to large cities."[48] He recommended bonuses as "an alternative to a raise in rates of pay or in connection with a raise in the rate of pay."[49]

Operators Organize and Strike

These paternalistic machinations failed to deceive the operators. From 1900 through 1907, operators' strikes in Texas, California, Montana, Iowa, Utah, and Idaho obtained higher wages, shorter workdays, and even union recognition in labor strongholds like Butte. After 1907, particularly in 1912 and 1913, operator activism was concentrated in Boston and the New England area. Organized in March 1912, the Boston Telephone Operators' Union negotiated an agreement with the company that maintained relative labor harmony from 1913 to 1919. Despite Bell System antiunion policy, and with the support of the Women's Trade Union League (WTUL) and other Boston trade unions, operators forced the New England company to bargain. Without striking, the operators won a wage increase, union recognition, and the establishment of an "adjustment board" through which the operators expected to address their other demands.[50]

Influenced by their New England sisters' success, St. Louis operators did not fare as well when they struck in 1913. Organized with the advice and assistance of the Boston operators and the WTUL, St. Louis operators supported an IBEW strike for union recognition and the reinstatement of fired union organizers. The strike failed when the company mobilized all of its resources against the union, and the men settled without allowing the operators to vote on the settlement.[51]

By 1917, operator militancy shifted to the Pacific Northwest where the IBEW organized locals at Aberdeen and other small Washington state and Idaho towns. Soon other locals formed in the larger Washington state and Oregon cities.[52] Some 9,000 operators and 3,200 plant men struck the Pacific Bell Telephone Company when it refused in November 1917 to negotiate with the men unless they abandoned the operators. The federal government intervened, and the strike ended with a settlement that awarded the operators and the men wage increases and union recognition.[53] Comptroller DuBois wrote to President Vail that, even in the South, there were "rumors and some more definite indication of unrest and even of attempted organization of operators coming from Arkansas, Georgia, Virginia and Philadelphia."[54]

Operators who struck Southern Bell Telephone and Telegraph Company in Jacksonville, Florida, in December 1917 failed to win their demands when the company brought in strikebreakers and refused to negotiate.[55] Chicago operators in April 1918 threatened a citywide strike for wages to meet the high cost of living. B. E. Sunny, president of Chicago Telephone Company, averted the strike when he announced that the company would discontinue free calls requesting time of day, "which would result in a considerable saving which we would give to the operators in the shape of a 10% increase in wages."[56] As the Bell System encountered more and more aggressive unionism, the federal government, alarmed at the potential disruption of wartime communications services, nationalized the telephone and telegraph industries from August 1, 1918, to July 31, 1919.

Government Control: Postmaster General's Reign

After nationalization, the Bell System came under the authority of the U.S. Post Office, headed by Postmaster General Albert S. Burleson, who took a strong antiunion stance that included firing operators who struck or joined unions. Burleson stipulated that all employees could join unions or any other organizations, but he would "not deal with persons not connected with the service, who often are authorized and seek to speak for and represent but a small percentage of those employed therein."[57] Burleson's actions helped defeat almost every strike during his reign.

Nevertheless, operators throughout the United States participated in the strike wave that affected many American industries during World War I. For example, St. Paul and Minneapolis operators, seeking a wage increase, struck in November 1918, were locked out for three months, and when some were reemployed, worked at the old wages and lost all seniority.[58] These abusive tactics so terrorized the operators that they met secretly after this strike.[59] Burleson justified his punitive measures with the opinion that the operators had shown "the most flagrant disregard for the rights of the public" by striking during a flu epidemic and especially after the company had promised a raise "as soon as an increase in rates could be obtained."[60]

Wichita operators struck Southwestern Bell Telephone Company on December 4, 1918, over the firing of a supervisor who had circulated a petition for higher operator wages. Burleson and AT&T officials humiliated these women when they decided that "only those who could satisfy management that they had been 'intimidated and misled' by 'ringleaders' [could be] re-employed."[61] "The interest of good discipline and administration," rationalized Burleson, "requires that organized employees must not be permitted to violate positive instructions . . . and expect to escape punishment by threats of or the calling of strikes."[62] Operators continued to organize, especially in the South where managers had always fiercely suppressed attempts at unionization. One Southern manager, in 1919, wrote to AT&T Vice President Thayer that operators had organized in Louisville, Nashville, Atlanta, Jacksonville, Florida, Waycross and Brunswick, Georgia, Meridian, Mississippi, Columbia, South Carolina, and Wilmington, North Carolina.[63]

In an imaginative twist of meanings, IBEW and other unionists used a bulletin issued by Burleson as one of its most significant organizing tools.[64] The Trades and Labor Council of Denver assured telephone workers that their right to organize had been "recognized and affirmed" by the National War Labor Board that President Wilson appointed. Furthermore, since the industry had been taken over by the U.S. government, "Woodrow Wilson, our great President, urges you to organize so you can all be dealt with as a unit."[65] The Chicago Federation of Labor passed out cards in October 1918 that read:

> *"HELLO GIRLS"*
> Be One Hundred Per Cent Americans. Join in a Union of the AMERICAN FEDERATION OF LABOR, by becoming members of the ELECTRICAL WORKERS' INTERNATIONAL UNION. The telephones of this country are now under the control of the United States Government. They will be glad to meet you, their employees, to adjust any grievances or wage demands that you may make, but you should have a good, strong Union to present your side of the case, if you expect any increase in wages or better working conditions.[66]

Workers frequently insisted on higher wages and better working conditions as government employees.

In April 1919, New England operators waged one of the few successful strikes during government control of the Bell System. Operators shut down service in five New England states for six days as the result of Burleson's refusal to recognize the direct bargaining procedures that the company agreed to and had been following since 1913. The chaos generated by Burleson's intransigence led the general public, businesses, labor councils, the mayor of Boston, and the Massachusetts governor to demand a resolution. Burleson acquiesced on the fifth day of the strike to direct negotiations that led to continued union recognition, wage increases, and no loss of positions or seniority for the operators.[67] This victory provided the impetus for telephone workers to organize and strike the Bell System across the country.

During the summer and fall of 1919, operators left their switchboards in the South (Atlanta, Columbia, South Carolina, Norfolk, Virginia, Jacksonville, Florida), the Southwest (Shawnee, Oklahoma), the Midwest (Cleveland and St. Louis), and the Pacific Coast, including California and other Northwestern states. Jacksonville, Florida, operators struck again in April 1919 when the company denied their request for a wage increase and dismissed thirty-eight union operators. Before the strike they informed managers that "the Company's position was not satisfactory, and that unless the proposed contract was executed, including the wage scale just as written, the operators would go on strike." Asked if they represented all the operators, they answered "yes." Asked when they would go on strike, they said they would not tell. Asked if they intended to give the company any notice, they answered "no."[68] Feisty, for Southern belles who, reputedly, were difficult to organize. The Bell System's ability to replace operators with strikebreakers and the failure of other unions to go out in sympathy ended this strike and others, either in total defeat or small wage increases.[69] Yet the operators' struggle against tyrannical management is admirable.

Operators Make Their Own Demands

The strike history of telephone operators from 1900 until 1920 demonstrates women's willingness to organize themselves into unions and to strike even against this most ruthless adversary. Even when men feared "petticoat rule" (women operators were far more numerous than male plant workers) and did not want women to be full members of their union, women accepted a separate department in the IBEW so that they could still have some organizational backing to attack the company.[70] Operators often struck in support of linemen, and, in 1913, they even helped to organize men in Boston.[71] Possibly inspired by the Suffragist movement and increasing trade union militancy, or simply weary of injustices, telephone operators expanded their "white lady" identities to engage in union struggles.

Unfortunately, these struggles were based on a trade union ideology that inadequately confronted the company on the issues particularly relevant to the well-documented effects on operators of technological changes. The solutions for lessening that impact, when addressed at all, were conceptually limited. In the trade unionist view, a shorter workday/week, higher wages, and union recognition held the highest priority and were expected to solve the important problems. In the short term, these goals reflected operators' concerns. Women working more than fifty hours a week for less than a living wage were certainly interested in such changes. The importance of higher wages and union recognition cannot be overemphasized, especially when all the forces of capital concentrated on suppressing wages and unionism. But in the long term, technology and changing working conditions, which unions' strategy failed to address, constrained operators more severely than the long hours and low wages.

The union's conceptualization of workers' problems generally, and of women's problems specifically, led to the failure to make demands that would fundamentally change the work process. Although "skilled" workers fought for the right to control their work, trade union ideology, as reflected by the American Federation of Labor, particularly at the turn of the century, still focused on narrow "craft" protections while it conceded to management the right to organize "unskilled" labor according to production needs. Because craft unions maintained some of their control and had their own work rules, their demands reflected the need for more money, a shorter workweek, and union recognition.

Thus, when the telephone operators joined the IBEW, a craft union, they adopted these types of demands. Craft ideology, for the operator, endorsed the quest for "adequate" compensation for the loss of workers' control rather than a change in the organization of production. Male telephone workers' jobs could be associated with electricians' work, and since the majority of repairmen still worked outside, they remained relatively independent despite company measures to control them. Male telephone workers who worked on lines, cables, and other equipment could not be timed precisely or speeded up by the use of technology.[72]

In general, male workers reluctantly organized and allied with women workers because they felt that women's work outside the home would conflict with their male ideals of the proper place for wives and mothers.[73] Some men also viewed women as potential competitors who would lower the pay scale for men. However, telephone men usually abandoned these fears in recognition of the operators' more powerful position in the highly segregated workplace. Often, men asked operators to join their unions because operators could shut down the telephone industry during strikes, not because they believed in solidarity with women. When telephone men organized women, they usually patronized and condescended to them, invoking the "white lady" image. Male trade unionists viewed telephone operators as "defenseless girls" in need of protection and guidance.[74] Many operators accepted this image of themselves.

Consistently, operators sought the help of outsiders, not just to increase their numbers, but to help them formulate their demands. Although they were helpful and supportive, male trade unionists and female reformers, encumbered with a nineteenth-century, middle-class definition of womanhood, offered strategies and demands that ultimately accepted operators' loss of control over their work.

In some instances, these conceptions actually changed operators' spontaneous demands so that they conformed more with traditional trade union ideas. For example, all but three Des Moines operators in June 1902 petitioned the Iowa Telephone Company for a change in wage and hours schedules and union recognition.[75] When notified that the company had practically conceded all of their wage demands, the operators insisted on union recognition. The company asked them "what recognizing the Union meant" to them. According to General Manager Smith "this question seemed a poser and they said they would let us know later on." After some consideration, a committee of women replied as summarized by Smith:

> that recognition of the Union meant that they, the operators, should elect their chief operator who would do the hiring and discharging of operators and that our operating room would be open at all times to their walking delegate or business agent. The committee was asked what would happen if the company saw fit to discharge an operator. They said the company could not do this, that they would have to file their complaint with the chief operator, who would take the matter up with the business agent who in turn would investigate the matter and decide whether the company could discharge an operator or not. If the company did discharge the operator against the advice of the business agent the operators would then all quit.[76]

The significance of the demand to "elect" the chief operator has to be assessed in the context of that job at the time. In some places, supervisors had not entered the corporate structure, which meant that chief operators continued to supervise operators directly. In addition to hiring and firing, chief operators monitored operators to insure that they worked quickly and followed all operating procedures. If operators controlled the person who disciplined them, they would control their work. These young women in Iowa, probably unaware of the significance of their demand in terms of "workers' control," simply proposed what they envisioned would make their working conditions better. The company "positively" refused to recognize the operators' union, and a strike ensued. These women had also been in contact with the Mutual Telephone Company (Independent) operators who walked away from their switchboards at the same time. Linemen, members of IBEW, also struck in sympathy with the operators. Strikebreakers were "roundly abused on the streets, in their homes and over the telephone wires."[77] Public opinion favored the "girl" operators, and the mayor had all the phones removed from the office of city hall, the police, and fire stations.

As soon as the operators went on strike, they requested the aid of the state Federation of Labor. This organization, along with the Trades and Labor Assembly, paid the operators $1.00 a day during the six months of the strike. These groups also took over negotiations and imposed their program on the operators. General Manager Smith described the meeting in which this change took place:

> On July 10th I had a conference with President Minton of the State Federation of Labor in Des Moines in which he said that the young ladies were wrong in having demanded that they be allowed to elect their chief operator etc., and that while they, the young ladies were under the impression that they would have a right to do this, *he had knocked that out of their heads* (my emphasis), saying that the chief operator was looked upon as an official of the company and they did not want her in the Union.[78]

In the end, the women won union recognition—but recognition as defined by male unionists, not by themselves. For the operators, union recognition meant having a voice in the selection of the person who supervised them. For male trade unionists, it meant a "closed shop." Women, inexperienced in trade union negotiations, had no knowledge of the trade unionists' ideology that accepted limitations on the kind of demands that could be put forward. Male trade unionists, as well as managers, accepted without question that the company would have total control over the person in charge. In the mind of the uninitiated operator, truly acting in her own interest, this was not preordained.

Iowa operators were not the only ones who wanted to have some impact on management's prerogatives. Against the counsel of male trade unionists, switchboard operators walked away from their boards in San Francisco at 7 A.M. on May 2, 1907. These women picketed until midnight, and, in the words of one manager, they and their sympathizers "almost at once resorted to lawlessness in the form of rotten-egg throwing, throwing of stones, refuse from the streets, dirt, etc."[79] Along with changes in wages and hours, they demanded that the Pacific Telephone and Telegraph Company "recognize an Operator's Union; withdraw Male Chief Operators from the San Francisco Offices; . . . cut out all Service Inspection in the City and abolish certain Operating Rules."[80] In addition to these demands, historian Stephen H. Norwood stated that the operators "called for a revision of the company's dress code, [and] a rearrangement of the switchboard so that operators would no longer have to 'stretch painfully' to reach numbers at the ends of their section."[81] Though some 450 of 525 operators struck for these demands, they were defeated by the company's overwhelming strength and ability to offer strikebreakers chauffeured automobile service to and from the office, sleeping facilities for those who chose to remain there, as well as a rented piano, gramophone, home-cooked meals, and "everything" to make "the surroundings pleasant and cheerful."[82]

Nevertheless, these demands indicated that when women articulated their own solutions to what they perceived as their problems, they voiced decidedly different ideas from those of men.[83] The San Francisco operators (unaware that they were attacking corporate structure, yet deliberately trying to change their working conditions) unwittingly attacked the very core of the Bell System's control over the workplace—the chief operator, service inspection, and operating rules. If the operators, in fact, did demand a rearrangement of the switchboard, it was the first indication that women sought to challenge the technological degradation of their work. Perhaps the operators had hoped that a female chief operator would be more lenient or understanding of their grievances.[84] Even if she had not been, working conditions would have been materially improved without the constant testing and the supervised enforcement of operating practices. Interestingly, even after male trade unionists had advised them against striking, refused to strike in sympathy, and voted against a telephone boycott, women operators still chose to "place leadership of the strike in the hands of a committee of Labor Council leaders."[85]

Another example of how women conceptualized their own organization differently from men was in the formation of Mutual Benefit Plans. Of more than a dozen such organizations established between 1890 and

1910, only one excluded men. The dues of its female members, free of company contribution, totally supported the Colorado Telephone Company Benefit Association located in Denver, which women organized in November 1906. The association had no age restrictions, compelled all new employees to join, and by May 1, 1910, had 542 members. This association was also the only one that made provision for 4.5 weeks of hospitalization in addition to the regular sickness and death benefits offered by most men's organizations. Women workers recognized the importance of providing for their own health care.[86] These examples illustrate how women workers, when left to their own organic and spontaneous responses, sometimes formulated demands and strategies that alleviated their specific problems.

Despite their enthusiastic advocacy for women workers, female reformers also failed to understand the demands formulated by telephone operators. Consequently, when the operators sought help from the reformers, their issues were redefined to conform with contemporary ideas about trade unionism and women's proper place.[87] The work of the middle-class women in the Women's Trade Union League, which was important and should not be minimized, illustrates this pattern. The WTUL helped to empower women workers by organizing, educating, and providing leadership opportunities to women throughout the United States. However, like male trade unionists, middle-class women viewed the operators as young girls who needed protection from managerial abuses in terms of wages, hours, and moral threats. They failed to understand the importance of addressing the technological pacing of work in addition to low wages and long hours.

For example, on March 26, 1912, twenty Boston operators, having independently organized themselves, went to the local chapter of the WTUL "looking . . . for advice and assistance." They told the secretary, Mabel Gillespie, "that they could no longer submit to excessive hours of exacting work performed under severe nervous tension; to unpaid overtime, to a petty system of penalizing, etc., . . . and announced their intention of striking that night."[88] Anxious to organize unions, the secretary persuaded the operators not to follow the course they had chosen. Instead, "WTUL officers decided that the telephone operators logically belonged to the . . . IBEW . . ." along with plant men. A male union official from IBEW, "summoned from New York" soon organized the Boston telephone operators into a sublocal of the linemen's local since IBEW had no constitutional provision for operators.[89] According to former operator and union leader Julia O'Connor, "the chief grievance and slogan of the new union was 'abolition of the split trick' " (an eight- or nine-hour workday split into two parts that resulted in a twelve- or fourteen-hour day).[90]

From March 1912 to April 1913, the Telephone Operators' Union leadership conferred with management of New England Telephone and Telegraph Company over the workers' demands. The company capitulated over wage demands, the eight-hour day, fifteen-minute rest breaks, and it promised not to assign operators with eighteen months or more seniority to split tricks. These promises fell through when the company appointed a new president who reneged on the agreements. On April 7, 1913, the operators voted to strike, and the next day the company began importing strikebreakers who management housed lavishly in the most luxurious hotels. The company's "harassment and intimidation" of the operators created a favorable public sentiment toward the operators.

The business community had suffered immensely from a strike by the Elevated Streetcar Workers the previous year. Hence, businessmen wanted no more city-wide disruptions of service, and they clamored for compromise. So did the newspapers, the mayor, and members of the state legislature. Various Boston trade unions were sympathetic to the operators, and many offered to strike if the operators struck.[91] But more importantly, this strike was one of the few times that male telephone workers had promised to strike in sympathy with the operators. Despite the importation of strikebreakers, the situation presented a most auspicious time for operators to strike and win. Indeed, the Telephone Operators' Union leadership as well as IBEW union officials and WTUL leaders had a difficult time keeping the operators at the boards in the face of the company's attempt to intimidate them.[92]

Instead of striking, the operators sought and accepted the advice of their allies. Even when they demonstrated independence by negotiating directly with management, the operators "during intervals . . . conferred with IBEW Vice President Gustave Bugniazet and the presidents of the Boston IBEW linemen's and cable splicers' locals."[93] Before the negotiations, the union "under the influence of the WTUL and IBEW organizers, . . . formulated standard trade union demands, including establishing a formal mechanism for collective bargaining, handling grievances, and improving wages and hours. There was no direct appeal by the union for restructuring of the work process—for example, by reducing excessive supervision or the pace of work."[94] In fairness to WTUL and IBEW, the list of demands they finally submitted did reflect most of the operators' initial concerns.[95] The settlement included a reduced workday (from nine and one-half hours to eight), wage increases based on skill and seniority, union recognition, and an adjustment board to handle other issues. "Split tricks" were "minimized" and made "non-compulsory" for those with eighteen or more months of service, but not abolished.[96] The settlement made no mention of the meticulous supervision, a system of penalties, or operating rules.

Operators had won major demands without striking and without attacking the technological pacing of their work because they had yielded the ideological leadership of their struggle to their allies. Even though telephone operators resisted male domination in the IBEW by accepting a separate department within the union, and even though they resisted the WTUL shift in focus away from organizing to legislative reform, operators still accepted an ideology that channeled their militancy away from their primary concerns. As they negotiated for themselves, they abandoned their own impulses in favor of an ideological point of view derived from male "craft" trade unionism that was inappropriate to their situation.

In 1921, operators repeated this pattern, even as their leader, Julia S. O'Connor, asked the Second Biennial Convention of the Telephone Operators' Department of the IBEW "to condemn the boycott against telephone companies," because it was not a tactic that "naturally suggests itself to our locals." Rather, she argued, "it is foisted upon them by well-meaning central bodies, or individual labor advisers who find the boycott effective in their own industry."[97] Cognizant of the union's failure to grant the telephone operators' "full recognition of [their] right, as well as [their] ability, to determine [their] own organizational policy," O'Connor appealed to women unionists to "patiently accept . . . for the present" that they would be receiving "gratuitous advice, protection and guardianship from all elements of the labor movement." She admitted that "we are still under the necessity of being saved from our friends," but that it was time that these friends recognize the operators' "right to adopt legislation and endorse policies which will best serve the interests of our movement." She declared that "the telephone operators are growing up!"[98] This critical assertion of operators' independence was not followed through in the actions that it suggests. Indeed, in the same report, O'Connor stated that "the perfection of the automatic telephone is far off," and that operators would continue "to be the heart of the service" for at least another generation. The union was evidently poorly informed about the Bell System's plans in 1921. Operators continued to follow outsiders.

Telephone operators, when organized by men or middle-class female allies, did not respond to the technological degradation of operators' work. One wonders why reformers and trade unionists, who were so aware of operators' strenuous working conditions, did not formulate a more effective strategy to alleviate these conditions. Part of the explanation certainly lies with the position taken by the President of the American Federation of Labor, Samuel Gompers. In an article headlined "Accept the Machine—Organize the Workers," he argued that the cigarmakers had struck and lost against the introduction of a cigar-rolling device (molds) because there was no way of stopping progress. "From that time," he stated, he "realized . . . that it was absolutely futile for workmen to protest against or go on strike against the introduction of a new machine, a new device or a new tool."[99] Under his leadership, most AFL unions sought to share in the profits of new technology rather than fight against it.[100]

The "protectors" of women (and sometimes the women themselves) erroneously believed that a shortened workday and more relief periods would lessen the stress. Yes, the long hours contributed to the nervous strain, but the required pace at which operators answered calls caused the greater amount of pressure. Even one hour of answering calls within a ten-second limit according to very strict guidelines under total supervision would produce nervousness. Less work per hour *and* shorter workdays would have been a better solution to the problem.

Unionists and reformers failed to conceptualize the technological possibilities that would encompass reducing the rate at which management compelled operators to answer calls. For operators, technology could have been a tool by which they changed their working conditions. A simple rewiring of the Intermediate Distributing Frame would have made operating less fast, but operators and their allies overlooked this possibility of relieving operators' stress. Even in a company like New England Telephone and Telegraph, where relative labor harmony existed between 1913 and 1919, or in Butte, where all labor was "union labor," the unions did not advance this strategy. A demand to slow the work pace was not more radical than the demand for an eight-hour day in the context of ten- and twelve-hour days for those working "split tricks." Yet it simply did not occur to unionists that they could change this aspect of the work.

As long as operators and unions accepted the premise that management could introduce at will changes in work organization or any type of technology it developed, they could not effectively resist the impact of technology. The power and resources at the company's disposal to suppress workers cannot be overlooked. Because operators for various reasons had never effectively addressed the speedups, the loss of autonomy, and the skill inherent in the new technology, the company successfully combined automation and personnel practices to eliminate most resistance. Regimentation, government control, and company antiunion practices had prepared the way, but automation, like common-battery systems at the turn of the century, gave the Bell System the technological means to enforce its policies.

PART TWO | The Dial Era, 1920–1960

Although the Bell System earned enormous profits under government control, it faced a severe deterioration in service, tremendous backlogs, and an unstable and demoralized workforce at the end of World War I. Telephone operators' frequent, militant, and sometimes effective resistance to Burleson's policies during the war alarmed Bell System managers. Even a flawed trade unionist strategy threatened profits and control over the workplace. Executives feared a costly and unruly operating force if they did not adopt appropriate technological and bureaucratic precautions to subdue the operators. Officials of AT&T determined that automation and representative associations (company unions) would be effective deterrents to independent unionism and rising wages. In the long term, automation would eliminate the reliance on operators, and in the short term, company unions would diffuse militancy and stabilize the workforce. When the government returned telephone service to private control in 1919, the first employee associations had been formed, and reliable and efficient automatic systems had been field-tested.

Neither company unions nor full automation had been Bell System objectives before the war. There had been no threat of widespread unionism and prewar automatic switching systems were inferior to manual systems.[1] The reasons for the Bell System's uncertainty about automation and its initial reluctance to accept it are this chapter's subjects. No attempt will be made to give an exhaustive account of the numerous types of automatic switching systems patented during this period. Instead, the process will be recounted and delineated by which AT&T executives simultaneously developed the technology and incrementally relaxed their ideal of personalized service.

Operators and their skills significantly shaped this process. Managers marketed telephone service based on nineteenth-century notions of servitude in which young, "compliant" women accommodated male subscribers' requests. Businessmen purchased Bell service with the expectation of receiving prompt, reliable, and confidential service without having to perform any action other than merely lifting the receiver. Of course, managers were reluctant to abandon the personalized service that had been a cornerstone in their defeat of the Independents. But then, the "ladies" revolted during the war and thereby contributed to management's acceptance of automation.

Ultimately, the convergence and evolution of several developments persuaded the Bell System to automate its local service in the post–World War I era. Most important, machine switching proved technologically and economically possible as a result of continuous experiments and investigations conducted by Bell System engineers. Second, management's perception of a shrinking labor pool, combined with a rapid increase in operators' wages and increasing militancy, intensified the sense of urgency among managers. And, finally, the Bell System progressively disassembled its long-established cultural links with subscribers by eliminating much of the customer contact and many of the free services that operators formerly provided. With the competition clearly defeated and the Bell System in control of the major portion of telephone service by the early 1920s, Bell managers felt comfortable about relaxing their strict standards of personalized service.[2] Telephone service had become an indispensable part of American life. Hence, AT&T gradually automated its switching exchanges as it became technically, economically, and culturally feasible.

Reluctant Observers: Evolution of Early Automatics

For nearly forty years after the first automatic system had been invented, AT&T remained indecisive about a fully automated telephone service.[3] The initial reluctance to automate was not caused by lack of familiarity with these systems. Even though imperfect in conception and implementation, the idea of automatic systems arose almost simultaneously with manual systems. M. D. Connolly, T. A. Connolly, and Thomas J. McTighe received the first patent granted for an automatic system in 1879, a year after the first successful manual exchanges had been in operation.

Like other early automatics, this system never actually operated on a commercial scale, but it did establish a foundation for later work. Indeed, technicians patented and offered for sale more than eighty-six automatic systems, devices, and improvements between 1879 and 1898. Thomas D. Lockwood, ABT's patent attorney, reviewed many of these new systems and approved the purchase of some as a safeguard against the future.[4] Lockwood, however, rejected the majority of the patent offers because he remained convinced that the company's aim "should in all cases be to secure simplicity in operation, and simplicity in mechanism, rather than complication; and to do nothing by machinery which can be as well, or more surely, done manually; . . ."[5] Nonetheless, ABT executives, cognizant of the many claims made by inventors of automatic features, permitted their own engineers to work on various design projects for such features.[6]

At first, Bell System engineers invented various types of automatics in an attempt to solve the high cost of service to small towns where not enough customers justified the salary of one operator, or even 24-hour service.[7] At this time, Bell managers viewed automatic switching systems as temporary measures to provide service for thirty to forty-five subscribers. These systems, they expected would inevitably be replaced by full manual systems when the number of subscribers exceeded these limits.

Furthermore, company officials, absorbed with solving the "big city problem," considered automatic switching impractical and unreliable for servicing urban areas. The "big city problem" was twofold. Unlike other industries, switchboard production suffered from a "diseconomy" of scale—the larger the number of subscribers, the more expensive the switchboard. And subscriber growth increased the number of telephone offices (exchanges) because calls could not be completed in one exchange. Equipment had to be provided to transfer calls to various exchanges via special lines called trunks, which led to more wiring and more errors as calls were transferred from office to office. "No intelligent person" who had experience in telephone exchange work, Lockwood declared, would "seriously entertain such a proposition" as using automatics for large exchanges.[8] Automatic systems required increased initial costs, high maintenance provisions, and extremely complicated equipment highly susceptible to breakdown. More importantly, it required the subscriber to make a number of sequential manipulations in order to complete a call. During this early period, Bell managers resisted automation based on the company's conviction that manual switching was technically superior and that an operator was needed to deliver high-quality, "personal service."

Not everyone, however, viewed depersonalization in negative terms. Almon B. Strowger (1839–1902), a schoolteacher turned undertaker, reputedly angered by an operator who "diverted" the family of a deceased friend to competitors, invented an automatic exchange in 1889 for the elimination of operators. Fortunately for the Bell companies, the first Strowger system needed solutions to a considerable number of operating problems before it could be truly competitive with the manuals. Initially, the Strowger automatic used five wires instead of the customary two found in manual systems, which substantially increased costs for installation, equipment, and maintenance. At the subscriber's station, local batteries remained necessary, creating further maintenance problems and burdens for the subscriber until 1892. Since the first Strowger systems also lacked dials, subscribers had to manipulate a number of buttons to complete a call. Independents introduced dials in 1896, but the Bell System found that the operation of dials created a considerable amount of work for the subscriber.[9]

Less than a month after Strowger received his patent, he sent a circular and his business card to ABT. Lockwood, the company's patent attorney, wrote the following assessment to ABT President Hudson: "There is nothing practical or meritorious about the peculiar form of apparatus described in this patent. . . . The patent would be of no use to this Company or to any of its affiliations."[10] Lockwood did not reply to Strowger. Snubbed by the Bell System, Strowger allied with two other inventors to form what became the largest and most successful automatic telephone company and telephone equipment manufacturer in the United States, the Strowger Automatic Telephone Exchange.[11] On November 3, 1892, that company installed the first commercial Strowger automatic exchange at La Porte, Indiana. This system and its numerous improvements established the foundation for all-automatic equipment of the step-by-step type.

Lockwood's assessment of automatic switching had been hasty, but his opinions reflect the reasons for ABT's initial reluctance to automate. Summarizing a report on the Romaine-Callender Automatic Exchange, Lockwood suggested why ABT ought to "decline to identify . . . with the invention":

the mechanism must be more costly than ordinary mechanism . . . , the said machine is inherently complex in the extreme.

The increased complexity involves increased liability to get out of order, and this in turn makes the practically constant attendance of a skilled artisan a necessity.

The strongest assertion made in behalf of the economy of such apparatus is that by its use, the operator may be dispensed with.

But the operator is not a very costly appliance, considering that she brings to her work (theoretically at least) a modicum of human intelligence, and introduces elements conspicuous only by their absence in the automatic apparatus, to wit, elasticity of operation, the power of meeting irregular and chance contingencies, and the power of dealing with the public. . . .[12]

Of course, "the power of dealing with the public" still concerned managers in 1893. While AT&T's long distance, toll, and other services continued to require operators, Independents could and did achieve savings because they operated few toll lines and provided no long distance service. On the expiration of the Bell patents in 1894, Independent companies hastily installed automatic exchanges to provide a more formidable opposition.

For the Bell System, however, the early automatics, compared with the manual systems, were as technically inadequate as they were economically unfeasible. Aside from the manual manipulations required by subscribers, the automatics provided none of the variety of services obtainable in manual exchanges. In addition to individual "personal service," manual exchanges offered such public services as party lines, coin boxes, pay stations (attended and nonattended), official rates, message rates, and flat rates.[13] Many automatic features long in use on the manuals were unavailable in automatic systems. Impractical and inflexible trunking inhibited connections between automatic exchanges and other automatic or manual exchanges; likewise, the bulky Strowger switches limited the size of automatic exchanges, whereas manual exchanges could accommodate up to ten thousand subscribers.[14] Also, few automatic exchanges offered any of these features at all before 1907.

Most Bell System managers, however, agreed with Lockwood that in exchange for the elimination of operators who earned small salaries, the first automatics offered higher installation, production, and maintenance costs because of the wages paid to skilled craftsmen, unreliable equipment, and limited types of services. As late as March 26, 1900, Lockwood argued against adopting automatics in small places, except in a small community where some service would be better than none, or in the case of competition, "which, even though done at a loss, or very little profit, is directly profitable as holding the field; and as teaching the community to use and depend on the telephone; and ultimately to want something better."[15] Economically, according to Lockwood, automatics were "no saving."

Of course, the Independents made claims of extraordinary savings and conveniences in their aggressive advertising campaign against the Bell System during the competitive era. The Automatic Telephone and Electric Company of Illinois, for example, promised:

> Immediate connection with the number desired. . . . Entire absence of the frequent tedious delays occasioned by indifference of operators or inability to handle business as promptly as desired, and the equally frequent and unsatisfactory response to calls "They're busy." . . . Absolute secrecy of conversation. . . . Continuous service, both day and night . . . lower rental. . . . Perfect adaptability to the smallest towns and villages, as well as cities. . . . Impossibility of interruption or disconnection during conversation. . . .[16]

Many of the automatic companies made similar promises, and they all emphasized the elimination of operators, reduced costs, and better transmission.[17] The Bell System challenged these claims by making their own cost comparisons, field investigations, laboratory experiments, and, finally, court briefs against Independent applications for charters and franchises.[18]

Even when challenging the competition, Bell System managers displayed an ambivalence about the elimination of operators. The Southern New England Telephone Company, in its brief against the Automatic Electric Company, clung to the necessity of having operators in the central office:

> The history of the manually operated switchboard abounds in instances where, in case of fire, assault and robbery, the manual operator has been able to summon assistance at all hours, day and night, and to

bring to the aid of the subscriber, in such cases, the help of neighbors, of the police or of the fire department or of all of them together. . . .

In rural districts, such as compose the principal part of the State of Connecticut, the telephone operator, who has been so derided and ridiculed by the promoters of this automatic system, has become a source of great protection to the community at large. . . .

If there were no operator, and the automatic machinery at the subscriber's station and at the central office were employed, the would-be telephone user, who is oftentimes a mother or daughter or child, alone in the threatened household, would, in the excitement or danger of the moment, be unable to manipulate the automatic machinery and to do correctly all of the other things required before a call for help can be sent. This automatic system cannot be operated by the subscriber in the dark.[19]

It is ironic that this argument was mainly based on the helplessness of women since it simultaneously affirmed the female operator as the protector of "the community at large." The telephone industry had a long way to go before it could give up its own nostalgia and mythology, created at a time when conditions required personal contact as a compensation for unreliable equipment.

The Bell System Experiments

Between 1900 and 1910, AT&T engineers conducted cost studies, laboratory experiments, and extensive field investigations of Strowger and other equipment developed for small towns.[20] The results convinced AT&T that automatic switching was not a viable method for providing service to small towns that would later need expanded service. Engineers realized that even improved automatics were really no less expensive for small cities than a manual board in the long term, because to increase subscribers in an automatic system required its total replacement, while additional positions could be added to a manual board. The failure of automatics on a small scale, in addition to the urgency to solve the "big city problem," persuaded Bell System engineers to reconfigure automatics for large, multiexchange cities.[21] The decision to pursue the development of automatic systems therefore did not indicate a total commitment to a fully automated service. While it clung to the nostalgic image of the operator, the Bell System, stimulated by competition and the consequent desire to raise capital for plant expansion, also had a practical need to increase profits and lower costs.

To solve this dilemma, managers had to keep most operators, introduce automatic equipment on a limited basis without requiring work by the subscriber, and bring savings in costs. Semi-mechanical switching systems in which operators, not subscribers, dialed calls represented the ideal solution to the Bell System problem. Simultaneously, the semiautomatics entailed a more efficient reorganization of the operators' work, a reduction in operators, and the most advanced and reliable technology available.[22]

At the September 1910 Conference of European Telegraph and Telephone Administration Technicians in Paris, John J. Carty, chief engineer of AT&T, opposed the fully automatic for the usual Bell System reasons, but he wholeheartedly endorsed the semi-mechanical for American cities. In 1909 he had argued that "if it [the semi-mechanical switchboard] were now in use in those places for which it is suitable, there would be a net saving of $2,500,000 a year."[23] An enormous outlay in capital to change subscriber equipment to dials could be avoided, and a reduction in operators would still occur, since their work would be reduced by the automatic equipment.[24] Technically, semiautomatic systems encompassed the capacities to handle the "big city problem."

In January 1906, AT&T engineers introduced a new type of automatic equipment that would be flexible enough to accommodate trunking complexities required by large cities.[25] The development of this technology progressed along two lines that eventually led to a rotary system and a panel system. Slightly more advanced at the time, a semi-mechanical trial of the rotary succeeded, and Western Electric decided to market it in Europe in 1911. For the United States, however, the Bell System decided in 1912 to adopt the panel system because of its larger capacity and trunking flexibility. Cost studies had shown that the panel would be less expensive than the rotary in large cities. Thus, panel switching systems became the focus of AT&T automatic switching developmental work.[26]

In the World War I period, the Bell System extensively studied the Strowger step-by-step and panel semi-mechanical exchanges. Through its acquisitions of Independents and experiments, AT&T had gained substantial knowledge of the development of Strowger equipment in operation.[27]

From 1900 until 1914, significant improvements such as a common battery, two-wire circuits, four-party full-selective ringing, automatic ringing,
a dial tone, an automatic busy tone, expanded network/traffic capacity,
and other improvements made it possible for Strowger equipment to
offer the same classes of service and features more economically than the
Bell System's.[28] Impressed by the improved Strowger apparatus, AT&T
ordered in 1917 an exchange for Norfolk, Virginia, that the Automatic
Electric Company installed within two years. The Bell System installed its
first step-by-step exchange in Dallas in 1921. Experience gained from
these installations and others acquired from the Independents enabled
the Bell System to make major changes in the Strowger system.[29] Step-by-
step equipment became the switching system of choice for small and
medium-sized cities over the next fifty years.[30]

AT&T installed offices in Newark, New Jersey (1915, 1917), and Wilmington, Delaware (1917), to test the efficiency of automatic call distribution and to assess how well the panel system worked in actual conditions
close to New York City. Operator loads did not reach the desired levels in
these systems, but "the trials demonstrated conclusively that the semi-
mechanical system, with panel equipment, could be depended upon to
render reliable and greatly improve[d] telephone service in an area where
the requirements were as severe as any in the world." These trials also
showed that fully automated systems could be implemented simply and
economically.[31]

On July 24, 1917, Plant Engineer Bancroft Gherardi confided that "the
work in the development of machine switching systems ha[d] reached a
point where definite recommendations [could] be made as to its use,"
based on city size.[32] He recommended the continuation of manual boards
for single-office cities because they provided better service at lower costs
than either the semi-mechanical or the full mechanical.[33] He endorsed
fully automatic switching systems for all but the very largest multioffice
cities. Gherardi suggested semi-mechanical switching systems for New
York, Chicago, Philadelphia, and Boston.

Management had preferred fully automatic systems, but Bell System
studies revealed that "the average telephone user could not keep more
than six digits in mind while dialing." Mechanically, machine switching
required seven-digit dialing in the largest cities.[34] Later in 1917, shortly
after AT&T President Vail had approved the engineering recommenda-

tions mentioned above, another AT&T engineer, W. G. Blauvelt, solved the problem with the idea of combining three letters of the exchange name with four digits. Subscribers, already familiar with exchange names, could easily remember four additional digits. With the technical barriers surmounted, automatic switching systems were capable of solving the "big city problem" by December 1917.[35]

Breakdown of Barriers to Full Automation

Conditions created by World War I hastened the breakdown of ideological and economic barriers to full automation. Equipment and labor resources had been drained from the industry to contribute to the war effort. The number of trunked calls had increased to 65 percent of all calls in the ten largest cities, and the number of exchanges had grown tremendously.[36] Consequently, service deteriorated everywhere. Under the pretense of meeting the government's request "that everything possible be done to conserve labor, material and capital during the war emergency," the Bell System exploited this situation to introduce new equipment and to reorganize work methods.

Traffic Engineer Waterson estimated that operating expenses could be reduced "at least $4,000,000 a year below what they would otherwise be," that the number of operators could be reduced by "about 6 per cent. or 6,000 employees," and that plant valued at $3,500,000 could be made available for future use that would avoid "new investment."[37] The technological changes required to obtain these savings and changes in the work process involved a conclusive break with the concept of personalized service.

Waterson's recommendations illustrate the progressive dismantling of personalized service accomplished by instructing operators to do less for customers. The time of day, for example, long given free of charge, was discontinued in all cities where it had not been stopped before the war. Waterson suggested that operators discontinue giving information such as sporting events or other information available in the telephone directory. Operators usually supervised a call and informed the customer of busy lines or "no answers." Waterson proposed the introduction of the "audible ringing signal" and the "audible busy signal," which would indicate a busy line or "no answer" to the calling subscriber. These automatic devices eliminated the operators' voluntary supervision. Waterson also instructed operators to discontinue supervision (callbacks) on busy calls and no-answer calls.[38] The practices introduced during the war eliminated all but the connecting part of the operator's job on manual boards. Clearly, the Bell System had overcome its philosophical objections to impersonal service.

During this period, Bell engineers also conducted studies to gauge subscribers' responses to machine switching. Their findings influenced AT&T's decision to abandon its policy against subscribers' participation in call completion. In 1919, Chief Engineer Gherardi assured associated company presidents: "From investigations which we have carried on throughout the country, I believe I can safely say that the automatic system will be acceptable to the public and that they will not object to dialing their own calls as compared with giving them to an operator."[39] Subscribers tended to think that they received quicker service because they ignored the time it took to dial the calls. The customers also blamed themselves rather than operators for wrong numbers and other problems.[40] The Bell System's enormous publicity campaign to convince subscribers of the advantages of the new equipment succeeded. With subscribers under control, management now directed its attention to operators.

The most important economic motivation for the introduction of fully automated systems was the dramatic increase in operators' earnings caused by wartime labor shortages. Operators' wages nearly doubled during the course of the war. At the Bell System Technical Conference, held in 1916, managers discussed the "sharp rise" in operators' wages and the "difficulty of securing and retaining an adequate number of operators." Waterson stated at this conference that "in 10 years, in 39 large cities, the number of telephone operators increased 160 per cent while population increased but 43 per cent."[41] He was concerned that wages showed no sign of going down and that the pool from which the Bell System chose its operators had shrunk. Telephone System Engineer A. F. Dixon articulated this idea from a statistical point of view:

The New York Telephone Company were using in 1910 a force of operators equal to 9½% of the total number of girls in New York who met the qualifications which they set up for satisfactory operators. In 1920 their force was equal to 19% of all who met such qualifications, and according to their best forecasts their requirements in 1930 will be equivalent to 43%. It is very obvious that such rapidly increasing requirements could only be obtained by the keenest competition with others employing similar grades of labor, and that the rates of pay would reach almost prohibitive heights. . . . Every means must be provided therefore, to prevent such an abnormal increase.[42]

If it had been merely a matter of a shrinking labor pool, the Bell System could have expanded the pool by including African American and other women who were literate but not single, white, young, and native-born. The Bell System's failure to employ from this larger pool belies the idea that the availability of cheap labor inhibits the introduction of new technologies. Racial discrimination influenced management's perception of the labor market and its cost. Consequently, the most significant economic reason for the adoption of automatic switching was the Bell System's desire to increase profits by reducing its operating workforce. In December 1919, Gherardi stated conclusively "that the only saving resulting from machine-switching operation, is the operator saving, including, of course, such traffic overhead charges as are affected. In all other respects, such as depreciation reserve, maintenance, etc., machine switching operation results in increased charges. The operating saving is, however, materially in excess of these increased expenses and an appreciable net saving results."[43] Though engineers adjusted the projections many times, a "conservative" ten-year projection made in 1923 estimated that the Bell System would reduce its "traffic" (operator) expense by at least $78 million.[44] By that time, it had been determined that operators' wages had "increased in a far higher ratio than ha[d] the cost of automatic equipment, reflecting development improvements and manufacturing economies."[45]

Not only rising operators' wages but increased operator militancy was another pressing reason for the Bell System to reduce its operating forces. In 1910, when J. J. Carty spoke in Europe, and even later, in 1912, managers did not view operators as a group from whom they would have much labor trouble, or at least any trouble that they could not handle.[46] Only in Butte, Montana, and Boston and its surrounding towns had there been any lasting union organizations among the operators. Operators, however, consistently challenged the Bell System and the federal government during World War I and its aftermath. Numerous strikes and other activities showed managers that a potential for long-term labor problems existed. No proof was evident that the employee associations (company unions) begun under government administration would provide a successful long-term solution to labor unrest. Automatic equipment, then, insured the continuity of service that the Bell System aspired to give.

Ideological, technical, and economic objections removed, engineers won approval in 1918 for the installation of the first Bell System automatics. However, labor shortages and the high cost and shortage of telephone equipment caused by the war prevented their installation until after 1920. The Bell System installed its first fully automated office on December 10, 1921, in Omaha. The New York Telephone Company made the first big city installation in New York City on October 14, 1922.[47] This marked the beginning of the "dial" era. It is important to remember, however, that the manual era did not end. Long distance, information, intercept, and other specialized operators remained in those jobs for which technology did not provide an alternative. Manual switchboards remained in use and continued to be improved throughout the "dial" era. Operators worked on manual boards in the New York metropolitan area until the last one was converted to "dial" in 1960.

Automation's Impact on the Work Process

Despite the slow to moderate pace at which dial conversions proceeded during the 1920s, these installations effected major changes in local operators' work. In some ways the transformation of operating work could be viewed as a process in which operators acquired additional skills, new knowledge, and more control over their work pace. An "A" operator in a machine-switching office, for example, learned several different operating jobs and used her judgment to determine what procedures to apply in specific circumstances. However, and equally important, the "enskilling" actually created more stressful working conditions. Traffic Engineer W. E. Farnham described in 1923 what he thought the future would hold as a result of dial conversions:

In general, the change when machine switching equipment is universal will be that, while under manual operation there was a large force handling comparatively simple types of work so that the problem was one of mass production and of proper supervision of a large force, with machine switching operation, there will be a smaller number of people in a large number of offices each doing work which is very much diversified and which is of a more or less complex character. It is necessary for each special operator in a machine switching office to know how to handle a variety of calls since the amount of this traffic in general is not great and specialization is not economical to the extent that is followed with manual operation. It is essential, therefore, that the degree of intelligence with which the operator works must be stressed rather than the degree of efficiency. The problem is one of a small force at any central office highly trained and capable of exercising considerable judgment as to the way in which they will handle traffic.[48]

Even though the equipment automatically processed calls, operators were needed to assist on some calls and to record and time calls for which there were charges. Management installed Dial Service "A" (DSA) boards in machine offices to handle these situations as well as to complete calls to manual offices. In addition to instructing customers in the use of the new dial phones, DSA operators performed information, intercept, and toll functions when a subscriber reached them by dialing "zero." Calls from manual to machine offices were completed by a "B" operator, who used a "cordless 'B' board" to "dial" the called subscriber, whose number had been given to her orally over either a call circuit or, later, through straightforward trunking methods.[49]

Operators gained more skills in a degraded work environment in which their smaller numbers could be more closely supervised by men and machines. Stating one of the sharpest ironies of dial conversion, Farnham assured other managers that even though the number of operators would be reduced, machine switching "[did] not mean . . . no traffic supervision. As a matter of fact the male supervisory employees today number about 1,900 and ten years hence we expect about 3,000 such employees."[50] The automation of various machine supervision capabilities aided these "males" in their tasks. Automatic peg counts and automatic call distribution provided the technical ability to monitor, speed up, and reorganize the operators' work. Automatic peg counts took away from the operator the task of counting her own calls. Management could use the knowledge gained through mechanical devices to establish operator workloads. To insure that each operator worked at the established speed, automatic call distribution mechanically directed calls to idle operators who could not "plug-up" because calls were directed only to positions where no calls were pending. When applied to the toll-recording operators' positions, automatic call distribution resulted in an estimated 20 percent increase in their loads.[51]

Soon after automation of local service began, machine switching and other mechanical devices were also applied to long distance. Methods to inaugurate toll-line dialing within a range of 100 to 200 miles were immediately investigated and installed. Dial apparatuses installed at toll centers made it possible for the outward operator to dial direct calls to both machine and manual offices without contact with other operators.[52] This change greatly increased the amount of work the outward operator could do, and it entirely eliminated the inward operator. Outward operators could also dial many "through" or tandem calls automatically by using codes to get them through the switching points.

Automation of Long Distance Service

Unlike the automation of local service, the automation of long distance involved problems that had to be solved on a nationwide basis. Full automation of long distance service, like local service, occurred in gradual steps as the solutions to various technical problems emerged. Among the features deemed essential to long distance automation were (1) a nationwide numbering plan that would provide each individual telephone with its own number; (2) adequate trunking and transmission facilities for handling nationwide traffic; (3) a switching system capable of automatically routing directly and indirectly as well as choosing alternative paths when the selected routes were found busy; and (4) an automatic means for recording, timing, and charging calls. Work had begun on these problems long before World War II, but it was after successful regional trials, and after the decision to pursue nationwide operator toll dialing, that engineers systematically designed a plan for operator toll dialing that "in all respects" would be "applicable to the future general extension of customer toll dialing."[53]

Like the automation of local service, the automation of long distance dialing depended on the design of a numbering plan that would make each individual telephone number unique. Engineers worked "to develop a universal system of numbering which would simplify the work of toll operators and which could later be used by customers."[54] The plan adopted formed two sets of nonconflicting three-digit numbers, one for identifying states or regions (area codes), and the other for identifying the local exchange (an office code). These six digits, in addition to four distinct digits peculiar to each subscriber, composed the ten digits dialed by operators.

When outward operators made long distance connections, they referred to a General Toll Switching Plan to determine how the calling toll center connected to the toll circuit network. To call from one toll center to another required a maximum of four switches using this plan. To provide adequate trunking and transmission facilities for nationwide dialing, engineers transformed the General Toll Switching Plan into a hierarchy of "interconnecting" networks of circuit groups designed to handle traffic on a "low delay" basis along predetermined traffic routes.[55]

The crossbar switch provided the foundation for an automatic switching system that could utilize the numbering plan, handle the toll network described above, and automatically route calls to the correct destination.[56] Crossbar switching had been developed during the 1930s, and it had been used extensively to replace panel and step-by-step systems for local exchanges after its first installation in Brooklyn in 1938. Composed of a mechanical switching unit, a No. 4 and a No. 5 switchboard, the No. 4 Toll Switching System first applied crossbar switching to intertoll service. Designed by Bell System engineers to confront high-volume toll traffic, this system was first installed in Philadelphia on August 22, 1943.[57] The No. 4 cordless, key-type switchboard component provided operators with the facilities to "function as combined inward, through and tandem operators—thus eliminating the provision of separate units to provide these particular services."[58] The outward position remained unchanged. Busy circuits and other types of delayed calls were automatically routed to the No. 5 switchboard where these situations were handled.

Though it played a significant role in the progress toward nationwide operator toll dialing, the No. 4 system required additional modifications to include features that would make it capable of "selecting the most direct route to a distant city."[59] A new No. 4A switching formed the basis of the operator toll-dialing equipment installed in New York and Chicago during December 1948. This toll network between New York, Chicago, and Philadelphia consisted of 125 toll centers through which more than

300 cities could be reached either directly or through switching centers.[60] Less than a year after these installations, coast-to-coast operator toll dialing began with the opening of the Oakland, California, toll-switching center in October 1949. Cleveland had been converted earlier in the year. Via this interconnected network and other smaller systems, operators could directly dial about 525 cities and towns. By November 1949, approximately 27 percent of all long distance calls were completed by operators using 4A equipment located at the five Control Switching Points (CSP).[61] The 4A equipment at these CSPs did "not . . . merely connect one toll circuit to another"; the switching equipment, not the operator, "interprets" the area code, "selects the route, operates the switches at intermediate points, tries alternate routes if necessary, and completes the call to the distant telephone."[62]

Obviously, the operators' jobs had become severely limited as a result of the introduction of this new switching system. Work previously "handled almost exclusively by human hand and brain power" was incorporated into the crossbar switches.[63] The Bell System Long Lines department proudly described its new equipment: the "brains of the No. 4 system is uncanny equipment called a 'marker,' which interprets the dialed numbers. A marker automatically selects the routing of calls and then tells a mechanism known as a 'sender' how to forward the signals that will reach the called telephone over the appropriate circuits."[64]

With her "brains" removed, little remained for the operator to do once she pulsed out the digits. An AT&T pamphlet explained:

> For most calls the operator does not have to talk on or listen on the connection—instead she watches her lamp supervision. The operator, therefore, has lost the opportunity to talk over the connection and, hence to exercise judgment as to whether transmission is satisfactory. The machine picks the first idle trunk in the routing pattern whether the trunk is suitable transmissionwise or not; formerly, the operator frequently could avoid specific trunks or connections which experience taught her were unsatisfactory. Furthermore, the operator is not conscious of customer difficulties until the customer signals a complaint. In order to reestablish the call the facilities used in the original connection which experienced trouble must be released; hence no direct investigation of the original connection by the testboard is possible.[65]

The end of operating had not come yet, however. From the revenue point of view, operators still performed the most important functions in long distance service. Operators recorded, timed, and charged all long distance calls. While the Bell System was well on its way to a Nationwide Operator Toll Dialing system, it could not further improve customer toll dialing without the automation of recording, timing, and charging.[66]

Automatic Message Accounting (AMA), developed for local crossbar offices, emerged in 1948 from numerous studies and experiments conducted at Bell Laboratories.[67] The AMA equipment automatically recorded all information relating to a call by punching holes in a coded pattern on a paper tape, which another automatic machine processed at an accounting center.[68] First installed at Media, Pennsylvania, for local crossbar dialing, AMA equipment was modified for the ten-digit dialing used by No. 5 crossbar switching and was installed in Englewood, New Jersey, in 1951 on a trial basis. Englewood subscribers could dial directly as many as eleven million other customers in cities such as San Francisco, Oakland, Boston, Cleveland, New York, Detroit, and Philadelphia.

In order to distribute the costs more effectively, the Bell System decided to install AMA equipment in regional locations where recording could be centralized to serve many local offices. A centralized automatic message accounting (CAMA) tandem office could handle as many as two hundred local central offices.[69] CAMA extended customer direct dialing to areas where it would not have been economically feasible, but it also momentarily reintroduced the operator into the connection. After the subscriber dialed the distant number, the operator, positioned at a specially designed console, cut into the connection to obtain the calling subscriber's number, which she then keyed into the recording machinery. Aside from this brief appearance by the operator, the remaining details were automatically recorded.[70] The Bell System first installed CAMA in Washington, D.C., in 1953. By the summer of 1955, installations had been made in Detroit, San Francisco, New York, Jersey City, Morristown, and Newark, New Jersey, Cleveland, and Pittsburgh.

Almost everything was in place for nationwide customer toll dialing except further adjustments and modifications in the AMA equipment to extend its usage to step-by-step switching systems and to automatically identify calling subscribers so that operators could be eliminated from the process. Local crossbar and panel adjustments to increase their capacities from seven-digit dialing to ten-digit dialing also had to be made. Investigations and field trials yielded solutions to these and other problems between 1955 and 1965 when 96 percent of Bell System subscribers had phones equipped for dial. For step-by-step systems, CAMA became available in 1961.[71] Automatic Number Identification (ANI) systems for panel, No. 1 crossbar, and large step-by-step offices had been developed and installed by 1960. Crossbar No. 5 systems were designed to include this feature. ANI enabled the equipment to identify the calling subscriber, which eliminated the need for the operator to cut in on the circuit for that purpose. In January 1965, when engineers installed the first ANI for small step-by-step offices at South Sioux City, Nebraska, Direct Distance Dialing (DDD) became possible for most Bell System subscribers whose numbers originated in a dial office.[72]

Automation Reinforces "White Lady" Image

The increased workloads and intensified supervision consequent to the introduction of automatic technologies threatened the "white lady" operator identity. For those operators that automation did not eliminate, a redefinition of skill ensued. Automated service shifted Bell emphasis away from "call connecting" to "secretarial assistance." Since subscribers dialed their own calls, the primary functions of operators changed to providing "personal assistance" on information, collect, charge, credit card, coin box, reverse charges, person-to-person, intercept, emergency, and other types of calls that required an operator's intervention. Long distance operators could connect most of their calls through the dial equipment without the assistance of two or three other operators. Hence, a different type of operator emerged from the dial era. The Bell System described her as a "service specialist" whose

> relationship with the customer has become more secretarial in nature than it ever was before. . . . Each call requires judgment, reasoning and tact. Every call is an important public relations contact requiring a helpful, understanding attitude on the part of the operator. She works more independently than ever before. She controls expensive, intricate equipment and her skill in its use and in detection of trouble contributes to greater equipment efficiency.[73]

Speed continued to be important, but the manual labor of plugging and unplugging cords or operating keys was alleviated by the new technology. In 1963, government investigators "agreed that the mental demands on an operator are greater than in earlier years, while the physical requirements are less rigorous. Today the operator does very little standing, stretching, and reaching" or monotonously "repeating numbers to other operators all day."[74]

Automatic switching systems transformed the girl operator into a machine operative with a "lady" veneer. The value of the "white lady" identity for the operator was that she did not work in a factory like the immigrants, and she was not a domestic like African American women. With their personal skills diminished in value, operators feared the loss of status. As the system became more automated, operators relied more on their white exclusivity to maintain what they perceived to be an elite position.

Even before dial systems became widespread, telephone operators embraced the company-constructed identity and protected it in a variety of ways. White operators insisted upon racial exclusivity, and they participated in creating negative and demeaning images of black people. In 1920, for example, when the telephone industry suffered a tremendous labor shortage and advertised for a thousand operators, militant white trade unionists ignored African American women's attempts to enter the occupation. An otherwise fiery and militant Teresa Sullivan, vice president of the Boston Telephone Operators' Department, IBEW, came to New York with a force of fifty other organizers to lure the 12,000 New York operators away from the company's employee association into the union. Acknowledging that the company had already raised New York City operators' wages above Boston's, Sullivan said: "It is not my business now to find fault with the New York Telephone Company. I am here solely to give the girls a chance to organize if they want to."[75] Occupied with the Telephone Operators' Union's narrow goal of trade union recognition, Sullivan not only failed to develop a powerful countertactic to the company's raise in wages, but she completely failed to address the contemporary controversy around hiring African American women.

It is unlikely that Sullivan was unaware of the New York Telephone Company's refusal to hire black women when Eugene McIntosh, proprietor of the Harlem Employment Agency, had publicly offered to supply it with "neat and intelligent . . . colored girls" free of charge.[76] To this offer of "100 per cent American" girls who would "prove competent and loyal," E. J. Anderson, the employment manager, replied that "while" the company had "given consideration to employing colored girls as telephone operators," it was "not in a position to do so at the present time."[77] Anderson gave no further explanation, but Mr. Schultz, assistant to the vice president, responded to a similar offer made by the League for Democracy by disclaiming any personal objection to black workers, asserting that the white operators would quit if they had to work next to black women, and further claiming that white women would not train black women.[78] Even though the company rationalized its own racist behavior by shifting the responsibility onto the operators, neither Sullivan nor any other union leader refuted the accusation. Certainly, Sullivan was cognizant of the injustice of barring African American women when the company advertised heavily, used "a 'flying squadron' of recruiting operators, [paid] premiums to employees who brought in new workers," "decidedly lowered the entrance requirements for applicants," and shortened the time spent in training school "to secure operators at any cost."[79]

Telephone operators not only failed to demand justice for black workers, but they actively defended their civilized "white lady" image by demeaning black people. Within seven months of its founding, the *Union Telephone Operator,* the national newspaper for telephone operators, serialized in three parts a story about a golden-haired beauty who was taken as a wife by a barbarian African chief whose tribe had killed her husband.[80] Although the offspring of this union eventually married a white man and thereby minimized any violations of social taboos, it is significant that a demand existed for this kind of entertainment. The story reinforced stereotypes about black people and reassured white women of their superior position. Not only did operators entertain themselves by reading about "savages," they also helped to create these images when they blackened their faces and staged minstrel shows that ridiculed African American people's intelligence, speech, and other behavior. From the 1920s through the 1950s, Bell companies sponsored these functions, to which they invited the public and about which they advertised and reported in company publications (including pictures).[81]

The need for white women operators to separate themselves from black women increased as automation progressed and black women continued to demand access to these jobs. White operators believed that the value of their jobs would decline if black women were admitted. Black women's work during this period was always the most menial, and white women recruited on the basis of racist selectivity would not accept that black women could meet the Bell System's elite employment criteria. Unable to challenge the company's continual degradation of their work, operators focused on maintaining their identity. Bell System paternalism (welfare programs) and employee associations provided company vehicles for accomplishing this task.

5 | The Bell System Family: The Formation of Employee Associations

In 1919, AT&T President Theodore N. Vail wrote to the president of each Bell System company instructing them to implement employee representation "to re-establish pre-war loyalty and efficiency."[1] Unlike the long-term results anticipated from automation, employee associations (company unions) would more immediately curb the operators' militancy and give managers the control they needed to improve and restore the system to normal. Rather than impose new policies by edict, Bell executives adopted the methods of the then-current corporate liberal reform movement that used industrial psychology as a means to develop employee "consent and cooperation" in the workplace.[2] Managers held many conferences during the 1920s at which they "constructed an ideology and a way of constraining their employees and of harnessing their energies for the expansion of the corporate enterprise."[3] This ideology elaborated the Bell System notion of "family" that originated in the companies' welfare programs. F. H. Bethell, vice president of the New York Telephone Company, boasted that "since the creation of the Employees' Benefit Fund we have felt more than ever that we are just one big family with every employee having a seat at the family table."[4] Consequently, the advent of employee associations among telephone workers signified the substitution of independent trade unionism with the Bell System concept of "family."

Bethell's meticulous choice of the family metaphor in 1915 became a cornerstone for the company's control over workers in the years following World War I. In their private conferences, managers developed techniques for persuading employees of their obligation to contribute to the family's prosperity. Employee associations established the organizational structure through which management disseminated this ideology. Managers couched policies on wages, hours of work, work methods, and technology in schemes intended to make the workers feel that the company extended itself as far as it possibly could to accommodate them, and that the success of the company depended on their cooperation. In association meetings, officials justified denials of system-wide raises, increased workloads, and layoffs. And, equally important, the associations engaged operators in activities that produced company loyalty and reinforced their "white lady" identity.[5]

To their credit, many operators did not immediately embrace the family concept. In areas such as New England, which had a strong union history and low turnover, operators resisted the associations. They stalled employee representation in the region until their major strike in 1923, when the company used intimidation, direct threats, and all of their other resources to defeat the women. E. K. Hall, an AT&T vice president, wrote "confidentially" to all the associated company presidents that the "plan" in this strike was "to fight it out to a finish and avoid any payment, settlement or compromise either as a result of threatened strike, actual strike or arbitration, so long as it is humanly possible to maintain such a position."[6]

New England Telephone and Telegraph Company President Matt Jones, on the eve of the operators' strike vote, wrote to the women stating that the company was "not in a position to reduce the hours of work or to make general wage increases," and furthermore "it should be very clear that a strike or threat of strike can not change the Company's position."[7] Striking operators, faced with the full and concentrated strength of the Bell System, with operator and craftsmen scabs, and with a lack of funds, failed to win any concessions from the company.[8] After this defeat, associations gradually replaced all traces of unionism in New England. Of course, in places like Canada where unionism had long been defeated, and in the South where it had not been very strong and patriarchy reigned openly, the companies easily established associations.

Forming Company Associations

These associations began forming in 1919 when Vail instructed each associated company president to have his "employees form associations which shall appoint representatives to discuss freely and frankly with the officials of the Company, questions affecting their wages and work."[9] Structured hierarchically along departmental lines, the associations con-

sisted of local chapters that were further divided into multilevel committees. Local conditions determined dues (never more than 25 cents per
month), the regularity of meetings, and election proceedings. Association
meetings were held only in local chapters, and individual complaints were
not considered (employees had to speak directly with their managers).[10]
Held on paid company time, attendance at these meetings was practically compulsory, and minutes of the proceedings recorded each person
present and his or her contribution. Associations denied membership to
high-level management and "any other Management Representatives or
employees who have advisory or supervisory positions with respect to
matters within the scope of the purpose of the Association. . . ."[11] Free and
frank discussions about general topics with low-level supervisors certainly did not empower employees to change their working conditions.

Operators in the Long Lines department organized one of the first associations. At their constitutional convention in December 1919, guided
by company samples, representatives adopted a constitution which recognized "that their interests and those of the Management are mutual in the
conduct of the operation of the Company. . . ."[12] This constitution, approved by AT&T, limited membership to "any white employee . . . after
active service of three or more consecutive months in the employing
Company. . . ."[13] The Bell family would continue to be white. Operators
had safeguarded their identity.

Having secured the operators to employee representation by guar-
anteeing racial exclusivity, AT&T Vice President and Chief Engineer Bancroft Gherardi expressed confidence in the Bell System's control over its
workforce:

> I do not worry about the plan resulting in employees taking over the
> management of the company; I do not worry about its interfering with
> discipline or impairing management responsibilities in any other re-
> spect. I believe it is an aid to management; I believe it will give us
> forces which will function more intelligently on their own initiative
> and carry out instructions more efficiently and cheerfully.[14]

The association constitutions merely granted employees an "opportunity to express their views" rather than an apparatus for negotiation.[15]

According to Bell System reports, subjects particularly relevant to
workers' welfare occupied less than 25 percent of the discussions between

Table 3. Percentages of Classified Subjects

Education	60%
Wages	7
Hours	8
Working conditions	9
Equipment and methods	10
Miscellaneous	6
	100%

Source: J. P. Downs, "Employee Representation," paper delivered as part of a larger discussion on this topic at the General Traffic Conference, April 1923, p. 616.

management and the employee representatives. A record of monthly meetings held by New York Telephone's traffic department in Manhattan for thirty-three months before April 1923 indicated that 3,225 subjects had been discussed in twenty-seven councils, with 306 employee representatives and alternates. The classification of subjects discussed is given in table 3 by percentage. It is not surprising that the association devoted so little attention to employee issues, considering that 60 percent of the representatives were supervisors, while 40 percent were operators, clerks, and others.

Although no major changes resulted, different types of representatives and a greater diversity of issues were discussed in other parts of the country where vestiges of independent unionism survived. One manager admitted that in some elections "individuals are selected who would not ordinarily have been chosen by us."[16] In fact, three employees wore union badges to the first employee representation meeting held in Denver in 1919.[17] And it should also be remembered that small independent unions remained throughout the dial era in Northwestern states like Montana.[18] These unions took no militant actions, but their existence may account for the diversity in subjects discussed in association meetings. For example, in the 152 joint conferences held in the Northwestern territory from May 1922 to February 1923, nearly two-thirds of the topics discussed were directly related to working conditions (table 4).

Perhaps influenced by IBEW craftsmen who maintained their union membership throughout this period, Chicago operators believed that they could at least wrangle some pleasantries from management.[19] Referring

Table 4. Percentages of Classified Subjects to Total
Subjects Presented

Condition of retiring room and operators' quarters	30.9
Hours of work	15.7
Condition of operating room	14.3
Service	8.5
Wages	7.7
Employment and welfare	6.3
Local operating methods	5.0
Miscellaneous	3.3
Equipment	2.8
Supervisors	2.1
Toll operating methods	1.8
Building	1.6

to Chicago, H. E. Eldridge reported: "At the start, our organization was, pretty much of a 'gimme club.' They wanted everything from dish cloths to pianos."[20] One should not hastily conclude from company summaries that genuine subject diversity or true compromises occurred in these meetings. .

While managers presented these reports as proof that serious issues important to operators were discussed, operators viewed the same discussions in a different light. Former employees who participated in these associations stated that they never discussed anything more important than "the pencil sharpener needed replacing or was dull." A New Jersey operator, for example, presented this picture:

> About the height of the complaints that ever got to management was that the toilet tissue in the bathrooms was too rough, or there wasn't enough sugar, or the food was cold in the cafeteria, and such trivial things as that. Nothing that had any bearing on your real working conditions. Elevators slow; clocks slow; not enough sheets for the night girls that had to work from 9 P.M. to 7 A.M. (They had a . . . two-hour sleeping period.)[21]

Bell System executives had constructed employee representation so that workers knew that attempts to discuss anything of substance would bring immediate reprisals in the form of warnings about production levels, removal of access to promotions, and even firings.[22]

Managers reported their successes to each other at various conferences held between 1920 and 1930. Their reports confirmed that by the use of the employee representation discussions, management had been able to reduce wages, take back bonuses and other monetary benefits, and, most importantly, increase work loads and introduce new technology with little overt resistance.

J. L. R. Van Meter, general traffic manager of AT&T's Long Lines Traffic Department, reported to the personnel conference held in 1922 the results of three years' work with the employee association. His report demonstrated how the company had been able to settle most simple complaints in the employees' favor, while those complaints pertaining to money and power ended according to the company's wishes. Management easily consented to rescheduling and posting hours, to providing new chairs when old ones damaged operators' clothing, and to firing an elevator man who flirted with the evening operators.[23]

However, when West Coast Long Lines operators complained that they did not receive the service anniversary payments some East Coast operators received, the association provided the mechanism whereby the payments were phased into the paychecks of those who were employed before the controversy and discontinued it for all others. These anniversary payments could have been extended to the others, but management felt that it had failed as a method of attracting more applicants and reducing turnover.[24] Companies in three states paid employees an Armistice Day differential, but Long Lines did not pay the differential even when the unfairness had been brought to their attention. Van Meter admitted that it was "particularly embarrassing," but he "felt that the best thing to do was to deal with all Long Lines employees alike and not to pay the differential anywhere in the System."[25]

At these conferences AT&T Vice President Hall frequently spoke on topics related to the Bell System "Personnel Policy" and "employee representation." For him:

The true function of the joint conference committees . . . is not to decide upon, but rather to talk things over with a view to coming to a mutual understanding and agreement.

To put it another way, the purpose of the joint conference committees is to prevent issues from arising rather than to settle them after they have been crystallized. A joint conference committee sometimes does settle real issues, but it seldom settles them on a mutual basis, or by reason of points brought out in a general discussion.

Issues are the special properties of unionism, and they are the kind of food which unions thrive on, and the theory of unionism is diametrically opposed to the theory of employee representation whatever its form may be. They don't need any outside organizers to convert them then. If they are thinking of issues all the time they are thinking in terms of unionism, of splitting the industry, of the industry being split instead of the industry working together. . . . The general purpose of joint conference committees, I would say, could be summed up as being advisory, informational and cooperative, rather than executive. There isn't any executive function in a joint conference committee.[26]

Workers who required executive decisions about issues usually handled by unions were advised to pursue their requests up the chain of command until the problem was solved. The personnel policy encouraged employees to view themselves as individuals who could resolve any problem by a private consultation with management and who could develop to his/her full potential as an individual within the Bell family. At the 1926 Bell System Educational Conference, Hall expounded on this philosophy as one which "seeks to bring out and develop the best qualities in each individual and to find ways and means to weld and integrate the individual performance of each into the competent, harmonious, team-playing cooperation upon which any successful group accomplishment depends."[27]

Despite the obvious control aspect of employee associations, Hall denied any antiunion purposes. He advocated using the associations to "educate" the employees regarding Bell System policies and plans. Hall emphasized that employee representation's purpose was not simply "to stall unionism" because a goal that simple would fail. Rather, the aim of the associations was "to tie" people together and to make them feel part of the system.[28] Therefore, he argued, "a good deal over 50 per cent. of the discussions in these joint conferences should be devoted to the local departmental job."[29] Education really meant brainwashing the employees into accepting changes not only without question but with enthusiasm. The Bell System strategy allowed the discussion of wages and working conditions within strictly defined limits. As members of the "Bell System family," employee acquiescence and submission served larger goals related to rates or public relations, new technology, and the general higher profits provided by keeping wages low.

Public Relations Goals of Employee Associations

As a part of the intense drive to create favorable public relations, Bell System managers advocated a personnel policy designed to transform each employee into an advertisement for the company. In order to divert these young women from unionism and to mold them into good, uncomplaining, and productive workers who would be good public relations examples and mouthpieces, managers devised several projects. A. C. Stannard stated:

> We finally hit upon a little stunt which served to arouse the interest of the force in the public relations movement and which, we feel, has been quite effective in helping to establish a closer relationship with the public. We call it the "What I Did Today Plan" which is predicated on the fact there are countless opportunities arising every day for us to do some little turn that will help the public—as individuals—to understand us better or like us better.[30]

In the associations, the company familiarized employees with first aid training, rest homes, the Pink Ticket Plan, "What I Did Today," company courses, picnics, and other entertainments in which their participation was expected. "What I Did Today" encouraged employees to "write a brief story, with no restrictions whatsoever as to nature of incidents to be reported, style, or length, . . . on any act which would help the public to a better appreciation of telephone service, policy and practices." Activities could be outside telephone service as long as "we let ourselves be known as employees of the telephone company when performing any service."[31] These stories were published in company magazines and made into posters placed in the central offices.

Each association had some variation of this plan, not only for public relations but also to keep their operators occupied in unthreatening activities and to keep them under Bell System surveillance. The "Pink Ticket

Plan" operated in a similar fashion except that it had been designed to elicit operators' suggestions for improvements in methods or solutions to any problems. Reversing the usual termination connotation of "pink slips," managers solicited ideas for improvements on pink slips. Of course, any suggestions particularly appealing to management's goals would be publicized with the operator's name and picture. The Bell System hoped to imbue a sense of participation, contribution, and gratitude in the operators by allowing these types of outlets.

Management wanted "to get every employee of the company in such attitude of mind that all of the contacts with the public will be of such a character as to enable the company to get as nearly as possible 100 per cent public relations."[32] Each operator, according to company propaganda, could make a difference since she had hundreds of contacts with subscribers daily. Why was it so important to have good public relations or to have more than 300,000 employees presenting a good public image?

AT&T Vice President Hall stated in 1923 that keeping the public satisfied with service was not enough:

> We now realize we have got to go a good deal further than that. If we double the size of the Bell System in the next 10 years, we have got to have successful financial performance; we have got to have a string of unfailing surpluses or margins at the end of every year in order to establish the credit to do it; we have got to have such public relations that the public will not only let us alone but if necessary will get behind us and say—"Give these telephone people a fair price." . . .
> If you can make your people understand this, I think that this understanding will go a long way toward getting them to do the thousand and one little things that they have opportunities to do in our contacts with the public.[33]

Hall assured other Bell managers that the "company's product was already sold, the point was to get a fair price for it which depended largely on the Company's Public Relations." Management persuaded operators who performed some simple favor on a train or in their communities to identify themselves as telephone workers. Countless stories about operators who helped a stranger to a new city, aided some sick person who needed a doctor, called the police or the fire department in an emergency, etc., filled Bell System literature. Public relations in Hall's estimation developed public opinion and the individual employee because the employee "lines up the Public with the Company and by his very act of so doing, lines himself up with the Company—with his associates—with the other members of his team."[34] Through this alignment, the Bell System prevented government interventions and therefore profited by regular rate increases and few, if any, wage increases.

Employee Representation: The Ultimate Diversion

Once the majority of employees accepted associations, the Bell System began to institute the strategies that had been formulated in conferences. At these conferences, usually held at vacation resorts, men discussed specific plans designed for what they perceived to be women's peculiar sentimentality.[35] The plans incorporated and reinforced patronizing, chauvinistic, and condescending myths about women. Referring to the complexity of the female employment problem, General Traffic Manager A. C. Stannard of Southwestern Bell Telephone Company stated that in addition to their youth, these women were "subject to all the peculiarities, both mental and physical, that are characteristic of the sex." For him, "temperament [was] one of the chief heritages of the Traffic Department."[36] He advised other managers who wanted to interest operators in public relations not to "think to do it by statistics but do it by appealing to her sentiment, her sympathy, the idea of neighborly service, her desire to do something for others, and then glorify her act by some special recognition, and you will have tapped the whole store of her imagination, pride and energy; her resources become yours and she displays an interest that is unbelievable and an inventiveness and resourcefulness that was unimagined."[37]

W. F. Cozad, general traffic superintendent of the Northwestern Bell Telephone Company, concurred:

> She wishes to understand her superior, her job, and what is expected of her. She wants to have the courtesies extended to her that any woman naturally deserves and expects. She wants to be surrounded with clean and wholesome working quarters and receive reasonable wages in payment. She wants a chance to talk over with her superiors, in an intelligent and fair manner, the things that she does not understand. She likes a word of praise when she has done an especially good job—and

all of this is very human. She is loyal, faithful, trustworthy, and when she feels her employer is square, she will sacrifice—for all women understand sacrifice—as long as that is necessary, and without grumbling, bickering and complaint.[38]

Bell System officials fostered this image of the quiet suffering "ladies," whose compliant personalities identified them as a stereotypical and homogenized group who could receive "a different kind of wage treatment."

Operators' earnings never captured any proportion of the large surpluses and profits that the Bell System achieved as a result of the labor peace enforced by the associations. Operators carried larger workloads at faster rates without any meaningful increases in their pay or major improvements in their work environment. Hall justified low wages by distinguishing a "public utility" from other businesses. He explained that "in working for a public utility, it is impossible to make big money. They pay good money and steady money but not big money."[39] According to Hall, employee cooperation in public relations work was rewarded with "a status which no other industry can give; a status in the biggest and most highly respected public utility in the country."[40] Managers thus used employee association discussions, not only to encourage participation in public relations efforts, but to rationalize low wages.

Employees who questioned their associations on the likelihood of a reduction in wage rates were told that present employees would probably not have their wages reduced, but they would receive fewer increases, and new employees would be given a different schedule. With employees so informed, J. L. R. Van Meter stated that there had "been no opposition anywhere" when management had "reduced starting rates or the wage schedules applicable to new employees at twenty offices, lengthened the steps in the schedule applicable to existing employees at four offices, and lengthened the intervals between wage increases to non-wage schedule employees at all offices."

Van Meter had absolute confidence in the company's ability to enforce its "wage policy" of paying as little as possible based on regional conditions of supply and demand. In regard to operators specifically, he said that there was "never . . . any disposition on the part of our Traffic employees to question the propriety of varying wage rates in different parts of the country, or the consistency or fairness of the rates established" since the start of the associations.[41] When market conditions made it difficult to attract operators, managers increased the starting rates, but it was "necessary to be just as prompt in lowering the starting rate to the normal rate when the pressure [was] over and going below the normal when conditions [were] easy."[42]

This policy also allowed them to place operators on different wage schedules based on "merit," thereby avoiding automatic raises such as those mandated by union contracts. For instance, Southern New England Bell Telephone Company had "no definite starting rate" and paid its operators increases according to "merit," not according to schedules. At a time when operators worked greater loads at faster rates, one would think that "merit" would warrant an increase in the Bell System payrolls. On the contrary, a Southern New England Telephone Company official estimated that his company saved in eight New Haven offices "at the rate of $16,000 less per year" without a progression schedule. The company saved another $50,000 to $60,000 in six other offices by not using a fixed schedule.[43] He concluded that their methods had been successful under considerable market fluctuations and that a fixed schedule under these conditions "would have cost us a great deal of money."[44] Furthermore, he claimed, "I have never had a complaint in regard to the wage situation from any of our employees although this schedule is talked over very openly and freely at all association meetings and students that come in know what they have got to expect. The psychological time to adopt such a plan is when a change is about to be made in fixed schedules. Our schedules have not interfered in any way with the company on either side."[45]

While managers continued to pay as little as possible on a regional basis, established maximum top pay rates, and fluctuated starting salaries, they further refined their wage policy based on differences in "vocation." In 1929, E. K. Hall presented to the associated company presidents certain "general principles for wage consideration" by which employees would receive raises in stages according to their progress and proficiency. Operators, however, could be exempted from the application of these principles, based on the following rationalization.

For example, the work of cable splicers and installers is essentially individual; improvement in individual performance is readily demonstrated and wage progress can, therefore, be satisfactorily administered on the basis of the individual employee. Improvement in individual performance may be demonstrated in different ways.

The work of telephone operators on the other hand is essentially group or team work. While this in no way lessens the requirement that each individual maintain a high standard of performance, it has not been found practicable or desirable to base wage progress on an individual record of quantity or quality of work. For employees who meet adequately the requirements of the position, experience has shown that the interests both of the employees and of the service are best met through the general application of wage schedules with increases at definite service periods.[46]

Sometimes supervisors even withheld these service period increases when they felt a particular operator had not met the standards to merit a raise. Not only did Bell System officials generally pay men almost twice as much as they paid women, but they refused to reward operators' individual performances. The unfairness of these practices was imperceptible to managers who measured women's work in terms of loyalty and ability to make sacrifices.

Like wages, reductions in employee numbers were also accomplished by methods worked out in the associations. Accordingly, when the Long Lines Department found in 1920–21 that it needed "to make pretty drastic reductions in the size of the operating forces, due to the combined effect of declining traffic, substantial improvements in force turnover and daily absenteeism," it appealed to the Executive Committees of the Employees' Association for their "suggestions as to how best to deal with the situation with a minimum of hardship to the force."[47] Each individual office decided how it would accomplish the necessary reductions. The executives based most of the furloughs on low seniority, but by Van Meter's account, the employees were so impressed by the opportunity to help the company that they made other kinds of arrangements as well. Older employees, for example, "even recommended that they be furloughed for longer periods than the younger employees, because their rates of pay were substantially higher and they would feel the loss of pay less keenly."[48] Employees had been successfully enlisted in reducing their own numbers.

By these methods AT&T laid off 500 people while increasing operators' loads. Another Bell System manager reported that association contacts between employees and managers had developed employee "initiative in producing quality and quantity" in their job performance without threats. He boasted:

I feel sure that in the Long Lines Department we could not, during the past 18 months, have raised our loads, increased our per cent. completed, decreased our expense—at least not to the extent to which it was done—if we had not first eliminated or explained away the many smaller causes of dissatisfaction, and through Executive Committees set forth the reasons for and the need for doing these things; otherwise, it would have looked as if we were merely taking advantage of the times, and we should have a dissatisfied force to deal with.[49]

The employee indoctrination accomplished by these "explanations" facilitated the unimpeded introduction of new methods and technologies. Local and long distance operators worked harder and faster, while their working conditions continuously worsened as a result of their inability to resist management manipulations.

Long distance operators experienced an increase in their loads and changes in their responsibilities after the introduction of straightforward trunking, Combined Line and Recording (CLR), and other long distance methods. The emphasis placed on speed in both local and long distance service necessitated a constant push for higher loads, either by forcing the operator to work constantly at the busy-hour peak capacity, or by introducing labor-saving devices to eliminate some of her tasks.[50] Management used both methods at different times.

The drive to increase loads received its impetus from the engineers' calculation that for each percentage point of increase in operators' loads systemwide, the Bell System saved $1 million annually.[51] This explains K. W. Waterson's exuberance when he reported to the Bell System Operating Conference in 1926 that while there had been a 3.2 percent increase in the number of operators in 1925, there also had been a 5.6 percent rise in their "units of work handled."[52] One official stated that his company had maintained high loads for financial reasons, and he had found that "operators readily carry 2 to 5 percent. overload." In his opinion, this overload was acceptable because "the strain" was "not on the operating force but on the male personnel and supervisory people."[53] One can only assume that, from his point of view, managers used more energy to speed up operators than operators used to work harder. Bell officials frequently believed their own propaganda.

The Bell System Concept of Family

At all times managers aimed to convince operators of the Bell System's concern for employee well-being. Official literature and presentations in association meetings constantly reminded operators of how well the company provided for them through various benefit and thrift plans. Management developed programs specifically to address what they perceived to be the "peculiarities" of the female sex. Management also presented rest homes and after-work courses as part of the company's effort to care for the perceived needs of operators. Besides fostering gratitude among the operators and good public relations, rest homes provided the companies with economic benefits. These homes insured that operators returned to work earlier from illnesses, decreased payments that otherwise would have to be made under the disability plan, and helped keep absences to a minimum.[54]

Courses offered in health and nutrition, presented to the women as concern for their health, formed yet another approach to absence control. In Hall's opinion, many women who were frequently absent had not "the slightest opportunity in the world, and never have had, to learn the ordinary common rules of hygienic living," and if they could "learn something more about how to take care of themselves, they [could] reduce the sickness, just on their own account. . . ."[55] Management rarely considered the idea that these women had illnesses that resulted from operating, and that no amount of hygiene would prevent stresses on a person's arms, ears, throat, and brain.

Bell System managers explicitly denied any "deleterious effects" as a result of telephone operating, even though they acknowledged in 1923 that there had been "one sickness disability case for every three or four operators" and that the "average duration" had been "over thirty days."[56] When evidence from all Bell System companies pointed in a different direction, one expert analyzed statistics from a single company that related to the causes of force loss due to disability to explain system-wide disability absences.

These data showed that a high percentage of the losses on account of disability were reported as due to nervous and run down condition, but from the nature of the material as a whole it was clear that this classification was very superficial. In a good many cases it appeared that the girls claimed they were in a nervous or run down condition when they did not know what was really the matter with them, or the underlying cause was in all probability some specific disease. . . . about half of the disability losses are clearly not chargeable to operating work but to such causes as appendicitis, heart trouble, tuberculosis, maternity, frail or nervous type girl, etc. 12% of all disability losses are cases in which there is no good evidence that telephone operating is not responsible, but, on the other hand, there is no evidence that the work is responsible.[57]

Distortion of the data (table 5) is only one problem with this analysis. Without resorting to female "peculiarities," how would one account for women not knowing that they were ill with appendicitis, heart trouble, tuberculosis, or maternity problems? These could not be considered benign conditions.

Ignoring the evidence presented by the operators about their own bodies and the statistics given by the whole Bell System, this expert concluded that the number of disability absences could be decreased through the "proper selection of new employees" "in order to eliminate the obviously frail and nervous individuals who have no business in a central office or probably any other form of indoor work."[58] And, of course, prevention through health education provided a "fine opportunity to obtain cooperation of employees' associations."[59]

The idea of using employee associations to effect a change in employee behavior did not originate with this expert, however. In 1929, when managers offered a nutrition course to the graduates of the General Health Course for Women, under "results hoped for" L. M. Smith stated:

Some of us feel that the Nutrition Course will, in time, become an important personnel activity; that it will not only tend to improve the general health of those who take it, but that it will have an important bearing upon the development of the individual along other important lines; that, like the Health Course, the new activity will tend to uncover

Table 5. Percentage of Losses Resulting from Female Employees' Sickness in Largest U.S. Cities (1921)

Clearly not chargeable to the work		51
Due in part at least to outside causes		8
Causes to which the work may have contributed		12
Eye trouble	1.2	
Ear trouble	3.2	
Throat trouble	3.6	
Nervous trouble, rundown condition, or	4.0	
loss of voice claimed by employee or her		
doctor to be caused by the work		
Insufficient data for classification		29
		100

Source: E. O. Raabe, "Sickness Disability Among Female Traffic Employees," paper presented at the General Traffic Conference, April 23, 1921, p. 426.

or develop leadership among the women employees; that it will serve as another medium of expression for those women who have ability beyond the requirements of the daily job. We hope also that it will serve as another proof to employees of the fact that the management is interested in them as individuals. . . .

If the Nutrition Course did nothing more than prolong the usefulness of a small percentage of those who will take it, its value as a personnel activity will have been demonstrated.[60]

That the company promoted women's health to keep them at work is practically insignificant given the failure to provide the majority with meaningful opportunities for advancement. The Bell System recruited and trained college men, held conferences on how to develop such recruitment and training, instructed non-college men in company courses on supervision and management, and generally offered men abundant opportunities for advancement, regardless of the level on which they were hired. Such efforts took place during the same period in which management offered women health and nutrition courses "to uncover and develop leadership" among them. Indeed, the expectations for women must have been based on perceptions of their "peculiarities." Managers rationalized these low expectations with affirmations about the youth and high turnover typical of the traffic department. They accused the young operators of having limited ambition.

The Assistant Chief Engineer stated at the 1923 Personnel Conference that "most of these girls do not expect to stay in the business very long. Someone has said that they consider it merely a transition between school and housekeeping. They are not heads of families but are young people who naturally think fully as much of having a good time as of work, and the great majority of them have little initial ambition for responsible positions."[61] This remark ignored the statistics compiled by the Bell System itself, which did not support the idea that marriage was the major cause of high turnover. Even during the 1920s when the percentages of married women increased, turnover was still high. Though turnover had been reduced from a system-wide average of 80–90 percent in 1920 to 40–50 percent by 1925, reasons for leaving remained the same.[62]

On occasion, when managers admitted that the company caused high turnover, they hastened to assign the problem to one location and to one set of managers who had not followed system guidelines. Hence, in its personnel, public relations, and wage policies, the Bell System persisted in attributing high turnover to "marriage" and not to "working conditions." As long as characteristics claimed to be inherent to women could be used to explain their actions, managers only had to invent health and nutrition courses and other association activities to accommodate women's needs.

Operators Embrace Public Relations Activities

While these ideas about women may have been imposed by larger social views, it must be emphasized that some women internalized these ideas. Even the most reluctant groups of operators eventually participated in the activities sponsored by the employee representation plans. Thousands of individual operators became representatives and participated in the joint conferences where they socialized with management. Many operators actually wrote brief essays describing "What I Did Today," contributed ideas to the Pink Ticket Plan, and attended the health and nutrition courses as well as taking part in other activities. Initially, a certain amount of compulsion would account for their behavior, but the stories written by these women reveal that often many of them absorbed the Bell System ideology and sought the praise and recognition offered to conformity. One enthusiastic operator reported:

I fell in company a few days ago with an elderly gentleman and, after having learned where I was employed, he seemed very much interested about our line of work.

He said, "I wish you would tell me how the Company in general treats its employees where the majority of them are girls." I explained to him all about our rest room, silence room and matron, and the care we received when ill. He said, "Do you mean that you have a rest room and beds and cafeteria furnished like that all at the expense of the Company?" I told him that was what I meant. He then asked if I was an operator, and I said I was a Maple operator. He said, "Well, don't you have chief operators and supervisors?" I said "Yes, sir." He asked how they treated us and I told him about how they took things up with us and how we could go to them with anything we could not solve ourselves. Then I told him about our Association and the entertainments it furnished.

I invited this gentleman up to our next open house and he said he certainly was coming and would bring his wife, and when I started to get out of the car he said, "Well, your Company has a wonderful system."—Vernal Black, Oklahoma City, Oklahoma[63]

Other examples graphically illustrate the operators' conscious desire to contribute their stories.

As I was waiting in the drug store one noon, a lady entered to use the public 'phone. After taking down the receiver, she put her packages on the counter, then placed her pocket-book on that. She had no more than placed the things until the pocket-book slipped to the floor. She set the telephone and receiver down. When she came back, of course she couldn't get central. She then made the remark of poor service. There was my chance of "What I Did Today." I explained the cause of delay. After placing the receiver back for a few seconds there was no trouble. She thanked me and said, "How easy to get central, and what a mistake I made."—Frances E. Miles, Arkansas City, Kansas[64]

Many other operator efforts to secure good public relations were reported. Aside from the typical help in emergencies, operators assisted subscribers in other ways while promoting the company. For instance, "while waiting at a railroad station Miss Edna Thompson met a woman who wished to place a long distance call but hesitated to do so on account of unfamiliarity with the use of the telephone. Miss Thompson advised her new acquaintance that she was an employee of the Telephone Company and her offer to file the call was gratefully accepted."[65] Two other operators increased the company income and provided a service to two subscribers when they suggested places where two new coin box stations were installed. AT&T managers had effectively designed their programs. Telephone operators by the end of the 1920s appeared convinced that their interests would be protected by Bell System policies. At the same time that unionism had been either eliminated or suppressed, Bell managers had successfully enlisted the aid of the workers in management's economic goals.

The Bell System Provides Family Support

Bell System paternalism improved some operating conditions to keep the operators lulled and also to prevent government intervention. Operators' salaries remained low compared to male craftsmen's, but most operators worked eight hours of a nine-hour day for six days a week, received either extra pay or a day off for Sunday work, and received paid holidays. One-hour lunches and two fifteen-minutes breaks had become common in most Bell companies. As the average age of operators rose because of lowered turnover, discrimination against married women lessened in many places during the 1920s. In 1926, about 48 percent of the operators in California were married, whereas only 9 percent of New York's operating force were married women. The general policy against hiring married women continued when single women were "available, except possibly where more mature people are desired, as, for example, the night tours."[66] A Bell System survey made in 1928 indicated that the percentage of married, widowed, or divorced women varied "from 3.1 to 34.4% by companies" and that 14 percent of all Bell System women fell into these categories. Before World War I, these categories of women represented only 2–3 percent of the workforce.[67]

Being a member of the white Bell family had certain "economic" advantages for workers. Two-week paid vacations had been institutionalized in the Bell System by 1929. In many areas of the country, operators could spend their vacations at camps or resorts provided by Bell. Operators with two or more years of service received sickness and disability benefits, while pension, stock, savings, insurance, and other thrift plans were improved for those eligible to participate in them. Although these plans failed to reduce turnover, many operators remained with the company. In the pages of the company magazines, dozens of examples can be found of telephone operators with more than twenty-five years of service who participated in the plans. These women were not only able to accumulate stock, eventually retire, and receive pensions, but they were able to benefit from mortgage plans that allowed them to buy homes, even though many of them were single.

Many operators found opportunities for advancement as clerical workers in the accounting, commercial, and plant departments that were growing as a result of business expansion and the various policies set in motion to gain public favor. And, above all else, young, single, and native-born operators continued to enjoy their elitist and racist homogeneity, created and fostered by Bell System hiring practices. More mythical than real, the aura of officelike working conditions delighted white telephone operators. They believed that the company hired only the best to become a part of the family, and the best did not include blacks or immigrants. Flattered in this way, suppressed in other ways, operators participated in the activities organized for them without making any attempts at union formation until after they had begun to feel the effects of the Great Depression.

Whether they genuinely believed in the family concept or not, operators conformed in their behavior. Hall stated conclusively in 1929 that management and the employees had a mutual "sincere confidence" in each other. He added:

> The management is no longer afraid of the employees or afraid of any particular groups among the employees, and the management does not today belittle the ability of the general forces to make real contribution to the objectives of the companies.
>
> Unionism has disappeared from the Bell System. The constant threat that used to influence and modify decisions and plans has in my judgment, forever disappeared from the Bell System. It is no longer an element or a problem in the managerial policy or program.[68]

As future events would prove, Hall had properly assessed the moment but not "forever." Indeed, the Bell System had doubled its wire mileage during the 1920s, "operating revenues jumped from $448.233 million in 1920 to [$1.095,000] billion by 1930, . . . declared dividends nearly quadrupled, $40 million to $156.625 million, [and] . . . average annual earnings of telephone workers rose, too, but not on such a grand scale, from $980 a year in 1920 to $1,497 in 1930."[69]

With levels of service far better than even before the war, workers under control, companies economically prosperous and expanding, and dial systems being rapidly introduced throughout the country, the Bell System could not have been better prepared economically or psychologically to face the Depression. Despite a temporary decline in telephone use and in expansion, the Bell System emerged from the Great Depression as it had from World War I, more secure economically and still in control of its workforce. Cloaked by these crises, the Bell System effectively instituted policies that otherwise would have been attributed to greed.

6 | The Dial Era

Sporadic subscriber objections to automation continued long after employee representation had effectively quelled any possibility of operator resistance. Whether representing their constituencies or themselves, elected officials denounced the elimination of "personal service" and the unemployment automation caused. On May 21, 1930, for example, when 31.8 percent of Bell telephones were dial, Virginia Senator Carter Glass (Democrat) introduced the following resolution to the U.S. Senate:

> Whereas dial telephones are more difficult to operate than are manual telephones; and
> Whereas senators are required since the installation of dial telephones in the Capitol to perform the duties of telephone operators in order to enjoy the benefits of telephone service; and
> Whereas dial-telephones have failed to expedite telephone service; therefore, be it
> Resolved that the sergeant-at-arms of the Senate is authorized and directed to order the Chesapeake & Potomac Telephone Co., to replace with manual telephones, within 30 days after the adoption of this resolution, all dial telephones in the Senate wing of the United States Capitol and in the Senate Office Building.[1]

Two hours later, North Carolina's Charles L. Abernethy (Democrat) introduced a similar resolution in the House of Representatives.[2] Neither the general public nor the politicians had completely accepted the Bell System's public relations campaign.[3] Aware of the impact of public pressure on rate increases and the introduction of new technologies, AT&T executives denied that dial phones caused individual job loss. They argued that long-term planning and the creative use of transfers, resignations, and retirements avoided massive layoffs. Bell System management manipulated public sentiment about larger societal issues to make these denials seem plausible.

Indeed, during the dial era (1920–60), social, political, and economic conditions provided managers with explanations for the fluctuations in the number of operators. For example, rapid telephone expansion in the 1920s created a higher demand for telephone operators than dial phones eliminated. The national economic decline of the 1930s obscured the rate of dial installations and the consequent decrease in operators. World War II and the Korean War required expanded telecommunications, which effectively halted dial installations and caused a temporary increase in operators. Only after the Korean War did the technological displacement of operators become so apparent that the Bell System could no longer attribute job loss to other causes.

In the period from 1920 until 1960, telephone operators experienced transformations in their responsibilities and work environments. They witnessed the gradual automation of both local and long distance connections. Operators acquired totally new skills and duties as a result of the introduction of new services such as overseas telephoning and the expansion of teletypewriters. Independent trade unionism recovered from its devastating defeat and became a powerful voice for telephone workers. The occupation of telephone operating opened for groups of women previously excluded, while other women left to take advantage of new opportunities. All of these things occurred within the context of 1920s' company unionism, the Depression, and World War II and its aftermath.

The Depression

In 1930, as American industries experienced severe economic decline, the Bell System initiated several measures to reduce traffic expenditures. Managers increased operators' loads, employed former operators on a part-time basis, and placed the workforce on a five-day week.[4] These measures saved money by reducing the number of full-time operators, minimizing the training of new operators, and increasing productivity by using part-time experienced operators to handle high-traffic periods. Both local and toll operators' loads increased approximately 29 percent from 1930 through 1933. Keeping in mind that each unit equaled $1 million, this increase in workloads saved the Bell System millions of dollars compared with 1930 and "dispensed with the services of over 30,000 operators."[5] Since the speedup reduced the need for large numbers of operators, and the lowered turnover in depressed conditions led to a more experienced operating force, management was able to save more money by decreasing its supervisory forces. AT&T attributed the increase in loads and general efficiency to improved operating methods, equipment, and management techniques introduced before the Depression.[6]

These payroll reductions bolstered low revenues, but the Depression provided the Bell System with an even greater opportunity to maintain profits and mask increased workforce reductions. From 1930 through 1933, the telephone industry experienced the worst part of the economic decline associated with the Depression and further decreased its workforce by one-third from the levels in 1929.[7] More than 77,000 experienced and student operators were among the total of 120,000 Bell System workers who lost their jobs during this period.[8] By the end of 1935, business had recovered within 10 percent of the 1929 levels, but employment continued to be reduced, and in 1937 it remained 25 percent lower than in 1929.[9] Increased loads and other managerial initiatives only partially explain these reductions.

Indeed, Bell System statistics reveal a correlation between dial conversion and employment. During the 1920s, an increase in the number of operators and the steady pace of dial installations resulted from rapid postwar expansion and enormous growth in telephone service.[10] After 1929, however, the rate of dial conversions continued, but the number of traffic employees declined. Between 1929 and 1939, more than 60,000 Bell System traffic employees lost their jobs, while the percentage of dial conversions more than doubled from 26.6 percent to 55.7 percent (see table 6). As conversions stabilized and the national economy recovered slightly, operating forces temporarily increased in 1937. When dial conversions accelerated during the 1937–38 recession, the numbers of operators fell again. Regardless of Bell System attestations to the contrary, the purpose and the effect of dial conversion eliminated operators. The Depression merely veiled this reality.

World War II and Its Aftermath

Unlike the Depression era, the period from 1940 until 1960 passed with almost uninterrupted economic expansion in the telephone indus-

Table 6

Year	Percentage of Dial Telephones	Total Number of Traffic Employees	Traffic Operators
1920	2.2	142,064	
1929	26.6	182,120	
1930	31.8	161,339	
1931	37.2	142,239	
1932	42.5	125,355	
1933	45.8	114,609	
1934	47.1	114,108	
1935	48.0	111,927	94,728[c]
1936	48.6	119,951	102,660
1937	49.8	126,187	107,923
1938	52.4	120,227	102,358
1939	55.7[a]	121,430[b]	102,415

[a] Taken from a chart in the proceedings of the President's Conference, Fall 1945, AT&T Archives, Box 69.

[b] AT&T, "Bell System Statistical Manual, 1920–1964" (New York: Business Research Division-Comptroller's Department, 1965), p. 706.

[c] Ibid., p. 708. No statistics are given for the number of operators before 1935.

try. War conditions (the need to rapidly move information, materials, and troops) and postwar prosperity overshadowed the technological displacement caused by dial telephones. By 1942, long distance calls alone had increased from 50 percent to 85 percent above 1939 levels in many places across the country.[11] The number of operators needed to handle this volume increased from 102,415 to 153,578. In the years immediately following World War II, the rush to fill backlogged orders, the end of overtime, the five-day week, large numbers of resignations, and continued growth contributed to the rapid increase in operators.[12] Dial conversions, which had practically halted during the war, increased slowly in the years immediately afterward. From 1948 to 1950, when conversions resumed a more rapid pace, the number of operators decreased. Later, during the Korean War, the increase in dial conversions continued at a steady rate, but the numbers of operators grew only temporarily as a result of demand associated with the war. After 1953, the rapid increase in local as well as long distance dial conversions caused a further decrease in operators by

Table 7

Year	Percentage Total of Dial Telephones	Total Traffic Operators
1940	53.6	108,375
1941	56.3	129,182
1942	58.2	153,578
1943	58.2	163,154
1944	58.6	159,157
1945	58.4	171,439
1946	59.2	223,824
1947	59.8	220,060
1948	62.4	223,413
1949	67.7	206,480
1950	70.7	208,139
1951	73.0	217,459
1952	75.1	222,732
1953	77.6	219,530
1954	80.7	204,062
1955	83.6	205,176
1956	86.6	203,285
1957	89.4	196,344
1958	91.9	173,218
1959	94.2	165,969
1960	95.9	159,954

Sources: AT&T, "Bell System Statistical Manual, 1920–1964," pp. 505, 708.

1960 (table 7).[13] In effect, the Depression and war conditions concealed the true impact of technology on operators' work during the dial era. Operators declined in numbers during a period when the number of calls handled monthly by an operator increased from 10,641 to 57,271, and the number of phones per operator rose from 63 in 1920 to 155 in 1950 and to 365 in 1960.[14] National economic conditions, whether depressed or thriving, provided the Bell System with the appropriate reasons for these changes. In contrast, labor experts said that the changes could "be attributed directly to the extension of telephones connected to dial equipment, to the extension of dial services, and to new operator methods such as marksensing."[15]

Bell System Denies Technological Displacement

In response to subscriber, congressional, and labor opposition to dial, U.S. Secretary of Labor W. N. Doak appointed a committee to investigate technological unemployment in August 1931.[16] He asked AT&T to supply information about the extent of conversions, their locations, and the numbers of employees affected.[17] Along with dates and places of past and future conversions, AT&T Vice President E. F. Carter replied that dial conversions during the past year had "reduced the requirements for operators by about 4,500," and that it was expected that another 2,500 more would not be required within the next seven months.[18] He attributed the reduction in "requirements" to the Depression rather than to the automation of telephone switching. It was important for the Bell System to deflect public scrutiny and to convince workers that their jobs were not in jeopardy.

Indeed, Carter claimed that management prevented massive technological displacement by hiring temporary part-time help, postponing retirements and resignations, and transferring surpluses to other departments or other cities.[19] Apparently, these arguments convinced Ethel L. Best, the Department of Labor investigator who conducted the study under the auspices of the Women's Bureau. After researching the methods and results of a single office cutover (conversion from one system to another) and a partial cutover in a multioffice city, Best concluded that more than two years of advanced planning had made it possible for the company to reduce its force at cutover time without laying off permanent employees. Employees hired two years before cutover, according to Best, "readily signed a clause stamped on the application blank that pointed out the short-term nature of the prospective job."[20] Neither Best nor the Bell System questioned the fairness of hiring women on a temporary basis and forcing them to sign away their right to permanent employment.[21] To avoid any unfavorable publicity, the companies transferred within the city or found jobs in other cities or in other industries for many of the temporary employees they released as a consequence of the cutover.

By emphasizing the planning procedures, Bell managers effectively obscured the fact that dial offices simply required fewer than half the operators required by manual offices. Despite Best's enthusiasm for the Bell System's methods, an injustice had been committed against both

Table 8. Effects of Change from Manual to Dial Operation

Operators	Total	Regular	Temporary	Occasional
January 1930	547	323	192	32
June 1930	534	312	179	43
January 1931	249	249	—	—

Source: Ethel L. Best, *The Change from Manual to Dial Operation in the Telephone Industry*, U.S. Department of Labor, Women's Bureau, Bulletin 110 (Washington, D.C.: GPO, 1933), p. 5.

the temporary and the permanent operators. Consider the statistics in table 8 for the single city cutover completed July 14, 1930. It is undeniable that the manual offices required 515 full-time and thirty-two occasional operators (who worked during peak traffic periods) to handle the traffic, whereas a dial office required only 249 full-time operators.[22] Even when the company retained operators to cushion the impact of the new system for subscribers, the numbers needed were small, and eventually the company laid them off as well.

Governmental approval of AT&T cutover methods did not quell public clamor. Bell System behavior during the Depression led many to question whether its employment and economic policies conformed to the standards expected of a public utility. AT&T had maintained its stockholders' dividends at $9 per share, while it also reduced the number of workers, decreased wages, demanded speedup of operators, and eliminated jobs through the introduction of dial equipment.[23] The newly created Federal Communications Commission launched a rigorous rate investigation into Bell System operations in 1935. Two reports resulted from the hearings.[24] Both recommended rate reductions and increased regulation, but Commissioner Paul A. Walker's *Proposed Report* attacked AT&T's dial program for having had "the effect of increasing the cost of telephone service to the subscriber, as well as of increasing unemployment [of operators]."[25]

Walker concluded that not only had AT&T executives been wasteful and inefficient in capital expenditures, but they also had predicted "a new era" of economic prosperity at the very moment that depression loomed. Indeed, Walker argued, their failure to make accurate long-range forecasts or to even comprehend the depth and extent of the economic decline resulted in high subscriber rates and severe consequences for their employees. Walker concluded that Bell System policies forced workers to pay for capital expansion begun in 1929 to meet an expected surge in telephone growth that did not materialize.[26]

Undaunted by this criticism, AT&T launched a propaganda campaign in which it aggressively justified its dividend payments and employee policy. Regarding the $9.00 dividend, managers answered:

> The management of the American Company does recognize an obligation to its stockholders, 650,000 persons, most of them small investors who have put their savings into a legitimate enterprise engaged in furnishing a necessary and valuable service to the public. It continued to pay the regular dividend through the years of depression. But it did not earn or seek to earn the full dividend during those years, and was able to pay it only by drawing upon its surplus to the extent of $141,000,000; a surplus which had been accumulated over the years against the time of such an emergency.[27]

Evidently, the Bell System had succeeded in accruing the "string of unfailing surpluses" that Hall spoke of in 1923. Although these surpluses had been accumulated at the workers' expense, AT&T felt obliged to distribute them to its stockholders.

As they had done during the 1920s, Bell managers held systemwide conferences to develop a unified response and to determine "the general public sentiment towards the telephone company, . . . the public's attitude towards the AT&T dividend, towards the employment policy of the telephone company, and toward rates."[28] They concluded that the dividend had not contributed to the "many agitations for reduced rates" and "nowhere ha[d] there been any unfavorable press reaction."[29]

Bell officials attributed their favorable image among "city councils, civic bodies and other organizations" to several factors:

> The participation of telephone employees and companies in unemployment relief has helped our public reputation and has drawn little fire upon the System's employment policies. . . . The figures in the annual report showing a reduction of 50,000 employees in the System have caused no comment in the press. The paragraph on a possible employment reserve produced four or five commendatory editorials and some comment but not much. . . . the reason that there was not

more comment is that the belief of last September that labor could be protected from further effects of this depression has been largely dispelled by events. There is a universal belief in the field, supported by a few pieces of evidence, that the spreading of work and the maintenance of the wage rate have been essential to our public relations.[30]

The misery suffered by workers thrown out of work and on to relief rolls concerned AT&T managers only if it affected the company's public image.

At the General Publicity Conference held in September 1934, Bell managers designed public relations answers to the question, "What Has the Bell System Done as a Citizen in the Depression?" Aside from asserting that the taxes and interest paid by the company helped to stabilize the national economy, managers argued that AT&T's employment and dividend policies were transformed into public and employee benefits. Some of the recommended answers stated that wages had not been cut, and an upward adjustment in wages for 278,000 employees had occurred; spreading the work had saved more than 42,000 jobs; 9,688 employees had been hired; $5 million had been paid in separation allowances; $136 million had been distributed from the Employee's Stock Plan; and $1.5 million had been spent for new construction.[31] And, of course, "efforts were made to confine lay-offs to those upon whom release would entail the least hardship," while the dividends had helped "thousands" with "the bare necessities of life."[32] These claims demonstrate how AT&T deliberately distorted the truth for publicity reasons.

To say that wage rates had not been reduced omitted the reality that workers accustomed to six-day weekly paychecks experienced an estimated 16.67 percent salary reduction when workweeks were reduced by the much-lauded "spread the work" program.[33] By the end of the Depression, AT&T claimed that by spreading the work, part-timing, and reducing the workweek, as many as 60,000 workers had been kept on the payrolls. What was not said was that the Bell System saved money by downgrading many of these employees into lower-level and lower-paying jobs, by suspending wage advances according to the wage increase schedules, and by forcing many to work overtime without pay.[34] "Upward adjustments of wage rates" did not necessarily mean wage increases, especially in light of the lost hours. Intentionally, the company claimed an increase in the number of employees without stating whether or not they were part-time.

Ten thousand new operators nationally would be insignificant during this period of accelerated dial conversion when the companies hired operators on a temporary and/or part-time basis.

How AT&T determined "those upon whom release would entail the least hardship" can only be conjectured. Norma Naughton remembered that the layoffs were "hit and miss and largely a matter of favoritism." She saw "girls dismissed with eighteen and twenty years' service and girls kept on who had only been there a couple of years." According to Naughton, "it was entirely up to the chief operator and the district man."[35] Returning employees' investments in the Stock Plan without penalty for premature withdrawal could be viewed as the only decent thing to do in a depression. The money spent on the construction program furthered the introduction of dial and expanded long distance lines that eventually led to a decrease in operators and certainly would not be viewed favorably by those women. The claim that the dividends "helped to provide the bare necessities of life" for "hundreds of thousands of small stockholders" crosses the line into fabrication. By definition, small stockholders could not receive enough in dividends to make any serious impact upon their lives during the Depression. Besides, it had been reasonably estimated that about 5 percent of individual stockholders received from 75 to 80 percent of the dividends paid.[36] The rich, not the small stockholder, benefited from the decision to maintain the $9.00 dividend. Obviously, the Bell System had been deliberately misleading in its public relations statements. As dial conversions proceeded, AT&T executives continued to create public propaganda to rationalize job losses.

Technological Displacement as Progress

When the Depression no longer provided a cover for technological displacement, Bell System managers returned to the theme that the introduction of new technologies indicated natural progress that benefited the whole society.[37] In 1940, in his testimony before the Temporary National Economic Committee, AT&T Vice President W. H. Harrison expressed this sentiment:

> The record shows that the Bell System has been alert to foresee and anticipate the needs and opportunities for technological progress. But more than that, it also has been the aim and policy to introduce into its

plant or practices those new technical developments which are clearly essential to progress, and to do this in such a way as to avoid or minimize any possible adverse effects in the nature of economic waste or human hardship. . . .

The long term effects of technological progress upon the scope, quality and cost of telephone service without exception have been beneficial to all participants in the business—employees, investors, customers—as well as the society as a whole. Similarly, it has created new investment opportunities and has expanded the demand for capital goods. Technology has made for advances in wages, shorter hours, more highly skilled jobs and many other betterments in working conditions; and these betterments have been realized without the use of "speed-up" systems.[38]

Aside from his duplicity about speedups, Harrison never quantified the beneficial effects of technological progress for operators. Instead, he rationalized job losses which resulted from dial conversion by emphasizing that proper planning had kept them to a minimum and that companies had paid lump-sum termination payments to individuals for whom layoffs had been unavoidable.[39] These "scattered" separations, he reasoned, were "offset, in part, by increased work for men."[40] Indeed, Harrison's rhetoric echoed male trade unionists' demands for the workers' share of the benefits. Workers, in unionists' and managers' minds, referred to men.

As long as they ignored how automation reduced women's work, telephone managers and workers could continue to measure technological progress in terms of more jobs for men. Rather than decreasing employment, Clifton W. Phalen, president of the Michigan Bell Telephone Company, stated that "the increased telephone usage resulting from scientific and technological progress has, in turn, helped to expand employment."[41] Phalen concluded that technological progress "created more jobs . . . better jobs—jobs that pay much higher wages and jobs that compare favorably with those in other industries."[42] Low-paying operators' jobs could be sacrificed at the altar of "progress."

Rebirth of Independent Unions

Bell System hypocrisy did not escape the attention of workers. As early as January and July of 1933, workers at employee representation meetings objected to "carrying a disproportionate share of the burden" of the Depression, and they questioned the "fairness of continuing the AT&T Company dividend payments at the present rate." These representatives stated "that no further reductions in payroll should be made unless the revenue of the company suffers further drastic contraction and the dividend rate has been reduced." They argued that "employees had not received "inflated" wages during the period in which the surplus was accumulated, and they felt that the surplus was built up of money "retained from employees in the same sense that it was created of money retained from the stockholders."[43] The lower-level managers at these meetings reassured the representatives that the maintenance of the dividend rate had not affected their "lot," that their wage rates had been maintained, and that telephone workers "felt the effects of the depression to a lesser degree than employees in most outside industries." Insulted, the representatives demanded that "their views be presented to the higher levels of management for earnest consideration."[44]

Representatives did not limit their comments to wage policies. In response to plant men's complaints regarding forced overtime, management agreed that "excessive" overtime without pay should be limited and requested that local management and employee representatives meet to "clear up the situation." Operators' complaints about their loads did not yield the same results. When they objected to the increase in their work caused by force reductions, management explained to them how their workloads were determined and what was expected of them.[45] Employee representatives initiated discussions related to further wage increases, cancellation of holiday pay, spreading of work, and employment of married women, but after each discussion, management effectively maintained its policies.

Bell System associations, for obvious reasons, did not provide the appropriate setting for addressing the unfairness of these policies.[46] Struck by the many injustices and conscious of their newly gained government protection as a result of the National Industrial Recovery Act (NIRA), employees gradually looked toward independent unionism as a solution. More than 1,800 Boston and other New England operators denounced employee representation and organized the United Telephone Operators of America in August 1933. These women, angered by the wage reduction

28. Operators working under extremely hot conditions. The windows are closed, and fans are blowing on ice, circa 1940s. (Courtesy of Communications Workers of America Collection, Robert F. Wagner Labor Archives, New York University)

concurrent with the workweek reduction, demanded that their salaries be maintained, even though their work hours would be reduced. They were especially incensed over these reductions because they already had worked one payless day weekly for the previous year and a half.[47]

Referring to their right to organize under the NIRA, the group's acting president, Grace Barry, informed AT&T to "communicate and deal directly with and through the United Telephone Operators of America and its designated representatives" "on all matters touching the interest of the operators working in the telephone service."[48] Management successfully suppressed this courageous but premature burst of unionism with "a systematic and persistent series of personal interviews."[49] But not for long. After the U.S. Supreme Court upheld the Wagner Act on April 12, 1937, independent labor organizations emerged throughout the Bell System.

Telephone operators became fervent organizers because of their outrageously stressful and degrading work environment. Helen C. Carmody, for example, remembered how management would turn on the heat and shut the windows on hot days when the humidity in her seashore area would adversely affect the equipment. She recalled:

> I know sometimes . . . they'd say, "Well, it's only ninety-six." Well, ninety-six, if you keep moving your arms up and down, you have somebody sitting on both sides of you, you know, and the humidity was bad, . . . they were just air-conditioning the equipment for a long time because they didn't want that to go bad. They didn't care about their human beings. I remember one time a girl fainted five times, and they'd take her out there and revive her, bring her back upstairs. Then they'd bring in the ice and put it in big buckets and put fans on the buckets, on the ice. They'd keep them on the job, but they had some rough times.[50]

These environmental conditions as well as the hours (split tricks, nights, Sunday and holiday work), physical immobility at the switchboard, and close supervision created bitterness and dissatisfaction among operators. For example, Nelle Wooding, who became an operator in 1914, expressed her resentment at company behavior during the Depression:

> here in Dallas for more than two years we worked only three and four days a week. After we did have a union, the company would tell us how good they'd been to us, and one day I got enough of that. We were in a meeting with the Texas traffic area director. . . . he was arrogant by telling us how good they were and so on. I said, "I want to ask you something. Did it cost the company any more to keep a hundred people on the payroll working those three days a week than it would have cost them to lay off half of them and keep fifty at six days a week." "Well, about the same." I said, "Of course, it was the same. The employees helped each other. It didn't cost the company a penny, and you had the advantage of keeping a trained force at your fingertips. And when the business picked up and you needed those people, you didn't have to employ or train anyone. You just let them work more days." I said, "Now, I don't want you to ever tell me again you helped us during the Depression. You didn't. We helped each other, and probably if we had to do it over, we'd do the same thing. I agree that part-timing is better than layoffs, but don't tell me you did something wonderful. You didn't."

Then another very serious thing during the depression: . . . Those progression increases were stopped completely for a period of three years. . . . The schedule was thirteen years long, and they added this three-year freeze. And when you came out of the freeze and they picked up progression increases, they didn't go back and make it retroactive. You just started fresh.[51]

The Bell System's systematic exploitation of its workers during the Depression provided the workers with the motivation—and the Wagner Act provided them with protection—to organize independent labor unions.[52]

Telephone operators helped to form these new organizations (either as all-female traffic locals or as mixed locals that included plant men), and they were essential to the building of a national federation. Women comprised more than one-fourth (eight of twenty-nine) of the delegates who convened on December 16–17, 1937, in St. Louis to form a National Assembly of Telephone workers.[53] This group met two times in 1938 and finally adopted a constitution under the name National Federation of Telephone Workers (NFTW) in New York City on June 5, 1939.[54] Convention proceedings document women actively engaging in the debates about union structure, bargaining demands, and issues specific to them.

During the first years of the NFTW, when members were ambivalent about the organization's purposes and still had not completely shed themselves of the timidity of company unionism, women helped to reshape the membership's attitudes. Autonomous NFTW locals refused to affiliate with AFL or CIO unions. Many members of these organizations abhorred strikes and looked to the organization merely as a means to share information and possibly develop strategies around common issues such as pensions. These workers desperately needed an education about "the history, goals, and aspirations of organized labor" as well as training in union operations and functions.[55] Women unionists made an enormous contribution to this educational process.

For example, as the NFTW educational director, Ruth Wiencek of Michigan traffic, helped write booklets and articles for the NFTW newspaper the *Telephone Worker*, helped affiliated organizations in conducting "officers' training programs," and held "period conferences to discuss programs and techniques."[56] Ann Herlihy, a research analyst, conducted the statistical research on which the new organization depended to formulate

Photos 29–32 illustrate the fervor with which the operators participated in strikes and other union activities after they had thrown off the yoke of company representation. 29. National Federation of Telephone Workers on strike, Washington, D.C., 1940s. (Courtesy of Communications Workers of America Collection, Robert F. Wagner Labor Archives, New York University)

30. Picketers take a break during 1947 walkout in New York City. (Courtesy of Communications Workers of America Collection, Robert F. Wagner Labor Archives, New York University)

31. The "Voice with a Smile" on strike, Roanoke, Virginia, 1953. (Courtesy of Communications Workers of America Collection, Robert F. Wagner Labor Archives, New York University)

32. These long distance operators not only refused to cross the installers' picket line, but they cheered others who supported them and booed those who crossed. New York City, 1957. (Courtesy of AP/Wide World Photos and Communications Workers of America Collection, Robert F. Wagner Labor Archives, New York University)

its bargaining demands. Under Sylvia Gottlieb, the subsequent director of the Statistics Department, the department functioned as a "co-ordinating agency, duplicating, and consolidating all statistical items, financial reports of the companies, interpretation of governmental orders, tax laws, reconversion information and other pertinent data."[57] As a result of their educational and statistical work, telephone women became even more aware of the need to address their own problems.

At the first meeting of the NFTW Executive Board, women delegates insisted on the election of one woman to the seven-member executive board and the formation of a traffic panel to address telephone operators' issues.[58] Within two years, when the Executive Board was increased to nine, women won another seat; they also pressured the editorial board to include two women associate editors on the staff of the federation's newspaper, the *Telephone Worker*.[59] As members of the NFTW executive board, the two women delegates constantly forced the board and the federation to consider "equal pay for equal work," reclassification of the operator's job and separation allowances for operators who were displaced by dial, as well as other important demands.[60]

During the war years, telephone women had to fight off efforts to lower operators' wages even further. For example, in 1940 the NFTW defeated an attempt by the U.S. Independent Telephone Association to pay "learner operators at less than the minimum," and it "intervene[d] in proceedings relating to requests for learner exemptions and the lengthening of the learning period."[61] Spokespersons for the NFTW frequently testified before government agencies to protest substandard wages. Leaders vigorously favored raising the minimum wage and supported the Equal Pay Act of 1945.[62]

Operators' "semi-skilled" classification provided part of the justification for their low wages. In January 1944, the NFTW telephone traffic panels successfully lobbied the Women's Bureau of the U.S. Department of Labor to conduct a job study for the purpose of reevaluating this designation. "Operators not only want[ed] to be classified as skilled workers— after the apprenticeship period— . . . they wanted to be classed specifically as 'telephone operators,' a designation of 'highly skilled and unique' work which was 'not comparable to that of any other industry and, therefore, the wages should not be compared with those of other industries.' "[63]

Ethel Erickson supervised the research and issued a report in July 1946, which affirmed that telephone operators' work "is a composite one involving manual dexterity, clerical ability, a knowledge of a variety of switchboards—the skills of the job are many, and the job is strenuous."[64] This redesignation provided bargaining leverage against the company's regional wage policy.

A downward reclassification of male-dominated work also suppressed women's wages during World War II.[65] When managers changed an insignificant detail of a job and assigned it to women at a lower wage, NFTW women appealed to the National War Labor Board to enforce its policy of "equal pay for equal work."[66] In wage disputes brought before the board, union leaders constantly sought to expand the application and enforcement of General Order No. 16 (adopted by the board on November 24, 1942), which affirmed women's right to equal salaries "for comparable quality and quantity" of work.[67] Appeals to government agencies, however, brought little remedy for these issues. Operators had to take to the streets before the government actively intervened.

On November 17, 1944, in the first major strike in the era of independent unionism, 500 operators in Dayton, Ohio, left their switchboards over unfair wage treatment and the failure of the War Labor Board to take corrective action in this case and others related to telephone workers' grievances. The company had effectively suppressed local operators' wages by paying an $18.25 living stipend to operators brought in from other states. This practice meant that an imported beginner could earn more than a local operator who had more than ten years of experience.[68] The strike ended eight days later, after spreading to all the major Ohio cities, Washington, D.C., and Detroit, and involving more than 10,000 telephone workers. The possibility of a nationwide strike forced the government to grant independent telephone unions representation in wage and labor disputes brought before the War Labor Board.

The settlement included an agreement that the War Labor Board would establish a National Telephone Panel (later called a "Commission"), which would have "the power to hear and determine and to issue directive orders in all labor dispute cases . . . [and] to make final rulings on voluntary wage or salary adjustments."[69] The Commission established that breaches of the "equal pay for equal work" principle were subject to contract grievance procedures and/or arbitration.[70] Unlike the War Labor Board, on which only AFL or CIO representatives sat, the Commission included NFTW representation. After telephone workers had fought indecisively for three years, operators won government and industry concessions.[71] The successful outcome of this strike earned the NFTW credibility among other telephone workers, and its membership grew rapidly.[72]

Despite the obvious value of women's union participation, telephone men feared domination by a female majority. It should be recalled that IBEW had created a separate department for operators during the World War I era to prevent women from having a controlling vote in that union. Joseph A. Beirne, who later achieved prominence as the president of the Communications Workers of America (CWA), remembered that "the men did not trust the women."[73] In 1939, when the new locals formed the National Federation of Telephone Workers (NFTW), the idea of a separate department for women surfaced again. This time the national assembly adopted "block-voting procedures" which prevented women from having the voting power their numbers commanded.[74]

According to male and female organizers, plant men often resisted women unionists and feared operators' militancy.[75] Differences in male and female working conditions account for their differences in attitude and focus. Men who worked independently, or with little supervision, were insensitive to the confinement, excessive monitoring, and other adverse working conditions that produced operators' militancy. Even technological displacement, a concern for all telephone workers, had a more immediate and direct impact on women.[76] While dial conversion could require the retraining of men, for the most part it created more jobs for them in manufacturing, installation, and maintenance, while it extinguished many operators' jobs altogether.[77]

In this environment of fear, mistrust, and differing interests, men gained control over the new independent unions. Even though their participation had been essential to building the NFTW, traffic women never achieved more than two representatives on the nine-member Executive Board.[78] When the CWA emerged, men again seized the major leadership roles, even in female locals.[79] As some women continued to fight for equitable representation, others, still under the influence of the "white lady" identity, imbued with the current social norms, and often burdened with domestic responsibilities, yielded to male leadership and, more importantly, to male-defined trade union priorities. Consequently, techno-logical displacement of operators continued to receive little attention from the union's leaders.

Independent Unions and Technological Displacement

Several explanations can be offered for the low priority given to the loss of operators' jobs and the misguided and ineffective strategy pursued by the unions to remedy losses. Adherence to craft union methods and ideology, the advanced progress of dial conversion, the undeveloped state of telephone unionism, a wartime increase in the number of operators, significant wage and benefit improvements, and a general acceptance by the union that automation meant progress partially explain the unions' actions. At its inception, independent telephone unionism faced a hostile employer and competition from older, more-established unions. Conse-quently, the new union leaders focused on union survival and traditional union demands.

The NFTW struggled with a lack of internal discipline (autonomous local affiliates) and unity, while AFL or CIO unions (NFTW unions could join neither) constantly raided its membership.[80] More importantly, the Bell System refused to bargain on the national level and constantly sought to pit one region against another. In this atmosphere, NFTW (and later CWA) leaders concerned themselves with increasing wages and pension benefits, seniority issues, increasing the membership, gaining union rec-ognition, adequate grievance procedures, formal written contracts, and achieving national bargaining with AT&T and its associated companies. Unfortunately, bygone tactics and strategies developed to protect male crafts proved ineffective for female service work in an industrialized set-ting. Indeed, telephone unionists failed to perceive the difference between protecting occupations in which work content was changing and preserv-ing an occupation that technology was abolishing.

The very first NFTW "Bargaining Objectives," designed "to reduce the inroads on employment due to technological advances and to assure that the benefits accruing from advances in methods, equipment, and par-ticularly efficiency of the workers, be shared by the workers," express an ideology which seeks compensation but not the cessation of job loss.[81] For example, the 1941 goals illustrate not only a traditional craft perspective that visualizes a shorter workweek as the most significant demand in the struggle to limit the effects of technological change, but a male bias as well.

One of the plans which the Federation advocates for offsetting reductions of employment due to technological improvements is the establishment of a seven-hour day, 35-hour week, without corresponding loss of pay. The Federation also is sponsor of the idea of a retraining program in order that older men can be made proficient in the operation of new type equipment, thus preventing force dislocations. The member organizations of the Federation composed of Traffic Department employees have been particularly active in attempting to minimize the effects of dial conversion programs, which in many cases sharply reduce the number of operators required. Collective bargaining effort along these lines has brought substantial benefits.[82]

Of course, retraining did little to protect the occupation of telephone operating, whereas it ensured that older men would be employable when new machines were introduced. The goals made no mention of preparing operators for different jobs. Nor did they quantify "substantial benefits" in light of the job losses involved.

Unionists expected a set of universal demands to cover the technological displacement of both women and men. Even the women on the National Traffic Panel Committee accepted this approach. Despite an otherwise commendable record of activism, the National Traffic Panel Committee minutes throughout its existence (1943–46) contain few references to dial conversion.[83] Engaged in the process of union-building, it is not surprising that these women concurred with overall union policy.[84]

Operators' identification with the craft model motivated them to demand a redefinition of their work so that it would be recognized as skilled labor. In 1942, for example, Norma Naughton urged the National Traffic Panel to decide "the length of the time . . . necessary to become a skilled worker. . . . three years or five years . . . because . . . on this decision would rest . . . final wage schedule requirements." She argued:

You will have to decide whether you have to have three years' learning period, or a two year learning period; and it would be necessary to request that the maximum salary be paid at whatever time you believe you are a skilled worker. That is only in line with craftsmen in the various other organizations; where after four years, an electrician or machinist or mason graduates from the learning period and becomes a skilled craftsman.[85]

The comparison with tradesmen illustrates how women tried to fit themselves into a model that only partially applied to their circumstances. The Women's Bureau reclassification of operators' work as skilled strengthened their demands for wage increases, but it diverted their resistance to technological displacement. The ineffective use of the reclassification of operators' work was as much a result of the inadequacy of using "skill" in the traditional sense as it was a reflection of the undeveloped state of independent unionism among telephone workers.

Despite their ineffective approaches, it is important to note that neither the NFTW nor the CWA had totally ignored technological displacement. Within a year of its formation, the NFTW went on record in favor of the "seven-hour day and 35-hour week without reduction in annual earnings."[86] At NFTW Regional Conference Traffic and Plant Panels, activity reports consistently show work toward these goals.[87] National and local union newspapers and newsletters carried articles that described job loss and the need to cushion its impact on "regular" employees. One headline in the CWA Weekly Newsletter exclaimed "Indiana Co. Shows Wrong Way to Deal with Force Cut in Mechanization" when that company followed "the letter of the contract" and refused to permit termination pay to older operators in Peru, Indiana. By insisting on "laying off in inverse order of seniority," the company would not allow older workers to leave and younger ones to keep their jobs.[88] A subsequent article showed that dial conversion would eliminate twenty-five or thirty-five of the eighty-five operators employed by the company. It ridiculed "AT&T propaganda" and stated that "the performance of the company is hardly living up to the promises made" that new technologies "would not have an adverse effect on employment."[89]

Even the local presidents declared that "the Bell System has demonstrated *a ruthless disregard* for the human element in its business by displacing large groups of employees through vast technological changes," and they resolved "that this Union do everything possible through Seniority provisions, clauses requiring union consultation and agreement etc., to reduce the *rude shock* of displacement resulting from technological advances" [my emphasis].[90] In a moment of unusual clarity, the *Telephone Worker* criticized the formation of postwar planning committees to study the problem. It stated: "this problem needs something more than committees. It needs the sober, careful thinking of all branches of the telephone labor movement working together to effect a lasting settlement."[91] This level of introspection and reconsideration of traditional trade union ideology and approaches never occurred.

Instead, local affiliates of the NFTW struck and threatened to strike throughout this period over union-building issues. In October 1945, for example, forty-three of the forty-seven NFTW affiliates held a four-hour meeting that crippled nationwide telephone service to the extent that only "extreme emergency" calls could be placed.[92] According to President Joe Beirne, this dispute had "nothing to do with wages" but with "deciding on a course of action in connection with the discriminatory treatment given to telephone workers by the NLRB."[93] This was not the only time that the union used a "meeting" to indicate to management the potential power of a nationwide strike. On January 17, 1946, the Washington, D.C., Telephone Traffic Union, led by Mary Gannon, began an "8 day meeting" in which 3,000 operators stayed away from their boards because of "sweatshop practices." Operators objected to the usual seating, voice, and courtesy requirements. Instructions such as "Do not change headset from one ear to the other without calling your supervisor," or "don't take an aspirin without being relieved from your position," were particularly offensive.[94]

Later in 1946, when company orders were backlogged and when a nationwide strike would have been equally effective, seventeen NFTW affiliates successfully bargained a significant wage increase for their workers and for other affiliates who had prematurely signed contracts for less money. Even in this position of strength, neither the all-female traffic locals nor the mixed locals formulated a specific demand to address the impact of automation on telephone operators. Mildred Beahm of the militant Washington Telephone Traffic Union had been on the strike committee that formulated the demands. And Dorothy Handy and Loreta E. Emnia of Long Lines participated in the bargaining with company officers.[95] Operators in Detroit, Cleveland, Washington, D.C., Philadelphia, and other large urban areas had begun to leave their switchboards as Joseph Beirne agreed to a settlement that made no mention of the impending technological threat to their jobs.[96] Indeed, most telephone unionists considered this strike a great success because it marked the first time that the company had bargained with a union on a nationwide basis.

The victory was short-lived. The following year, when the workers' bargaining power had diminished, 350,000 telephone employees (230,000 operators) struck nationally for the union shop, nationwide bargaining, a wage increase, better vacations, higher pensions, and other demands.[97] However, dial systems, which affected 65 percent of all telephones, neutralized the effect of the strike on local service. Defeated by technology and defections by affiliates, workers returned to their jobs after six weeks, having gained an average weekly wage increase of $4.00 and "practically nothing on their nonmonetary demand." The American Communications Association, CIO, criticized the NFTW leadership as "incompetent, bungling and irresponsible," for sitting around in Washington, D.C., hotel lobbies while the rank and file across the country "waged a magnificent fight" "against the nation's most powerful monopoly." The ACA claimed that "had the courage of the rank and file been supplemented with united organization, intelligent planning and preparation, and responsible leadership genuinely dedicated to the welfare of the rank and file, the strike nationally and on the Coast could have been won completely." Instead, the national leadership reduced the wage demand from $12 to $6 and allowed the affiliates to bargain locally when the strike had been called on a nationwide basis.[98] This defeat temporarily weakened telephone unionism, but it also motivated union leaders to correct the NFTW's internal organization. The Communications Workers of America, a centralized national union, emerged from the decaying NFTW one week after Western Electric workers settled the last strike in Lincoln, Nebraska, on June 2, 1947.[99] The formation of the CWA represented the entry of telephone workers into the era of modern unionism.

In effect, it could be argued that independent unions developed too late to develop a strategy that would help telephone operators. World War II labor demands and the postwar expansion of toll usage caused the number of operators to double between 1940 and 1948 (see table 7). Although unionists were aware of the long-term effects of dial conversions, technological displacement could hardly become a pressing priority in this climate of growth. By the end of World War II, when independent unions had matured, more than two-thirds of local calls were dialed, long distance dialing was imminent, and the Bell System had long defined and established the principles and procedures for implementing the conversions.

Certainly it is debatable whether any union demand restricting dial technology would have been considered under these conditions. Telephone workers in the preceding two decades had acquiesced to the Bell System's definition of the issues. Consequently, the new unions could only "disagree with particulars" or "protest specific applications and oversights" within parameters set by management.[100] In essence, "union action ha[d] been restricted to reducing unilateral management policy to contractual terms, improving existing benefits, and introducing seniority into the transfer process."[101] Sylvia B. Gottlieb, director of the Research and Statistics Department, advised local unions that "one of the most reasonable and effective ways you [unions] can protect yourself from undue hardships and unfair treatment when layoffs appear imminent is the inclusion of a strong clause covering 'Reduction in Force' in your union contract."[102] Sadly, these clauses were hopelessly ineffective in protecting operators' jobs.

The NFTW and CWA force adjustment clauses illustrate how management set restrictions on negotiable items. A New Jersey Bell Telephone Company contract stated that the "Company shall decide the necessity for and shall determine the extent of . . . force adjustments."[103] After the company made such a determination, other clauses stipulated that the union should be notified and established the time limits for notification. For example, union contract language required Michigan Bell Telephone Company to notify the union "in writing not less than ninety days in advance of the scheduled cutover date" when "a force surplus condition, brought about by a dial conversion program is anticipated by the Company."[104] Force adjustment clauses pertaining to layoffs, transfers, part-timing, retraining, seniority, bumping rights, rehiring, pensions, and termination pay usually contained language that ceded to the company the right to "determine the extent of the reductions required, the effective date or dates thereof, the exchanges, and the job classifications involved."[105]

Even the best of "Force Adjustment" clauses merely provided an orderly method for compensating, laying off, and firing operators. In many cases, management used these very clauses to circumvent other clauses that guaranteed employees' rights. Local 1150 received many complaints about AT&T's practice of firing temporary workers in order to break off their employment before one year so as to avoid making them permanent employees. "Under the terms of the contract the company may not maintain an employee on temporary status more than one year, and the dismissal of an employee with more than one year's service can be made only on the basis of just cause with the right to arbitrate the dismissal in the event of disagreement between the union and the company." Thus, the policy was to "fire them . . . , break their service, rehire them and still retain the right to get rid of them without having to worry about the protection of the union."[106]

When Beirne appointed the Dial Conversion Committee within a few months of the formation of CWA, the committee also reflected the boundaries established by telephone management.[107] The purposes of the committee were to "study conditions surrounding . . . Conversion programs," "the effect of these conversion programs upon the national economy, and employment opportunity," and to "develop a . . . program . . . wherein the undesirable results of rapid technological improvement, can be minimized."[108] The committee met several times and constructed a resolution that the CWA annual convention later adopted.[109] The resolution recommended the continuation of the dial committee, that the Research and Statistics Department "be authorized and directed to ascertain" more information on the impact of dial conversions on operators, and, most importantly, that "the Executive officers be directed to study and recommend their conclusions to the Executive Board for approval, bargaining items which would include a 30-hour workweek, jurisdiction of work, voluntary retirement after 25 years of service with a minimum pension of $100 per month and such other provisions as may be necessary to reduce the impact of dial conversion upon our members."[110]

The demand for a thirty-hour workweek and a meeting with AT&T certainly demonstrates the willingness of the women on this committee to extend but not to surpass the usual trade union solutions. Bargaining as unionists, rather than as operators acting in their own interests, these women, like their predecessors on the National Traffic Panel, accepted the parameters set by management and craft union ideology and confined themselves to the study of what they already knew (dial conversions caused job losses) and making ineffective recommendations. The Third

Annual CWA Convention adopted this resolution, and no further mention in union documents was made of it or the Dial Conversion Committee after 1950.

In an equally misguided proposal to combat technological displacement, the unionists suggested that the Bell System slow the pace of dial conversions.[111] At their November 2–4, 1943, meeting held in Chicago, women on the Traffic Panel endorsed the idea "that efforts should be made to spread dial conversions and other technological changes over periods long enough so that serious force dislocation would not result."[112] In September 1946, a Central Regional Conference delegate, responding to an AT&T proposal to issue $1.5 million worth of stock, accused AT&T of having "the primary purpose of [using] this money . . . to convert to dial within the next five years all remaining manual telephones." Indicating a monumental job loss for operators and massive layoffs of plant men once the installation of the new equipment was completed, the delegate proposed "to spread this program not over a five year period but a fifteen year period, in order to prevent a wide spread dislocation of the nation's economy and to eliminate the fear of unemployment in the present worker's mind."[113] The Central Regional Conference adopted a motion favoring this proposal, which stated that "it be transmitted immediately to the headquarters of the NFTW . . . [for] immediate action."[114] It is ironic that unionists would propose the slow introduction of dial when this was exactly what the Bell System had been doing since 1921. Indeed, management had consistently argued that in this way they saved individual jobs and avoided massive layoffs. These misdirected craft strategies only partially explain why the new unions gave dial conversions so little genuine contemplation.

CWA Welcomes New Technology

Union acceptance of technological displacement solidified during the dial era. Like telephone company managers, union leaders viewed technology as a part of a continuum called progress. Union leaders generally agreed with the position outlined by Clifton W. Phalen. For example, forty women delegates to the NFTW Traffic Panel meeting on November 2–4, 1943, "went on record as not disapproving . . . technological improvement, but proposing that the gains resulting from such improvements be shared with workers, as for example, in a shorter work-week."[115] Even the

NFTW Postwar Planning Committee could only propose to "study poten-tial effect of technological changes in their relation to postwar unemploy-ment and make recommendations in respect thereto."[116] A CWA booklet issued to clarify the union's position in 1950 contract bargaining stated that "CWA does not oppose technical improvement but rather welcomes it, provided the proper share of the benefits go to the workers."[117]

Although the union estimated in 1950 that 100,000 telephone opera-tors would become "victims of unemployment" within the next few years, and that in some places "hundreds of operators have been forced to part time because of dial conversion changes," it still welcomed auto-mation.[118] Why? In a booklet published by the union in the early 1960s, Beirne answered: "For ourselves, we welcome automation because we see in it a lever for higher wages, longer vacations, shorter hours, and ultimately, greater security for ourselves and the American people."[119] He agreed with the company that there had been "an over-all job move-ment towards the higher paying departments within the major telephone companies. . . ."

> Between 1945 and 1958, the switchboard operators—the lowest paid group in the telephone industry—decreased from 52% of the work force to 32%. The higher paid Plant Department increased from 22% of the work force to 32%. The Plant Department's average pay in 1958 was $2.68 an hour compared with the telephone operator's average of $1.75. Increases also took place among clerical, business, sales and professional workers.[120]

Without analyzing the loss of women's work or the unequal pay, Beirne looked to what he thought were the long-term benefits of automation—higher-skilled and higher-paid work mostly for men. He would not even entertain a discussion of the possibility of another approach to automation.

For example, in 1952, at the annual convention, Delegate Sacha of Local 4350 "directed a proposed amendment to the attention of the chair," which resolved "that the Research Department of the CWA investigate the possibility of a method or methods to combat the dangerous strike break-ing mechanization of the telephone industry during an authorized strike and that the instructions arrived at be forwarded to the locals."[121] Presi-dent Beirne interrupted before the amendment could be seconded and suggested that it not be accepted in "haste" and that "it would be in the best interest of the Union if the Executive Board studied that amendment . . . and take whatever action on it, . . . as the Board in its judgment, . . . might deem desirable."[122] The motion failed without a second, and another motion passed which resolved that "the entire matter be referred to the CWA Strike Director for his study and disposition."[123] Beirne had suppressed this courageous attempt to conceptualize an alternative resistance strategy.[124] Thus, the CWA would continue to watch and study as operators' jobs diminished.

The CWA formalized this approach in the early 1960s when it created an automation committee to "maintain surveillance over employment, working conditions, technical changes and other matters relating to automation in the communications industry."[125] It also established a job structure committee to survey and evaluate "changing technology and methods in the communications industry and the effects these changes ha[d] on the overall job structure." Policy recommendations for solving problems created by new technology formed the basis of the committee's duties. Beirne stated unequivocally that it was "not the purpose of this Committee to resist change but rather to be certain that human values receive at least the same amount of consideration as mechanical and financial values."[126]

Although this approach protected operators' jobs insufficiently, many did receive "consideration" as changes occurred over the course of the dial era. In the midst of the development of independent unionism and the struggles for recognition, operators obtained many of the traditional union protections and benefits. For example, grievance procedures corrected many injustices in the assignment of tours, hours, pay treatment, and penalties of all types. On the national, industry-wide level, bargaining achieved higher wages, a forty-hour workweek, shorter wage progression schedules, time and a half for overtime, night and evening differentials, better pensions, improved sickness and disability benefits, more vacation time, holidays and other paid time off from the job.[127] Operators and other women profited from these reforms as well as from the large variety of jobs generated by service expansion and a general increase in clerical work.

The simultaneous expansion of occupations in the Bell System and the achievement of many union demands obscures the true extent of the technological displacement of operators. During the early years of the dial era when new technologies provided different types of services to subscribers, opportunities as other types of operators within the Bell System became available to white women. Up to 1950, expansion in long distance usage led to an increase in the number of toll operators. Overseas connections, begun in 1927, required specially trained operators to complete such calls. Conference calling in which up to fifty subscribers across the country could speak together, first offered in the early 1930s, required a specially trained group of operators to get all of the parties on the connection. Teletypewriter (TWX) service, greatly expanded in the 1930s, offered operators who had typing skills positions in large teletype exchanges. Telephone companies also supplied and trained TWX operators for their customers. Special assistance to complete collect, third-party-billed, and credit card calls also provided operating jobs. As the 1960s progressed, this variety in operating jobs gradually gave way to dialization and other technological changes that either eliminated operators or transformed their work processes.

As dial conversions whittled away operators' jobs, other opportunities opened for white women, either as operators in outside businesses or as clerical workers in other departments of the Bell System. Private Branch Exchanges (PBX) hired as many women as the Bell System, and in large cities PBX hired more.[128] In New York City, for example, 19,000 operators worked for the telephone company, while 37,000 worked as PBX operators in 1925.[129] Bell System companies in all large cities maintained a department that trained and supplied permanent, temporary, and vacation relief operators to the Private Branch Exchanges.[130] As dial conversions progressed, outside businesses became one of the sources of jobs for displaced Bell System operators. In many ways, a transfer to a PBX for an operator about to be displaced could be seen as a promotion.[131] Opportunities for these jobs contracted and expanded along with the national economy. For the most part, however, opportunities remained abundant well into the 1960s when technology displaced PBX operators as well.[132]

Clerical work in the accounting, commercial, and plant departments of the various Bell System companies provided the majority of available jobs. A Women's Bureau study of six Bell System operating areas, conducted in 1944, found women composed 87.5 percent of the accounting departments and 63.8 percent of the commercial departments.[133] The proportion of clerical workers among telephone women increased from 20 percent to 34 percent, and the proportion in the business office and sales doubled from 4 percent to 8 percent between 1945 and 1960.[134]

While offering little prestige and often even smaller pay, the quality and relative status of clerical jobs varied. Frequently, women moved into jobs formerly held by men.[135] Women, of course, received neither the power nor the salaries that men had enjoyed. In 1944, the Women's Bureau found examples of "separate wage schedules for men and women covering the same or very similar jobs in the commercial department."[136] Whether or not management promoted them to supervisors, women welcomed other benefits of clerical work. Mary E. Gannon, chairman of the National Traffic Panel Committee of the NFTW, confirmed that "many clerical jobs pay no more than operators are paid but it is considered a step upward. To secure one of these jobs is a step toward a higher promotion. There are such advantages as 8 hours a day, no holiday or Sunday work, ½ day off on Saturday (pre-war). It is considered a definite promotion."[137] Agreeing with Gannon, a telephone company manager stated that the clerical jobs were preferred "because there are also more privileges—girl can walk around, call home etc."[138] Usually an operator would be transferred to the plant department first, then to accounting or commercial. These transfers were "defined as promotions."[139]

Women, even up to the 1970s, attained few real promotions either as higher-paid craft workers or as higher-level career managers. Craft jobs, which paid more, offered greater opportunity for advancement, and provided "more challenging and satisfying" work than operating, were barred to women.[140] Supervisory positions open to women involved maintaining order and production, not policy- and decision-making. In 1970, 95 percent of women managers worked in entry-level positions from which further advancement could not be expected.[141] Despite their position as the majority of telephone workers, women merely moved from one low-paying, tedious, and unpromising job to another whether they were managers or not.

Hence, for women, new technologies and the expansion of telephone service provided few of the high-paying, skilled jobs that Beirne predicted. Perhaps, caught up in the optimism of the 1950s that viewed technology as progress, he failed to see that the "promise of abundance" in the "age of automation" would have a limited distribution. Union achievements did not outweigh the degradation and displacement that women experienced in the telephone industry. "Meaningful" or fulfilling work did not result from the introduction of new technologies. Unfortunately, for the operators of the future, union ideology had not formulated a strategy in the face of technological change. Consequently, management's technology and the union policy led to the further decline of telephone operating in the post-dial era.

PART THREE | The Computer Era

7 | Racial Integration and the
      Demise of the "White Lady" Image

The entry of African American women into telephone operating
occurred nearly half a century after the struggle against the industry's discrimination began. As early as 1910, black women
had sought entrance into the switchroom but met rejection by managers
and the operators. Bell System management used several ploys to avoid
hiring black women during the 1930s, but Bell finally capitulated during
World War II under the pressure of labor market changes, black people's
efforts, and Fair Employment Practices Committee (FEPC) investigations.
White women and their unions also continued to resist the employment
of black women as operators. They relented as other opportunities became available and as dial conversions decreased their ranks. The absolute number and proportion of black operators remained small during
the 1950s and early 1960s. However, social movements (civil rights),
technological change, and demographic transitions in larger urban areas
led to the almost complete transformation of the operating forces from
white to black during the late 1960s.

Even before this transformation became apparent, racial integration
had made the "white lady" telephone operator image untenable. Bell
System management slowly abandoned the image in places where it no
longer met business needs. Attitudes toward the occupation changed.
For the black operators, this change meant that the job did not bring the
same prestige and deference as it had for white women. Predictably,
managers found it wasteful to continue providing special recreational
activities and conveniences to an integrated workforce. As subscribers
became aware of the changing racial composition of operators, many
abused the black women with obscene remarks and racial epithets. And
white telephone operators as well as other white workers showed their

resentment and lack of respect for black women by refusing to accept them as equals in the workplace.

The racial integration of telephone operating and the subsequent decline of the "white lady" image are manifestations of the Bell System's restructuring of its workforce in the context of workers' resistance. However, neither African American women's success in integrating the job nor white women's attempts to maintain segregation significantly changed the outcome. As it introduced new labor-saving technologies, the Bell System continued to use race as a divisive force.

Bell System Continues Racist Hiring Practices

At the beginning of the 1930s, blacks made up 9.7 percent of the American population, but only .7 percent were Bell System workers, and no blacks were telephone operators. Even though blacks worked at a variety of menial jobs in different operating companies, the "white lady" operator prevailed as Bell managers continued to justify the exclusion of African Americans by alluding to tradition/custom, black women's incompetency, and white women's refusal to work with black women. Indeed, New York Telephone Company, perceived by many to be progressive and liberal, pioneered in rationalizations for black exclusion.

For example, in 1927, when George S. Schuyler of the *Messenger* inquired about the number of blacks employed by the company, Vice President T. P. Sylvan replied that some blacks were on the payroll "assisting . . . in the conduct of . . . restaurant and lounge facilities."[1] To Schuyler's follow-up letter asking why no blacks worked as operators, Sylvan answered that he had already discussed this matter with other "distinguished" blacks and that he believed that he had "satisfied them that the position which we have taken with reference to their employment has been a proper and necessary one."[2] Even after New York state passed a law in 1933 that forbade public utilities to "refuse to employ any person in any capacity, in the operation or maintenance of a public service on account of the race, color or religion of such person," the exclusion of black women from the operating forces continued.[3]

According to a Mayor's Commission Study in New York in 1935, "Mr. R. H. Boggs, Vice-president in charge of personnel of the New York Telephone Company did not regard the exclusion of Negroes . . . , as discrimination but only as a customary practice."[4] Indeed, during the 1930s, in testimony given before government investigators, New York Telephone managers insisted that the absence of African American women from operating and clerical jobs was an indication of black women's incompetence.[5] Consider the testimony of Walter D. Williams, New York Telephone's general traffic manager before the New York State Temporary Commission on the Condition of the Urban Colored Population in 1937:

Q. What explanation have you for the failure of any Negro telephone operator to be employed out of those 4500?

A. That in the opinion of the interviewers, they are not qualified to fill the position of telephone operator. . . .

Q. Have you ever had a Negro Telephone Operator who has been qualified, in your experience?

A. Not in my experience.

Q. What prevents them from being qualified, in your opinion?

A. Our job, of course, in the Central Offices, is to give telephone service; that is done by a group of girls and we work together. They are white girls, and in our judgment it would not be possible to give a proper grade of telephone service if we put the Negro girls in with the white girls.

Q. Upon what is your judgment based, Mr. Williams, what fact, if any, have you in your possession upon which you base your judgment?

A. Business judgment over a number of years.

Q. I ask you if you are in possession of any facts?

A. I am not. . . .

Q. I understood the tenor of your remarks to be, Mr. Williams, that even if an applicant should possess all other qualification, the fact that such applicant was colored—a colored applicant—would in your judgment be a proper reason for refusing employment because of what you feel—of seating that colored employee next to a white person in the switchboard exchange.

A. That is correct.

Q. In other words, having perfectly competent colored applicants, you would feel it your duty to refuse to accept those applicants, and you would feel it your duty to give those jobs to white applicants, of no better or equal qualificants, merely because of that fact?

A. That is correct, yes, I would say.[6]

Throughout his testimony, Williams asserted that the company had the right to exclude black people and that it was not in violation of the law.[7] Furthermore, he maintained that his judgment was in no way affected by the knowledge that black and white women worked side by side in civil service and other government jobs.[8] He even acknowledged that hiring African Americans would be just, but concluded that "it is a matter of a practical condition that we have before us, and unfortunately all the things in this world are not decided on straight questions of justice."[9]

AT&T and its associated companies shared New York Telephone Company's rationalizations. As late as July 1943, August B. Haneke, vice president and general manager of the Chesapeake & Potomac Telephone Company in Baltimore, stated that his company had not employed blacks as operators and "could not do so for three reasons: (1) The white operators refuse to work with Negroes. (2) There had been a great deal of community resentment against using Negroes as operators. (3) The persons who would have to train operators refuse to instruct Negroes."[10] Haneke argued that because operators sat so close to each other, their work could not be compared to other work where blacks and whites were not in such "proximity." He feared that "white employees would walk off the job if Negroes were placed as operators," causing "a major tie-up of communication facilities."[11] Two years later, he reiterated the same excuses but added that the company feared the strength of the newly formed unions and that he believed that "an educational program was necessary before Negro operators [could] be employed without friction and without the danger of a walkout."[12] He indicated that the company had made significant progress by pointing out that blacks had been hired into clerical and supervisory jobs. These jobs, however, were in a "separate commercial office and . . . a segregated accounting unit."[13] The entire staff of twenty-five blacks had been hired in a newly opened office in a black section of Baltimore.

Walter Gifford, AT&T's president, assured FEPC investigators that he "was personally in complete sympathy with the hiring of Negro girls in telephone exchanges," but AT&T corporate structure prevented him from making directives that required associated companies to do so. Unlike U.S. Steel, which "has one central Board of Directors," he stated that "in the case of AT&T each State has its own Board of Directors made up of local residents and not "dummies."[14] He promised FEPC officials that he would "continue to pass the word along to State telephone officials indicating his own attitude on the matter."[15] Of course, he neglected to mention that AT&T Long Lines also did not hire black women as operators for the long distance service. Indeed, the uniformity of the rationalizations and excuses given by the entire Bell System makes it difficult to believe that this policy was not developed and directed by AT&T as all other policies were.

Ample evidence shows that these notions about racial exclusivity prevailed throughout the Bell System. A study of forty-four cities conducted by the Urban League concluded that "available information is sufficient to substantiate the fact that Negro workers have been systematically excluded from employment in this industry in many cities."[16] Consequently, the report continued, "prior to 1940, no Negro switchboard operators were employed in any of the exchanges" investigated. And, "in fact, there is no record of the employment of Negro operators in any city in the country before that date."[17]

Managers resorted to an assortment of tactics to hold the line against hiring black women as operators. One tactic that persisted in some places well into the 1960s was to hire black women clerical workers to justify their exclusion from operating by saying that the clerical jobs were better. Another method to delay hiring black women was to continuously refer to white women's objections to working closely with black women. For instance, J. N. Stanbery, general personnel manager of Illinois Bell Telephone Company, indicated that his policy was to hire blacks in as many other jobs as possible because he believed that "after Negroes have been observed by white operators to be employed in most all other categories of the company, then the white operators will be unlikely to object to the hiring of colored operators."[18]

Even during the severe labor shortages of World War II, New York Telephone continued to reject African American women as operators.[19] In 1940, when blacks comprised 10 percent of the nation's population, they still represented .7 percent of telephone workers and were still segregated in the lowest jobs.[20] By 1944, the FEPC conducted an investigation into the personnel practices at New York Telephone; it found that the company had begun to employ African Americans as clerks, typists, messengers, kitchen men, lounge attendants, stenographers, tellers, coin collectors, and business representatives and matrons, "but not as operators."[21] Despite company reports that it had "difficulty filling labor needs for operators due to relatively low wage[s]," managers claimed in November 1943 that they could not "hire Negroes because of speech and diction limitations."[22] On July 20, 1944, managers explained to FEPC investigators that they were willing to hire black operators "if given just a little time."[23] D. McClure, assistant to the first vice president, stated "that the company for the present felt it better to place non-white workers on individual jobs and not on "team play" jobs. . . . a great deal of cooperation was necessary in the operation of a switchboard where a large group of operators is employed and . . . Negro and white workers would not get along well on such a board."[24] Four days later, when pressed further by FEPC investigators, McClure claimed that the company had already agreed to a program "for a slow, gradual process whereby Negroes would be hired in other divisions of the company and gradually moved into operators jobs."[25] Stonewalling persisted as the company's preferred strategy to keep black women barred from operating work.

Like most other Bell companies, Pacific Telephone and Telegraph Company simply ignored Executive Order 8802 and 9346.[26] On April 13, 1944, the company wrote to the FEPC that the "Company's practice and policy" was not to discriminate, but it added this caveat: "We are sure, however, you appreciate that as responsible managers of a public service which is of great importance to the war effort, in administering our employment practices and policies we must continue to exercise our best judgment as to where in our organization we can use most advantageously the various individuals who apply to us for available employment."[27]

In the post–World War II era, Southern telephone operating companies were able to stall integration by using a single "moral" standard in addition to physical, mental, and voice qualifications to bar African American women as operators.[28] The "white lady" image was integral to maintaining control in Southern society. As "part of the effort to maintain a work force of persons of high moral character," Southern Bell, and later South Central Bell, refused to hire women with "illegitimate" children.[29] Even women whom personnel evaluators deemed "co-operative," "industrious," and in good "health" with an appropriate "appearance" were rejected for "lack of integrity" if they were unwed mothers.[30] Despite management's statement that they had "never applied this practice in order to discriminate with regard to either sex or race," the policy was both racist and sexist.[31] The requirement was never applied to men.

And, the EEOC investigation conducted during the late 1960s found that "throughout the South . . . [the policy] has tended to exclude Negro females to a far greater extent than whites. Indeed, the Commission has never been presented with evidence of any white woman being rejected on this ground."[32] Relentless pressure by the EEOC and civil rights organizations forced Southern Bell and South Central Bell to "reconsider" the "moral" requirement in 1970.[33] This victory had been won after decades of agitation for integration.

African Americans Demand End to Racist Employment Practices

From the 1910s through the 1970s, African Americans fought to change Bell System employment practices. Invoking the ideal of justice, they participated in boycotts, all-night vigils, mass bill pay-ins (sometimes in pennies), mass phone-ins to tie up the equipment, protest stickers attached to phone bills, demonstrations, and legal complaints to various government agencies.[34] Their protests were national in scope and included men and women from all sectors of the community. Protesters based their demands on the fundamental principle of equality, their rights as citizens who fought in American wars, and who paid thousands of dollars in public utility bills to companies licensed by their governments.[35] In many instances, simply applying for operators' jobs—as the seven African American women whose applications were rejected in 1910 because they were "colored" had done—was a challenge to the Bell System's discrimination policy.[36] One patriotic black woman in Cleveland, whose application also had not been accepted, questioned: "Does it make any difference . . . what nationality helps to bring this most awful war to an end?" She believed that black women should not be denied their right to wartime jobs or to contribute to the war effort, especially because "our girls have brothers, sweethearts, and husbands over there fighting for democracy for all nationalities."[37] Even though this argument had been effective in opening doors to other workplaces, it failed to change the Bell System's hiring policies. Disappointed but not disillusioned, African American women continued to confront this injustice.

In what would become a nationwide strategy against telephone industry discrimination, highly qualified black women in New York City began applying for operators' jobs right after World War I. During the postwar labor shortage, they answered New York Telephone advertisements for

"1000 operators needed" and used their rejections to rally publicly for justice. Agitation continued in New York City into the 1930s when a group of civic and political leaders met at the Bethel A.M.E. Church on February 22, 1931, in support of legislation barring discrimination in public utilities.[38] Assemblyman J. Edward Stephens of the 19th District in Harlem introduced a bill to the New York Assembly the next day, and he continued to do so for three sessions of the legislature until it was finally passed on April 8, 1933. However, the passing of civil rights laws guaranteed neither compliance nor enforcement.

Individuals, politicians and organizations employed several tactics to force the New York Telephone Company to obey the law. After appeals to the New York State Public Service Commission resulted in no action, "the New York and Brooklyn Urban Leagues, the YWCA, YMCA, the City-Wide Citizens' Committee on Harlem, the Welfare Council, the NAACP, and the National Negro Congress" all "attempted to negotiate with the company."[39] As others chose to go through the "normal" channels, the Peoples' Committee and the Coordinating Committee for Employment, directed by Congressman-elect Adam Clayton Powell Jr. launched a "Don't-use-your-phone" drive. This direct action called on customers to refuse "to dial numbers and insisting upon personal attention from an operator every time they made a call."[40] Historian John Henrike Clarke recalled another New York campaign in which protesters tried to jam the lines with calls at the times when stock quotes were sent to the West Coast.[41]

African Americans in St. Louis used tactics similar to those employed in New York, and they pioneered their own tactics as well in their fight against discrimination. In the summer of 1943, when Southwestern Bell Telephone advertised widely for operators but refused to hire qualified black applicants, the local chapter of the March on Washington Movement launched a protest campaign.[42] They called on all citizens to place a sticker in one corner of their telephone bills or their mailing envelopes. The sticker read: "Discrimination in employment is undemocratic—*I protest it!* Hire Negroes now!"[43] Referring to Executive Order 8802 and President Franklin D. Roosevelt's affirmation of the telephone industry's status as a defense industry, the St. Louis protest leaders appealed to both black and white organizations, churches, and individuals to support them in their fight against the company's "undemocratic un-American and pro-Hitler employment policy."[44]

On June 12, 1943, after company officials had refused to answer registered letters requesting a meeting to discuss hiring black women, more than 300 African Americans marched to the Southwestern Bell Telephone Company building carrying placards and banners that demanded: "How Can We Die Freely for Democracy Abroad If We Can't Work Equally for Democracy at Home?" and "25,000 Negro Subscribers Deserve Consideration."[45] The picketers (mostly black women, judging from the photographs) encircled the block-long building, declaring that "$4,000 Spent Daily by St. Louis Negroes for Phones! Yet Not One Decent Job for Us."[46] T. D. McNeal, director of the local March on Washington unit, stated: "The pigeonholing of applications due to race, creed or color, is an undemocratic, un-American and pro-Hitler employment policy and is retarding the progress to better service."[47]

MOWM leaders claimed widespread support for their movement in the white community. The Church Federation of St. Louis had "cooperated" with the movement "by conducting a survey in white neighborhoods to determine the attitude of white St. Louisians toward the integration of Negroes in jobs with public utilities."[48] A "smaller scale" survey had previously shown that "80% of white St. Louisians" wanted integration of the public utilities, and "a large number" of white organizations had sent messages of support to MOWM headquarters.[49] Leaders of MOWM stopped short of describing whites as participants, but they stated that "a large crowd of white sympathizers . . . milled around in the main lobby of the company, confusing clerks and exciting company officials," on September 18, 1943, when more than 200 people arrived at the Southwestern Bell building to pay their telephone bills. Some paid in pennies so as to "slow up the process of collection." Although the surveys may have been less than scientific, and perhaps MOWM leaders exaggerated the magnitude of their white support, their allegations do show an attempt to legitimize their struggle through interracial cooperation. According to McNeal, this demonstration successfully "dramatized this un-American situation and forcibly called to the attention of the telephone management the fact that Negro citizens . . . have an abiding determination to see this fight against the telephone company through no matter how long a time or what sacrifice might be entailed."[50]

Black women expressed the same determination when they also marched into the streets of Baltimore during the summer of 1943. More

than two hundred women took turns in 24-hour picketing of the Chesapeake & Potomac Telephone Company in an effort to gain access to jobs
as operators. Like the St. Louis managers, the c&p had advertised for
applicants to train as operators but turned away qualified black women.[51]
Complaints against the c&p had been filed by the Urban League as early
as July 29, 1942. Other organizations, such as the Union for Democratic
Action and the *Baltimore Afro-American,* in addition to twenty-four black
women who had been refused employment, had continued filing charges
before the mass picketing started.[52]

Indeed, African American women across the United States combined
their mass protests with complaints to appropriate levels of government.
For example, on March 19, 1935, many participated in the rebellion
against employment discrimination and other injustices in what has been
called the 1935 Harlem Riot. In a subsequent investigation into the cause
of the "riot," blacks testified before the Mayor's Commission on Conditions in Harlem about "the discrimination, the Jim-Crowism, and all
the forms of oppression to which they had been subjected."[53] Many of
these blacks received the opportunity to question managers from the utilities. As Williams's testimony illustrates, African Americans had forced
the telephone company to admit that their policies were unjust. Over the
course of the next three decades, African Americans filed suits with the
FEPC, EEOC, and local and state equal employment opportunity agencies.

During World War II, when the telephone industry denied that it was a
defense industry and therefore not subject to Executive Order 8802, African Americans appealed directly to President Roosevelt. He affirmed that
communications were vital to the war effort and therefore the order was
applicable to the telephone industry. This decision opened the door for a
flood of complaints against the Bell System. Following the strategy of
sending only the most-qualified applicants, African American organizations across the country filed complaints. When the Urban League answered an advertisement in a Louisville newspaper by sending ten qualified applicants, the applicants were refused jobs, and Bell management's
only explanation was that the ad was a mistake and no openings were
available. The Urban League reported the company to the FEPC.[54] Complaints to the FEPC initiated by Alma Illery, president of the Housewives
Cooperative League, resulted in the hiring of twenty-four black women

clerks at the Bell Telephone Company of Pittsburgh in the winter of 1943.[55] By the end of the war, Bell System companies in every region had faced FEPC charges of discrimination.

Even after the first operators were hired and the FEPC dissolved, African Americans continued to request government intervention. In May 1948, Marian Wynn Perry, NAACP Assistant Special Counsel, reminded R. E. Gilmore, president of the Plainfield, New Jersey, branch: "It is important that the telephone company have no loophole for finding the applicants unqualified. Therefore, they should be unmarried, high school graduates, of medium build (particularly not stout), have pleasant voice and no noticeable accent. If the applications are still turned down, *a complaint should be filed with the New Jersey Division Against Discrimination . . .*" [my emphasis].[56] During the 1950s, women filed charges with the New York State Commission Against Discrimination (Division of Human Rights) against both the New York Telephone Company and AT&T.[57] And, of course, later when the federal government established the Equal Employment Opportunity Commission, African American women initiated hundreds of cases during the early 1960s when they still were hired only in small numbers for the operators' jobs.

White Operators Resist Black Inclusion

For white women operators who had experienced the destruction of their independent unions, had seen the imposition of company unions and the specter of automation during the 1920s, and finally had felt the loss of jobs to automation during the Depression, the importance of the "white lady" image—as reflected in racial exclusivity—intensified. Even though operators' jobs paid less than some clerical work and required longer and more irregular hours, operators continued to resist integration. For these white women, it was not simply a matter of economic competition; it was a matter of preserving an identity. Evelyn N. Cooper explained that "the real reason for the separate treatment of the operator job category . . . seems to lie in a long standing Bell System policy . . . the companies have provided the operators with exceptionally nice rest room[s], recreational and eating facilities, thereby giving them a sort of compensatory 'social status' among telephone company workers."[58] White women perceived African Americans' demand for inclusion as a threat to that

33. White women performing minstrel show (*Telephone Review,* December 1949, p. 20). (Image from a New York Telephone Company magazine that is now defunct)

"social status" and, more significantly, as a threat to the last portion of their working environment over which they believed they had some control. Furthermore, even within the context of degraded work, the operator's job was still a good one compared to factory and domestic work, and most white women wanted to keep it exclusively theirs. Consequently, they actively resisted black inclusion by their continued participation in the creation of demeaning images of black people, exclusion of anti-discrimination clauses in their new independent union contracts, strikes, and threats of strikes.

As they had during the 1920s, the Depression, and afterward, white women continued to perform in minstrel shows that ridiculed black people. For example, in 1939, the *Telephone Review* reported that "the old south," complete with plantation, Aunt Jemima, and "Lazybones," was a "principal feature" of the annual Christmas party held for operators in Buffalo, New York.[59] As late as September 1955, the "Sodus Minstrels" staged "minstrel shows for Pioneer parties, the Business and Professional Women's Club and the Grange."[60] The names of many of these performers suggest that they were the native-born children of immigrants, who themselves were only one generation removed from exclusion; and therefore sought to identify with the "white lady" image as part of their Americanization process and as an entry into the mainstream white world.[61]

Even when these women formed their new, independent unions during the late 1930s, they maintained a very strong stance against inte-

34. Fargo, North Dakota, operators held a show that included one operator in black-face and one dressed as a Native American, circa 1950s. (Courtesy of Communications Workers of America Collection, Robert F. Wagner Labor Archives, New York University)

gration. At a time when the CIO made racial unity a cornerstone of its organizing drives, the overwhelming majority of unions affiliated with the NFTW omitted antidiscrimination clauses from their constitutions, and some explicitly excluded black members.[62] Racism was so rampant in the NFTW that at the 1943 National Assembly, union members openly discussed how to evade Executive Order 8802. One representative assured the audience that the FEPC had no enforcement powers and that "it is up to the spinal cord and rigidity thereof of your company. If your company doesn't care about bad publicity . . . , you won't have the problem."[63] In effect, he advised the membership to collude with sympathetic companies to keep segregation in the workplaces.

Telephone workers and their union representatives made it clear to companies considering integration that trouble would arise if blacks were hired. D. McClure, assistant to the first vice president of the New York Telephone Company, told FEPC investigators on July 24, 1944, that he "would be willing to hire Negroes as operators . . . except for the very determined attitude of the telephone operators' union that Negroes not be put on such jobs."[64] When the FEPC investigators discussed these allegations with representatives from the Telephone Employees' Association (representing 98 percent of the operators):

> it was discovered that a very large percentage of the operators now employed by the company are Catholics and that many of them had been originally recruited through various Catholic churches. It was also learned that a very large proportion of them had at various times expressed themselves as vehemently opposed to the introduction of Negroes as telephone operators, either individually or in groups. The union representatives felt that it was almost certain that there would be violent opposition to the introduction of Negro workers on to the company's switchboards if attempted at this time. They said, however, that they would be willing to undertake an educational campaign among the operators to convince them that their fears were ungrounded. They suggested that we secure the cooperation of religious groups in furthering such a program of education.[65]

The union never established an educational program, which indicated a rhetorical rather than genuine commitment to integration. Formed after the Wagner Act granted the right to organize independent unions in 1935, this union's constitution contained no antidiscrimination clause.[66] Union officials disavowed discrimination on their own part, claiming that they represented blacks employed by the company and that they were in the process of revising the union's constitution to include a nondiscrimination clause. Indeed, the Telephone Employees' Association, like other telephone unions, denied having any control over the company's hiring policy.

Despite union disavowals, evidence indicates that the Bell System had reason to fear work stoppages and other union actions against the employment of African Americans. An example was the foreboding tone evident in a resolution adopted by the Pennsylvania NFTW. At its annual convention in 1945, the delegates acknowledged the existence of the FEPC but reiterated the union's duty to "safeguard the interests of all workers." Accordingly, they resolved that "in that connection that the Council be consulted and its written consent be obtained before any change in the status of workers be effectuated by the Company through arrangements with the FEPC or any other Government Agency."[67] Union officials who generally denied having power over hiring practices in cases where black workers demanded an end to discrimination, asserted authority over that same process when white workers believed their exclusivity was in jeopardy. And they sought to enforce their authority.

Union officials and union members threatened various companies with disruption throughout the war. Evelyn N. Cooper, hearing examiner of the Legal Division of the FEPC, reported that "a strike is reported to have been threatened by some of the national officers of the union at the time Negro operators were first employed in New York, and in Baltimore it is claimed that there is now more tension among the white operators than before."[68] George M. Johnson, deputy chairman and acting chief of the FEPC's legal division, who had investigated hundreds of complaints and corresponded with dozens of managers, stated: "in every instance refusal [to hire black women] has been based on the alleged possibility of a strike among white operators if Negroes [were] brought into work with them."[69] White female accounting clerks participated in a one-day wildcat strike in Camden, New Jersey, on May 3, 1943, after the New Jersey Bell Telephone Company announced that it would hire African American women as clerical workers.[70] The company insisted that it was complying with Executive Order 8802 and refused to capitulate. The strike failed, but white women had demonstrated their willingness to strike against the employment of African American women.[71]

Again, on August 12, 1943, thirty-five white women refused to work with a black woman who had been hired as an inspector at the Western Electric Company in Baltimore. They demanded separate rest room facilities and stayed off the job for three days. The company insisted that Executive Order 8802 would be violated if they assented to the women's demand. The Point Breeze Association (the women's union) supported the walkout and prepared "a lengthy brief opposing the company policy."[72] V. L. Dorsey, the union's director, requested a meeting with Clarence Mitchell, the FEPC's Associate Director of Field Operations, and company representatives to discuss the situation based on a letter that Dorsey had received from the War Production Board in June 1942, which stated that "separate facilities would not violate Executive Order 8802 if the facilities were equal."[73] Since no separate facilities existed at that time, the FEPC informed the union that the situation was in conformity with FEPC policy and that "the adoption of separate facilities [would be] a step back from the equal treatment of employees."[74] No meeting occurred, and the women continued to work.

Black Women Hired as Operators

Finally, in December 1944, the New York Telephone Company hired the first black operators in the Bell System. Small numbers of African American women gained entry into AT&T Long Lines and some of the operating companies, but it is not clear whether this resulted from FEPC pressure or the scarcity of female labor during and immediately following the war. Although the long period of African American agitation against Bell System discrimination had an effect, it is likely that the alternative opportunities offered to white women, the extraordinarily high turnover, and the overall expansion of telephone use in the war period all combined to create an economic motivation for the Bell System to reconsider its discriminatory personnel policies.[75]

As the 1950s progressed, the demand for operators in large urban areas led to another small percentage increase of black women operators. Between 1950 and 1960, 2.5 percent of the telephone workforce consisted of black workers concentrated in New York City, Philadelphia, Detroit, Chicago, and Los Angeles.[76] Southern operating companies hired no black women, and they actually reduced the number of black men.[77] The trend toward hiring black women as operators only, and mostly in Northern industrial centers, emerged clearly during the 1960s. Up to that time, black males had been more numerous than black females "by a sizable proportion."[78]

Southern Bell and Southwestern Bell continued to exclude blacks from all except the most menial jobs. A look at those companies' records during the 1960s is illustrative:

> In the entire state of Mississippi, Southern Bell employed no blacks in any entry-level job above service worker or laborer until June, 1965. In New Orleans, Southern Bell hired its first black above service worker or laborer in November, 1963, and its first black Operator one year later. The Company hired its first black Operator in Florida in March, 1964; and in South Carolina in July, 1964. Southwestern Bell hired its first black Operator anywhere in Kansas in 1963. The first black Installer employed in Kansas was hired in June, 1969. No black above

service worker or laborer was hired in Arkansas until 1964. The first black Operator in Oklahoma was hired in March, 1964.[79]

Neither general employment trends nor the Civil Rights Act (1964) affected Southern discrimination until the early 1970s, when the companies' black employment patterns mirrored those in other areas.

African American women and men, in addition to large groups of Spanish surnamed people in various parts of the country, were systematically excluded from craft and upper-management positions. Intelligence tests and arbitrary academic credentials barred most nonwhites from the higher-paying and more desirable jobs in the telephone industry. Craft jobs, the highest-paying nonmanagement jobs, and almost the exclusive domain of white men, opened to a few nonwhite men, but black operators, like white operators, did not have a real chance at these jobs before the 1970s. And the few black men who did achieve craft status remained in the lower crafts. Even in such companies as New York Telephone, where blacks had worked since the 1940s and where large numbers of blacks were employed, they were underrepresented in management jobs. At the end of 1969, only 4.4 percent of New York Telephone's black employees held management positions, as opposed to 27.2 percent of the white employees.[80] In the South, 0.6 percent to 0.9 percent of the blacks held management titles.[81] Regardless of location, blacks remained trapped in the lowest-paying jobs.[82]

At the height of the civil rights era (1960–70), the Bell System rapidly increased its black workforce (4.0 percent of all employees in 1963, 4.6 percent in 1966, and 9.8 percent in 1970) without changing the pattern of occupational and geographical segregation.[83] New York operators interviewed for this study stated that the transformation to a black force of operators happened in no more than the last four or five years of the 1960s. Bernard E. Anderson, an expert on black telephone industry employment, substantiates this claim with census and other data.[84] An EEOC investigation into Bell System discrimination confirms this observation for the largest non-Southern urban areas. Of the black Bell System employees who worked for the New York Telephone Company in 1967, 92 percent were women. White women constituted only 50 percent of all white telephone employees.[85] Most of the large non-Southern cities in 1967 followed this same pattern, with women ranging from 72 percent to

92 percent of the black workforce, compared to 48 percent to 61 percent for the white one. In the entire Bell System at the close of 1970, 43.9 percent of the black workforce were operators.[86]

The explanation for the change from white to black operators during the late 1960s lies in the changing nature of the urban labor market, coupled with the Bell System's persistent drive to increase profits by maintaining a favorable public image and stabilizing its control over workers and the workplace. As other industries were moving to the suburbs, the telephone companies continued to install major switching systems in or near large cities where an untapped black labor pool resided.[87] From 1960 to 1970, the number of young black city dwellers increased by 78 percent, while the number of young whites increased only by 22.8 percent.[88]

Technological innovations made it possible to locate call-processing equipment at any location without diminishing the quality of service. Indeed, an AT&T manager confirmed that "the System has maintained the large work force in the cities by implementing technology that allows the System to concentrate work activities."[89] By 1977, "81.1% of the total work force [was] concentrated in the large cities or in the close proximity to a large metropolitan area."[90] AT&T managers deliberately kept their switching systems in the central cities because, as Vice President Walter Straley so eloquently stated: "to transplant our operations from the cities to the suburbs would in the long run put us at the mercy of a labor market in which our kinds of entry level jobs would be even less attractive to the people looking for employment."[91] Managers knew that white men and white women living in the suburbs gladly commuted to the cities for the higher salaries offered in the upper-level jobs. It was not the lack of white workers, but the lack of white workers who would work for low wages, that led the Bell System to integrate black urban dwellers into their segregated wage system.

The restructuring of low-level clerical work and telephone operating was cloaked in equal opportunity rhetoric for the general public, but in private among company presidents, Straley spoke without inhibition in October 1969:

> Population and labor force projections are not at all encouraging. The kind of people we need are going to be in very short supply. . . . Most of our new hires go into entry level jobs which means we must have

access to an ample supply of people who will work at comparatively low rates of pay. That means city people more so than suburbanites. That means lots of black people.

There are not enough white, middle class, success-oriented men and women in the labor force—or at least that portion of the labor force available to the telephone companies—to supply our requirements for craft and occupational people. And from now on, the number of such people who are available will grow smaller even as our need becomes greater. It is therefore perfectly plain that we need nonwhite employees. Not because we are good citizens. Or because it is the law as well as national goal to give them employment. We need them because we have so many jobs to fill and they will take them.[92]

Faced with unusually high turnover and white flight from operating, Straley questioned who would be "available for work paying as little as $4,000 to $5,000 a year."[93] Noting that two-thirds of the people in urban areas available for such low rates would be black, he answered, "It is therefore just a plain fact that in today's world, telephone company wages are more in line with black expectations—and the tighter the labor market the more this is true."[94]

Unaware of the Bell System's hiring policy that consciously segregated them into dead-end jobs, these new "expectations" of better job opportunities created a tidal wave of black female applicants for telephone operating. Job opportunities that were higher-paying, less stressful, more varied, and available in the limited sphere of telephone women opened mostly for white women.[95] However, black women, many of them recent emigrants from the South, searching for an escape from agricultural and domestic labor, believed that operating elevated their social status. And this was true from the very first group. Anne Walden, hired in 1946, confirmed: "When I came to New York and went to work for the telephone company, I was very appreciative . . . cause I had a good job. . . . this was considered an upward movement for a black woman."[96] Employed ten years later as a clerk, Harriet Tubman expressed that her "parents were proud" because "status was involved" and the money was "pretty good."[97]

Nearly twenty years after the New York Telephone Company hired its first black operator, Bea Miller, seventeen years old in 1963, was especially proud because she started at a weekly salary of $67 while her mother who had worked more than twenty years in various factories received only $65. She knew from her mother and aunt that this job "compared well with other jobs" available to African American women. She understood what it meant to have benefits such as medical and life insurance and a stock plan. Indeed, Miller said that she was very "pleased . . . because if you got a job in a place like New York Telephone Company, . . . the banks loved you . . . it meant a house, furniture, car. . . ."

Even later, African Americans in their early twenties with previous work experience found Bell employment highly attractive. Geneva Tucker, hired in 1969 during the hiring rush, had worked in restaurants, factories, and cleaners. She thought "at first" that "there was a lot of opportunity," and $84 a week "seemed like a lot of money." Ron Tyree, a military veteran with college credits, earned $127 weekly when he started as an AT&T overseas operator in 1973. He had worked for the U.S. Post Office and believed the telephone job to be better. From television ads and people he knew, he formed the impression that the company offered good benefits and a chance to advance, and that it "rarely failed people. . . . it was a life time job." At the beginning of their telephone careers, most African Americans believed that employment by the Bell System opened the way to new and greater possibilities compared to other workplaces. Only after they experienced unfair treatment and understood the limitations on those possibilities did they become disillusioned. The Bell System's selection, timing, and introduction of new technologies contributed to the stagnation of such opportunities.

Replacement of Switchboards

Direct Distance Dialing (DDD) had reduced the total number of long distance calls requiring operator assistance by 50 percent, but coin, collect, credit card, third party, and person-to-person calls continued to require an operator for connections, timing, and charging.[98] Searching for a way to further decrease the number of operators and speed up the service, New York Telephone engineers conducted an experiment in 1958 that used specially designed equipment to determine if operator-assisted calls could be conducted on a dial basis. The success of this experiment and a similar one in the smaller residential city of Poughkeepsie, New York, provided the information for changes in method and equipment

35. The changing face and technology of Bell System operators. African American woman operator working on TSPS. Note the "plantronics" headset. (Property of AT&T Archives; reprinted with permission of AT&T)

that led to the development of Traffic Service Position (TSP), an entirely new concept.[99]

Operators no longer made connections because TSP's were not switchboards. These new machines were cordless consoles equipped with special buttons that indicated information for billing to the dial equipment. *Bell Telephone Magazine* explained that "the switching or connecting of telephones is done in the dial equipment. Calls do not go through the TSP as they go through a switchboard. With the TSP, the calls go through the dial equipment. The only time the TSP is connected is when it is necessary for the operator to assist the customer or to exercise control over the call." TSPs automatically computed time and charges, displayed the telephone numbers of called and calling parties, disconnected completed calls, and continuously distributed incoming calls to operators who were "not han-

36. When these paired TSP's were introduced, the switchroom had an officelike atmosphere that looked very different from the crowded rows of switchboard panels long associated with telephone operating. (Property of AT&T Archives; reprinted with permission of AT&T)

37. However, even this mid-sized city (Albany, New York) office seemed packed by 1972. (Property of AT&T Archives; reprinted with permission of AT&T)

dling a call at the moment."[100] The first Traffic Service Position office opened in New York City in October 1963. It made possible the introduction of Expanded Direct Distance Dialing, which provided the facilities for subscribers to dial their calls with a minimum of operator assistance.

Operators in the majority of cases either had been eliminated from the process or their functions had been reduced to the smallest possible part of the connection. At this point, an increase in the rate at which operators could work and at which calls could be processed through the equipment reemerged as the major focus of Bell System engineering activity.[101] The automatic electromechanical switching systems (whose moving parts took time to function) driving TSP and the operating methods used with those systems had reached their performance limits. Engineering efforts materialized in a new computerized switching system (integrated circuitry did not move) that operated in time factors of micromilliseconds. The No. 1 Electronic Switching System (No. 1 ESS) replaced the electromechanical systems (crossbar and panel) as the switching system of choice when it was introduced in metropolitan areas in 1965.[102] Successful installations of electronic switching systems between 1958 and 1965 marked the transition from automation to computerization.

The application of electronic switching technology to TSP (Traffic Service Position Systems-TSPS) and to toll switching systems (No. 4 ESS-4E) achieved the "jet-age" speed and reliability that Bell System engineers had sought. The advantages of TSPS over TSP included increased speed, more economical installation, adaptability to new features, and compatibility with any toll-switching system (unlike TSP, which was limited to electromechanical systems). The first 4E machine, installed in Chicago in January 1976, processed 550,000 long distance calls per hour, four times as many as the 4A crossbar system.[103] Computerization completed the process of transferring responsibility for telephone connections from operator to subscriber. The advent of 4E and, later, more sophisticated, electronic switching systems made possible the closing of many toll centers and the routing of their calls to considerably larger regional or national centers. By 1980, the Bell System had established customer direct dialing to most places in the world, and it had also made significant inroads into reducing the remaining information, intercept, and overseas operators.[104]

TSP reduced local and long distance operating to jobs of selecting the correct buttons to push in "a matter of moments, a few words, [and] a few movements of her fingers."[105] Equally important, TSP transformed the operator's typical work environment and the methods by which operators were trained to use the new equipment. Bell System managers boasted that the new console had been "designed with the operator in mind and included consideration of human engineering practices"; "the varying arm and leg dimensions of operators was one of the most critical points."[106] Engineers added adjustable foot rests, ergonomically designed chairs, sight-saving digital light indicators, and other features to reduce eyestrain and fatigue.[107] The console's "light beige textured vinyl finish" and the seventy-six multicolored lamps and keys mounted on it reflected a deliberate move away from the solid black switchboard. Consciously, managers fostered the idea that the freshly deskilled operators, renamed "service specialists," required a more officelike atmosphere. The new consoles resembled desks, which reinforced an appeal to modernity and class status that sought to ward off potential resistance to the job loss effects of these machines.[108]

Automatic training further instilled the ideas of a "jet-age" society in which operators, using programmed equipment, could teach themselves how to operate the TSP console. Rather than the one-to-one instruction formerly given to toll operators, education experts developed "a faster, more effective way, both for deciding if a new girl will make a good operator and for getting her ready to do a top job."[109] Bell managers eliminated human instruction, except in special situations, on the stated belief that "the automated 'teacher' has infinite patience, is tireless, immune to distraction, and can have . . . as thorough knowledge . . . as any expert."[110] Influenced by their own propaganda, managers asserted that not only were the operators "more relaxed" and could "concentrate more fully" with their machine teachers, but "program-trained girls [were] more accurate than . . . girls trained the old way."[111] Of course, computerization made it even easier for Bell System methods to secretly monitor these machine-trained operators.

New Technology: The Cost to Bell System Women
Always stressful, operating with the new Traffic Service Position Systems (TSPS) reached limits of absurdity beyond those experienced by even the fainting operators of the early 1900s. TSPS operators automatically

receive calls sent to them by an Automatic Call Distributor. They have no control over when to take the next call because the machine within a micro-second recognizes when the previous call has ended and immediately sends another. Unlike the flashing light signals on the cord boards, TSPS operators know they have another call when they hear a "beep" in their earphones. Keep in mind that these operators still worked according to the pre–World War I standard under which they were expected to answer the "electronic beep" within three seconds and no later than ten seconds. TSPS stole even the few seconds of peace that cord board operators had been able to pilfer between the physical operations of plugging and unplugging cords. Even worse, computers made it possible to automatically measure the amount of time spent on each call. Operators' average work times (AWT) could be measured every fifteen minutes and AWTs above thirty seconds per call could result in disciplinary actions against the operator.

Obviously, this level of stress resulted in a decline of job satisfaction and created a multitude of health problems for operators. Telephone women who work at some type of video display terminal (VDT) are subject to significant health hazards, including miscarriages, eye strain, backaches and back strain, headaches, stress, and burning and itching eyes. Environmental problems include extremes in temperature, inadequate illumination, and poorly designed work spaces.[112] Directory assistance operators, who are confined to one position for up to 2.5 hours without a break and work at a constant pace under extremely tight surveillance, have been especially susceptible to carpal tunnel syndrome and other VDT illnesses.[113]

While physical health remains a central issue in the era of computerization, mental health has become equally important. One National Institute for Occupational Safety and Health (NIOSH) study found "that people who work on VDTs face higher stress than any other occupational group, including air traffic controllers."[114] Other NIOSH research concluded that VDT workers suffered from "anxiety, depression, irritability, monotony, fatigue, and lack of inner security."[115] Bell System monitoring and production standards have contributed to high levels of drug abuse and alcoholism among its workers as they try to cope with the stress. The Connecticut Union of Telephone Workers found that among two hundred Southern New England Telephone service representatives "37.2 percent were taking tranquilizers or other nerve medicine, 39.3 percent had increased their consumption of alcohol since starting on the job and 12.3 percent were using both—a potentially lethal combination."[116] Company medical offices, perhaps illegally, dispensed "greenies" (aspirin and caffeine packaged under the Bell logo), Valium, Darvon, Lomotil, codeine, and other drugs to workers in recognition of their stress but also to get them back on the job. Nervous breakdowns and disorders have been frequent among service representatives and among operators who have computer-monitored preset time limits in which to answer and service calls.[117] The Bell System, of course, does not publicize these problems, but it does maintain relations with numerous psychiatric, alcohol, and drug treatment centers where workers are sent under health plans offered in the benefits packages.

These degraded working conditions indicated a new managerial perspective regarding operators. Operators were no longer needed as they had been in the nineteenth century to sell the service, nor were they essential to deliver it. Hence, management's motivation for perpetuating the "white lady" image of the telephone operator atrophied and the disintegration of that identity commenced.

Disintegration of the "White Lady" Image

As the racial transformation of operating personnel progressed, a gradual decline in respect for operators followed, as did the level of esteem for the position's status. Changes in Bell System workplace policies, customer attitudes, and white telephone operators' sense of prestige reflected the fading away of the "white lady" image. Racial integration meant that employer control over white workers through exclusivity disappeared. Consequently, management increasingly withdrew the "privileges" that had been used to appease white operators. By the 1970s, for many subscribers and telephone workers, the operators' reputation had changed from the selfless white heroine to the incompetent, lazy, rude, and undeserving "hardcore" black woman. Although region and local practice often determined the extent and the rapidity with which this process occurred, the Bell System dismantled the internal workplace features of the "white lady" image at a much faster rate than its external public relations indicated.

Hence, the Bell System quickly degraded working conditions in places where black women worked, while to the public it continued to represent the operator as a "lady." For example, on May 11, 1972, Pernella Wattley made a deposition to the EEOC in which she compared working conditions in 1945 when she was first employed as a telephone operator with those in 1972. According to Wattley's testimony: "the conditions of work . . . have deteriorated considerably since 1945." She said that the company no longer sterilized headsets nor kept surplus sets available in case of malfunction. In the past, stations had been cleaned daily, whereas in 1972 they were "only cleaned by demand—our demand." She cited differences and unfairness in sick pay, night differentials, and training policies.

But the real indication that the job was no longer viewed as a "lady's" job is that "rest rooms with chairs and coaches [sic] have been replaced by locker rooms without enough chairs. Most dining rooms have been replaced by expensive canteens with poor quality food." All of these things marked an enormous difference from the matrons and free refreshments and inexpensive, or free, freshly cooked lunches. Wattley also stated that one of the "company's policies which ha[d] the most dehumanizing effect on the operators [was] that there is only one bathroom and we have to ask permission and then we are timed and reprimanded when we go too often."[118] South Central Bell even refused to supply taxis or armed guards to escort African American women to "places of safety," whereas managers supplied these services freely to white women who worked at night.[119] The Bell System eventually abandoned all of these costly perks since they no longer served as methods of control.

However, Bell managers found it less cost-effective to immediately abandon the idea of the female operator. The public bought telephone service based on assistance received from women, and management saw no reason to change that notion unless forced to do so. On April 6, 1965, immediately before Title VII of the Civil Rights Law became effective, Pacific Bell held a company conference in which management "reviewed the anticipated problem areas." Noting that the EEOC had "absolutely no judicial or even quasi-judicial powers," and that any individual seeking redress from discrimination incurred enormous financial burdens, the managers decided not to "go off 'half cocked' and to wait until they were 'challenged.' "[120] They acknowledged that "no bonafide occupational qualification . . . would limit the Traffic operator's job to a female," but they stated: "however, since thousands of dollars have been spent building the image of the 'voice with a smile' we shouldn't be in any hurry to recruit men operators!"[121]

Indeed, Bell companies wanted to preserve the female image by prescribing operators' attire. In 1970, Illinois Bell forbade women to wear slacks based on the following rationale: "It's not our purpose to limit merely for the sake of limitation; instead, we wish very much to preserve the image of the operator which the public generally carries in its mind, that of an employee who is not only efficient and courteous, but is also feminine and well groomed according to prevailing standards for most places of business."[122] Of course, clothing requirements did little to protect black women from the unfair treatment they received as the job became increasingly identified with them.

Helen Dunbar in testimony before the FCC stated that in her eight and a half years as an operator for the New York Telephone Company, "the job has actually deteriorated."[123] She explained that once the majority of operators were black, the administration of company policies in respect to stock ownership and other benefits had changed, and an increase in supervision and production standards occurred at the same time that managers implemented a more vigorous and unfair enforcement of production standards, constantly changed rules, and reinforced the absence control plan. When asked, "Have there ever been any comments made to you by any management people referring back to the black women in the office?" Dunbar answered "yes," and she explained: "When I became shop steward and really started to fight to get whatever benefits or considerations I could for the girls, I came across one particular—I guess you would call it a cliché. Regardless of what the situation is, the answer is: They are not worth it. This is referring to the operators."[124] Obviously, lower-level managers resented having to work with people for whom they felt hiring standards had been lowered. Racist stereotypes lingered in many of these managers' minds, and they treated the women accordingly. Dunbar's recollection of her experiences as a shop steward elucidates this point.

Dunbar recalled that when she approached management about the operators' grievances, they attacked the women. Managers accused the operators of "playing" with the elevators, stealing "cheap" cafeteria uten-

sils, and leaving hair that "looks like steel wool" in the bathroom sinks![125]
Therefore, lateness—even as a result of slow or broken elevators—was
penalized; cold, stale food continued to be left in vending machines without provision of utensils; and permission to leave the operating position
to go to the bathroom was still granted at the discretion of the supervisor.
Management did nothing about the food that made the operators sick.[126]
Instead, they blamed "new" operators for poor service.[127]

Indeed, the company found that "every source of measurement of
customer opinion indicates that there has been a very noticeable increase
in the incidence of operator discourtesy. Letters received, complaints to
the Customer Service Bureau and Central Office customer contacts demonstrate that there appears to be more of an inclination on the part of
operators to enter into arguments and to challenge rather than accept
customer demands."[128] These findings may have indicated both an unwillingness on the part of poorly trained staff to adhere to past practices,
and that customers became abusive when they recognized the changed
racial composition of the operating force. Discourtesy may have been the
operators' response to changes in their working conditions in the operating room as well as what they tolerated from customers.

Unfortunately, black women began to dominate operating at a time
when the industry faced severe service crises as a result of increased
demand. This coincidence made it easy to scapegoat the operators. Dunbar remembered that when she had been hired eight and a half years
earlier "an operator was respected by the customers, [and] she was respected generally in her office. This is not the case any more. I've read
many articles about the service not being what it was because minority
groups are now handling these calls. Naturally, when this happens, the
attitude of the customer changes. Certainly, being operators, we can tell
this."[129]

In one such article dated August 1, 1973, the New York Times sympa-
thetically repeated the company's explanation for "quietly mov[ing] parts
of its directory assistance operations, for area code 212, out of New York
City." Along with photographs of black operators at work in New York
City and white operators in Babylon, Long Island, the Times explained
that the company had been "plagued with rising costs and an inability to
find qualified personnel in the inner city" in the previous three years,

even though they had "kept . . . employment offices open six days a week and sent out mobile employment vans."[130] African Americans disagreed with this assessment and registered their grievances with the NAACP.

Herbert Hill, at that time the National Labor Director for the NAACP, stated that his organization had received complaints that "blacks and nonwhite workers were being phased out of the directory assistance operations," and "investigations . . . suggest the Bell companies have not stopped their discriminatory practices, they have merely changed the format. They are now engaging in more sophisticated practices, but the consequences for blacks and other minorities are the same." Hill's evaluation was correct not so much because there was an immediate threat of the company making a mass exit. In fact, 2,200 operators still remained in the city, whereas only 400 had been moved to outlying areas. However, the technological flexibility of switching systems amplified managerial control over black and white workers.

Implicitly, the company promised to move jobs to upstate areas where unemployment was high and presumably more "qualified" and compliant white workers could be hired; at the same time, this tactic maneuvered criticism for poor service onto black operators. The effectiveness of this propaganda on the public and white operators was affirmed by one of the Babylon operators (a former New York City operator) who said, "we do have fewer customer complaints out here." According to the *New York Times*, the company had experienced "sharp criticism over many of the minority-group operators they [had] hired. Callers [had] complained that the new operators were unwilling or unable to handle the queries of callers or, in some cases, to make themselves understood."[131]

Angered over poor service and indoctrinated with Bell System propaganda about the massive hiring of unqualified "hardcore" women, racist subscribers mercilessly abused African American operators. Before the FCC, Gay Semel explained that "an operator is expected to be polite no matter what is said to her, and, over and over again, people complained about having to listen to racial and sexual abuses. For example, you know, people will call up and, . . . say 'You are all a bunch of niggers,' or more obscene things, . . . about wanting to go to bed with you or something like that, and you are supposed to take that, you are not supposed to respond in any way."[132] She described one case in which a woman could not be heard, but when the woman was called back and informed that she could not be heard because of a malfunction in the phone, the woman shouted, "That's because I don't talk nigger talk like the rest of you."[133] Clearly, this subscriber held no "white lady" image of this operator.

Bea Miller also witnessed a change in customers' responses "when the company brought women from the deep south who had regional accents—not necessarily uneducated but a regional accent."[134] "The public began to harass them, talked to them very nasty and treated them as though they were servants and sex objects. Men would come on and say nasty obnoxious things . . . would call them a bitch." This seemed to be the favorite epithet, as Gabrielle Gemma also testified that "operators were often forced to endure such epithets as 'you black bitch.' "[135] Social relations between operators and customers hardly resembled those of twenty years earlier.

Maternalistic and personal relationships between the chief operators and their workers also degenerated as the operating force changed to a black majority. In the past, companies had fostered the type of relationship in which operators told all of their problems to the chief operator, who with the power of the Bell System behind her could find a solution. Bea Miller remembered the chief operator as a powerful person who, "if your husband beat you . . . made calls to the local precinct and it stopped." Miller's chief operator signed for her to buy her first house. Miller was careful to say, however, that she was "not sure that everybody got the treatment" that she received, but she was sure that "personal involvement broke down . . . once blacks became a majority" of operators where she worked. Indeed, management did not think they were "worth it."

Many white operators absorbed this point of view and ruthlessly attacked black women. For example, Dorothy J. Mitchell, who had been employed with the Bell System in Columbus, Ohio, moved to Natchez, Mississippi, where she was belittled and mistreated by management and workers. Mitchell said that she had been "elbowed" and "jostled to keep [her] out of the operating room" so that she would be reprimanded for being late. Her superiors neither investigated nor sought to punish anyone when Mitchell reported these incidents. She claimed that she was "constantly harassed by three of the supervisors," who consistently refused to consider her for promotions. After she had been "kicked" at the switchboard and received no consideration from her supervisor, Mitchell appealed to the traffic manager, who told her that she "misunderstood everyone's motive." He assured her that it was just a matter of the supervisor being "prejudiced to the south as compared to the north."

Mitchell's nightmare continued. She stated that the night of Martin Luther King's assassination, she refused to work overtime and was told to "get out." The next day, constant slanders against Dr. King made her ask to go home, but she was not allowed to leave until her supervisor found it convenient for her to do so. Mitchell said that "all day I heard so-called jokes about killing coons out of season." Finally, when her endurance failed, she sought medical attention and was given tranquilizers. She resigned. Her affidavit states that she knew two other women who had had closely similar experiences.[136] Mitchell's is an extreme case, but it is indicative of the many others that can be found in the boxes of EEOC evidence, the author's own interviews, and from other sources. It also demonstrates how racial integration could be used as a method of control as powerful as racial exclusion.

Neither racial integration nor the decline of the "white lady" image lessened the Bell System's ability to maintain control over the workplace by manipulating white anxiety against the opening of opportunities to women and minorities. This control perpetuated the Bell System's freedom to introduce new technologies that eliminated jobs and sped up, fragmented, and deskilled work. Indeed, management turned every gain won by workers (integration, affirmative action, technology clauses, etc.) into a weapon against workplace unity. In the twenty years following the hiring of the first black operators, Bell managers carefully chose how and when they would hire African Americans. They introduced black people in such a way as to intimidate white workers. The Bell System's administration of affirmative action programs exemplifies how management manipulated employee racism as it integrated the workforce for greater control and ease in the implementation of new technologies.

In less than ten years African American operators replaced white
operators in the major American cities as a result of a hiring
policy that segregated most of the African American women into
one department and one kind of job. The Bell System in its public relations statements attributed this metamorphosis to its desire to conform to
the civil rights movement and laws. The real reasons had more to do with
the Bell System's profit-driven need to hire inexpensive labor as it implemented new technologies into a work environment in which it could
control worker resistance. Simultaneously, the Bell System hired African
American women to work switchboards, and it incrementally introduced
computerized equipment (TSPS) along with the practice of charging for
directory assistance. All of these changes reduced the need for operators.
In effect, as soon as job opportunities opened for black women, computerization and occupational segregation closed them. Between 1960 and
1981, women operators in the Bell System decreased by one-half, while
the total number of operators fell by 40 percent. Managers deliberately
hired African American women into an occupation that not only paid low
wages but was becoming technologically obsolete.

An enormous public relations campaign obfuscated this travesty of
inclusion. To the general populace, the Bell System represented itself as a
community-spirited company that pioneered in equal employment and
promotion opportunities for minorities and women. After they instituted
their affirmative action program, managers advertised their alleged nondiscrimination policies through print and television media. In places
such as New York's Harlem, they sent vans to recruit African Americans
off the streets. Of course, women and minorities flocked to the industry in

the mistaken belief that they could advance themselves. Publicity obscured the fact that integration not only supplied the industry with an inexpensive labor force for whose training the company received government funds, but that it also made possible a favorable public image that expedited rate increases. And, equally as important, the publicity helped management divide the workforce by using integration as a threat to white workers' job security.

White workers, especially males, believed company rhetoric about hiring and promoting black people, and they perceived these new policies as a hindrance to their own advancement. The Bell System's successful manipulation of white workers' fears allowed the industry to restructure its workforce and work environment unimpeded by workers' resistance to the implementation of various new technologies. Union officials, reflecting the attitudes of white workers long accustomed to segregation, defied gender and racial integration rather than rebel against technological redundancy.

Big Change in Image, Little Change in Practice
It is not surprising that black workers would believe that they had a genuine chance for advancement in the telephone industry. Bell managers used the gradual inclusion of blacks, especially women, to project themselves as leaders in providing employment and advancement opportunities. Managers cited numerous government or private business-sponsored hiring programs in which the telephone companies participated. The president of AT&T, H. I. Romnes, along with presidents of seven other operating companies and the U.S. vice president, Lyndon B. Johnson, inaugurated a "Plan for Progress" in 1962 to insure equal employment opportunity to all qualified persons. Various Bell companies held "Equal Employment Fairs" and hired "Negro employment interviewers" as part of their effort to give visibility to their alleged "commitment." Indeed, AT&T, in its own estimation, had not only perfected "minority" recruitment, but it had become a leader.

To be certain that our hiring practices are widely publicized and understood, and as a further means of obtaining assistance in recruiting qualified employees, personnel people in all Bell System companies maintain cordial and productive liaison with Negro leaders throughout the communities which the companies serve. In addition to the usual sources, such as state employment agencies, religious leaders are contacted for assistance in the general program, as are business and professional groups. Extensive use is also made of such especially created services as the Urban League's National Skills Banks (with which a number of Bell System volunteers are associated in staff and tutorial positions). So successful has the overall activity been in some locations that other employers have actually called on Bell System companies for help with their own programs.[1]

Clifton W. Phalen, president of the New York Telephone Company, the largest Bell operating company and the largest employer of African Americans, also signed the "Plan for Progress" agreements. According to the company, this was a "voluntary commitment," which "marked no departure from the policy of the past," but was "instead, a reaffirmation of our long-standing code of conduct."[2]

Confident in their new leadership role, AT&T managers boasted of their participation in the National Alliance of Businessmen (NAB), "a government-industry partnership dedicated to finding permanent jobs for the 'hardcore' unemployed and summer jobs for urban youth still in school."[3] In 1968, Bill Mercer, AT&T's vice president of personnel relations, stated that the company had made a commitment to help improve educational and vocational opportunities for minorities trapped in the slums. Aside from the introduction of more flexible entry requirements, the company agreed to introduce "special pre-employment and remedial training programs to provide skills, confidence, and good job orientation."[5] Racial paternalism aside, on paper these plans promised substantial progress and provided substantial public relations benefits as it divided the workers.

Directed at "poor persons who do not have suitable employment and who are either school dropouts, under twenty-two years of age, 45 years of age or over, handicapped, or subject to special obstacles to employment," the program did not recruit from the same age and educated groups (among black people) that had previously succeeded (among white people) in the Bell System. Regular Bell System employees resented the program—in some instances because of racism—but also in other instances because they thought it was unfair to "lower" the standards when other qualified people were available. Indeed, the Bell companies could have upgraded operators soon to be displaced, if they had been truly committed to creating more opportunities for blacks. New York Telephone employees, white and black of both sexes who worked during this period, felt that the company had lowered the standards to the point of hiring people who really could not do the job. These regular employees felt that they would then have to work harder to compensate for workers hired under special programs. And, more significantly, they thought the "hardcore" had special privileges in relation to the "authoritarian" rule they had long suffered.[6] Frank Novotny, the national director of the CWA's Sales Bargaining Unit, described these employee feelings in an interview with John Schacht in 1970:

> Of course, we're having problems with it today because the company, in our opinion, has gone overboard, and actually the pendulum of discrimination, based on our experiences during the past two years, is going the other way, not only against white employees of long years' service, but against black employees of long years' service. Because the so-called hardcore people of short years' service are being given very— well, for want of a better term, treatment with kid gloves; whereas, our long service employees, faithful employees, skilled employees, are still being treated the same way. And, of course, it's only natural, when our long service employees and our long service members see these so-called hardcore people come in and get away with "murder," so to speak, and they, the long service employees, being written up for every slight infringement: coming in late, smoking on the job, talking back to a boss—and they see these short service employees being given extra privileges—this, of course, has caused a lot of problems for the union.[7]

From one unionist point of view, concern for long-service employees had a certain amount of legitimacy.[8]

On the other hand, many black employees believed that the "hardcore" programs were a means of keeping the best jobs for whites. Some thought that the Bell System deliberately put unqualified black people into positions in which they would fail, to thereby prove that no blacks could do the work. Regular African American employees felt that these hiring practices barred them from advancement, and the "hardcore" felt that no sincere effort had been made to incorporate them. In fact, union/company agreements, and company designations such as "trainee" or "hardcore," stigmatized these new hires, causing them to be singled out for unfair treatment by both lower-level management and other workers.[9] Among the many complaints before the EEOC related to this issue, one charge that surfaced consistently was that those labeled "hardcore" were punished more harshly than others, particularly whites.[10] In a study conducted by the CWA, "over three-fourths of the Locals gave poor ratings to such training programs. Also more than a majority reported that management expects too much too soon from newly trained employees."[11] Of course, their long probationary period (compared to that of regular employees) exposed the unprepared trainees to greater opportunities to be penalized or fired. Many lower-level managers, responsible for the implementation of the new programs, had not been able to throw off the effects of years of discriminatory practices necessary to treat African Americans fairly.

In the minds of many, however, full inclusion was never the goal. Company rhetoric and workplace manipulations convinced many African Americans that Bell System policies were hypocritical, and, in fact, designed to exploit a specific group of black people. Eugene Mays, former CWA Assistant to the Vice President, District 1, had strong opinions on this subject. He said, "I think the Bell System, per se, gets an awful lot of credit which they are not entitled to. I think that they have exploited the hard-core area. And I think they have done what they have done because they had to do it. They had no other source to get help. So what they have found themselves in, from the public's point of view, is a very enviable position: getting a lot of credit for doing something they had to do."[12] The economic benefits of the Bell System's undeserved public relations credit were not only reflected in their rate increases; Bell companies also received compensation for hiring and "training" the hardcore.

Bea Miller, who worked more than thirty years for New York Telephone, claimed that the motivation was $6,000 per person that the company received from the government for its participation in the "hardcore" hiring programs. She said that the company sent vans to poor neighborhoods and took any "body" they could find in order to garner the federal funds.[13] AT&T's Bill Mercer explained these policies as part of an effort to confront "the need to hire 'unemployables'—people not simply unskilled but altogether unaccustomed to work disciplines." Less magnanimously, New York Telephone described these recruiting methods as a need to hire large numbers of people to provide a rapidly expanding service.[14]

Monetary compensation for training the "hardcore" or "disadvantaged" was conspicuously missing from Bell System public relations propaganda, but Jules Cohn, an expert witness on the company's behalf, gave explicit evidence of monetary compensation in his written and oral testimony before the EEOC hearings in 1972.[15] He attributed the acceptance of government monies to "increased availability of Federal funding" and rising costs.[16] Cohn stated:

> Companies participating in the JOBS program have had to allocate as much as $3,000–$4,000 per trainee though normal training costs for similar jobs are less than half that amount. In the early days of the JOBS program, some large companies were willing to meet the dramatically increased costs themselves. AT&T and its associated companies were among those that did not seek government aid when they set up special programs. Subsequently, however, as it became clear that costs could be twice the normal ones, and in the face of the general economic downturn, more and more companies, Bell included, have accepted subsidies.[17]

Under cross-examination, Cohn admitted that he had no assurance that "AT&T's decision not to seek Government aid in the early years was not at all influenced by . . . other factors" such as a desire to remain independent of government supervision and interference.[18] Government subsidies may have covered costs, but greater economic motivations played a part in the Bell System's active participation in numerous government-financed training programs.[19]

The substantial publicity for "progressive" hiring policies tended to neutralize criticism of AT&T's employment practices and service inadequacies by diverting public attention from the actual positions that these new hires received to the varied problems of dealing with this population. Aside from providing jobs and training, the Bell System claimed that "providing service to ghetto customers is more costly and more difficult" due to the high cost of protecting "plant and people," vandalism, high turnover of workers, higher training costs of the so-called disadvantaged, and difficulties in collecting payment for telephone bills.[20] And, more importantly, as we have witnessed all along, the Bell System prized a favorable public image, for its rate increases were more easily obtained when government agencies were not receiving complaints. Indeed, New York Telephone requested a rate increase based on the extensive training it provided because "in recent years, prospective employees in greater numbers lack the basic skills, educational background or work habits that telephone work requires."[21]

However, the parent company became extremely alarmed when the EEOC, supported in petitions by the NAACP, California Rural Legal Assistance, the American Civil Liberties Union, the National Organization for Women's Legal Defense and Education Fund, and other organizations, challenged an AT&T long distance rate increase request before the FCC. Striking a theme present in all the petitions, the NAACP charged the Bell System with engaging in "pervasive, system-wide and blatantly unlawful discrimination in employment against women, blacks, Spanish-surnamed Americans, and other minorities."[22] These petitions further declared that "the Commission is under a statutory obligation to find the proposed rate increase unlawful," and they demanded that the FCC "suspend the rate increase, hold hearings on AT&T employment practices, grant . . . permission to intervene at those hearings."[23] In defense of the Bell System, H. I. Romnes, chairman of AT&T, submitted a statement to the FCC declaring: "The EEOC's intervention in proceedings before the FCC on grounds of discriminatory practices by the Bell System is outrageous."[24] He cited the Bell System's participation in various programs as an indication of its record as "leaders" and "pioneers in developing training and remediation programs to help the disadvantaged qualify for employment and advancement in our business."[25]

Indeed, AT&T's *Bell Telephone Magazine* did not hesitate to describe the company's financial support of another training program from which it recruited only a few employees. Bell System operating companies, according to William T. Patrick Jr., AT&T's community relations director, had been among the first supporters of Opportunities Industrialization Centers (OIC), an African American–initiated, self-help training program begun in the late 1950s. Patrick asserted that among other things, Bell companies had given financial support, technical assistance, and surplus equipment for training to the OIC and hired an unspecified number of its graduates. Bell companies, he emphasized, had contributed more than

$100,000 in 1973 and loaned technical experts to teach in classes offered by the OIC. Despite all of this self-praise, the intent and extent of the Bell companies' participation in the OIC, besides the public relations benefits, can be ascertained from their surplus equipment donations. Executives boasted: "in at least four cities—Boston, Wilmington, St. Louis and Baltimore—associated companies have loaned and installed switchboards used by the local centers for telephone operator training. Other training equipment—ranging from key punch and teletype machines to teletraining units in clerical training has also been donated or loaned by local Bell Companies."[26] The Bell System directed its aid toward developing operators and low-level clerical workers at a time when managers knew that few possibilities existed for moving beyond these entry-level jobs slated for technological redundancy.

The goals of Bell System participation in these training programs were not only to obtain low-wage workers and to maintain favorable public relations, but they also sought to hire a malleable workforce. Initially, this meant that they hired lighter-skinned black women with a certain image, Southern migrants, and, later, Caribbean women who possibly feared deportation.[27] Management selected African American women who could accept the Bell System discipline for a number of reasons. For example, Anne Walden, hired in 1946, remembered that she felt that she "had to set an example . . . to make them be able to hire other black people," that they "had to excel" and could not "be average or ordinary."[28] Consequently, she did not present any discipline problem at that time. Indeed, Evelyn Holton stated: "You have got to understand, I mean how you were raised. I was raised by my grandmother, I was raised in the South and there were things that you just didn't do. . . . So I was a disciplined person. . . . My background was disciplined." Furthermore she said, "maybe because of my upbringing" . . . "I didn't come in with an attitude every day."[29] Evelyn claimed that because of her self-discipline, a supervisor never called her out or chastised her about doing anything wrong.

In addition to a "good attitude," other qualities that may have suggested potential for conformity were attractive to the Bell System. Harriet Tubman, who was hired as a clerk in 1956, confirmed that "they liked the way I looked and spoke." She "presented a certain image . . . ," "because [she] was light skinned and well spoken without a southern accent." Tubman believed that managers and workers "received" her "very warmly . . . almost solicitous" because "in a way [they saw her as] a novelty, [who] wasn't a threat" and "was able to get along."[30]

Bea Miller, who was escorted to the employment office in 1963 by her aunt Merenthia Jones, also presented the right image. Jones had received a master's degree in English from a Southern black college, but the only job she could get in the telephone company in the early 1950s was as a directory assistance operator. She left in 1961, but she knew enough about the company to dress Miller in a hat, white gloves, and stockings when she took her to a New York Telephone employment office in Long Island City. Miller, at seventeen, had been raised in a family of educated blacks, spoke clearly, and scored well on the tests. She easily rose to a position as training supervisor (of the hardcore) and was also an ideal employee for the first five years of her thirty-year tenure in the Bell System. Indeed, Miller, Walden, and Tubman had been exactly what the company wanted until the late 1960s. Miller remembered, "I was becoming conscious. . . . Adam Clayton Powell and Martin Luther King were on the scene . . . more and more [I] decided [that I] didn't want to be anything in the company." She "witnessed a woman with an afro get fired . . . another one [who wore] pants," and she "started to become a rebel." "I started to see some of the things managers were expected to do to other people."

Bell System management was acutely aware of the changing consciousness in the black community. Researchers for AT&T methodically studied African American communities, organizations, thought, and behavior as they simultaneously assessed urban labor market conditions and the possibility of urban social unrest.[31] In one pamphlet, "The Black Militants/The Negro Moderates," these researchers described differences among African American organizations and concluded that the militants differed in objectives and methods from the moderates. Emphasizing the militants' openness to the use of violence and rebellion, the pamphlet clarified that "the moderates advocate equality and a multi-racial society, while most militants advocate equality with some form of separation from the white power structure and self-determination for the blacks."[32] AT&T management decided on a strategy to dilute resistance as much as possible by propping up those it considered "moderate."[33] Their rationale was explicit: "In light of what has transpired in the past three or four years, it may be that today's moderate leadership, unless it receives encouragement in the form of money, public acknowledgement and help in conducting programs, will be succeeded by figures that will make Stokely Carmichael seem moderate."[34]

Obviously, managers fully understood the implications of hiring "militants" and took precautions against doing so.[35] For example, in 1971, Ohio Bell used an interview form asking "the interviewer to evaluate the applicants' 'radical views.' "[36] Even with these precautions, little could be done about the transformation of African American women's consciousness on the job, which is what made Walden, Tubman, and Miller three of the most radical fighters during the 1970s.[37] Management, however, could manipulate white workers' feeling about this militancy and the "opportunities" offered to blacks.

Integration allowed managers to manipulate, threaten, and control white workers who believed their job security was jeopardized by the new employment programs. First and foremost, the Bell System continued to divide its workers by reassuring whites of their supremacy and by denigrating black people in company publications. Even in 1972, a company magazine could portray black people as follows: "Many young black high school graduates have never had to achieve. When they go to work for the telephone company, it is often the first time they have ever been asked to meet high standards of any sort. Many come from an environment where they have never heard a polite word spoken. The idea of simple courtesy, especially to a faceless voice on the phone, may be as foreign as Sanskrit."[38] Although one wonders how high school graduates "never had to achieve," Bell System literature during this period is filled with images of unqualified black people hired for jobs that white people formerly held.

Eugene Mays described white fear in his explanation for employee resistance to the "hardcore" hiring policies. He stated: "telephone people, by virtue of the paternalistic training of Ma Bell and having grown out of an atmosphere of employment that over a number of years has been lily white, still accept the fact that a telephone company job is basically a white person's job. I have found, and I have been startled to some degree, that there's a very strong undercurrent of racism that prevails among telephone people."[39] Management successfully tapped this current during the civil rights era.

AT&T and the EEOC

As the Bell System proceeded in the restructuring of its workforce, women and minorities filed discrimination complaints with the EEOC. Unable to effect change on its own, the EEOC requested the FCC to investigate charges of discrimination before it granted an AT&T long distance rate increase. On the completion of hearings in 1971, the FCC concluded that AT&T and its associated companies had systematically discriminated against women and minorities. Without any admission to previous unfair practices, AT&T signed a consent decree with the EEOC, the U.S. Department of Labor, and the Department of Justice, which was approved by the U.S. District Court for the Eastern District of Pennsylvania on January 18, 1973.[40] The degree awarded workers $38 million in wage compensation and called for complete reorganization of personnel procedures to reduce the racial and sexual job segregation so long practiced in the telephone industry.[41] Subsequently, the Bell System's failure to fully implement the intent of the agreements necessitated two more consent decrees.[42]

The original consent decree granted AT&T and its operating companies six years to hire, transfer, and promote a "targeted" number of women and "minorities" into higher-paying management and craft jobs as well as to place men in some of the female-dominated jobs. The Bell System constructed an "Upgrade and Transfer Program" (UTP), and it used government-approved seniority "overrides" to obtain the "targets." Under these new programs, some women and minorities gained access to jobs from which they had formerly been excluded. However, the general economic conditions, union legal interferences, technological displacement, and entrenched/structural sexism and racism severely limited the extent of these new opportunities. Women's "proportion within the work force declined from 52 percent to 51 percent."[43]

Nevertheless, researchers agree that white women were the "big gainers from the consent decree," because the government's "first and foremost" intention was to "get something done for women."[44] White women, regardless of their educational levels, moved more rapidly, and in larger numbers, into the higher-level and craft occupations than did "minority" women. As the more highly educated white women moved into upper management and sales positions, inexperienced and unskilled white women advanced into craft jobs.[45]

Of the total number of women employed in the Bell System, those in upper management categories such as "officials and managers" increased from 9.7 percent in 1973 to 13.4 percent in 1979. (Men went from 31.5 percent to 34.2 percent.) Women held 24.5 percent of the jobs in this group in 1973 and 29.1 percent in 1979. Of this distribution, white women constituted 22.5 percent (37,054) in 1973 and 24.9 percent (47,713) in 1979. African American women comprised 1.5 percent (2,390) in 1973 and 2.9 percent (5,627) in 1979. Hispanic and other "minority" women increased from 0.6 percent (902) in 1973 to 1.3 percent (2,370) in 1979. These numbers should be viewed with some skepticism, because secretaries and other administrators were counted as "officials and managers" when they really had no decision-making powers; they simply were not in the unions.

In the "outside craft" occupational group, the total number of Bell System women increased from 0.2 percent to 1.5 percent in 1973 and 1979, respectively. Their distribution increased from 0.7 percent to 4.7 percent. The change for white women was from 0.6 percent (879) to 3.8 percent (5,138). African American women moved from less than a tenth of 1 percent (57) to 0.5 percent (742). Hispanic and other "minority" women also comprised less than a tenth of 1 percent (36) in 1973 but increased to 0.4 percent (433) by 1979.

In 1973, 2.5 percent of the total number of women worked in the "inside crafts," increasing to 4.3 percent in 1979. In those same years, their distribution jumped from 10.7 percent to 17.9 percent. Of this distribution, white women comprised 9.2 percent (8,957) and 14.3 percent (14,015). African American women constituted 1.2 percent (1,140) and 2.5 percent (2,419). Hispanic and other "minority" women's part changed from 0.4 percent (354) in 1973 to 1.1 percent (1,072) in 1979.[46]

After a detailed statistical analysis by region and occupational group, economists Herbert R. Northrup and John A. Larson concluded that when white women were hired, promoted, or transferred into craft jobs, the percentage of white male applicants entering these jobs decreased from 83 percent in 1973 to 56.3 percent in 1979.[47] They noted, however, that some less-educated white women may have lost clerical and administrative opportunities to men since white men hired into introductory clerical jobs increased from 17 percent in 1973 to 43.7 percent in 1979.[48] Affirmative action had favorable results for both white men and white women, even though some occupational shifting did occur. And more important, racial segregation did not change significantly.

As these numbers indicate, African Americans and other "minorities" experienced a more ambivalent improvement in their status and in the numbers hired during the years of the consent decrees. As with white women, the numbers of more highly educated nonwhites in the higher job categories rose as a result of the protection afforded by the required targets.[49] Minority women advanced remarkably in craft jobs, given how few there had been in 1973.[50] White women's shift away from low-level clerical work is illustrated in the increase in nonwhite women, who numbered 39,818 in 1973, and 53,158 in 1979.[51] Despite these improvements, minorities, especially women, tended to remain disadvantaged as the occupational groups in which they were concentrated suffered enormous losses.[52] Between 1973 and 1979, the number of operators decreased by 28.7 percent and service workers by 53.8 percent.[53]

Scholars offer several explanations for this pattern of sex and race stratification. Northrup and Larson, for example, applauded the results of the consent decree since the results had been obtained in a period of employment stagnation (total Bell System employment increased by less than 2,000 employees) and at a time when the total percentage of telephone women declined.[54] They minimized the racial segregation by emphasizing the increase of minorities in the rapidly expanding higher-level positions. Predicting that future telephone workers would have to be "more sophisticated" in the changing labor market, they attributed the decrease in operators to "automatic systems and charges for directory assistance." Apparently, these authors accepted technological displacement as part of a continuum of wider "technological progress" in which change occurred as a result of historical momentum rather than as a consequence of human managerial choices.[55]

Unlike Northrup and Larson, who viewed technology as a basically benign progression (an independent variable), Sally L. Hacker identified "technology as an intervening variable" in the sex stratification of the telephone industry. She "discovered" that "planned technological change would eliminate more jobs for women than affirmative action would provide."[56] Hacker's other findings indicated that jobs in which large numbers and proportions of minority women worked best predicted "slow growth or decline."[57] Hence, she concluded that "displacement struck most sharply where minority women worked."[58] Indeed, Hacker asserted that "the corporation planned to hold growth or cut back on jobs at occupational levels employing large numbers of females, and to increase jobs at levels employing large numbers of white males."[59] Furthermore, technological change displaced both management and nonmanagement women because the new computerized systems eliminated both low-level clerks and the women who supervised them.[60]

Affirmative action had protected only middle-management females, while it had opened entry-level, traditionally female jobs to men. Indeed, according to Hacker, nonmanagement women suffered excessively since "affirmative action placed thousands more men in traditionally women's work than it placed women in traditionally men's work."[61] Not only were men moving into traditional female jobs, but they also were progressing up and out of these very jobs at a faster rate than women had. These dead-end jobs had become stepping-stones for men.[62] Sex discrimination had decreased, but only because men had replaced women in their work, not the reverse.

For different reasons, white and black women telephone workers decreased in numbers during this period. African American women replaced many white women in the lowest levels of telephone work. Although sexist managers continued to place white women in jobs that were already segregated by sex, or in low-level craft work that would later be negatively affected by technology, these jobs were better-paying with more opportunities for advancement than those for which African American women were selected. Racial ideology severely eroded any opportunities based on sex for African American women.

Managers' racial attitudes also determined how the Bell System used affirmative action "targets" to maneuver women into rapidly changing male craft jobs. Under the guise of upgrades and promotions, managers placed both white and black women in jobs that new technologies changed. Personnel departments across the country hired women as pole climbers, installers, and frame technicians at the very time that the Bell System planned to eliminate this work by introducing new technologies and changes in customer services.[63] As the Bell System encouraged women, mostly white, to use the upgrade and transfer programs to enter these higher-paying craft jobs, they also encouraged "minority" women to accept "targeted" upgrades and transfers into clerical jobs created by the fragmentation and deskilling of male craft work. Bell managers tracked women into these jobs because of the expected high turnover among them and because women's work did not receive adequate union protection. Black and "minority" women suffered more severely since they worked in the lower-paying and the more stressful and highly supervised jobs with the least union protection.

Dave Newman, a switching technician at the New York Telephone Company, gave a vivid illustration of this process in the case of deskmen or testers who had been responsible for locating troubles on customer lines.

This has been one of the most highly skilled craft jobs. It is being virtually eliminated by MLTS (Mechanized Loop Testers), which are operated by clerks earning significantly lower wages. But money is not the only loss incurred by the workers involved. Testers utilize their knowledge and experience to interpret meter readings and to work with other craftspeople, while a clerk simply dials a line into the machine, cross-references the response against a chart without knowing what it means, and dispatches the trouble to the appropriate craftsperson without knowing what that person's job involves or understanding how it is related to the trouble. Also, testers are overwhelmingly white and male; the maintenance administrators who operate the MLTS tend to be black and female.[64]

Similar fragmentation and deskilling of switching technician's work and other crafts have led to the creation of whole departments at New York Telephone in which only black women work. More than 75 percent of these jobs require women to remain seated at video terminals where they key in data at company-established productivity rates. White men (who had been skilled craftsmen) and frequently white women supervise these departments. Computerized work measurements and strict supervision combine frequently with racism and sexism to form a virtual hell for most of these women.[65]

Objectively, these women work in degraded, deskilled, and dehumanized jobs, but subjective conditions compel some caution in presenting this point of view. African American and other "minority" women who had worked in the low-paying operator and clerical jobs jumped at the opportunity to work in the deskilled craft jobs, just as they did when the

Black Operators in the Computer Age | 241

opportunity to work as operators first became available. Higher wages, and in some cases more routine hours, made these jobs highly attractive to women who were often single mothers. They earned less than skilled craftsmen, but their wages were greater than those of most other clerical workers. These new jobs represented an upgrade into higher-paying craft work long unobtainable for "minority" women.

Regardless of the women's own subjective perceptions and conditions, the new jobs amounted to nothing more than another set of positions with little upward mobility. No question, Bell managers used racial and sexual divisions to achieve their aims, and they diverted and manipulated equal opportunity goals to ensure that African American and other "minority" women remained at the bottom of the Bell System hierarchy in jobs adversely affected by new technologies. Managers not only decided which new technologies would be introduced, but they determined who would work in which occupations. Upgrades and "targets" merely placed a numerical goal on positions planned and designed by Bell engineers.

Locally, many lower-level managers found ways to subvert even the limited goals planned by Bell System executives. Frequently, local managers left African American women's "upgrade and transfer" applications unprocessed. Completed applications would be rejected at a later stage in the bureaucracy, either because a manager intentionally failed to fill it out properly or because he simply did not care enough to follow it through. In many cases, by the time all of the paper shuffling was finished, someone who had completed the application earlier had filled the job. African Americans also complained that even after their applications had been successfully recorded, unfair testing procedures often eliminated them.[66] Affirmative action provided the Bell System with the legal sanction to continue, in a different form, long-established practices. Management's power to deploy the consent decrees to their own interests expedited their strategy to engender the kind of jealousy and confusion that would provoke the unions to fight affirmative action rather than fight management over technological change.

CWA Opposes Consent Decrees

The administration of affirmative action guidelines created division, fear, and feelings of unfairness among telephone workers. Perceiving the protections provided to women and minorities by the Civil Rights Act of

1964 and the investigatory authority of the EEOC as an attack on their privileges, white males responded by filing charges of sex discrimination with the EEOC based on the "special privileges" granted to women. One man complained about the "special rooms and taxis" provided for women as well as the company's denial of the opportunity to become a telephone operator and the perpetuation of the image of an operator as female.[67] Clarence W. Bailey Jr. of New Orleans charged that Southern Bell discriminated against him because of his sex "by following a policy, practice, custom and usage of harassment and intimidation by applying unrealistic norms for illness and incidental absences against men more severely than against women. The company is following the practice of allowing women six (6) absences and men three (3) absences per year. . . ."[68] Others found that men did not receive the same treatment under disability provisions as women received for pregnancy. They objected to such things as lower retirement ages, lower weightlifting requirements, rest breaks and lounges for women, and the dispensation given to women not to report in emergencies.[69]

The effect of this backlash decreased workplace unity, and it gave the company an excuse to take privileges away from women that should have been extended to all workers. Indeed, these types of charges became so common that New Jersey Bell adopted recommendations to handle them. Management decided to "increase female compulsory retirement and voluntary retirement ages to agree with male requirements," to "eliminate "break periods" for female employees," to "open women's lounges to all employees on an equal and non-discriminatory basis," to "eliminate rules which would preclude having women report for emergency assignment on a basis different than that expected of male employees," and to consider physical limitations of all individuals in relation to heavy weights.[70] Racial tensions had similar, if not worse, results for African Americans specifically as well as for workers in general. White males and females filed charges of race discrimination when they believed they were passed over for a transfer or promotion in favor of a black person.[71] The Bell System tightened discipline, introduced new technologies, and decreased its workforce as workers fought each other over dwindling jobs. The consent decrees frightened white workers even more because they believed that their contractual rights were being abrogated.

Alarmed over the possibility that "targets" threatened job security, unions, particularly the CWA, which had already failed to protect operators from technological displacement, now openly challenged affirmative action. The CWA refused to attend the EEOC negotiations, although it had been asked along with the IBEW to participate in the formulation of the consent decrees.[72] Instead, CWA sought "to block the implementation of the decree on the grounds that: (1) it infringed upon their bargaining rights and (2) it was not consulted on areas in which it had a vital interest such as issues affecting wages, hours, and conditions of employment."[73] Unsuccessful in this attempt, the CWA initiated a suit in 1973 against AT&T to reverse the consent decree, especially the "override," which the union charged "violated the seniority provisions of the unions' contracts and caused the company to engage in sex-conscious and color-conscious 'preferential treatment' that was proscribed by Title VII of the Civil Rights Act and the U.S. Constitution."[74]

After five years and numerous appeals up to the U.S. Supreme Court, the CWA lost, and the "override" remained in place along with the other provisions of the consent decree.[75] These legal defeats only exacerbated white fears. And management's hiring and promotion of a few women and blacks into highly visible jobs and into selected craft work added to male feelings of victimization. After the courts affirmed the consent decrees, union practices often contributed to the company's ability to suppress African American advancement. Union failure to represent African Americans has been evidenced in the hundreds of charges of discrimination filed against the Bell System that also included charges against the union.[76] From stewards to local presidents, union leaders frequently challenged female and nonwhite craft upgrades in order to have a white male upgraded first. Alleging "reverse discrimination," most of the challenges were based on seniority or some other supposedly outstanding qualification that led to a high success rate of grievances initiated for those reasons. And in many shops on an individual basis, whites unified so that white women could be used to block the progress of nonwhites. Often white male managers promoted white females to the disadvantage of nonwhites, which, of course, tended to destroy any unity between the two disadvantaged groups. Because whites benefited from the unfair administration of upgrades and promotions, the union did not challenge the company's right to promote to management at its own discretion without regard to seniority.

The explanation for the union's sexist and racist behavior lies in the composition of the CWA leadership and the leaders' unchanging trade union ideology. Like most high-level company executives, up to the 1980s most CWA national officials were white and male. White males continued to represent the largest single interest group, although they did not out-number women and nonwhites. The leadership did not reflect the member-ship, which partially explains why the union sought to protect what it perceived to be the rights of white men over the rights of others.

As the Bell System manipulated women and nonwhites into jobs ad-versely affected by technological change, the union leadership made no genuine protests because these changes did not affect white male jobs. Automation, in its initial stages (when it only affected women), had been welcomed by the national leadership. In 1965, CWA President Joseph A. Beirne expressed minor concern over the loss of eighty thousand jobs because he felt that "frankly, most of the losses had been handled by attrition since technological innovations affected telephone operators and clerical operations where turnover was high."[77] Management had decided to give these very jobs to African American women. Beirne admitted that "what most disturbed us in 1963 was that we saw where future innova-tions might affect the most highly skilled occupations where turnover was much slower."[78] In 1963, the more highly skilled occupations employed white males. The failure of CWA leaders to address technological redun-dancy is comparable to their failure to organize African Americans dur-ing the early phases of integration.

On the local level, white male *and* female union leaders, protective of their power bases, did not encourage nonwhite union participation. Union leadership feared the voting power of nonwhite people, especially women, to the point that many nonwhite employees remained unor-ganized well into the 1970s. This was especially true in places where the membership had rapidly changed from white to black and where the leadership consisted of long-entrenched white union bosses. Lavie Bol-ick, an assistant to a district vice president in 1970, referring to Atlanta and other Georgia offices where black operators had become a majority, confirmed:

the old administration don't want to stress organizing in those offices because they foresee that the power is going to be there, and *they* ain't going to be able to set on their asses and hold their jobs down because they're going to be threatened by a union member. And as long as he's a nonmember, he's not a threat to their reign, and I hate to put it that way, but as I see it from where I sit. In a lot of our large offices, this is about the way it would sum up if the people would tell the truth.[79]

Although the traffic department had been better-organized than the plant twenty years earlier, most of Atlanta's black operators remained nonunion in 1970 because local leaders would not ask them into the union.[80] Union policies based on racial prejudice and exclusion, like company policies, were not peculiar to the South.

In Northern cities, white female leaders who had historically headed the operators' locals fought against nonwhite leadership and participation, while they also neglected to fairly represent nonwhites. The CWA's large traffic local in Newark, New Jersey, experienced near destruction in 1970 when its white female leadership resisted a black majority membership effort to achieve representation in the leadership.[81] New York City operators (nearly 75 percent of whom were black) belonged to a near company union (Telephone Traffic Union–TTU), whose white leadership, according to Lessie Sanders's recollections, failed to represent them on the job and never sent the operators out on strike.[82]

TTU members resorted to wildcat strikes at the end of their contracts because their leadership failed to fight for operators' demands. "We didn't wait for our union," according to Sanders, "when we had a fight we went out to try to force the company to see our position because the union would never do it."[83] For the seven years she worked in directory assistance, Sanders recalled "no elections," and she believed that the leaders "were appointed."

Sanders participated in two CWA organizing campaigns between 1970 and 1975 to win operators from TTU. To Sanders's disbelief, each failed. "I can't understand how we lost those elections [campaigns]. . . . It seemed like the ideal thing to get out of TTU." When asked if she felt that the CWA had made an all-out effort to win, she responded that "they spent the money to do it but it was the operators who went from building to building, took leaves of absences and worked for it. CWA never came to us saying they wanted all of us in one union. We went to them. They made the funds available."[84] Besides allocating the money, CWA leadership could have done more. By Sanders's analysis, "they could have had more of their members to join in on the campaign staff . . . maybe it would have been more convincing. It was just operators talking to operators about a union they knew very little about."[85] During these campaigns, Sanders did not "see very much resistance" on the part of the white male membership, and she remembered receiving "a lot of support from CWA black males." Whether it was a fearful leadership or, as Eugene Mays assessed, a matter of an unattractive "conservative image" that caused New York City operators to reject the CWA, one of the nation's largest groups of African American operators received inadequate representation until the early 1980s.[86] And, ironically, New York City's white male unionists lost much of their strike efficacy as a result of their failure to convince black operators that they would be better represented in the CWA than in the company-minded TTU.[87]

This picture, of course, would not be complete without some mention of those unionists who did abandon their own racism and fought racist company hiring practices and working conditions. Indeed, these cases were rare and exceptional, and they occurred in isolated communities, but they did happen. Scott Stephens, a retired CWA international representative, acknowledged that racism existed in Indiana but that the union there had fought it. He asserted:

> under the direction of Mae Mann, we constantly argued with the telephone company for better positions for the black people, better understanding of their needs, and that there were well-educated people among them. So in the plant department there were jobs created by negotiations, upgraded jobs, for colored people. In the traffic group, girls were interviewed for operators. And in one of our most southern cities, Evansville, Indiana, the company introduced the first colored operators.[88]

Stephens and Mann followed through with the company and the local presidents. Mann, according to him, guaranteed that the local presidents would not give the company any trouble. Stephens and Mann personally introduced the first black operator in Evansville, and they also convinced the reluctant local leaders that this move presaged the wave of the future.

Although evidence exists for other examples of initiative shown by individual unionists or local leaders, telephone unions in general throughout the 1960s and most of the 1970s never pursued strong equal opportunity goals. Without concerning themselves with unfair racist and sexist hiring and promotion practices, most union leaders maintained that African Americans and other "minorities" received the same union protections and benefits won by national contractual provisions for all workers. Despite the fact that contracts had been bargained mostly in the interest of white males, nonwhites and women at least theoretically received the same benefits and protections. Indeed, the cwa gained a public reputation for bargaining contracts that included high wages, above-average benefits, and in the 1980s significant protections against technological change.

CWA Bargains Technology Clauses

Like other unions, the cwa has been criticized for its aggressive pursuit of "economic" gains at the expense of neglecting concerns over technological displacement. Partially reversing this trend, the cwa, which was mostly concerned about the impact of technology on its craft workers, bargained several new contract provisions in 1977 and 1980. Ronnie J. Straw, the cwa Director of Development and Research, in testimony before the House Subcommittee on Science, Research, and Technology, stated that the 1980 cwa/at&t contracts contained clauses that provided "benefits and ways for our members to deal with the human impact of technological change."[89] These clauses included such income protections as the Supplemental Income Protection Plan (sipp) for workers "declared" surplus (technologically displaced), the Reassignment Pay Protection Plan (rppp) for downgraded workers, and Technological Displacement allowances for workers who chose termination rather than transfers or downgrading. Other provisions upgraded the service representatives in 1977 and the operators in 1980 (both jobs dominated by black women by this time and increasingly besieged by technology), eliminated certain types of remote monitoring, and prohibited outside contractors from performing telephone work.[90]

The 1980 contract contained letters of agreement that established joint Technology Change Committees in the Bell operating companies, weco and Long Lines, a national cwa/at&t Working Conditions and Service Quality Improvement committee, and a national cwa/at&t Occupational Job Evaluation Committee. Technology Change Committees discussed "employment and training for workers affected by technology and . . . possible applications of existing programs such as sipp, rppp and transfers."[91] Another provision of the contract obligated the company to give the union six-month advance notice of any technological change that might affect its members. The Working Conditions and Service Quality Improvement Committee sought employee participation in what the name implies. And the Occupational Job Evaluation Committee had the responsibility of evaluating and creating new job titles and classifications in light of technological change.[92] These committees and the other contractual provisions have been applauded by the labor movement as a real advance in the technological struggle.

Dave Newman, a former cwa steward, critic, and activist, also conceded that the cwa had "pioneered in winning contract language which seeks to minimize the harmful impact of technological changes."[93] Newman, however, voiced several objections to the committees mentioned above:

> While virtually the entire membership supports such protections as rppp, sipp, layoff procedures by inverse seniority, etc., there is increasing concern and understanding that the amelioration of negative company actions is not the same thing as fighting the actions. These programs and procedures do not constitute job security, nor do they protect job content or skills. The three committees . . . are seen as impotent (having advisory power only), and the high union officials on these committees are viewed with skepticism, since they are the same officials who are seen as having done nothing previously to combat technological change and its negative effects.[94]

Acknowledging the economic gains, Newman criticized the general failure of these new contract provisions to protect all workers. Union contracts affected nonwhite workers differently, for protective clauses, like eeoc "targets," must be administered.

Ideally, the new but inadequate, technology clauses should have protected any group of workers experiencing technological change. But frequently, management unfairly manipulated these clauses against the interests of women and nonwhites. During the 1980s, well after nonwhites and women had become union members, union neglect and apathy created conditions conducive to the continuation of company racism and sexism. The closing of the AT&T New York City International Operating Center in 1983, and the continued technological displacement of low-level clerical workers in the operating companies, provide examples that demonstrate how even these objective clauses can be administered in a subjective and racist manner.[95]

Closing of the New York IOC

Long distance operators, particularly overseas operators, were the last large group to experience technological displacement. International Direct Distance Dialing (IDDD) and International Service Position Systems (ISPS similar to TSPS for local offices) eliminated overseas operators in the 1970s and 1980s, just as "dial" and DDD had eliminated local and long distance operators earlier. In the largest cities by this time, nonwhite women had replaced white women as the majority of operators. Nationally, AT&T had operated at least a half-dozen international operating centers to process calls from different parts of the country to various overseas points.[96] The most advanced technology allowed operators anywhere in the country to place overseas calls, which led to the shifting of work from one region to another.

Gradually, AT&T had begun phasing out these centers for reasons other than a surplus of workers. According to Pat Meckle, who was an operator and also Secretary Treasurer of CWA Local 1150 during this period, the Oakland IOC "did not stay open too long" because the company took "a beating" from the militant operators out there.[97] When AT&T decided to close its New York IOC and move the work to other points (especially Springfield, Massachusetts), Meckle attributed the move to the company's continuous quest for cost effectiveness. In other locations, she believed the company could pay less for rents, salaries, and other facilities. Another reason for the closing may have been the desire to close before the upcoming divestiture of the Bell operating companies. And, equally as important, Meckle stated, "they also felt they didn't have such militant people in some of the other locations as well."[98] Ron Tyree, vice president of Local 1150, one of the first male operators and a steward at that time, also suspected that the company especially wanted to get rid of the black operators because of their militance and their willingness to act on it.[99] The Bell System had initially hired African American women in the belief that these women would not only be a source of cheap labor but compliant labor as well.

Managers were deeply surprised and disappointed after these women had attained large numbers in the operating jobs. For example, in December 1979, three-quarters of New York City 10c operators, angered over the job pressures brought about by a company speedup, as well as excessive supervision and unfair suspensions and dismissals, carried out a militant three-day wildcat strike. The operators also were incensed by the death of a sixty-two-year-old operator who had worked thirty-six years for the company and was only a few weeks from retirement. A few days before her death, the operator had been suspended because she "had briefly 'plugged out' her position while filling out a repair ticket."[100] The suspension, in addition to the close supervision she experienced on her return, had made her "nervous and upset." Her sister operators were convinced that the company had killed her, and after a week of seething over it and other grievances, they struck. It took a federal injunction to end their wildcat action. Thus, AT&T had reason to fear militance from this group.

Anne H. Walden, CWA Local 1150 section vice president of traffic, wrote in 1983 about a number of ways the company manipulated the contract to create confusion, fear, and frustration among operators soon to be laid off as surplus. Walden recalled that when the company first notified the union of the closing on August 30, 1982, management indicated that it would "make an attempt to place the employees in other jobs including a few thousand downgraded clerical jobs in New York Telephone without the benefit of the Reassignment Pay Protection Plan."[101] By February 1983, the company announced that these jobs would not be available since New York Telephone also had a surplus. The company gave no explanation for why the operators would not have received RPPP benefits (a contract violation) if these jobs had become available.

Other possible opportunities proved equally elusive. Some upgrades to service representative became available, but few operators passed newly required tests. In another attempt to "provide alternatives," the company offered a "crash typing course" for which, by Walden's assessment, there did not "appear to be any jobs that require[d] these skills."[102] Upgrades to craft jobs, even by operators who had already passed the tests, rarely happened. Eventually, AT&T pressured some operators to accept entry-level clerical jobs often at great distances from their homes or former jobs. The company induced others to quit with a "Separation Payment." In reality, the new union contract clauses had little meaning for these women.

Since many of these workers had already achieved an operator's top salary, moving into entry-level clerical positions entailed a reduction in income. For those with less than fifteen years of service, RPPP protected their pay for only one year. Many black women did not have enough years of seniority. "The Company," concluded Walden, "was quite successful in their SIPP offer as a majority of the eligible employees took the offer and said Goodbye."[103] Again, black women hired in the 1960s could not take advantage of the retirement benefits under SIPP. Eventually, the closing of the IOC caused more than 1,200 women to be transferred to new locations, downgraded, or forced to resign. The company laid off as many as 300 of these women.

Meckle, who had nearly forty years of service at that time, stated that none of the IOCs before or after New York had been closed in the same manner.[104] Somehow, all of the people in the other IOCs received other jobs. As far as Meckle was concerned, race and sex had everything to do with the closing of the New York IOC. She believed that "they zeroed in on New York IOC . . . because it was predominantly black." The women affected were either older white or younger black women. The white women, still willing and able to work, had the ironic fortune to be able to retire when they could not be placed within the company. Black women, on the other hand, who had come to dominate the IOC, found it economically difficult to relocate to other company locations such as suburban New Jersey, White Plains, New York, and Long Island.[105] With premium pay for working weekends and other than normal hours, these women earned salaries they could not expect to get in other jobs or other industries. The company snatched away black women's jobs without following union contractual procedures.

Meckle acknowledged that the union had been criticized strongly for the layoffs, scattered transfers, and lack of demonstrations and political agitation. She argued that the criticisms had been misdirected since "so many did get jobs because [the union] persisted and persisted and argued and fought . . . they got a lot of concessions out of the company . . . they got a lot things that had never happened before . . . that was over and above anything that was just there in the contract at that time."[106]

The Local 1150 Vice President in 1990, Ron Tyree, voiced a considerably different assessment of how the union handled the closing:

> I believe the national union including my local could have fought a lot better . . . for jobs and for the IOC. . . . There are certain things we could have done . . . there were no research committees that I know of that ever said . . . let us go into this work and see what we can do and see if we have to move all of this work. . . . As far as I know and I was a worker there and no body ever said to me as a worker . . . what do you think . . . do you have a better idea . . .
>
> I don't think we could have completely changed what happened but we could have made it easier . . . we could have prepared people a lot better. . . .[107]

According to him there were no slowdowns or plans for slowdowns, few demonstrations, and not even informational picketing. Neither the national nor local leadership made any plans or took any aggressive action on behalf of these operators.

Local union complacency and unwillingness to take any independent initiative in addition to the corporate terror campaign paralyzed the operators. Operators feared losing their jobs to such a degree that they refused to sign a petition circulated by Anne Walden on their behalf to be presented to the union Committee on Equity.[108] At an unusually well-attended Local 1150 meeting held in May 1983, hundreds of operators, described as "angry about a multitude of broken promises and facing a 4-day week (and eventually a 0-day week)," demanded a "No Layoff, No Downgrade, No forced-transfer" clause in the next contract. They also sought "a strike over the closing of the N.Y.-I.O.C., a demonstration to show the city that N.Y. is going to lose another 500 jobs. . . ."[109] According to Tyree, union officers Walden and Meckle were the only operators who voted for a strike. He attributed this disaster to the actions of Chester (Chet) L. Macey, the local president at the time. Macey told the operators that if they voted for a strike, the company would simply close the IOC earlier. Angry but afraid, operators defeated the strike vote. A local president, either through lack of concern, ineptitude, or perhaps ambition for a position in the company, asserted his authority to suppress dissent instead of rallying and directing the workers toward resistance.[110] And the national leadership did nothing about it.

As a result, the company could abuse contract provisions by simply ignoring them (RPPP) or using them (separation payments) to force the operators to quit. And more importantly, the provisions themselves had been conceptualized with seniority prerequisites when black women with lower seniority worked in the very jobs slated for technological displacement—supposedly the type of jobs intended for protection.

Contrast this AT&T closing with the introduction of MLTS, which displaced test desk technicians, a largely white male group who tested lines and dispatched the trouble to the appropriate technician. According to Newman, some of these men retired under SIPP, and others accepted downgrades under RPPP or transferred to test bureaus in areas yet unaffected. Significantly, Newman admitted: "It is important to note that whatever the inadequacies of the union's response, no testers lost their jobs as Bell System employees."[111] Other major work reorganization as a result of technological changes also did not deprive the craftsmen of their jobs. Crossbar switchmen, for example, have been retrained for the latest digital switching systems. Before the 1990s, the majority of white men suffered few pay reductions and no loss of individual jobs. Yet massive deskilling, centralization, and computerization have increasingly diminished their control over their work. At the start of the year 2000, craft jobs were under the same technological onslaught that displaced operators. However, in the period under study, the protections of the union's technological provisions, however small and inadequate, were greater for white male craft workers than for women and nonwhites.

Changes in Union Behavior

In fairness to the union, it must be acknowledged that on a case-by-case basis, union performance in some regions and in some instances should be congratulated. In the case of the MLTS, the women who replaced the men achieved higher salaries (though significantly below those of testers) than they would have as regular clerks.[112] Even as their numbers decreased, operators' salaries increased. One study stated that in 1985, operators represented by CWA earned "wages that equalled those of the average male worker in the labor force as a whole" and "significantly more than the average woman earns in the U.S."[113]

Indeed, the cwa, having bargained the highest wages for women in female-dominated service work, envisioned itself as a leader in the struggle for higher wages for all women. In 1986, when the telephone industry felt that it paid its operators, office clericals, and sales representatives 20 percent to 40 percent above the current market rates and demanded a pay cut for these female-dominated jobs, the cwa responded with a three-week national AT&T strike. Convinced that the company had made these retrogressive demands because women in other service industries earned so little, the cwa felt compelled to maintain a standard for other industries to follow.[114]

The cwa also has sought to improve the wages and working conditions of women by its participation in special committees, conferences, and community coalitions. In the early 1980s, the cwa began to adjust its outlook to reflect an awareness of the special problems presented by its female and nonwhite membership. Working with AT&T in the Occupational Job Evaluation Committee and the Quality of Worklife Committee, which was established in 1980, the union sought to establish principles of "comparable worth" and to address other problems in the workplace. Prompted by the demands of the union's now more diversified membership, the national cwa leadership expanded its previously established women's committees and committees on equity. Alone and in conjunction with the Coalition of Labor Union Women, the cwa has sponsored several national women's conferences to discuss issues such as pay equity and new technology. However, on the local level, the impact of the cwa's new equal opportunity rhetoric has been almost imperceptible. Bell System divestiture, continuous technological displacement, and unstable national economic conditions have neutralized the implementation of these rather tardy corrections of past practices.[115]

New Consent Decrees: Same Old Results!

Even with the cwa's public compliance and cooperation, government intervention in the Bell System's employment practices failed to modify patterns of racial and gender segregation. A renewal of the consent decrees in 1982 helped to change the percentages of women and minorities in the Bell hierarchy, but it did not seriously alter their numbers in the lower-paying and powerless positions. Statistics released by the New York Telephone Company reveal increases in management, but these are lower levels of management, and the largest increases have come among administrative workers and secretaries—nonunion members—designated as managers but not as decision-makers. As women's participation more than doubled, "minority" numbers in the skilled crafts virtually stagnated. This growth in women's participation appears more significant than it actually was because so few women worked in the skilled crafts before the consent decrees. In reality, the difference in the number of women is only slightly more than five hundred.

Just as in the early 1970s, the numbers of women in the female-dominated occupations (service representatives and operators) decreased at a faster rate than they increased in male-dominated crafts. Men benefited quantitatively more than women by the renewed consent decrees, because the entry of men into service representative and operator jobs proceeded at higher rates than occurred among women entering male-dominated skilled crafts. Overall, unionism and affirmative action helped to increase the numbers of women and nonwhite people in jobs from which they had been historically excluded. Yet the company continued its sexist and racist practices under government observation, and even after the union supposedly had adopted equal opportunity as its own goals. The Bell System complied with government mandates only enough to avoid government intervention in rate increases and to receive the money to train a less expensive labor force. Besides, government nondiscrimination regulations lacked either strict enforcement or provisions to address specific problems of technological displacement and racial and sexual stratification within the workplace.[116]

The experience of women and minorities in the telephone industry exposes the government's failure to interfere with power relations in the workplace. Historically, the government presented no threat to the Bell System's control over its workforce. We have seen that the New York Public Utilities Commission did little to make the New York Telephone Company comply with the state's civil rights laws during the 1930s. Even the Fair Employment Practices Committee's World War II success in bringing about the integration of the operating forces is clouded by the fact that few African Americans were hired before the late 1960s. As automation and computerization advanced during the 1950s and 1960s, state FEPCS and other equal opportunity agencies did little more than document charges of discrimination against the Bell System. And, of course, the federal government agreed to affirmative action programs in the 1970s that ultimately facilitated the technological restructuring of the telephone workforce.

Heavily dependent on Bell technologies for national defense, the government would have been the last critic of the Bell System's research and development choices and policies. State and federal investigations have consistently minimized technological displacement and echoed Bell System explanations for it.[117] Preoccupied with racial and sexual integration, the government neglected technological displacement, promotion opportunities, and job satisfaction. At no time did any government agency, committee, or commission seriously challenge the Bell System's right to organize its work environment according to its business needs. For women and minorities, especially black women, the federal government's supervision of the telephone industry contributed to the continuation of the Bell System's policy of racial and sexual segregation in the workplace. Rather than scrutinize the impact of telephone technology on workers, the government has concerned itself with other Bell System personnel policies. Investigators and other reformers have occupied themselves with working conditions and compliance with poorly conceived equal opportunity laws. As we have seen, this narrow (and admittedly important) focus has inspired consent decrees that have opened opportunities for some women but have had little impact on technological displacement and degradation of work.

Former operators, black and white, have stated that the Bell System chose young white (in some places Roman Catholic) women when its workforce was segregated, and it chose Southern black women (sometimes Caribbean women) when it first decided to integrate, because these groups of women were considered more obedient as a result of their cultural indoctrinations.[1] As these pages have shown, neither group of women was as malleable as the companies wanted. Even when TSPS and other computerized equipment forced women to work at inhuman speeds, most of them found ways to cope and resist without lapsing into dependency on drugs or other abnormal behavior. Bereft of adequate union leadership and direction to resist the introduction of new technologies and the concomitant speedups, black women adopted attitudes and techniques of resistance similar to those of nineteenth-century women who "threw up" the annunciators.

For example, Geneva Tucker, after more than twenty years with the New York Telephone Company, expressed the desire to just get out and go back down South to live. She did not expect to advance any further, and she made no requests for an upgrade to craft work. Her plan to escape was her way of coping. She typified many of the women in the clerical force.

Many other women resisted passively by refusing to take the initiative or to correct inaccuracies in their supervisors' instructions. With the new technology assigning tasks, women assumed the attitude that they would do only what they were assigned and nothing more. After all, they believed that taking the initiative and trying to do a good job could possibly end in punishment. Winifred King best exemplified this attitude. Bitter over poor training, racism/sexism, and the lack of opportunities for advancement, King stated: "as long as they pay me my salary, I will stay here and do what I can, but I have no incentive to be outstanding . . . or gung ho . . . or motivated to do anything more than I have to do." She also looked forward to accumulating "enough time [seniority] . . . where I can retire and relax."[2]

Even those women who denied feeling pressured by supervision and technological changes, and who in fact welcomed the changes, unconsciously thwarted the company's attempts to control all of their actions. Evelyn Holton, hired as an operator in 1961, advanced to clerk and then to a craft position, claimed that she never felt pressured by the supervision and that she "did not find being an operator a demeaning job."[3] Yet she described how she talked at the cord board, even though it was strictly forbidden.

> I had a ball, we had fun . . . great bunch of women . . . we talked if it was slow . . . as long as your eyes were on the board . . . Of course you could talk to a person . . . I sat with cord in my hand at all times . . . but . . . there is always a way to do things. . . . I could talk to a person on either side of me and never look at them or never turn my head and they talked to me the same way. . . . It's not that we were yelled at or anything. This is what we did. I talked to the person next door to me without even turning my head looking at them. . . . We could talk and the supervisor would not even know you're talking. Because no one could, no one will stop me from talking. [laughter] I guess I would have been fired. [laughter] . . . there are always ways to get around anyone . . . it's just how you do it.[4]

Holton learned how to cope in a disciplined manner.[5] She did not feel pressured because she had found a release valve, as she has probably done in all the jobs she has had since operating.

When they did not quit, many women engaged in another form of passive resistance: "playing" the Absence Control Plan. The plan is a progression of five stages leading to termination. Every absence (of any number of days) creates a step that has to be cleared by a three-month period without another absence, otherwise that step advances to the next one. Employees take off sick days, get paid, and wait until their step clears before they are absent again. In response, the company has introduced obligatory visits to its medical offices and other regulations to prevent employees from manipulating the system. Managerial discretion has been instituted, which can hurt someone with genuine problems related to health, child care, or other causes. But for those who use absence as a means of resistance, the plan merely controls the frequency, not the number, of their absences.

More overt forms of resistance include willfully performing work incorrectly, or simply not doing it. The narrow management/worker ratio precludes the effectiveness of this tactic. If discovered, the individual would certainly be punished and made an example. Alternatively, employees sometimes perform their tasks strictly according to the procedures described by the "Bell System Practices" (manuals that tell how to do everything from climbing stairs to using an oscilloscope). Such actions significantly increase the time to complete any task.

On the shop floor, stewards initiate grievances for all types of work-related pressures. Often, they advocate medical and pay benefits for employees victimized by substance abuse. And, of course, operators have participated in slowdowns, wildcat strikes, and other more militant actions when they believed management had committed some especially grievous act. However heroic, these spontaneous individual and group acts of resistance have not altered the impact of technology on telephone operators' work. Sadly, black operators, like white women before them, never enjoyed the union leadership required to protect their jobs and their work process.

Before the 1980s, upper-level union leaders did not even contemplate strikes or other more militant actions against the introduction of new technologies. More recently, the CWA has acknowledged that "historically, American unions have left the choice to management. We traded control of technology for better wages. Today this trade-off is no longer in our best interest. Choices about the type of technology to be used are too important to leave solely to management. Left in their hands, new technology can be a potent weapon used to destroy union jobs and union security."[6] Although union leaders' interest in preserving their own jobs is painfully apparent in this admission, the CWA's leadership by the mid-1980s instituted a training program on technological change. Designed for union activists, the course espoused an ideology and an ambitious course of action that remain goals at the start of the twenty-first century.

The instructor's manual, for example, stated clearly that workers should have some control over the introduction of new technology, and it outlined a list of strategies and tactics that included an innovative set of demands. With the aim of increasing "worker and union involvement in new technology," making jobs "meaningful," and sharing the "benefits of changes," the manual proposed "redesigning work," "legislative and political action," and community "coalition building" in addition to the usual collective bargaining demands for training, a shorter workweek, and advance notice of the introduction of new technologies.[7]

Whatever the merits of these new strategies and tactics, they may have come too late for telephone operators. The human telephone operator is almost extinct. The few who still exist work at electronic speeds, under both human and inhuman supervision. Machines time how long they take to answer and complete calls. Supervisors monitor what they say to customers. Operators are still confined to their positions, unable to leave or disconnect themselves from the position without their supervisors' permission. Lunches, relief periods, days off, and vacations are all scheduled by the "traffic curve," not by human needs. Personal contact has been made completely unrewarding by the thirty-second time limit for getting the customer off the line. And, Directory Assistance operators face an even deeper dehumanization because they are forced to allow electronic voices to complete their sentences.

The technological deskilling and degradation of operators' work is only one example of what is happening to telephone workers. Craft work, formerly dominated by men, as well as all types of female clerical work are increasingly under technological assault. Behind their technological barriers, postdivestiture telephone companies appear invincible to strikes and other forms of resistance. As they enter the twenty-first century, telephone workers are still disgruntled about how the machines are taking over their jobs, scheduling their lunches, timing their breaks, tracking their whereabouts, measuring their productivity, and defeating their strikes. The CWA and other unions that represent telephone workers must not only adopt new demands, they must find new ways to bring their aims into existence.

Hence, the study of Bell System telephone operators can be instructive because it contributes another paradigm for analyzing race, gender, and technology in the workplace. Telephone operators' experiences inform us about the obstacles to creating and maintaining avenues of redress in a workplace in which continuity and change occur in relation to the impact of technology. As service goals required more efficient machines, Bell System managers expanded and contracted possibilities for operators' initiative and judgment while they never lost sight of the quest to control workers with technology and organizational structure. For well over a century, AT&T executives used race and gender ideologies to restrain the development of an awareness of genuine common interests among workers. Under varying circumstances, managers also used paternalism, racial exclusion, and gender segregation when it was convenient to do so. Consequently, women were either technologically displaced, or the job opportunities that opened to women as a result of new technologies did not change the sexual and racial division of labor that relegated women to lower-paid, repetitive, machine-paced, dead-end jobs.

As social and economic conditions permitted, operators accepted, accommodated, or resisted management's goals and strategies. The historical dynamic between managerial aims and telephone operators' responses illustrate that ideas that people bring to work about race, class, and gender are important in shaping both an integrated and segregated workplace. From vastly different class perspectives and objectives, white managers and workers shared similar ideas about race and gender. As a result, management could use racial and gender exclusion as a reward and inclusion as a threat to workers' job security. Simultaneously, the construction of a gendered and racial identity for operators inhibited their ability to resist not only management's policies, but the craft ideology of male-dominated trade unions.[8]

Telephone operators' history suggests that unions, as they have previously existed, may not be the best ideological and organizational structure for all workers. Nineteenth-century strategies and tactics designed to protect crafts deteriorated into twentieth-century methods of safeguarding union recognition, economic gains, and white male jobs. Women and people of color benefited from these methods if they were among the small numbers who entered the more powerful unions. For the most part, however, trade union definitions of skill, priorities for bargaining, and methods of resistance were inappropriate for addressing telephone operators' issues. Consequently, the unions' failure to develop an effective strategy to defend operators' jobs meant that unions were virtually unprepared when technological change threatened male telephone jobs.

The CWA's new outlook does represent some progress, but on the question of technology it is clear that workers must be in on the conceptualization of new technology as opposed to merely choosing from among the options that management creates. The postdivestiture proliferation of new telephone companies requires that unions insist on this level of participation.[9]

NOTES

Preface

1 After a period of adjustment, we [craftswomen] began to explore the building. Often we heard rumors about the operators. One had died because she was not permitted to go to the bathroom. Another had miscarried for the same reason. They had a company union, and they wanted to join ours. Occasionally, we would see an operator in the vending machine room when we worked nights—they were always hurried. We never got to know them. I noticed that they were mostly young black women.

2 When overtime was scarce, this meant that women could not qualify for the work. During this early period we were not particularly resentful because most of us made more money than we ever had in any other job.

3 In essence, I had moved from the secondary labor market into the subordinate primary labor market as described by David M. Gordon, Richard Edwards, and Michael Reich, *Segmented Work, Divided Workers: The Historical Transformation of Labor in the United States* (New York: Cambridge University Press, 1982).

Introduction

1 The Bell System was composed of American Telephone and Telegraph Company (AT&T) and twenty-two associated companies that provided service throughout the United States. This study does not include the history of the operators who worked for Independent companies.

2 Venus Green, "The Impact of Technology Upon Women's Work in the Telephone Industry, 1880–1980," Ph.D. Diss., Columbia University, 1990. Studies related specifically to the telephone, technology, culture, and society include articles in Ithiel de Sola Pool, ed., *The Social Impact of the Telephone* (Cambridge, Mass.: MIT Press, 1977); Alden Atwood, "Telephony and Its Cultural Meanings in Southeastern Iowa, 1900–1917," Ph.D. Diss., University of Iowa, 1984; Claude S. Fischer, "'Touch Someone': The Telephone Industry Discovers Sociability," *Technology and Culture* 29 (January 1988): 32–61; Carolyn Marvin, *When Old Technologies Were New* (New York: Oxford University Press, 1988); and Claude S. Fischer, *America Calling* (Berkeley: University of California Press, 1992). Lana F. Rakow, *Gender on the Line: Women, the Telephone, and Community Life* (Urbana: University of Illinois Press, 1992) and Michèle Martin, *Hello Central? Gender, Technology, and Culture in the Formation of Telephone Systems* (Montreal: McGill-Queen's University Press, 1991) discuss the role of women in shaping the uses of the telephone.

3 This study focuses on sexism and racism directed mainly against African Americans, but Native Americans, Mexican Americans, Puerto Ricans, and other Spanish-surnamed Americans, as well as homosexuals, all filed discrimination charges against the Bell System. The usual anti-immigrant and racist ideology barred other "minorities," but homophobia invoked explicit regulations. For example, in 1966, New Jersey

Bell decided on some "basic rules" to follow in considering applications by either sex for jobs traditionally dominated by the other. One manager stated the policy: "We will not hire a man to fill a job normally held by a female if the applicant is seeking the job solely *to satisfy an emotional condition* or is applying as a 'test case' " (my emphasis). During the mid-1960s, it was still socially acceptable to explain homosexuality as a "psychological" problem. See G.W.G., "Problems Under Title VII of the Civil Rights Act of 1964," February 14, 1966, Records of the Equal Employment Opportunity Commission, Record Group 403, National Archives (hereafter EEOC), Box 99, Folder "Miscellany," R-1054, p. 3. Without the appropriate legal protections, one man, Kenneth E. Nash, filed charges of sex discrimination (instead of antigay) after he was denied a position as a directory assistance operator. In his charges, he stated: "I passed the test but during the interview I indicated that I was homosexual. They refused to consider me further for this reason. I belive [sic] I was not hired because of sex—male." It is more likely that he was not hired because of his sexuality, but no provision within EEOC guidelines allowed him to protest that fact. See Case File No. TSf1-8845, September 16, 1970, EEOC, Box 109.

4   See Sharon Hartman Strom, *Beyond the Typewriter: Gender, Class, and the Origins of Modern American Office Work, 1900–1930* (Urbana: University of Illinois Press, 1992). According to Strom, office managers actually requested "white-skinned [young women] with thin and straight mouth[s]," p. 400.

5   See essays in Martha Blaxall and Barbara Reagan, eds., *Women and the Workplace: The Implications of Occupational Segregation* (Chicago: University of Chicago Press, 1976); Donald J. Treiman and Heidi I. Hartman, eds., *Women, Work, and Wages: Equal Pay for Jobs of Equal Value* (Washington, D.C.: National Academy Press, 1981); Barbara F. Reskin, *Sex Segregation in the Workplace: Trends, Explanations, Remedies* (Washington, D.C.: National Academy Press, 1984). Barbara F. Reskin and Patricia A. Roos, *Job Queues, Gender Queues: Explaining Women's Inroads into Male Occupations* (Philadelphia: Temple University Press, 1990), use the concept of labor, job, and gender queues to explain the feminization of male jobs. "Labor queues order groups of workers in terms of their attractiveness to employers, and job queues rank jobs in terms of their attractiveness to workers," p. 29.

6   Margery W. Davies, *Woman's Place Is at the Typewriter: Office Work and Office Workers, 1870–1930* (Philadelphia: Temple University Press, 1982), suggests that the availability of young, common-school-educated women who would work for low wages led to the feminization of clerical work. Ruth Milkman, *Gender at Work: The Dynamics of Job Segregation by Sex During World War II* (Urbana: University of Illinois Press, 1987), looks at women workers in the manufacturing sector (auto and electrical) and criticizes other theories of sex segregation for paying insufficient attention to "the effect of industrial structure on the sexual division of labor and on the struggles that take place over 'woman's place' in the labor market," p. 7. Milkman claims that regardless of workers' efforts, managers insisted on a sex-segregated workplace. See Alice Kessler-Harris, *Out to Work: A History of Wage-Earning Women in the United States* (New York: Oxford University Press, 1982), for a general discussion of how,

after the introduction of new machinery, women were hired into areas of work formerly dominated by men. Articles in Reskin and Roos; Cynthia Cockburn, *Brothers: Male Dominance and Technological Change* (London: Pluto Press, 1983); and Barbara S. Burnell, *Technological Change and Women's Work Experience: Alternative Methodological Perspectives* (Westport, Conn.: Bergin & Garvey, 1993), all argue that in the workplaces they examined, new technologies facilitated the feminization of male occupations but did not decrease sex segregation because men would leave the occupations when women entered.

7 Here I am using David Gartman's distinction between forms of control "beyond that necessitated by mere production" (repressive) and that which is necessary to increase the "productivity of labor" (nonrepressive). As Gartman states, this difference is "analytic" not "physical or organizational." Gartman, *Auto Slavery: The Labor Process in the American Automobile Industry, 1897–1950* (New Brunswick, N.J.: Rutgers University Press, 1986), p. 8.

8 Harry Braverman's *Labor and Monopoly Capital: The Degradation of Work in the Twentieth Century* (New York: Monthly Review Press, 1974) is the seminal work and the point of departure on the degradation of work. Braverman has argued that employers used scientific management in conjunction with new technologies to degrade and deskill work by separating "conception from execution." Other labor historians have tested Braverman's thesis in different workplaces and have arrived at similar conclusions. See the essays in Andrew Zimbalist, ed., *Case Studies on the Labor Process* (New York: Monthly Review Press, 1979); David Noble, *Forces of Production: A Social History of Industrial Automation* (New York: Knopf, 1984); Harley Shaiken, *Work Transformed: Automation and Labor in the Computer Age* (Lexington, Mass.: D. C. Heath, 1986). Braverman's thesis was challenged and modified by writers who expanded definitions of skill, evaluated governmental/political influences on technological development, and analyzed workers' behavior to determine the workers' agency in accepting, resisting, and transforming managerial control. Among this group are Kenneth Kusterer, *Know-how on the Job: The Important Working Knowledge of "Unskilled" Workers* (Boulder, Colo.: Westview Press, 1978); Charles Sabel, *Work and Politics: The Division of Labor in Industry* (Cambridge: Cambridge University Press, 1982); Larry Hirschhorn, *Beyond Mechanization* (Cambridge, Mass.: MIT Press, 1984); and Michael Burawoy, *Manufacturing Consent: Changes in the Labor Process Under Monopoly Capitalism* (Chicago: University of Chicago Press, 1979). Feminist scholars have criticized labor process literature for omitting gender from their analyses. See note 13.

9 Referring to telephone operators specifically, labor historians have argued that AT&T introduced automatic switching to replace operators and to intimidate the ones who remained. See Maurine Weiner Greenwald, *Women, War, and Work: The Impact of World War I on Women Workers in the United States* (Westport, Conn.: Greenwood Press, 1980), pp. 230–31; Amy Sue Bix, *Inventing Ourselves Out of Jobs: America's Debate Over Technological Unemployment, 1929–1981* (Baltimore: Johns Hopkins University Press, 2000), pp. 22–26; and Stephen H. Norwood, *Labor's Flaming Youth:*

Telephone Operators and Worker Militancy, 1878–1923 (Urbana: University of Illinois Press, 1990), pp. 254–65. More recently, Kenneth Lipartito has challenged the labor control argument. He states that enormous growth along with system complexities were the primary reasons for the introduction of automatic switching, not labor control. See Kenneth Lipartito, "When Women Were Switches: Technology, Work, and Gender in the Telephone Industry, 1890–1920," *American Historical Review* 99 (October 1994): 1075–1111.

10   After Braverman, many scholars sought to refine various points of interpretation regarding the interconnections among skill, work degradation, and workers' control. David Montgomery, *Workers' Control in America: Studies in the History of Work, Technology, and Labor Struggles* (New York: Cambridge University Press, 1979), challenged the idea that managers have unlimited power and argued that when workers resist, managerial aims are transformed. In *The Fall of the House of Labor: The Workplace, the State, and American Labor Activism, 1865–1925* (New York: Cambridge University Press, 1987), Montgomery examines not only the actions of skilled workers but the actions of common laborers and factory operatives in their struggle for control of work and the workplace. Richard Edwards, in his *Contested Terrain: The Transformation of the Workplace in the Twentieth Century* (New York: Basic Books, 1979), portrayed the workplace as a scene of continuous conflict in which various managerial methods of control (simple, technical, and bureaucratic) evolved. David Noble weighed the importance of profitability, efficiency, deskilling, and the need for control over the workplace as influences on managerial decisions to design and implement new technologies. In his study of numerically controlled machine tools, he concluded that managers' desire for control over the workplace was paramount. See Noble, *Forces of Production*. In a later study of the same industry, Shaiken, *Work Transformed*, arrived at a similar conclusion. David Gordon, Richard Edwards, and Michael Reich, *Segmented Work, Divided Workers: The Historical Transformation of Labor in the United States* (New York: Cambridge University Press, 1982), refined Richard Edwards's (*Contested Terrain*) argument to include the notion that managers sought to control the workplace with a division of the working class based on varying levels of opportunity—market segmentation. Workers compete in either primary markets (which through strong unions offer job security, higher pay, health and other benefits—mostly white men) or secondary markets (women, "minorities," and the unskilled have few of the benefits of those in the primary unionized sector). They argue that workers divided by sex, skill, and race are more easily controlled.

11   For an elaboration on the construction of the servant image, see Venus Green, " 'Goodbye Central': Automation and the Decline of 'Personal Service' in the Bell System, 1878–1921," *Technology and Culture* 36 (October 1995): 912–49.

12   For examples of the argument that cheap labor stalled the introduction of labor-saving technologies, see Gary Kulik, "Black Workers and Technological Change in the Birmingham Iron Industry, 1881–1931," in Gary Fink and Merl E. Reed, eds., *Southern Workers and Their Unions: Selected Papers, the Second Southern Labor History Conference, 1977* (Westport, Conn.: Greenwood Press, 1981); and Roger Waldinger,

"Another Look at the International Ladies' Garment Worker's Union: Women, Industry Structure, and Collective Action," in Ruth Milkman, ed., *Women, Work and Protest* (Boston: Routledge & Kegan Paul, 1985).

13   Feminist scholars who have analyzed the impact of technology on women's work in a variety of occupations, especially clerical work, have come to similar conclusions. Most question technological determinism but agree that technological development is gendered in favor of men and therefore reinforces sex segregation and powerlessness in the workplace. New technologies, they argue, will have different consequences for men and women workers. Women are likely to suffer loss of jobs, lower pay, greater deskilling, and loss of autonomy and control. Despite this grim picture, they also employ the concept of "social shaping of technology" to assert that women are not passive in this process. Even though men create the new technologies and women operate them, it is in the actual use of the machines that women can sometimes change the technology's original purpose. For many examples of this literature, see Reskin and Roos; Burnell; Cockburn; Webster; articles in Barbara Drygulski Wright, ed., *Women, Work, and Technology: Transformations* (Ann Arbor: University of Michigan Press, 1987); Heidi I. Hartmann, Robert E. Kraut, and Louise A. Tilly, eds., *Computer Chips and Paper Clips: Technology and Women's Employment*, vol. 1 (Washington, D.C.: National Academy Press, 1986); Heidi I. Hartmann, ed., *Computer Chips and Paper Clips: Technology and Women's Employment*, vol. 2 (Washington, D.C.: National Academy Press, 1987); and Joan Rothschild, ed., *Machina Ex Dea: Feminist Perspectives on Technology* (New York: Pergamon Press, 1983).

1. "Hello Central": The Beginning of a New Industry

1   For histories of the Bell System, see J. Warren Stehman, *The Financial History of the American Telephone and Telegraph Company* (Boston: Houghton Mifflin, 1925); N. R. Danielian, *AT&T: The Story of Industrial Conquest* (New York: Vanguard Press, 1939); Joseph G. Goulden, *Monopoly* (New York: G. P. Putnam's Sons, 1968); John Brooks, *Telephone: The First Hundred Years* (New York: Harper & Row, 1975); Horace Coon, *American Tel & Tel: The Story of a Great Monopoly* (New York: Longmans, Green, 1939); Robert W. Garnet, *The Telephone Enterprise: The Evolution of the Bell System's Horizontal Structure, 1876–1909* (Baltimore: Johns Hopkins University Press, 1985); Neil H. Wasserman, *From Invention to Innovation: Long Distance Telephone Transmission at the Turn of the Century* (Baltimore: Johns Hopkins University Press, 1985); George David Smith, *The Anatomy of a Business Strategy: Bell, Western Electric, and the Origins of the American Telephone Industry* (Baltimore: Johns Hopkins University Press, 1985), Kenneth Lipartito, *The Bell System and Regional Business: The Telephone in the South, 1877–1920* (Baltimore: Johns Hopkins University Press, 1989).

2   M. D. Fagen, ed., *A History of Engineering and Science in the Bell System: The Early Years (1875–1925)* (N.p.: Bell Telephone Laboratories, 1975), pp. 9, 25–27.

3   Stehman, p. 8, and J. E. Kingsbury, *The Telephone and Telephone Exchanges: Their Invention and Development* (London: Longmans, Green, 1915), p. 180.

4   Kingsbury, p. 179.

5   Elisha Gray and Amos E. Dolbear each had patented devices for improvements to the "harmonic telegraph."

6   Joseph C. Goulden, *Monopoly* (New York: G. P. Putnam's Sons, 1968), p. 36.

7   Smith, p. 47. Blake's transmitter was "clearer in sound and easier to adjust than Edison's. . . ." On Francis Blake's death in 1912, AT&T President Theodore N. Vail said, "Mr. Blake's invention not only came opportunely, but was so superior to all other transmitters then in existence, that it soon became a very large factor in the upbuilding of the Bell System as it is today." AT&T Annual Report, New York, March 19, 1913, p. 39.

8   From 1878 to 1898, the Bell companies filed more than 600 patent infringement suits against various would-be telephone inventors. Goulden, p. 41. For an analysis of how AT&T used patents to monopolize and control the telephone industry, see David F. Noble, *America By Design: Science, Technology, and the Rise of Corporate Capitalism* (New York: Oxford University Press, 1977).

9   Fagen, pp. 31–32.

10   Ibid., p. 120.

11   Critical innovations such as loading coils (1900), mechanical repeaters (1906), vacuum tube amplifiers (1907), and the adoption of underground cables gradually created a transcontinental service. Fagen, p. 34.

12   Richard Gabel, "The Early Competitive Era in Telephone Communication, 1893–1920," *Law and Contemporary Problems*, Spring 1969, pp. 3893–94.

13   Gabel, p. 3899.

14   Stehman, pp. 60–61.

15   Alfred D. Chandler, *The Visible Hand: The Managerial Revolution in American Business* (Cambridge, Mass.: Harvard University Press, 1977), p. 201. Vail spent two periods in the industry. The first was from 1878 to 1887 when he had been general manager of ABT and later president of AT&T. The second was from 1907 to 1919 when he was president of AT&T. In 1902 he also served on the AT&T board of directors. John Brooks, p. 124.

16   By 1913, thirty-four states had some type of public utility supervision of the telephone industry. In 1917, more than forty states, at least eight cities, and parts of Canada made provisions for the regulation of the business. Federal regulation that placed the telephone industry, a public utility, under the authority of the Interstate Commerce Commission was established by an amendment to the Act to Regulate Commerce in 1910. Stehman, pp. 166–67.

17   Coon, p. 137–38.

18   Stehman, p. 153.

19   Competing Independents allied with the Bell System in 1921 to request Congress to pass the Willis-Graham Act to modify the Kingsbury Commitment to allow "the merger or consolidation of competing telephone companies." Stehman, p. 153, Gabel, pp. 3902–3.

20   Licensees could no longer go directly to Western Electric to order equipment. Orders first had to be approved by AT&T's Engineering Department. Coon, pp. 104–5.

21 In 1910, for instance, the combined AT&T and WECO engineering departments consisted of 192 engineers, whereas in 1916, 959 men were engaged in theoretical experimentation. Danielian, p. 105. In 1919, AT&T's engineering department was expanded into two departments, one for operation and engineering, and the other exclusively for development and research. In 1924, AT&T and WECO consolidated all of their engineering into Bell Telephone Laboratories. Coon, p. 198–99.

22 See Noble, *America By Design*, for an excellent analysis and elaboration of this point.

23 Predecessors to the first genuine telephone switchboard included the use of burglar alarm and telegraph wires connected to Bell phones in private homes, drugstores, and other public locations. These early systems did not provide constant telephone service, which alleviated the need for a trained operator. Fagen, pp. 476–77, and Frederick Leland Rhodes, *Beginnings of Telephony* (New York: Harper and Bros., 1929), p. 149.

24 Emma M. Nutt, "Reminiscences," enclosed with a letter to W. L. Richards, dated February 15, 1925. AT&T Archives, Box 1124.

25 Ellen Considine, another pioneer operator, claimed that "the majority of messages were repeated by the operators." J. Leigh Walsh, *Connecticut Pioneers in Telephony* (New Haven, Conn.: Pioneers of America, 1950), p. 168.

26 Switchboard development involved different switchboards and improvements which are far too numerous to detail here. This study analyzes the impact of the major inventions on operators and their work process.

27 Election results, sports scores, time, weather, local news, fire, police, and other information services, as well as special exchanges for "bankers and brokers" or "produce and commission merchants," were among the conveniences offered. See National Convention of Telephone Companies held at Niagara Falls, N.Y., September 7–9, 1880. Record of the Organization and First Meeting of the National Telephone Exchange Association (hereafter the proceedings of the meetings of this group are referred to as NTEA). Report by Henry W. Pope, general superintendent, Metropolitan Telephone and Telegraph Company, p. 160, and Venus Green, " 'Goodbye Central': Automation and the Decline of 'Personal Service' in the Bell System, 1878–1921," *Technology and Culture* 36 (October 1995): 9–12.

28 R. T. Barrett, "The Changing Years as Seen from the Switchboard: Part 7, Personalized Service and Public Relations," *Bell Telephone Quarterly* 14 (October 1935): 278.

29 Poor signaling, transmission difficulties, primitive switchboards, and various kinds of electrical interference frequently required that operators transmit conversations verbally and repeatedly reconnect poor connections and cutoffs. For a discussion of the terms "social abilities" and "emotional labor," see Cobble, pp. 5–6.

30 Bell System authorities knew well the importance of operators' skills and called for schools to better train and discipline operators. See for example, Charles E. Scribner, "The Multiple Switchboard System, Its Requirements and Its Limitations," a paper read at the Switchboard Conference in 1887, pp. 48–49.

31   For a discussion of how gender determines skill in the workplace, see Anne Phillips, and Barbara Taylor, "Sex and Skill: Notes Toward a Feminist Economics," *Feminist Review* 6 (October 1980): 79–88. Phillips and Taylor argue (p. 79) that "the classification of women's jobs as unskilled and men's jobs as skilled or semi-skilled frequently bears little relation to the actual amount of training or ability required for them. . . . Far from being an objective economic fact, skill is often an ideological category imposed on certain types of work by virtue of the sex and power of the workers who perform it."

32   Walsh, p. 168.

33   "When 'The Voice with the Smile' Arrived," *Telephone Review* 14, no. 10 (October 1923): 311.

34   "Proud of My Long Service," *Telephone Review* 25 (January 1933): 11.

35   Central Union Telephone Company's "Local Operator Examination of Bulletin No. 2" contained sixty nonmultiple choice questions, among them the following:

No. 2. What are the seven essential elements of good and satisfactory service? Give them in order of their importance.
No. 34. How do you give a number over a call-circuit? How would you give 105-2?
No. 40. Is an operator supposed to assist a neighboring operator in making disconnections? In making connections?
No. 56. What does green mark, at right hand side of jack, denote?
Central Union Telephone Company, "Local Operator Examination of Bulletin No. 2," AT&T Archives, Box 1379.

36   Electricians, inventors and other technical men developed and manufactured numerous switchboards "almost exclusively in small workshops operated virtually on an artisan basis." Robert J. Chapuis, *100 Years of Telephone Switching (1878–1978), Part 1: Manual and Electromechanical Switching (1878–1960s)* (New York: North-Holland, 1982), p. 49.

37   See Theodore N. Vail's (then general manager of the Bell Company) letter of June 1879 to H. W. Pope (general superintendent of the New York Telephone Company), quoted in R. T. Barrett, "The Changing Years as Seen from the Switchboard: Part 3, Why Women Entered the Telephone Service," *Bell Telephone Quarterly* 14 (April 1935): 114.

38   Lockwood, "The Evolution of the Telephone Switchboard," paper presented at the meeting of the American Institute of Electrical Engineers, New York, January 23, 1903, p. 4, AT&T Archives, Box 1056.

39   Fagen, p. 473. I.e., vibrating bells and buzzers, simple switches, and annunciator drops and relays.

40   Rhodes, pp. 168–69.

41   Barrett, "The Changing Years as Seen from the Switchboard," p. 116. This was the Chinnock board installed in New York City in 1879. "New England central offices utilized the Williams board while the Gilliland and Post boards were popular in the Middle West, sometimes in New England and in Canada. Law boards (although they

had originated and achieved perfection of operation in New York) were used in the South and Southwest."

42 Lockwood, "The Evolution of the Telephone Switchboard," pp. 6–7.

43 Walsh, p. 133.

44 Fagen, p. 491.

45 Fagen, p. 494. This is what the Bell System considered the standard reach for an operator.

46 A trunk is a line used to connect subscribers either on switchboards in a central office not connected to each other or to switchboards in distant central offices. Trunks thus provided the means for communication between two central offices. Later on, tandem offices, which consisted only of trunks going to different central offices, were installed. Tandems obviated the need for each central office to have direct trunks to every other central office.

47 A simple call from Manhattan to Brooklyn required the subscriber's operator to make the connection to the toll board where the toll operator would determine what trunk to use and make the connection to the distant incoming toll operator by cranking a hand generator to signal. The incoming operator would determine if a direct connection could be made, or if another trunk was required. For a direct connection, the call would be transferred to the incoming subscriber's operator, who made the final connection. The recording operator's desk would receive the call to take down the appropriate information for billing purposes. Disconnecting this call required reversing this noisy process.

48 Henry Metzger, quoted at the Switchboard Conference, 1887, p. 91.

49 NTEA, April 1881, p. 140. Hall said operators in large exchanges handled 23 subscribers, while those in small exchanges handled 43. NTEA September 1881, pp. 46–48. In New York City (23 subscribers to an operator), it took 60 seconds to make local connection. In Clinton and Lyons, Iowa (106 subscribers to an operator), it took 2.7 seconds to make a local connection.

50 Thomas D. Lockwood quoted at the Switchboard Conference, 1887, p. 17.

51 Edward J. Hall, president of the Buffalo Exchange, "Rates Committee Report," NTEA, 1880, p. 165, and C. N. Fay, president and general manager of Chicago Bell, "Central Office Systems and Apparatus, and Exchange Committee Report," NTEA, September 1882, p. 48.

52 See Milton Mueller, "The Switchboard Problem: Scale, Signaling, and Organization in Manual Telephone Switching, 1877–1897," *Technology and Culture* 30 (July 1989), 534–60.

53 As early as 1880, Bell System executives lamented that rates throughout the country were insufficient, and that it cost even more to provide service for large city subscribers who paid the highest fees. Edward J. Hall quoted at the NTEA, 1880, pp. 164–65, and Thomas D. Lockwood, "Ten Years of Progress in Practical Telephony," paper read at NTEA, 1887, p. 50.

54 Leroy B. Firman, general manager of the American District Telegraph Company in Chicago, experimented with various designs in late 1878 and installed two

boards at 118 La Salle Street, Chicago, in early 1879. Patents for the Multiple were not granted until 1882, and the board itself did not come into general use until the late 1880s. Fagen, p. 490.

55   Under the authorization and guidance of AT&T, The Metropolitan Telephone and Telegraph Company built and installed a board of that size at the Cortlandt Street Exchange in New York City in 1887. Though it was not filled to capacity until the turn of the century, this board demonstrated the full potentiality of the Multiple principle. Fagen, pp. 493, 496, and Chapuis, p. 55.

56   C. H. Barney, quoted at the NTEA, 1886, p. 60.

57   The reports gave no reason for the reductions in the number of subscribers per operator between 1886 and 1887. Nevertheless, it remains clear that the Multiple outperformed the Standard in these two areas.

58   John J. Carty, "The Multiple System of Switchboards," a paper read at the NTEA, 1885, pp. 147–48.

59   Improvements such as signal lamps and common batteries that dramatically changed the physical work content will be discussed later.

60   C. H. Wilson, quoted at the Switchboard Conference, 1887, p. 92.

61   Thomas D. Lockwood, "Conclusions Reached by Conference," synopsis of the Switchboard Conference, 1887, p. 5, and Wilson, quoted at the Switchboard Conference, 1887, p. 92.

62   Charles E. Scribner and others, quoted at the Switchboard Conference, 1887, pp. 40–50.

63   For the individual subscriber the most significant and troublesome problem occurred in the case of a false busy-line indication caused when dirt became lodged in the spring contacts of the "series" wired jacks. An exchange of 5,000 subscribers had at least thirty-two different contact points for each line. If dirt or any other debris became lodged inside of a subscriber's jack on any section of the "Multiple," that subscriber was out of service on every section because it was difficult to isolate a short circuit. J. E. Kingsbury, *The Telephone and Telephone Exchanges: Their Invention and Development* (London: Longmans, Green, 1915), p. 339.

64   Switchboard Conference, 1887, p. 227.

65   Edward J. Hall to John E. Hudson, November 14, 1891, AT&T Archives, Box 1259.

66   Kingsbury, p. 355.

67   Hammond V. Hayes, "Mechanical Department Annual Report," March 19, 1894, p. 2, AT&T Archives, Box 2021. Hayes stated: "for this system it was necessary to design new apparatus throughout, including transmitters, receivers, bells, line and clearing out annunciators, also proper methods of protections."

68   Before centralized power supply, operators communicated with each other and with subscribers by means of a hand-cranked magneto generator, energized by local battery supplies for the operator in the central office, and for the subscriber at home. Fagen, p. 497.

69   Hammond V. Hayes, "Mechanical Department Annual Report," March 7,

1892, p. 3, AT&T Archives, Box 2021. Hayes stated that "an entirely new system of telephone exchange has been devised, in which the battery is placed at the central office with the telephone induction coil, the subscriber's apparatus consisting only of a bell, transmitter and receiver."

70   Telephone managers first discussed these lamps for telephone signaling in October 1891 at the second meeting of the Switchboard Committee. C. H. Wilson, general superintendent, Chicago Telephone Company, reported that lamps had been used for more than a year in Chicago for trunking indications between operators who made interexchange calls. Wilson, untitled paper read at the Switchboard Committee meeting, October 1891, pp. 327–34.

71   For trunk operators the introduction of lamps made it unnecessary to verbally attract the attention of a distant operator to disconnect, and these signals significantly decreased busy testing work. Fagen, p. 499.

72   R. B. Hill, "A Brief Survey of some of the Important Inventions that have been made in connection with the Art of Telephony in the United States," "The Automatic Hook Switch," p. 1, AT&T Archives, Box 1122.

73   Hammond V. Hayes, "Mechanical Department Annual Report," January 1, 1897, p. 2, AT&T Archives, Box 2021.

74   Kingsbury, p. 388.

75   Arthur Vaughn Abbott, "The Evolution of the Telephone Switch Board," *Electrical Engineering* 4 (September 1894): 112–13, AT&T Archives, Box 1266.

76   American Telephone and Telegraph Long Lines Department, "Telephone Company Administrative Practices" (a training course), September 1924, p. 213.

77   A toll call, for example, could occur between two exchanges in the same city or with a surrounding suburban area, while a short haul call could be at a greater distance within the same associated company or between thirty and fifty miles. A long haul call involved distances of more than 400 miles. Fees for these services decreased after 5 P.M. in graduated steps, so that service between midnight and 5 A.M. was the least expensive.

78   Transmission includes signaling, cabling, trunking, and other devices such as coils that made speech clearer.

79   A. S. Hibbard, "Some Practical Results in Long Distance Telephoning," paper delivered at the NTEA, September 1885, p. 63.

80   Walsh, p. 115.

81   The technical discoveries and applications that finally made transcontinental conversation possible in 1915 included hard-drawn copper wire (1877), metallic circuits (1881), underground cables (late 1880s), loading coils (1900), mechanical repeaters (1906), and vacuum tube amplifiers (1907). Cable improvements and other major developments such as carrier, radio transmission and phantom circuits also greatly advanced the science of transmission but are beyond the scope of this study.

82   Fagen, p. 616.

83   The solutions cost much more to manufacture and install than local plant. Aerial and underground cable construction over long distances required more work-

ers and more time to complete than the installation of a local switchboard. A. S. Hibbard, "Long Distance Telephoning, and the Present Operation of Toll Telephone Lines," p. 120.

84 Randi Simson, "Overseas Bridge Spans 56 Years of Memories: New York IOC 1927–1983," final issue of *IOC Magazine*, 1983. Thanks to Mrs. Anne H. Walden, a retired operator, who gave me this magazine.

85 Like local service, toll service required different types of arrangements depending on traffic volume. In small cities and towns, toll service could be provided by simply adding a toll board section to the local switchboard lineup. This section had a full subscriber "multiple" which permitted the operator to connect the subscriber directly with a toll circuit. In larger multioffice cities or toll centers a separate toll switchboard connected by trunks to the local switchboard provided the switching for long distances. Toll sections added to local lineup initially included several designs, i.e., 1B, No. 2, No. 9C, etc. These boards were replaced in the mid-1920s by No. 11. Fagen, pp. 642, 647.

86 Fagen, p. 643, and M. B. McDavitt, "Machine Switching and Revenue Accounting," p. VIII-2, AT&T Archives, Box 2051. A cordless toll board tried in Philadelphia in 1943 was discontinued after World War II.

87 Fagen, p. 617.

88 No source, including the official Bell System history of the company's own technology, discusses in any detail the evolution of toll switchboards. The Bell history discusses only two before 1925. Fagen, pp. 615–59.

89 A Multiple toll board, for example, multipled trunk lines instead of subscriber lines. The methods of operation included up to five operators, in contrast to the single operator required for a local connection.

90 A. S. Hibbard, "Some Practical Results in Long Distance Telephoning," paper delivered at the NTEA, September 1885, pp. 65–66.

91 Ibid., pp. 64–66.

92 For example, traffic engineers in 1922 estimated that the dispatch method increased the operating expense by 40 percent. AT&T still profited because there was an estimated reduction in annual circuit charges of $4.8 million and $1.1 million for the associated companies. E. A. Gray, "Development, Status and Application of the Dispatch Method," paper delivered at the Traffic Engineering Conference, December 1922, p. 205.

93 Fagen, pp. 34–35. Soon after AT&T became the parent Bell System company on December 30, 1899, executives saw the need for a special department to handle long distance service. On October 1, 1900, AT&T formed the Department of Long Distance Lines. The name was changed to the Long Lines Department on November 14, 1917.

94 AT&T, "Operating Rules," "approved to take effect December 1, 1904," and updated in January 1910, illustrate the latitude of operators' discretion within set procedures. Operators were ordered to change circuits, hold other operators on the line, and otherwise "locate and remove" troubles. AT&T, "Operating Rules. Instruc-

tions to Chief Operator," December 1, 1904, section titled "Instructions to Operators," pp. 14–17, AT&T Archives, Box 1309.

95   Long distance operators were subject to service observing and the same intense supervision local operators endured.

96   From 1923 to the introduction of customer direct distance dialing, the Bell
System maintained a policy of "personalizing the service." Managers aimed "to make
the toll service as a whole more pleasing to the customer . . . , and to remove every
possible source of irritation to the customer." They introduced a more flexible policy
of allowing the operator to tactfully address the customer by name in the process of
making a connection. In many instances, operators continued to perform special
favors for the more frequent users such as businessmen and others who used hotel
phones. "Further Improvements Are Made in the Toll Board Operating Methods and
Practices," *Headquarters Bulletin* 5 (February 1931): 6.

97   AT&T, "Operating Rules. Instructions to Chief Operator," December 1, 1904,
section titled "Instructions to Operators," p. 12.

98   AT&T, Long Lines Department, "Traffic Department Operating Instructions,"
October 1, 1917, p. G-7, AT&T Archives, Box 2055.

99   A recording operator had to closely follow the procedures, including abbreviations, to complete a ticket accurately. Nevertheless, as more operating methods came
into usage, she had to decide which method to use so that the ticket would be sent to
the proper outward operator.

100   Central Union Telephone Company, "Instructions for the Information and
Guidance of Toll Operating-Room Employes," Operating Bulletin, No. 4. August,
1904, pp. 19–21. There were more than thirty-six abbreviations: "by" for busy, "cf" for
cannot locate, "wh" for we have, etc.

101   Ibid., p. 8. In a section under Instructions for Information Bureau Clerks.

102   AT&T, Traffic Department, "Operating Instructions," Section G, "Time Allowances," p. G-57.

103   Fagen, p. 618.

104   Ibid.

105   Unpaid circuit time included the time that long distance lines were used to
pass the preliminary information to the distant end, to report on delays consequent to
busy lines, unavailable parties, etc., and the time when a long distance circuit was held
to insure its availability when the parties were ready to talk. At all times, the Bell
System worked to reduce this unpaid period either by new technology or new operating methods.

106   See Traffic Department Students' Text Book, March 1, 1912, which lists more
than twenty-five routines and the updated version dated December 24, 1914, which
lists more than forty routines. AT&T Archives, Box 2055.

107   "A morse down call is a call between two correspondents on a leased morse
wire to complete which the morse wire is taken down at the request of the party
calling. . . . may be completed over a local exchange telephone loop when the special

terminal loop is busy or in trouble." American Telephone and Telegraph Company Traffic Department, "Operating Instructions," section entitled "Instructions for Operators," p. 25.

108   Sherwood, "The Suburban Toll Line Problem," p. 24, AT&T Archives, Box 1376. Signaling for disconnections depended upon the type of switchboard and toll trunks. In magneto systems and if several through operators made connections, the outward operator rang the inward or through operators to disconnect the connections (the ringdown methods). After the introduction of common battery systems, lamps signals indicated to toll operators the need for disconnects. The "unguarded interval" when the subscriber's line could be connected to another call was removed by the introduction of a special tone test that indicated that the line was waiting for a long distance connection.

109   Sherwood, "The Suburban Toll Line Problem," p. 21.

110   AT&T Company Long Lines Department, "Telephone Company Administrative Practices," September 1924, p. 224, AT&T Archives, Box 1026.

111   J. L. R. Van Meter, "The Handling of Long Haul toll Traffic," in Proceedings of the Traffic Conference of Bell Telephone Companies, February 1905, p. 200. Before this method was adopted universally, an interim method ("Method 102") in which the inward operator made a skeleton ticket existed for a short time. The drive for standardization led to the abandonment of the interim method. Thereafter, operators only made an inward ticket for delayed, appointment, and collect calls. AT&T, Long Lines Department, "Telephone Company Administrative Practices," September 1924, p. 224.

112   The Morse wire (Method 104) and call circuit Methods 105, 106 and 107 sought to conserve toll circuit time by using call circuits. For a detailed and specific description of these methods, see Green, "The Impact of Technology Upon Women's Work in the Telephone Industry," chap. 9; E. A. Gray, "Development, Status and Application of the Dispatch Method," paper delivered at the Traffic Engineering Conference, December 1922, p. 205; Van Meter, "The Handling of Long Haul toll Traffic," pp. 203–5; AT&T Traffic Department "Operating Instructions," section titled "Instructions for Operators," p. 25; AT&T, Long Lines Department, "Telephone Company Administrative Practices," pp. 224–25, AT&T Archives, Box 1026.

113   D. S. Raynor, "Straightforward Trunking and Restricted Repetition: Service and Cost Results," paper delivered at the General Traffic Conference, November 1927, p. 1.

114   K. W. Waterson, "Improvement in Toll Service Through Combined Line and Recording Method," Bell Telephone Quarterly 5 (April 1926): 71–73.

115   Vice President and Chief Engineer Gherardi to AT&T President W. S. Gifford, April 1, 1927, p. 4, AT&T Archives, Box 54.

116   Fagen, p. 624.

117   Waterson, "The Functions and Management Problems of the Traffic Department," p. 60.

118   K. W. Waterson, "Review of Traffic Results for 1925 and Opportunities for Further Improvement," paper printed with the proceedings of the Bell System Plant and Engineering Conference, June 1926, p. 56. (Actually delivered at the Operating Conference at Absecon, May 1926.)

119   E. E. Browning Jr., "Toll Board Operation," paper presented at the General Traffic Conference, November 1927, p. 10.

120   Ibid., pp. 4–5.

121   Vice President and Chief Engineer Bancroft Gherardi to President W. S. Gifford, April 1, 1927, p. 4, AT&T Archives, Box 54.

122   American Telephone and Telegraph Company, Department of Operation and Engineering. "Combined Line and Recording Text Book," June 1, 1928, updated February 1, 1929, AT&T Archives, Box 2055.

123   In Ohio, for example, Bell Telephone Company operators received five weeks of CLR on the job training and practice, spending only an hour in the classroom daily. F. R. Eckley, "Meeting CLR Problems," paper presented at the General Traffic Conference, November 1927, p. 30. The introduction of CLR contributed to the eventual demise of operator training schools. By 1930, when practically the entire country had adopted CLR, Bell System managers realized that classroom training did not sufficiently prepare the student for the actual work. Classroom instruction and practice switchboards declined in usage. Instead, student operators received most of their toll training "at the toll board in the actual handling of commercial traffic." T. F. Davis Jr., "Toll Training Methods," a paper presented at the Toll Training Conference for Operating Men, May 1928, p. 3.

124   See reports and minutes of the National Telephone Exchange Association, 1887 Switchboard Conference, and the Switchboard Committee meeting where Bell executives discussed these issues privately.

125   Thomas D. Lockwood quoted at the Switchboard Committee meeting, July 1891, p. 14.

126   Edward J. Hall, vice president and general manager, American Telephone and Telegraph Company, quoted at the Switchboard Committee meeting, October 1891, p. 165.

127   Thomas D. Lockwood quoted at the Switchboard Committee meeting, October 1891, p. 166.

128   Hall, quoted at the Switchboard Committee meeting, October 1891, p. 117.

129   Switchboard Committee meeting, October 1891, pp. 113–22.

130   I. H. Farnham, quoted at the Switchboard Committee meeting, March 1892, p. 5.

131   At the 1887 Switchboard Conference, managers stated that operators' reach limited the size of the Multiple. Switchboard Conference, 1887, p. 41. These limits also affected how many subscribers could be placed upon the board because subscriber jacks occupied a lot of space. To overcome this problem, inventors created smaller jacks and plugs.

132   D. R. Henry to J. P. Davis, September 22, 1899, AT&T Archives, Box 1318.

133   John J. Carty to F. N. Bethell, July 26, 1915, AT&T Archives, Box 8.

134   AT&T Archives, Boxes 1353 and 1379, contain numerous letters under the heading "Operator's Chairs Development."

135   Managers even surveyed operators and used the findings to modify typewriters' chairs adopted in 1911. After operators complained that the backrests were "uncomfortable in that no support is given to the hips," engineers redesigned adjustable chairs in 1913. See J. J. Carty, chief engineer, to R. W. Devonshire, general manager, September 28, 1911, AT&T Archives, Box 1379, and Carty, October 12, 1913, AT&T Archives, Box 1379.

136   The Gilliland harness of 1880 weighed six pounds and rested on the operator's shoulder and waist. C. E. Scribner, "Log Fire Reminiscences of a Pioneer," *Western Electric News,* October 1927, p. 19, AT&T Archives, Box 1046.

137   Hammond V. Hayes to Joseph P. Davis, April 28, 1899. Hayes to John E. Hudson, May 26, 1899. A. S. Hibbard to Davis, April 19, 1899. Hayes to Davis, April 28, 1899. Hayes to Hudson, May 26, 1899. Thomas D. Lockwood to Hudson, June 15, 1899. These letters and others in this file show that some consideration was given to the operator at the same time that managers dealt with the business problem of efficiency. AT&T Archives, Box 1259.

138   H. D. McBride to Joseph P. Davis, August 20, 1903, AT&T Archives, Box 1331.

139   This type of information "gives the direction and general scope of the business," helps to "ascertain whether the operator is overcrowded or not," and also enables managers to "calculate with some degree of certainty what additional facilities were necessary." W. D. Sargent quoted at the Switchboard Conference, 1887, p. 212.

140   Later on, peg counts were used to part-time and swing-shift operators. At this point they were used in a simple straightforward manner. See H. W. Trafford, "Report on Chicago Express System," September 1, 1896, p. 23, for first mention of the idea to "hire operators by the hour," AT&T Archives, Box 1276. AT&T, Engineering Department, "Local Traffic Records, Bulletin No. 3," p. 1, AT&T Archives, Box 1359.

141   Switchboard Conference 1887, pp. 8, 75, 85–88.

142   Fagen, pp. 529–31.

143   A. S. Hibbard, quoted at the Switchboard Committee meeting, October 1891, p. 296.

144   Lockwood, "The Evolution of the Telephone Switchboard," p. 28.

145   Hammond V. Hayes noted that operators completed 500 calls daily on the Standard board, 800 on the Multiple, 1,000 on the Branch Terminal, and 1,400 on the latest Common Battery board. Hayes to John E. Hudson, March 27, 1899, AT&T Archives, Box 1329.

146   Lockwood, "The Evolution of the Telephone Switchboard," p. 23. Also John S. Stone to Hammond V. Hayes, June 1, 1896, AT&T Archives, Box 1259.

147   Hibbard quoted at the Traffic Conference, 1905, p. 89.

148   AT&T, Engineering Department, "Local Telephone Service, Bulletin No. 5," p. 1.

149   Central Union Telephone Company, "Rules and Instructions for the Guidance and Information of Managers and other Employes" (Chicago: 1888), passim, AT&T Archives, Box 1040.

150   Delaware and Atlantic Telephone and Telegraph Company, "Rules and Regulations, 1890," p. 1, AT&T Archives, Box 1028.

151   Ibid., p. 10.

152   Wiley W. Smith, general superintendent, Missouri and Kansas Telephone Company, quoted at the Switchboard Conference, 1887, p. 203.

153   Her duties: (1) To see that signals are answered promptly in the order of their importance, and that good team work is secured. (2) To assist in disconnections. (3) To relieve the operators of any details which will tend to prevent the prompt answering of signals. (4) To see that the established operating rules are properly observed. AT&T, Engineering Department, "Local Telephone Service, Bulletin No. 5," February 1903, p. 9, AT&T Archives, Box 1359.

154   At the 1887 Switchboard Conference, Lockwood explicitly stated that a competent man, not a boy, sufficiently mature so as not "to lose his balance of mind when thrown into such a bevy of feminine charms as we find in some of our offices" should be in charge of the operating room. Lockwood felt that the person in charge "should in all cases be a male" because electrical knowledge was required, and it was rare to find a woman capable of understanding it. He also thought "operators will be more readily amenable to proper discipline when exercised by and insisted upon by a man." Switchboard Conference, 1887, p. 202. Lockwood changed his attitude considerably by 1891, when he thought women chief operators should be in charge of men.

155   "Rules and Instructions," p. 1.

156   "Rules and Regulations," pp. 2, 6.

157   Other rules were directives regarding the chief operator's responsibilities, operator's tasks in connecting calls, maintaining the switchboard and customers' lines, reporting times and duration, ringing procedures, subscriber conversations, and pay station procedures. New York and New Jersey Telephone Company, "Instructions for the Guidance of Employes," January 1, 1893, p. 28, AT&T Archives, Box 1021.

158   The degree to which the Bell System sought to establish preset terminology was demonstrated in 1899 when New York Telephone's (Westchester division) prohibited the use of "Hello" for "any purpose or at any time." According to the Yonkers superintendent, the word was "not only meaningless," but it was confusing to the subscribers and also caused a delay in the service. Superintendent to L. W. Johnson, manager, Yonkers, N.Y., February 25, 1899, AT&T Archives, Box 1021.

159   Ibid., p. 31.

160   Ibid., p. 29.

161   AT&T, "Rules for the Employes of the American Telephone and Telegraph Company," in effect September 1, 1895, p. 6, AT&T Archives, Box 1014.

162   Ibid., p. 7.

163   Ibid., p. 6.

164   Central New York Telephone and Telegraph Company, "Rules for the Govern-

ment and Information of the Employes," in effect June 1, 1897, pp. 17–18, AT&T Archives, Box 1021.

165   Charles Cutler to John E. Hudson, June 2, 1893, AT&T Archives, Box 1257.

2. "Hello Girls": The Making of the Voice with a Smile

1   Under no conditions could operators relate information overheard in a conversation to a third party. The concept of "personal service" entailed strict confidentiality. Operators were specifically instructed "that all communications over the Company's lines must in all cases deemed to be private between the parties communicating." General Order no. 60, September 28, 1889, quoted in Jasper N. Keller, general manager, NET&T to Thomas Sherwin, president, NET&T, June 6, 1893, AT&T Archives, Box 1257.

2   Cecil W. MacKenzie, who became an operator on April 1, 1879, in Buffalo, claimed that boy operators, "of necessity, had to have some Morse or telegraph knowledge as when on late night duty we had to signal every half hour to show that we were awake." Cecil W. MacKenzie, "Early Days of Telephone in Buffalo, 1878–1926," typescript, p. 27, AT&T Archives, Box 1127.

3   For some time, long distance calls between Buffalo and Rochester were completed by sending a telegraph message to the distant end "telling them to 'cut in telephone' on the wire." Ibid.

4   Ibid., p. 29.

5   Ibid., p. 23.

6   Frank Rozelle, as quoted by Fred DeLand, "Telephone History, 1877–1908," volume I, book III, typescript, p. 4, AT&T Archives, Box 1109.

7   DeLand, p. 3.

8   R. T. Barrett as quoted in MacKenzie, p. 30.

9   John J. Carty, quoted by R. T. Barrett in MacKenzie, p. 29.

10   Katherine M. Schmitt, "I Was Your Old 'Hello' Girl," *Saturday Evening Post*, July 12, 1930, p. 121.

11   See NTEA, 1880, p. 160; and "Switchboard Meeting No. IV: Report," May 1892, p. 341, AT&T Archives.

12   For the feminization of telephone operating as a method of winning over subscribers, see Venus Green, "The Impact of Technology Upon Women's Work in the Telephone Industry, 1880–1989" (Ph.D. Diss., Columbia University, 1990). Other studies of telephone operators include a pioneering study of telephone operators by Maurine Weiner Greenwald, *Women, War, and Work: The Impact of World War I on Women Workers in the United States* (Westport, Conn.: Greenwood Press, 1980), which analyzes questions of female segregation and substitution in traditional male jobs in the context of the war; Stephen H. Norwood, *Labor's Flaming Youth: Telephone Operators and Worker Militancy, 1878–1923* (Urbana: University of Illinois Press, 1990), traces the rise and decline of unionism among operators; and Michèle Martin, *"Hello Central?" Gender, Technology, and Culture in the Formation of Telephone Systems* (Montreal: McGill-Queens University Press, 1991), in her history of early

Canadian operators, explores how women changed the intended uses of the telephone. Although Martin examines changes in work organization, her focus is on the larger society. The Greenwald and Norwood studies are limited to World War I and the immediate postwar era.

13 Nathaniel W. Lillie, "Reminiscences of the Telephone in Boston, 1877–1914," typescript, p. 32, AT&T Archives, Box 1116.

14 NTEA, 1880, p. 160.

15 Frank Rozelle as quoted in DeLand.

16 B. E. Sunny, quoted at the 1887 Switchboard Conference, p. 207.

17 MacKenzie, p. 28.

18 MacKenzie, p. 21, and Lillie, p. 32.

19 Lillie, p. 32.

20 Walsh, p. 133.

21 The International Brotherhood of Electrical Workers (IBEW), founded in 1891, first organized telephone workers who were their members and working as linemen or other craftsmen. IBEW first struck the telephone industry in St. Louis in 1898. John N. Schacht, *The Making of Telephone Unionism, 1920–1947* (New Brunswick, N.J.: Rutgers University Press, 1985), p. 7.

22 Throwing up the annunciators meant disconnecting the subscriber without acknowledging the call.

23 Switchboard Conference, 1887, pp. 74, 82–83.

24 Telephone "girls" and factory "girls" received low wages, but the first operators enjoyed considerably better working conditions, more control over the pace of their work, greater prestige, and possibilities for advancement. Other white-collar professions such as grammar school teaching had become oversaturated, while newly available office work and dry goods store clerking offered fewer opportunities for advancement. And the "extremely low status" of domestic work, another female-dominated field, could not satisfy the ambitions of a native-born white girl with a grammar school or high school education. See David M. Katzman, *Seven Days a Week: Women and Domestic Service in Industrializing America* (New York: Oxford University Press, 1978), for a detailed discussion of how the menial status of domestic workers deterred most women, even though the pay often compared favorably with the wages of the average woman worker.

25 See General Manager W. H. Eckert to Miss Luella Austin, January 12, 1880; General Manager W. H. Eckert to Miss Luella Austin, February 3, 1880; "Oldest Living Telephone 'Girl' Served in Cincinnati Exchange," *Southwest-Times Record*, May 16, 1926, 39, AT&T Archives, Box 1037.

26 Schmitt, "I Was Your Old 'Hello' Girl," pp. 18–19, 120–21.

27 R. T. Barrett, "The Changing Years as Seen from the Switchboard Part 5, Training Methods—Then and Now," *Bell Telephone Quarterly* 14 (July 1935): 203.

28 For examples of women who had as many as fifty years of service and who advanced in the Traffic, Accounting, and Commercial Departments, see Walsh, pp. 378–79; "Thirty Years Under the Blue Bell," *Telephone Review* 8 (July 1917): 166; M. A.

Jones, "Looking Backward," *Telephone Review* 8 (May 1917): 139; "She Made Friends by Being a Friend," *Telephone Review* 27 (July 1936): 8; and Anna Millett Higbee, "Early Telephone Day," typescript, pp. 1–5, AT&T Archives, Box 1015.

29   Nathaniel W. Lillie said that women managers in Boston offices "answered all calls, did the switching, looked after the messenger boys, and waited on the patrons who frequently called to telephone." Lillie, "Reminiscences of the Telephone in Boston, 1877–1914," typescript, p. 32, AT&T Archives, Box 1116.

30   The Independent competition sparked by the expiration of the first Bell patents in the 1890s created new types of services that men were not very successful at selling. The Chicago Telephone Company in an effort to promote its new party-line system in 1895 hired two women in addition to the male canvassers. The company found that when the women took "a telephone and transmitter in a hand bag," they got "an opportunity to present their case where a man could not." Memo to C. Jay French, American Bell Telephone Company general manager, May 2, 1895, AT&T Archives, Box 1276.

31   For example, Charles L. Smith, a black man and President Vail's protégé, was hired in the late 1880s and worked as the receptionist for the executive offices in Boston for more than twenty years. See Joseph A. Gately, "Telephone Reminiscences," 1939, pp. 20, 59, AT&T Archives, Box 1013.

32   Norwood, *Labor's Flaming Youth*, p. 42.

33   W. F. Cozad, superintendent of traffic, Colorado Telephone Company, made a trip East in 1904. He observed in New York City "a goodly number" of foreign-born operators. Cozad, "Notes on a Trip East," 1904, p. 55, AT&T Archives, Box 1044.

34   A picture of a black operator in Pittsburgh is dated 1891 in the AT&T Archives, and the 1900 census lists 11 "Negro" telephone and telegraph operators, a decrease from the fifty-six listed in 1890. It is probable that these "Negro" telephone and telegraph operators worked for the Independents. Black telephone operators also could have been working in black firms as PBX operators. U.S. Department of Commerce and Labor, Bureau of the Census, *Statistics of Women at Work*, pp. 158 and 159. It is extremely unlikely, but African American women may have "passed" as they had in retail, textile, and clerical work. See, for example, Cheryl I. Harris, "Whiteness as Property," *Harvard Law Review* 106 (June 1993): 1707–91; Rosalyn Terborg-Penn, "Survival Strategies Among African American Women Workers: A Continuing Process," in Ruth Milkman, ed., *Women, Work and Protest: A Century of U.S. Women's Labor History* (Boston: Routledge and Kegan Paul, 1985); and Susan Porter Benson, *Counter Cultures: Saleswomen, Managers, and Customers in American Department Stores, 1890–1940* (Urbana: University of Illinois Press, 1986), p. 209.

35   U.S. Senate, *Investigation of Telephone Companies*, S. Doc. 380, 61st Congress, 2nd sess., 1910, p. 20. The largest groups of women rejected included those who were too small (544), too old (53), too young (436), of insufficient education (519), and of poor appearance (169). Doctors refused only one for poor hearing, but they excluded 151 for poor sight and 43 for physical defects. Six applicants refused vaccination, 82 had poor voices, 7 refused night work, 36 were not willing to wait, and 74 others were

rejected for miscellaneous reasons. The city to which these statistics apply is not identified in the report.

36 U.S. Bureau of the Census, *Statistics of Women at Work* (Washington, D.C.: GPO, 1907), p. 34. Although telegraph operators are included with telephone operators, women telegraph operators were really very few at this time. The census data are used to show trends not exact numbers.

37 Ibid., p. 168.

38 The 1900 census gives family living arrangements by selected cities not by national numbers. Of 506 operators (480 single) employed in Boston, one of the largest cities, 421 lived with a parent or some other relative, 79 were boarding or living with their employers, and only 6 were heads of families living alone. This pattern was followed in other places as well. Ibid., p. 222.

39 McBride, quoted at the Traffic Conference, 1905, p. 42.

40 Bell managers did not hire "mature" women because managers thought that older women lacked the physical dexterity, speed, and energy required for operating. Linemen, repairmen, and construction teams were limited to younger men also because this work required "strength, skill and courage." See Bell System pamphlets prepared for the Louisiana Purchase Exposition, 1904: "Operating," p. 2, and "Trouble-shooter," pp. 5, 7, AT&T Archives, Box 1061.

41 Open houses also were held where the public, especially parents, were invited to the telephone exchanges to view the places where their daughters worked. A. S. Hibbard to P. L. Spalding, April 19, 1913, AT&T Archives, Box 2018.

42 For example, Cecil MacKenzie's mother "had the good luck to get [him] a job as an operator" in Buffalo on April Fool's Day in 1879. And she monitored his promotions closely. MacKenzie, p. 19.

43 McBride, quoted at the Traffic Conference, 1905, pp. 40–41.

44 Ibid., p. 41.

45 Large numbers of family members who worked together exerted control over the individual whose actions could adversely affect the whole family.

46 Up to the early 1960s, companies advertised for operators in the female section of the classifieds.

47 J. F. Dwinell, supervisor of traffic, "Relations of the Traffic Department to the Commercial Department," paper presented at the Second Convention of District and Exchange Managers of the New England Telephone and Telegraph Company, Boston, August 11–13, 1910, pp. 160–61.

48 H. D. McBride, superintendent of traffic, Boston, "The Selection and Training of Operators," paper read at the Traffic Conference, 1905, p. 39.

49 Marion May Dilts, *The Telephone in a Changing World* (New York: Longmans, Green, 1941), p. 101.

50 Schmitt, "I Was Your Old 'Hello' Girl," p. 121.

51 Engineers incorporated discipline into the very design of the classroom, which was furnished with common school desks placed in double or single rows like a typical schoolroom. By 1920, the Engineering Department's manual on the "Selec-

tion and Arrangement of Space" stated that "students should be seated so that they will not face the windows. The entrance door should be at the corner of the room." When schools became larger and more classes were held, "students usually march[ed] in regular order" to and from classrooms. AT&T Engineering Department, "Local Training Department Equipment and Space," sec. 11, pp. 2, 4, AT&T Archives, Box 1353.

52 J. L. Turner, "The Art of Expression As Applied to the Work of the Telephone Operator," *Telephone Review* 2 (October–November 1911): 236–38.

53 Ibid.

54 See below. AT&T required answers within 10 seconds, but New York Telephone required operators to answer all requests within 3.5 seconds.

55 Instruction manuals taught the method for doing this as follows: Main 4350— Main four three five oh. Walnut 2311—Walnut two three double one. Lindell 3307— Lindell double three oh seven. For more on these instructions, see McBride, quoted at the Traffic Conference, 1905, p. 51; Central Union Telephone Company, "Instructions for the Information and Guidance of Local Operating-Room Employes," 1903, p. 5, AT&T Archives, Box 1333; Illinois Bell Telephone Company, "Local Operating Practice- Manual Offices 'A' Operators," Div. II, sec. 2, p. 1, Library of Congress.

56 Norwood, p. 27, and traffic operating training circa 1915 to 1927. Photograph sent to the Japanese government in response to its request "for information on the training of telephone operators in American cities." AT&T Archives, Box 2048.

57 For example, operators in Boston, Chicago, and New York worked mostly on Chinnock boards until they were replaced by the Standard board and its successors. New England operators worked the Bell patentees' recommended Williams board. The Gilliland and Post boards were dominant in the Midwest and, to a lesser extent, in New England and Canada. Barrett, "The Changing Years as Seen from the Switch- board," p. 116. The South and the Southwest stubbornly held on to the Law board even after the Bell system began its standardization policy. See Kenneth Lipartito, *The Bell System and Regional Business: The Telephone in the South, 1877–1920* (Baltimore: Johns Hopkins University Press, 1989), pp. 69–70.

58 Regular operators worked Sundays, taking scheduled turns with no extra pay, in places as scattered as Albany, Denver, and St. Louis. In New York, Washington, D.C., and Chicago, the regular force of operators worked Sundays, also taking turns, but with extra pay. An extra force of operators in Cincinnati worked only on Sundays with no extra pay. Albany, Cincinnati, Boston, Denver, and New York provided paid vacations of one week to ten days with pay. San Francisco and Washington, D.C., gave vacations without pay, and St. Louis made no provisions for vacations. Length of service determined length and pay of vacations in other places. George N. Stone, general manager, American Bell Telephone Company, "Comparative Statement of Pay, etc., of Lady Operators," March 8, 1892, AT&T Archives, Box 1146.

59 Operation of cordless boards like the Post, Gilliland, and Williams differed greatly from that of a cord board such as the Chinnock. Connections between local lines and suburban or toll lines also were made differently.

60   This practice continued until wages were standardized by collective bargaining in the late 1950s.

61   The company started operators at a monthly salary of $10, which gradually increased to $30 by the end of the first year. A special promotion merited $35. Chief operators, at this time mostly men, started at $40 monthly and reached a maximum of $65 per month.

62   NTEA, 1881, p. 112. Bell Telephone of Missouri's manager, George F. Durant, stated that his company recruited all of its managers and operators from the male messenger forces.

63   NTEA, 1885, p. 79. The Central Union, Missouri and Kansas, Pacific Bell, and the Southern New England companies did not send any reports.

64   Age discrimination and segregation, more than gender discrimination, typified management's attitude during this period.

65   Managers' salaries, for example, ranged from $50 to $100 monthly. Linemen and battery men earned from $50 to $75 monthly, and helpers received from $1.25 to $1.50 per day, allegedly "because of the more complicated nature of their duties and necessity for greater experience." NTEA, 1880, p. 160.

66   Wage comparisons among women in various feminized occupations is complicated by region, race, ethnicity, and degree of feminization. Nevertheless, it is fairly accurate to say that telephone operators earned less than most clerical workers (even within the Bell System), compared favorably with the average saleswoman, and earned more than waitresses, most factory workers, and domestics (if we omit room and board). This pattern holds from the 1880s to the 1940s. On the national level, however, the social status of the telephone operator far outweighed that of most women workers, except for elite clerical workers such as secretaries. See Sharon Hartman Strom, *Beyond the Typewriter: Gender, Class, and the Origins of Modern American Office Work, 1900–1930* (Urbana: University of Illinois Press, 1992); Benson, *Counter Cultures*; Dorothy Sue Cobble, *Dishing It Out: Waitresses and Their Unions in the Twentieth Century* (Urbana: University of Illinois Press, 1991); Katzman, *Seven Days a Week*; Norwood, *Labor's Flaming Youth*; and Green, "The Impact of Technology Upon Women's Work in the Telephone Industry."

67   City and Suburban Telephone Company Historical Pamphlet, pp. 25–26, AT&T Archives, Box 1203.

68   See instances of management's handling of personal circumstances in cases of aging, death, and illness of heads of household in Thomas D. Lockwood to R. W. Devonshire, January 8, 1900, AT&T Archives, Box 1345. Also Mrs. Marsh to President Vail, January 19, 1911, and Comptroller Charles G. DuBois to Vice President U. N. Bethell, January 24, 1911. Both letters are in the AT&T Archives, Box 1377.

69   George C. Maynard to D. C. Patterson, July 9, 1880. Maynard to Warren Choate, chief operator, July 9, 1880. Maynard to Patterson, July 10, 1880. These letters can be found in the AT&T Archives, Box 1139.

70   Other types of arrangements may have been made in other locales, but for most Bell System employees before 1913, no company provision was made for protec-

tion against sickness, accidents, or death. W. H. Forbes to Edmund Dwight, June 13, 1882, AT&T Archives, Box 1214.

71   "Rest Room—195 Broadway Building," an announcement issued November 1, 1916, AT&T Archives, Box 2019.

72   Rocky Mountain Bell Telephone Company even considered the advantages of installing bathtubs in restrooms. George Wallace wrote to President Frederick P. Fish that he wanted to be put on record as "saying that . . . it is our *duty to do everything we can to get the best class of operators,* and the way to get the best class of operators is to offer them every possible convenience and comfort; and the expense of $35.00 or $40.00 in a *bath tub* is a very small item compared with the class of operators we hope to get by offering such conveniences." This argument was ignored. Operators did not get bathtubs. F. A. Pickernell to F. P. Fish, April 26, 1905. George Wallace to F. P. Fish, May 1, 1905. Both letters are in AT&T Archives, Box 1353. Also Hammond V. Hayes to President Fish, May 5, 1903, AT&T Archives, Box 1353.

73   Schmitt, "I Was Your Old 'Hello' Girl," p. 121.

74   For example, "Accounting Bulletin 108A" lists under Clerical Employees (a class divided into five subclasses) ten different subclasses of Cashier titles, twenty-five Supervising Clerk titles, fifty-one Clerk titles, ten Stenographer and Typist titles, and eight Office Boy and Messenger titles. Bell Telephone System, "Accounting Bulletin 108A—Standard Occupational Classification of Telephone Employees," September 1, 1917, pp. 13–16, AT&T Archives, Box 1376.

75   "Accounting Bulletin 108A," pp. 20–21. The operator titles included "Senior Operator, Operator, Local Operator, Information Operator, Multiple Marking or Change Number Operator, Official PBX Operator, Tandem Operator, Trouble, Complaint, Desk, Test, Hospital or Voltmeter Operator, Toll Operator, Recording Operator, Directory Operator, Rate Quoting Operator, Routing Operator, Line Operator, Inward Toll Operator, Incoming Ring Down Operator, Morse or Telegraph Operator (if not testboardman), Relief Operator (Sunday or vacation), Substitute Operator, Toll Substitute Operator and Combination Operator."

76   Created by the functional reorganization of the companies, the Traffic Engineering Department studied and compiled statistics for future planning. It designed apparatus as well as space. These engineers also wrote the rules and regulations for operators.

77   An AT&T chief operator, for example, was mandated to "keep informed on and be governed by the following instructions":

Traffic Bulletins addressed to Chief Operators.
Traffic Circular Letters addressed to Chief Operators.
Instructions in the Tariff and Route Book.
Instructions in the Special Route Book
Operating Instructions
   —General
   —Chief Operator

—Supervisors

—Recorders

—Line Operators

—Information Operators

—Methods in Use at her station

All other instructions issued for her guidance.

AT&T, Traffic Department Operating Instructions, Approved November 1, 1910, pp. D1-2, AT&T Archives, Box 1305.

78 J. L. Turner, "The Art of Expression as Applied to the Work of the Telephone Operator," p. 236.

79 AT&T, "Traffic Department Operating Instructions," November 1, 1910, p. A-3, AT&T Archives, Box 1305.

80 Ibid., p. A-4.

81 The Pacific Telephone and Telegraph Company, Traffic Department, "Local Operating Practice for the Information and Guidance of the Central Office Operating Forces," div. 2, sec. 1, p. 1, Library of Congress. Illinois Bell and New England Bell also required operators to sit with cords in hand.

82 H. D. McBride, "The Relation Between Service and Operating Loads," paper read before the Telephone Society of New England, November 10, 1903, pp. 2–3, AT&T Archives, Box 1359.

83 Ibid., p. 10.

84 Ibid., p. 11. One operator had handled 405 calls during the busy hour, but this rate was exceptional, and it was clear even to McBride that she could not continuously work at that level.

85 Joseph P. Davis to Frederick P. Fish, November 13, 1903, AT&T Archives, Box 1359.

86 If the operator completed all 100 calls free of "irregularities," she received her $35 monthly regular salary. When she erred, managers made $2.50 reductions in compliance with six grades of service. Rogers, engineer of the Nebraska Telephone Company, quoted at the Traffic Conference, 1905, p. 71.

87 Traffic Conference, 1905, pp. 77–90.

88 Nelle B. Curry, Investigation of the Wages and Conditions of Telephone Operating, U.S. Commission on Industrial Relations Report (Washington, D.C.: GPO, 1915), p. 41.

89 Grace Dodge et al., What Can Women Earn? (New York: Frederick A. Stokes, 1898), pp. 169, 277.

90 Curry, Investigation, p. 30.

91 U.S. Senate, Investigation, 1910, pp. 45–47.

92 C. F. Sise to Frederick P. Fish, February 20, 1907, AT&T Archives, Box 1050.

93 Most of them felt that women between the ages of seventeen and twenty-five by nature were "peculiarly sensitive" to nervous stress. Dr. Robert Dwyer, Associate Professor of Clinical Medicine at the University of Toronto, stated that neither the telephone company nor the doctors who worked for them saw the final result of the

tension induced by telephone operating. He said: "after these girls have gone on for four or five years and served the company, and they get married or for other purposes leave, then they turn out badly in their future domestic relations. They break down nervously and have nervous children, and it is a loss to the community." Department of Labour, Canada, *Report of the Royal Commission on a Dispute Respecting Hours of Employment Between the Bell Telephone Company of Canada, Ltd., and Operators at Toronto, Ontario* (Ottawa: Government Printing Bureau, 1907), p. 74.

94 Ibid., pp. 62–64.

95 Ibid., pp. 57–59.

96 Elizabeth Beardsley Butler, *Women and the Trades: Pittsburgh, 1907–1908* (New York: Charities Publication Committee, 1909), pp. 291–92.

97 AT&T's J. D. Ellsworth was so comforted by the report that he wrote to President Vail that it was "on the whole commendatory of the Bell System." In the same letter he conceded that the Royal Commission's medical finding "stands against us and I know of no systematic study now in existence which could be used against this and carry equal weight." J. D. Ellsworth to Theodore Vail, September 9, 1912, AT&T Archives, Box 8.

98 Josephine Goldmark, *Fatigue and Efficiency* (New York: Charities Publication Committee, 1912), pp. 43–53.

99 Curry, pp. 34–39.

100 The possibility that underpaid women would resort to prostitution constantly worried female reformers. Curry, pp. 5–10.

101 The District Attorney of the AT&T Legal Department, David F. Hall, to the U.S. Commission of Industrial Relations, August 7, 1915, and Basil M. Manly to David F. Hall, August 11, 1915(?), AT&T Archives, Box 26. See the exchange of letters that discussed the seriousness of the investigation and fear of unionization: B. E. Sunny to N. C. Kingsbury, July 23, 1915, N. C. Kingsbury to B. E. Sunny, July 24, 1915, and B. E. Sunny to N. C. Kingsbury, July 24, 1915, AT&T Archives, Box 26.

102 Jessie Mix, quoted in J. Leigh Walsh, *Connecticut Pioneers in Telephony* (New Haven, Conn.: Telephone Pioneers of America, 1950), p. 133.

103 Walsh, p. 133; Cecil W. Mackenzie, "Early Days of the Telephone in Buffalo, 1878–1926," typescript, p. 22, AT&T Archives, Box 1127.

104 Schmitt, "I Was Your Old 'Hello' Girl," p. 120.

105 Katherine M. Schmitt knew one of her customers so well that each morning she would sequentially call each person he spoke with without being told to do so.

106 Hammond V. Hayes to John E. Hudson, March 27, 1899, AT&T Archives, Box 1329.

107 For instance, as late as 1897, AT&T's "Rules for the Government and Information of the Employes" instructed operators on how to perform their daily tests of each subscriber's line. Chief operators provided operators with the testing equipment to determine working lines and instruments, grounded, crossed, or open lines, drop troubles, or blank wires. In addition, operators performed cord tests to find defective

cords, subscriber loop tests to discover defective instruments and loops, and trunk tests to locate defective local or office trunks. AT&T, "Rules for the Government and Information of the Employees," 1897, p. 16, AT&T Archives, Box 1021. Also see the 1895 version in Box 1121, p. 5.

108 Stephan Harlan Norwood, "The Making of the Trade Union Woman: Work Culture and Organization of Telephone Operators, 1900–1923," (Ph.D. Diss., Columbia University, 1984), p. 138.

109 *Boston Post*, quoted in Norwood, p. 138.

110 Ibid.

111 *Boston Globe*, quoted in Norwood, p. 135.

112 Butler, *Women and the Trades*, p. 285.

113 John J. Carty to President Thayer, March 1, 1909, AT&T Archives, Box 1357.

114 David Roediger described his recently deceased 83-year-old great-aunt as someone who had "worked much of her life as a telephone operator," and was "a staunch trade unionist." Even though it was for only ten hours each week, she employed a black domestic "through most of her working life." She achieved middle-class status by hiring black labor. Consequently, she "fiercely opposed integrating the ranks of telephone operators, drawing on arguments in which whiteness and class defined each other." See David Roediger, "Race and the Working-Class Past in the United States: Multiple Identities and the Future of Labor History," *International Review of Social History* 38, supp. (1993): 127–43. As Roediger and others have documented, telephone operators were not the only poorly paid white workers who sought to enhance their status by hiring black domestics. This practice was common among Southern textile workers.

3. The "Ladies" Rebel: Unions and Resistance

1 See, for example, *PACT News*, "Traffic Spread," 7 (June 1944): 10, for humorous definitions of jack, plug, tip, multiple markings, repeater, ring, etc.

2 These assertions are based on examinations of the *Union Telephone Operator*, the *Telephone Review*, *Bell Telephone Magazine*, *Headquarters Bulletin*, *CWA News*, *UNION VOICE*, *FTWP News*, *PACT News*, *The Associate*, *The Relay*, and other company and union communications.

3 The "Something for the Girls" column in AT&T's *Headquarters Bulletin* is a good example of the types of subject that management fostered.

4 Loretta M. Baker, "Driftway," *Union Telephone Worker* 1 (February 1921): 19–20. The proud operators named their possession "Driftway." It was located at Scituate, an "hour's ride from Boston."

5 "Bryn Mawr," *Union Telephone Operator* 8 (September 1921): 8.

6 NTEA, 1887, p. 58.

7 Katherine M. Schmitt, "I Was Your Old 'Hello' Girl," *Saturday Evening Post*, July 12, 1930, p. 120.

8 See Charles E. Scribner, B. E. Sunny, and others, quoted at the Switchboard Conference, 1887, pp. 5, 15, 42, 82–83, 91–92.

9   H. W. Trafford, "Report on Chicago Express System," September 1, 1896, p. 26, AT&T Archives, Box 1276. Thanks to Milton Mueller for giving me a copy of this report.

10   W. R. Westcott to Hammond V. Hayes, October 3, 1899, AT&T Archives, Box 1203.

11   Stone submitted his findings in a comparative statement to C. Jay French, assistant general manager of ABT, on March 8, 1892. George N. Stone to C. Jay French, March 8, 1892, AT&T Archives, Box 1146.

12   Memo to Samuel M. Bryan, September 1, 1894, AT&T Archives, Box 1146.

13   "The Telephones Silent," *Indianapolis Sentinel*, July 29, 1892, photocopy found in AT&T Archives, Box 1257.

14   Beach expressed surprise that local management "should not have had such a control of the affairs there as to have advised themselves of such a state of feelings before it had developed into a strike." F. G. Beach to C. Jay French, August 2, 1892, AT&T Archives, Box 1257.

15   U.S. Senate, *Investigation of Telephone Companies*, S. Doc. 380, 61st Congress, 2nd sess., 1910, p. 53.

16   Ibid., pp. 53–54.

17   See a memo by Waterson, "Summary and Discussion of Data on Employment Conditions of Operators," July 13, 1915, included in a letter from J. J. Carty to all the associated companies, July 26, 1915. AT&T Archives, Box 8.

18   Teresa Sullivan quoted in the *Evening Journal* (?), "Telephone Company and Its Operators in Battle Over Union," February 24, 1920. Several newspaper clippings in this folder lack the precise newspaper name. "E. Journal" is written on the article from which this quotation was taken. AT&T Archives, Box 1363.

19   See Waterson, "Summary and Discussion of Data on Employment Conditions of Operators," AT&T Archives, Box 8.

20   Nelle B. Curry, *Investigation of the Wages and Conditions of Telephone Operators*, U.S. Commission on Industrial Relations Report (Washington, D.C.: GPO, 1915), pp. 7–8.

21   Judith Long Laws, "The Bell Telephone System: A Case Study," in Phyllis A. Wallace, ed., *Equal Employment Opportunity and the AT&T Case* (Cambridge, Mass.: MIT Press, 1976), p. 159.

22   Ibid.

23   The company completely replaced the operators at Waco with a new operating force. Galveston operators did not belong to the union. Twelve or fifteen men were discharged in Dallas to forestall any "intention" they "may have entertained of precipitating a strike." Frank B. Knight to ABT, November 13, 1900. In Dallas and Fort Worth, operators also did not go out on strike. Knight to ABT, November 23, 1900. Austin telephone workers refused to join the union. Knight to ABT, December 11, 1900. Knight's letters can be found in AT&T Archives, Box 1304.

24   All except Charles R. Smith, who ended up killing a policeman and wounding a striker. The company had him cleared of all charges. Frank B. Knight to ABT, November 30, 1900, and December 15, 1900, AT&T Archives, Box 1304.

25   Frank B. Knight, a special agent, and other Southwestern Bell managers consistently complained to ABT managers in Boston that local police, city governments, and small businesses sympathized with the strikers. See letters in AT&T Archives, Box 1304.

26   Frank B. Knight to ABT, November 10, 1900, November 22, 1900, January 2, 1901, February 9, 1901. "No Progress in the Strike," *San Antonio Daily Express,* November 15, 1900, AT&T Archives, Box 1304.

27   Martin Wright, president, Local No. 60, IBEW, to F. B. Clyde, manager, Southwestern Telegraph and Telephone Company, October 1900, AT&T Archives, Box 1304.

28   J. E. Farnsworth to F. B. Knight, November 6, 1900, AT&T Archives, Box 1304.

29   Martin Wright et al., quoted in "Business Men Take a Hand," *San Antonio Daily Express,* November 14, 1900, and H. J. Pettingill, quoted in "The Telephone Strike," *San Antonio Daily Express,* November 13, 1900, AT&T Archives, Box 1304.

30   "To Push It, Striking Linemen Decide to Be Aggressive," *Duluth Evening Herald,* July 3, 1901. Linemen first decided to strike the independent Zenith Telephone Company before turning their attention to the Duluth Telephone Company (a Bell System firm), AT&T Archives, Box 1322. No information has been found on the outcome of this strategy at Duluth, but in Des Moines, operators struck both the independent Mutual Telephone Company and the Iowa Telephone Company (Bell System) and won their demands against Mutual first. David F. Hall, special agent to General Edward P. Meany, assistant manager, August 23, 1902, AT&T Archives, Box 1155.

31   E. B. Smith, general manager, to C. E. Yost, president, Nebraska Telephone Company, August 14, 1902, described the Iowa strike. AT&T Archives, Box 1155. Also see Stephen H. Norwood, *Labor's Flaming Youth: Telephone Operators and Worker Militancy, 1878–1923* (Urbana: University of Illinois Press, 1990), pp. 73–82, for a detailed description of these strikes.

32   George Y. Wallace, president, Rocky Mountain Bell Telephone Company, to Theodore N. Vail, president, AT&T, October 21, 1907, AT&T Archives, Box 1365.

33   Letters can be found in the President's Letter Books (AT&T Archives) addressed to the following associated companies: Nebraska Telelephone Co., Northwestern Telephone Exchange Co., Michigan Telephone Co., Rocky Mountain Bell Telephone Co., Missouri and Kansas Telephone Co., Central District and Pittsburgh Telephone Co., Central Union Telephone Co., Cumberland Telephone & Telegraph Co., Pacific States Telephone & Telegraph Co., and Iowa Telephone Co.

34   F. P. Fish to E. B. Smith, June 24, 1902, President's Letter Books, AT&T Archives.

35   F. P. Fish to E. B. Smith, August 21, 1902, President's Letter Books, AT&T Archives.

36   J. K. Turner, general manager, Manufacturer's Information Bureau (main office, Cleveland) to H. J. Pettengill, general manager, Western Telephone and Telegraph Co., December 9, 1902. The Manufacturer's Information Bureau to President Vail, May 25, 1907. J. F. Pelan, president and general manager of the Maintenance Company, Bridgeport, Conn., to Theodore Vail, August 1, 1907. Despite its innocuous

name, the Maintenance Company declared its purpose "to check, fight, and crush the ever growing demands of organized labor in all the Electrical trades." AT&T Archives, Box 1365.

37 G. P. Robinson to A. J. Steiss, both of Pacific States Telephone & Telegraph Company, October 25, 1904, AT&T Archives, Box 1369.

38 D. S. Murray to George Y. Wallace, October 14, 1907, AT&T Archives, Box 1365.

39 George Y. Wallace to F. P. Fish, April 18, 1903, AT&T Archives, Box 1314.

40 George Y. Wallace to Frederick P. Fish, March 18, 1907, AT&T Archives, Box 1307.

41 J. D. Ellsworth to Theodore Vail, April 6, 1910, AT&T Archives, Box 47.

42 B. E. Sunny of Chicago advised President Vail that AT&T should not pay for the plan directly since in regard to rate regulation the local company "would not be entitled to any consideration for the amount paid out by the AT&T." B. E. Sunny to Theodore Vail, October 14, 1912, AT&T Archives, Box 47. Vice President Thayer replied that the plan had been worked out in "accordance" with Sunny's views. H. B. Thayer to B. E. Sunny, October 16, 1912, AT&T Archives, Box 47.

43 AT&T, "Plan for Employees' Pensions, Disability Benefits and Insurance," January 1, 1913, p. 1, AT&T Archives, Box 47.

44 Ibid., pp. 2–4.

45 AT&T, "Plan to Aid Employees of Bell System to Become Stockholders of American Telephone and Telegraph Company," January 1, 1915, p. 1, AT&T Archives, Box 2054.

46 AT&T General Superintendent of Traffic Van Meter to General Superintendent C. H. Wilson, December 30, 1912, AT&T Archives, Box 2019.

47 AT&T Vice President N. C. Kingsbury to Senior Vice President U. N. Bethell, December 31, 1912, AT&T Archives, Box 2019.

48 H. B. Thayer to B. E. Sunny, March 12, 1913, AT&T Archives, Box 2019.

49 Ibid.

50 Norwood, pp. 121–22. Norwood gives the best description of this near-strike and the days of bargaining, including all of the union, WTUL, local and state government, as well as Bell System officials involved. See pp. 91–122.

51 See Norwood, pp. 130–32, and a synopsis of the strike from management's point of view in a letter from Eugene D. Nims, first vice president and treasurer, Southwestern Bell Telephone System, to H. B. Thayer, vice president, AT&T, August 23, 1913, AT&T Archives, Box 2018.

52 Comptroller DuBois to President Vail, August 30, 1917, AT&T Archives, Box 12.

53 Norwood, p. 158–59, and Greenwald, p. 210.

54 Comptroller DuBois to President Vail, August 30, 1917, AT&T Archives, Box 12. Norwood described a community-based strike in Fort Smith, Ark., in which operators struck for three months with the support of a general strike that "lasted less than a week." This operators' strike was totally defeated because the Bell System used the full weight of its financial power to do so. See Norwood, pp. 160–62.

55 Southern Bell Telephone & Telegraph Co. President J. Epps Brown to AT&T Vice President Thayer, June 10, 1919, AT&T Archives, Box 2.

56 B. E. Sunny to Vice President N. C. Kingsbury, April 29, 1918, AT&T Archives, Box 4.

57 Postmaster General Burleson to Secretary of Labor W. B. Wilson, March 15, 1919, p. 4, AT&T Archives, Box 2.

58 Elizabeth Faue, *Community of Suffering and Struggle: Women, Men, and the Labor Movement in Minneapolis, 1915–1945* (Chapel Hill: University of North Carolina Press, 1991), pp. 47–50. Faue depicts this strike as an example of community and labor solidarity. She also points out women's use of "their own symbols of solidarity— tooting horns and waving rattlers, singing and posturing on the picket line . . .," p. 50.

59 Norwood, p. 166.

60 Burleson to Wilson, p. 10.

61 Norwood, pp. 166–67.

62 Burleson to Wilson, p. 11.

63 J. Epps Brown to H. B. Thayer, June 10, 1919, AT&T Archives, Box 2.

64 On October 2, 1918, Burleson issued Order 2067, which stated that the government would not discriminate against union members. This statement in no way recognized a "closed shop," nor did it agree to negotiate with union leaders outside the company. Burleson made it clear that he would settle each case individually, not in groups.

65 The Trades and Labor Assembly, Open Letter, October 4, 1918, Denver, AT&T Archives, Box 14.

66 See cards in AT&T Archives, Box 14.

67 Norwood, pp. 193–94.

68 J. Epps Brown to H. B. Thayer, June 10, 1919, AT&T Archives, Box 2.

69 Norwood, p. 208.

70 Ibid., p. 136.

71 Ibid., p. 105.

72 Computerized monitoring and other technological problems came much later for men. Because they had not worked out an effective strategy during the 1900s regarding female operators, and because they had accepted management's right to introduce new technology as management saw fit, men were almost defenseless in the face of the computerization of their work in the 1970s and 1980s.

73 For an excellent analysis of how women were excluded and discriminated against by organized labor, see Alice Kessler-Harris, "Where Are the Organized Women Workers," *Feminist Review* 3 (Fall 1975): 92–105.

74 Norwood, p. 107.

75 Norwood says that the first operators' union was organized in Butte in December 1902. Des Moines operators appear to predate the Butte operators' union. Des Moines operators, however, may not have affiliated with a national union as had the Butte operators.

76 General Manager E. B. Smith to Nebraska Telephone Company President C. E. Yost, August 14, 1902, p. 2, AT&T Archives, Box 1155.

77 Ibid., p. 4.

78 Ibid.

79 The Pacific Telephone and Telegraph superintendent of traffic, J. P. Downs, to Thomas B. Doolittle at AT&T, June 26, 1907, pp. 1–2, AT&T Archives, Box 1369.

80 Ibid., p. 1.

81 Norwood, p. 85. No citation substantiates this claim. Letters between the relevant managers do not include these demands.

82 Downs to Doolittle, p. 2.

83 According to Norwood, male telephone workers voted against a sympathy strike and a "proposal to boycott the Bell Telephone." After two months, male telephone workers finally walked out in support of the operators, p. 86.

84 Norwood, without a citation, states that the operators demanded "the replacement of male chief operators to eliminate sexual harassment," p. 85.

85 Ibid., p. 86.

86 "Welfare Plans in Use Among Bell Telephone Companies," Appendix E, pp. 59–60, AT&T Archives, Box 47.

87 See Nancy Schrom Dye, *As Equals and As Sisters: Feminism, the Labor Movement, and the Women's Trade Union League of New York* (Columbia: University of Missouri Press, 1980), p. 3. Dye argues that the middle-class WTUL's "devotion" to the AFL "prevented [it] from realizing how inappropriate craft unionism was for unskilled, poorly paid, and irregularly employed female industrial workers." When WTUL did become "aware of the limitation of AFL-style unionism, most members could envision no viable alternatives." Or, as Alice Kessler-Harris remarked, working-class women who became associated with the WTUL "moved quickly from working class militance to the search for individual social mobility through vocational training." See Kessler-Harris, "Where Are the Organized Women Workers?" p. 102.

88 Mabel Gillispie, "The Telephone Operators," *Life and Labor* 2 (August 1912): 252.

89 Norwood is the expert on this situation. I rely on his version, except where I have found primary evidence, p. 101.

90 Julia S. O'Connor, "History of the Organized Telephone Operators' Movement," part 1, *Union Telephone Operator* 1 (January 1921): 14.

91 For example, the Boston Hotel Workers' Union, the Commercial Telegraphers' Union of America, and the Boston Central Labor Union supported the operators. Operators in Lynn and Springfield also promised to strike in sympathy. Norwood, pp. 114–15.

92 Norwood, p. 114, and O'Connor, "History of the Organized Telephone Operators' Movement," part 2 (February 1921), pp. 15–16.

93 Norwood, p. 117.

94 Ibid., p. 103.

95   They demanded "the abolition of the split trick, the eight-hour day, the establishment of a Board of Adjustment, and an increase in pay." O'Connor, "History of the Organized Telephone Operators' Movement," part 1, p. 14.

96   Ibid.

97   Julia S. O'Connor, president, "Report of Officers and Convention Proceedings to the Second Biennial Convention of the Telephone Operators' Department of the International Brotherhood of Electrical Workers," St. Louis, October 31–November 3, 1921, p. 17.

98   Ibid.

99   Samuel Gompers, "Accept the Machine—Organize the Workers," *American Federationist* 30 (September 1923): 718–21.

100   Gompers and other union leaders accepted the idea of new technology and labor-saving devices as steps toward progress and the lessening of arduous work, but they objected that all the benefits were going to the capitalists. During the 1920s, various union leaders wrote articles suggesting ways to offset the impact of technology. For example, when automatic glassblowing machinery was introduced, the Glass Bottle Blowers' Association negotiated a settlement that included a wage reduction, retraining for skilled workers to become semiskilled machine operatives, and continuous running of the machines to increase the need for more workers. See Harry Jenkins, secretary, Glass Bottle Blowers' Association, "Meeting Job Displacement Brought About by Introduction of Automatic Machinery," *American Federationist* 34 (September 1927): 1054–57. Pressers in the cloak-and-suit industry accommodated automation by accepting a 20 percent wage reduction that was placed in a fund to assist unemployed pressers. See Max D. Danish, International Ladies' Garment Workers' Union, "Taxing Machines to Relieve Jobless," *American Federationist* 39 (October 1932): 1104–6. The Cigarmakers also proposed a relief fund for displaced workers to be financed by a tax on machine-made cigars. I. M. Ornburn, president, Cigarmakers' International Union, "Men Before Machines," *American Federationist* 41 (February 1934): 141–47. AFL leaders changed their emphasis in different periods, but they stuck to the traditional demands of "the five-day week with no reduction in pay, a shorter work day and further restriction of immigration. . . . Vacations with pay, unemployment insurance, liberalization and extension of retirement plans, [and] elimination of seasonal fluctuations in operation and employment." Also see these articles, which appeared in the *American Federationist*: L. E. Keller, statistician, Brotherhood of Maintenance of Way Employees, "Efficiency and Unemployment" 37 (June 1930): 676–80; Carl Huhndorff, research director, International Association of Machinists, "A Few Remarks on Automation," 61 (May 1955): 31; O. William Blaier, second general vice president, United Brotherhood of Carpenters and Joiners, "Will Automation Wipe Out Your Job?" 62 (December 1955): 28–29. By the 1960s, unions concentrated on "advance notice" of impending automation. See "The Impact of Automation—A Challenge to America," 72 (December 1965): 13–17; Rudolph Oswald, "Easing Job Changes by Advance Notice," 68 (Au-

gust 1961): 12–19; and Markley Roberts, "Adjusting to Technological Change," 80 (February 1973): 13–18.

4. "Goodbye Central": Automating Telephone Service

1   Employee representation will be discussed in chapter 5.

2   In 1920, the Bell System controlled 61.2 percent of U.S. telephone service, and in 1924, 69.6 percent. AT&T, *Bell System Statistical Manual, 1920–1964* (New York: AT&T, 1965), p. 503.

3   A fully automated system eliminated an operator completely by allowing the subscriber to access the central office switching equipment, which processed the call. In a semiautomatic system, subscribers continued to give the operator their requests, and she accessed the automatic switching equipment to complete the call.

4   R. B. Hill, "Early Work on Dial Telephone Systems," *Bell Laboratories Record* 31 (January 1953): 28. Thomas D. Lockwood to President Hudson, December 3, 1887, AT&T Archives, Box 1253. Lockwood recommended the purchase of the McCoy patent for automatic switching. He argued that these systems would never achieve any practical use, but at some time in the future the Bell System might want to install an automatic exchange "for some special purpose." Furthermore, since ABT owned none of the other patents for automatics, it would be wise to buy this one in case some part of it might be used in the future.

5   Lockwood to Hudson, June 7, 1888, AT&T Archives, Box 1244. Lockwood wrote in response to a review of a patent for an automatic annunciator that he did not think it should be bought. He thought that Western Electric should get a chance to look at it because it was applicable to multiple switchboards. On June 13, 1888, Western Electric President E. M. Barton wrote to Hudson that he also did not think the patent would be immediately useful. He suggested that it should be bought at a small price to insure that the Bell System had it if some use did arise in the future.

6   Lockwood rejected the Strowger, Bishop, Romaine-Callender, and the Smith-Vassar automatic systems. Thomas D. Lockwood to ABT President John E. Hudson, December 3, 1887, and November 9, 1892, AT&T Archives, Box 1253; September 9, 1893, Box 1274; and November 9, 1896, Box 1315. Hammond V. Hayes, the electrical engineer, rejected the Clark Automatic. Hayes to ABT President F. P. Fish, January 10, 1902, AT&T Archives, Box 1366. Even Thomas D. Lockwood received two patents in 1886–87 for automatics that never achieved any commercial use. Hill, p. 24.

7   M. D. Fagen, ed., *A History of Engineering and Science in the Bell System: The Early Years (1875–1925)* (N.p.: Bell Telephone Laboratories, 1975), pp. 46, 546; Hill, pp. 23–24; and two letters to President Hudson, one from the electrical engineer, Hayes, and the other from Devonshire, both dated May 10, 1889, AT&T Archives, Box 1228.

8   See Milton Mueller, "The Switchboard Problem: Scale, Signaling, and Organization in Manual Telephone Switching, 1877–1897," *Technology and Culture* 30 (July 1989): 534–60; Green, chaps. 2 and 3, for an analysis of this problem. Lockwood to Hudson, November 25, 1892, p. 3, AT&T Archives, Box 1253.

9   Chapuis, p. 64; Fagen, p. 549; and J. E. Kingsbury, *The Telephone and Telephone*

Exchanges: Their Invention and Development (London: Longmans, Green, 1915), pp. 400–401.

10   Lockwood to Hudson, April 11, 1891, AT&T Archives, Box 1286; Fagen, p. 545. Strowger applied for his patent on March 12, 1889, and received it on May 10, 1891.

11   The Strowger Automatic Telephone Exchange was incorporated on October 30, 1891. In 1901, the Automatic Electric Company was formed to manufacture and sell Strowger automatics, and in 1908 it took over full ownership of Strowger Automatic Telephone Exchange. Two types of automatic systems achieved wide commercial use: the Strowger step-by-step system and the panel system created by the Bell System.

12   Thomas D. Lockwood to John E. Hudson, September 9, 1893, AT&T Archives, Box 1274.

13   R. B. Hill, "The Early Years of the Strowger System," *Bell Laboratories Record* 31 (March 1953): 100. Also see E. B. Craft, L. F. Morehouse, and H. P. Charlesworth, "Machine Switching Telephone System for Large Metropolitan Areas," an article presented at the Mid-Winter Convention of the American Institute of Electrical Engineers, New York, February 14–17, 1923.

14   Fagen, pp. 564–69. The early Strowger automatics did not have common battery power, automatic ringing, automatic busy signals, and operator assistance for information, time, weather, private branch exchange service, toll calls, long distance, and "personal service," all of which were customary for manually operated boards before 1900.

15   Thomas D. Lockwood to W. W. Hutchinson, March 26, 1900, AT&T Archives, Box 1253.

16   See advertisement in AT&T Archives, Box 1109.

17   See the United States Automatic Telephone Company of New York, the Eastern Automatic Telephone Company of Massachusetts, and the Strowger Automatic Telephone Exchange (and its descendant the Automatic Electric Company) advertisements in AT&T Archives, Boxes 1291, 1109, 2026, and 1152.

18   Southern New England Telephone Company, "Brief: The Automatic System in Connecticut," 1904, p. 1, AT&T Archives, Box 2026; and New York Telephone Company, "Supplementary Brief of New York Telephone Company with Special Reference to the Automatic Telephone System," presented to the Board of Estimate and Apportionment in Committee of the Whole on the Application of the Atlantic Telephone Company for a Franchise, AT&T Archives, Box 1325.

19   "Brief: The Automatic System in Connecticut," p. 38.

20   See letters and engineers' reports sent to President Fish from 1900 to 1904, which discuss the technical and economic advantages and disadvantages of various automatic systems, in AT&T Archives, Box 1366; M. B. McDavitt, "Rebuttal," p. II-2, AT&T Archives, Box 2051; W. G. Freeman, "History of Development of the Panel Dial System," p. 2, and "Chronology of Machine Switching Development," AT&T Archives, Box 1014; William Girard, "Auto-Village Days in Rockaway," *New Jersey Bell*, April 1930, pp. 13–14, AT&T Archives, Box 1325; Fagen, p. 547; New England Telephone and

Telegraph Company, "Questions and Answers for Commercial Department Examination, December 28–29, 1911," pp. 36–37, AT&T Archives, Box 1015; and "Dial: Queens Had It in 1902" (no author or journal citation), AT&T Archives, Box 1325.

21   Fagen, p. 573.

22   In the prewar period, Bell System engineers invented, improved, and adopted many labor-saving devices (automatic features) to enhance manual systems. They investigated and experimented with various methods to improve or to implement automatic ringing, automatic listening (by operators), private service (operator lockout), automatic call metering (to eliminate the operator's job of making tickets for each call), automatic disconnects (enabling the subscriber to receive or initiate calls before the operator took down the cords of a previously completed call), automatic peg counts, and automatic call distribution. For automatic ring patents and improvements, see AT&T Archives, Boxes 1308 and 1296. For a discussion of toll registers or call counters and call registers, Boxes 1292 and 1361. The need for automatic call distribution is discussed in a letter from Traffic Engineer K. W. Waterson to Chief Engineer Joseph P. Davis, January 7, 1904, Box 1359. Discussions of methods for equalizing loads are in Boxes 2, 1274, and 1295.

23   J. J. Carty to H. B. Thayer, April 8, 1909, p. 12-A, AT&T Archives, Box 1.

24   Chapuis, pp. 78–81; Fagen, pp. 551–52; and Kingsbury, pp. 410–16. See letter from Vice President John J. Carty to Vice President and Chief Engineer Bancroft Gherardi, dated August 7, 1920, in which Carty clarifies why he favored the semi-mechanical over the fully automated system in 1910. AT&T Archives, Box 56.

25   Freeman, "History of Development," p. 3.

26   Ibid., pp. 5–6; E. F. Barron, "Bell System Automatic Telephone Installations," typescript, 1947, AT&T Archives, Box 1116.

27   Freeman, "History of Development," pp. 10–11. "Among others there were two studies in 1912, one in 1915, three in 1916 and one in 1917. . . . investigations of the step-by-step system under actual operating conditions were made at Lincoln, Neb. in 1912, Defiance, O. in 1915 and St. Paul, Minn. in 1918. . . . An exhaustive study of the North (Clement) automanual system was made in 1915, based on the installation at Lima, Ohio. In 1917, a study of the possibilities of this system, as applied to the largest multioffice areas, was made."

28   Fagen, pp. 569–71.

29   C. F. Cozad, "Notes on a Trip East," p. 107, AT&T Archives, Box 1044. Cozad indicates that the Bell System obtained experienced men with expertise in Strowger automatics when they acquired Independents during the early 1900s. Also see "Chronology of Machine Switching Development," p. 12. In June 1918, the Bell System gained 62,000 automatic stations (in addition to the 91,000 the system had in 1915) through consolidation with Los Angeles Independents.

30   Chapuis, pp. 209–10; M. B. McDavitt, "Machine Switching and Revenue Accounting," p. II-3, AT&T Archives, Box 2051.

31   Freeman, "History of Development," p. 8.

32   Bancroft Gherardi to J. J. Carty, July 24, 1917, p. 1, AT&T Archives, Box 1014.

33   Ibid., pp. 1–3.

34   Ibid., p. 12; Freeman, "History of Development," p. 17.

35   Freeman, "History of Development," pp. 17–18. In addition to perfecting the actual switching equipment, other technical problems were solved as part of automatic development. To make a call from a manual to a dial office or vice versa required the development of special equipment. "Call indicators" were the devices invented to receive dial pulses and convert them into visual indications on a special panel at a manual office. Operators in dial offices worked at "cordless 'B' boards" where they received numbers orally from manual offices and then punched keys to cause the dial equipment to complete the call. Automatic equipment had to be compatible with "all types of offices, local, tandem and Long Distance, in both directions." Provisions for all types of operator assistance also had to be made. Operators had to be retrained, and, more importantly, the subscriber had to be educated about the use of the new dial equipment. For documentation on the various problems involved in the transition to dial, see a memo for Root, Ballantine, Harlan, Bushby, and Palmer titled "Problems of Interconnection Between Telephone Offices in a Metropolitan Area," AT&T Archives, Box 2021.

36   Freeman, "History of Development," p. 16.

37   K. W. Waterson to J. J. Carty, May 22, 1918, AT&T Archives, Box 3.

38   Ibid. See also a May 29, 1918, letter from Chief Engineer J. J. Carty to First Vice President U. N. Bethell in which Carty approves of Waterson's recommendations. AT&T Archives, Box 3.

39   Bancroft Gherardi, "Machine Switching Program," paper delivered at the Bell System Presidents' Conference, New York, December 8–10, 1919, pp. 29, 30, 38, AT&T Archives, Box 52. On September 24, 1919, AT&T First Vice President N. C. Kingsbury sent a letter to all of the associated companies with detailed instructions, including questions and answers, on how to handle any unfavorable responses to the introduction of automatic switching. The package was to serve as a "guide for making public statements where such statements become necessary." AT&T Archives, Box 56.

40   Ibid., pp. 30–31. See also Bancroft Gherardi to J. J. Carty, July 24, 1917, pp. 7–8, AT&T Archives, Box 1014.

41   K. W. Waterson, quoted in Freeman, p. 14.

42   A. F. Dixon, "Future Development in the Art of Communication—Central Offices," paper presented at the Telephone Department Conference at Lake Placid, N.Y., October 11, 1922, pp. 1–2, AT&T Archives, Box 1055.

43   Gherardi, "Machine Switching Program," p. 34. A Federal Communications Commission (FCC) rate investigation, conducted from 1935–37, concluded that AT&T executives had consistently underestimated plant and *personnel* costs related to panel automatic switching. The investigators argued that even the "savings" in operators' wages would be "offset by the fact that during the program of conversion from manual to automatic operation the average rate per hour of the remaining operators [would be] materially increased" as the result of higher salaries based on seniority. However, the FCC provided no figures on which it actually calculated the difference

between the salaries of women who remained and the possible number of women who would have been employed without dial. See FCC, *Proposed Report: Telephone Investigation (Pursuant to Public Resolution No. 8, 74th Congress)* (Washington, D.C.: GPO, 1938), pp. 312–14.

44   See memo for Bancroft Gherardi from the Plant Engineer dated July 6, 1923, "Data Relating to Machine Switching Equipment," AT&T Archives, Box 56.

45   McDavitt, p. II-1. These estimates are based on the costs of Bell System panel switching manufactured by Western Electric rather than step-by-step equipment made by independent manufacturers. FCC investigators claimed that step-by-step switching was less expensive at that time. See FCC, *Proposed Report,* p. 315.

46   Vice President H. B. Thayer to Bell Telephone Company of Canada President C. F. Sise, May 14, 1912, AT&T Archives, Box 47. Thayer said that the situation in Europe was different from that in Canada or the United States. "Government owner-ship of telephone service involves civil service rules with regard to operators which makes the operator question much more serious than with us and therefore the various European governments are looking toward the automatic as a possible relief from trouble."

47   Fagen, p. 585.

48   W. E. Farnham, "Traffic Responsibilities Under Machine Switching Opera-tion," paper delivered at the General Traffic Conference, April 1923, p. 451.

49   Fagen, pp. 602–3.

50   Farnham, p. 451.

51   The need for automatic call distribution is discussed in a letter from Traffic Engineer K. W. Waterson to Chief Engineer Joseph P. Davis, January 7, 1904, AT&T Archives, Box 1359. Methods for equalizing loads are discussed in Boxes 2, 1274, and 1295.

52   Call indicators at manual offices automatically showed the inward operators what numbers to connect.

53   AT&T Department of Operation and Engineering, "History and Development of the Nationwide Toll Dialing Plan," p. 8.

54   Ibid., p. 9.

55   AT&T, Department of Operation and Engineering, "Notes on Nationwide Dial-ing," 1955, pp. 8–10. The entire description given here of the hierarchy of toll centers was taken from this pamphlet.

56   Step-by-step equipment serviced small areas on a very limited basis because it required a different set of digits for each through or tandem switch that a call would pass through. Crossbar switches could use the digits and pass them on so that a large number of digits were not necessary to pass a call through several switches. The crossbar became the standard system for toll-switching.

57   Howard L. Hosford, "A Dial Switching System for Toll Calls," *Bell Telephone Magazine* 22 (Winter 1943–44): 229–30.

58   Ibid., p. 230. Key pulsing equipment had been developed in 1930 as part of the general effort to "ease" operation and improve speed. See "Key Pulsing Equipment

Developed," *Headquarters Bulletin* 4 (February 1930): 8. Operators using the No. 4 equipment did not dial in the sense that is usually implied by that term. Instead, a ten-button key set was used to pulse out the digits. It was claimed to be twice as fast as dialing.

59   James J. Pilliod and Harold L. Ryan, "Operator Toll Dialing—A New Long Distance Method," *Bell Telephone Magazine* 24 (Summer 1945): 111.

60   Ernst F. Guengerich, "Toll Dialing by Operators Reaches Some 300 Places," *Bell Telephone Magazine* 27 (Winter 1948–49): 231.

61   "Long Distance Operators Now Can Dial from Coast to Coast," *Headquarters Bulletin* 23 (November 1949): 7, 14.

62   Ernest W. Baker, "Toll Dialing Is Expanding Throughout the Nation," *Bell Telephone Magazine* 30 (Winter 1951–52): 257.

63   AT&T, Long Lines Information Department, "Information About New Method by which Operators Dial Long Distance Telephone Calls," sec. 3, "New Operator Toll Dialing Equipment," 1949, p. 1.

64   Ibid., p. 5.

65   AT&T, "Notes on Nationwide Dialing," 1955, p. 26, AT&T Archives, Box 1122.

66   New York Telephone installed the first electromechanical counting device that counted message units (the Multiunit or Zone Registration system) in New York City in 1931. The message registers could automatically count units but were limited to bulk billing between zones that used the same rate structure. The Bell System introduced the automatic ticketer, which could produce a ticket, to Culver City, California, in 1944. However, it was designed for step-by-step equipment when panel and cross-bar systems were prevalent. Robert G. Elliott, "Dial Service Is Extending Its Reach," *Bell Telephone Magazine* 34 (Summer 1955): 112–13, and O. A. Friend, "Automatic Ticketing," *Bell Laboratories Record* 22 (July 1944): 445–46.

67   AT&T, Department of Operation and Engineering, "History and Development of the Nationwide Toll Dialing Plan," p. 13. Robert G. Elliott, "Dial Service Is Extending Its Reach," *Bell Telephone Magazine* 34 (Summer 1955): 114.

68   Elliott, p. 114.

69   F. H. Martin, "Centralized AMA Switchboard," *Bell Laboratories Record* 32 (October 1954): 371.

70   Elliott, p. 116. This arrangement was temporary since the Bell System was actively developing equipment to automatically identify the calling subscriber's number.

71   A. S. Martins and R. G. Ruwell, "CAMA for Step-by-Step Inter-Toll," *Bell Laboratories Record* 40 (1962): 59.

72   P. A. Ghiloni and H. R. Moore, "ANI For Small Step-By-Step Offices," *Bell Laboratories Record* 44 (February 1966): 204.

73   Peter B. Howell, "The Modern Telephone Operator," *Bell Telephone Magazine* 29 (Autumn 1960): 16.

74   Caroline C. Cherrix, *Women Telephone Workers and Changing Technology*, U.S. Department of Labor, Women's Bureau, Bulletin 286 (Washington, D.C.: GPO, 1963), p. 23.

75   Boston operators received $21 weekly (beginners, $13), whereas New York operators' wages were increased to $23 (beginners, $15). Teresa Sullivan, quoted in the *Evening Journal*(?), "Telephone Company and Its Operators in Battle Over Union," February 24, 1920. Several newspaper clippings in this folder lack the precise newspaper name. "E. Journal" is written on the article from which this quotation was taken. AT&T Archives, Box 1363.

76   "Phone Co. Won't Hire Negroes to Meet Shortage," *New York Call*, March 1920, p. 2.

77   Quoted in ibid.

78   Ibid.

79   Consumers' League of the City of New York, "Light on the New York Telephone Situation," *Consumers' League Bulletin*, July 1920, p. 2.

80   See Holja Pookaw, "In Dark and Deepest Africa, A Story in Three Parts," *Union Telephone Operator*, August 1921, pp. 7, 25; September 1921, pp. 23, 25–27; October 1921, pp. 18–21, all in vol. 1, nos. 7, 8, and 9.

81   For example, see "The Minstrelettes at the Richmond Hill, Virginia and Cleveland Central Office Party," *Telephone Review* 19 (March 1928): 97.

5. The Bell System Family: The Formation of Employee Associations

1   President Theodore N. Vail to Associated Companies Presidents, June 3, 6, and 7, 1919, AT&T Archives, Boxes 2 and 15.

2   See David F. Noble, *America By Design: Science, Technology, and the Rise of Corporate Capitalism* (New York: Oxford University Press, 1977), chap. 10, for a discussion of the rise of industrial psychology.

3   Thomas R. Brooks, *Communications Workers of America: The Story of a Union* (New York: Mason/Charter, 1977), p. 25.

4   *Telephone Review* 6 (April 1915), p. 134. F. H. Bethell, vice president, New York Telephone Company, address before the Albany Chamber of Commerce, March 22, 1915.

5   After a successful campaign designed to flatter the operators into believing that they were part of something important, management was able to make its own desires the priorities of discussion. Individual and group pictures displayed on the bulletin board, auto trips to different locations, picnics, parties, and minstrel shows convinced the young women to follow the company's agenda. This agenda included discussions of the Big Sister Plan, Prevention of Colds, Force Schedules, Stock Plan, Telephone Study Club, Quiet Operating, Force Losses, Importance of Peg Counts, Overlap Ringing, Pay Station Shortages, Explanation of the Dispatch Method, History of Development of the Telephone, Organization of Company, and Pink Ticket Plans.

6   E. K. Hall to James T. Moran, president of the Southern New England Telephone Company, June 14, 1923, AT&T Archives, Box 6. Sent to presidents of all associated companies.

7   President Matt Jones to all operators, June 15, 1923, AT&T Archives, Box 6.

8   John N. Schacht, *The Making of Telephone Unionism, 1920–1947* (New Brunswick, N.J.: Rutgers University Press, 1985), p. 17.

9   President Theodore N. Vail to Associated Companies Presidents, June 3, 6, and 7, 1919, AT&T Archives, Boxes 2 and 15.

10   Schacht, p. 41.

11   "Constitution of Association of Employees," Long Lines Department, American Telephone and Telegraph Company, p. 7, AT&T Archives, Box 6.

12   Ibid., p. 1.

13   Ibid., p. 6.

14   Bancroft Gherardi, "Some Suggestions and a Summary of the Discussion of Employee Representation and Personnel Work in the Bell System," paper delivered at the Personnel Conference, October 1923, p. 2.

15   Schacht, p. 41.

16   W. F. Cozad, "Employee Representation," paper presented at the General Traffic Conference, April 1923, p. 621.

17   Ibid., p. 1.

18   Schacht, p. 17.

19   Ibid.

20   H. E. Eldridge, "Employees Federation, Chicago Suburban Division," paper presented at the General Traffic Conference, April 1923, pp. 631, 633. During 1922, the Traffic Employees Federation discussed issues divided along the following lines:

Operators' quarters (restrooms, dining rooms, lavatories, etc.)	45.2 percent
Working conditions, compensation, etc.	15 percent
Activities in connection with the federation itself	14 percent
Switchboard equipment, toll lines, etc.	10.8 percent
Service, local and toll	5.2 percent
Social (picnics, dances, parties, etc.)	4.6 percent
Social service, Christmas boxes, funds for disabled soldiers, visits of sick committees, etc.	3.7 percent
Public relations	1.5 percent

21   Quoted in Schacht, p. 42.

22   The telephone company in Arkansas fired "every one" of a "group of desperate Arkansas operators" who left their switchboards "in a protest over wages and working conditions." Nelle Wooding, a long-time operator and eventual CWA official, remembered that the company imported operators from as far as Dallas to replace the strikers. In a policy similar to that assumed by the New England Telephone and Telegraph Company in 1913, Southern Bell managers paid the strikebreakers higher wages and spared no expense because they could not permit independent unionism— or even the idea of it—to thrive anywhere. Thomas R. Brooks, p. 22.

23   J. L. R. Van Meter, "Employee Associations in the Traffic Department of the Long Lines Department," paper presented at the Personnel Conference, April 1922, pp. 12–13.

24   Ibid., pp. 15–16.

25   Ibid., p. 17.

26   E. K. Hall, "Analysis of the Personnel Policy of the Bell System: Joint Conference Committees," paper delivered at the Bell System Plant and Engineering Conference, June 1926, pp. 5–6.

27   E. K. Hall, "General Personnel Problems and Policies," paper delivered at the Bell System Educational Conference, June 1926, p. 244.

28   E. K. Hall, "Personnel and Public Relations," paper delivered at the Plant and Engineering Conference of the Bell System, May 1923, pp. 7–9.

29   Ibid., p. 11.

30   A. C. Stannard, "Personnel Work in the Traffic Department of the Southwestern Bell Telephone Company," paper delivered at the Personnel Conference, October 1923, p. 12.

31   Ibid., p. 13.

32   Bancroft Gherardi, "Some Suggestions and a Summary of the Discussion of Employee Representation and Personnel Work in the Bell System," p. 1.

33   E. K. Hall, "Personnel and Public Relations, Summary and General Statement," paper delivered at the General Traffic Conference, April 1923, pp. 643–44.

34   "Summary of the Conference," summary of the papers delivered at the Personnel Conference, April 1922, p. 15.

35   Pauline Goldmark of AT&T's Department of Operations, Mary T. Reuse, assistant to the vice president, and Evelyn R. McGath from the vice president's office attended the 1922 Personnel Conference as "invited guests." Other than stenographers, they appear to have been among the few women who ever attended these conferences; they presented no papers. In 1929, Miss L. M. Smith did present a paper on the new women's nutrition course at the Personnel Conference.

36   Stannard, "Personnel Work in the Traffic Department of the Southwestern Bell Telephone Company," pp. 3–4.

37   Ibid., p. 12.

38   W. F. Cozad, "Employee Representation in the Traffic Department of the Northwestern Bell Telephone Company," paper presented at the Personnel Conference, October 1923, p. 5.

39   E. K. Hall, "Personnel and Public Relations, Summary and General Statement," p. 644.

40   "Summary of the Conference," summary of the papers delivered at the Personnel Conference, April 1922, p. 15.

41   J. L. R. Meter, "Employee Associations in the Traffic Department of the Long Lines Department," p. 20.

42   E. O. Raabe, "Some Employment Problems," paper presented at the Bell System General Traffic Conference, June 1925, p. 5.

43   Moore of the Southern New England company spoke in a general discussion on the "Question as to Advisability of Introducing Factor of Merit as well as Length of Service in Determining Operator's Wage Payments." This talk took place in a special "Separate Session of General Traffic Managers and Superintendents," held at the General Traffic Conference, April 1923, p. 30.

44   Ibid., p. 31.

45   Ibid.

46   Vice President E. K. Hall to all Associated Company Presidents, August 1929, AT&T Archives, Box 52.

47   Ibid., pp. 20–21.

48   Ibid., p. 22.

49   Hermann Thomas, "Service Committees, The Experience in the Long Lines Traffic Department," paper delivered at the Personnel Conference, April 1922, p. 14.

50   Switchboards with new lamps and other modifications made possible "a distribution of the traffic over the several 'B' positions in accordance with the loads they handle which results in a maximum occupied time by the 'B' operator and permits loads in the neighborhood of 575 calls per hour." Combined with "restricted repetition," straightforward trunking also made it possible to increase "A" operators' loads by 8 to 10 percent, which also increased the net profit for this new method from 20 to 32 percent. W. E. Farnham, "Local Traffic Engineering Problems," paper presented at the Bell System General Traffic Conference, June 1925, p. 12.

51   "Outline of Discussions at Separate Session of General Traffic Managers and Superintendents," paper delivered at the General Traffic Conference, April 1923, p. 1. In a discussion on operators' loads, K. W. Waterson stated: "The importance of . . . one unit in the overall Bell System load means extra expense or saving of about $1,000,000. a year." Other engineers and executives alluded to this saving whenever they discussed loads.

52   K. W. Waterson, "Review of Traffic Results," paper presented at the Bell System Operating Conference, May 1926, p. 44.

53   "Outline of Discussions at Separate Session of General Traffic Managers and Superintendents," p. 3. Statements made by J. H. Brace, general traffic superintendent, Bell Telephone Company of Canada, in discussions of operators' loads.

54   "Bell System Medical Department Administration and Practices," committee report prepared by W. F. Armstrong, C. F. Brisbin, F. W. Willard, and H. W. Bang, chairman, and presented by the Chairman at the General Personnel Conference, October 1929, p. 21.

55   E. K. Hall, "Certain Matters in the Personnel Program," paper presented at the Bell System Operating Conference, May 1926, p. 13.

56   E. O. Raabe, "Sickness Disability Among Female Traffic Employees," paper presented at the General Traffic Conference, April 1923, p. 423.

57   Ibid., p. 426.

58   Ibid., pp. 427–28.

59   Ibid., p. 428.

60   L. M. Smith, "The Nutrition Course," "talk" presented at the General Personnel Conference, October 1929, p. 7.

61   K. W. Waterson, "Traffic Administration and the Personnel Job," paper delivered at the Personnel Conference, October 1923, p. 3.

62   An analysis made of two multioffice cities in 1925 demonstrated that 5–7

percent of the women left to marry, 10–11 percent to attend to home duties, 2–3 percent to return to school, 5–12 percent to leave the city, 3–4 percent became disabled, 3–5 percent because of employment conditions, and more than 12 percent for miscellaneous reasons. E. O. Raabe, "Routine and Special Analysis of Force Conditions," paper delivered at the Bell System General Traffic Conference, June 1925, p. 8.

63   Vernal Black, "What I Did Today," quoted in A. C. Stannard, "Personnel Work in the Traffic Department of the Southwestern Bell Telephone Company," paper delivered at the Personnel Conference, October 1923, pp. 45–46.

64   Frances E. Miles, "What I Did Today," quoted in Stannard, p. 47.

65   M. D. Sedam, "Employee Representation in the Traffic Department of the Chesapeake and Potomac Telephone Company," paper presented at the Personnel Conference, October 1923, p. 13.

66   K. W. Waterson, "Review of Traffic Results for 1925 and Opportunities for Further Improvement," paper delivered at the Bell System Operating Conference, May 1926, p. 54.

67   "The Bell System Benefit Plan," committee report prepared by J. T. Sheafor, J. E. Macdonald, and L. S. Crosby, chairman, presented to the General Personnel Conference, October 1929, p. 3.

68   E. K. Hall, "Opening of the Fifteenth Personnel Conference," at the General Personnel Conference, October 1929, p. 3.

69   Thomas R. Brooks, pp. 25–26.

6. The Dial Era

1   "Glass Launches Crusade on Dial Phones in Capitol," *Washington Post*, May 22, 1930, pp. 1, 4. President Hoover also disliked the dials.

2   "Dial Phones, Banned In Senate, Stir House," *Washington Post*, May 23, 1930, pp. 1, 7. Abernethy's resolution went further than Glass's by adding that dial telephones "increased unemployment." When this point was brought to Mr. Glass's attention, he responded, "I know that and I object to being transformed into a telephone operator myself without compensation," p. 7. These resolutions launched a citywide debate among elected officials, businessmen of all kinds, and local residents. Many people felt that the dial simply represented progress that could not be stopped. Among the defenders of the dial was New York Representative Fiorello H. La Guardia (Republican), who commented that "any member of the House who hasn't enough sense to operate a dial telephone ought to go out and get himself another job." "Roll Your Own Phone Keeps Users Arguing," *Washington Post*, May 24, 1930. pp. 1, 3. The senators who wanted dial phones introduced an amendment to Glass's resolution that "allow[ed] the dial telephones to stay except in the offices of Senators who specifically wish[ed] their removal." See Arthur W. Page, AT&T vice president, public relations, to All Presidents, "Official Telegram," May 1930, pp. 2–3, AT&T Archives, Box 67.

3   See Venus Green, "Goodbye Central: Automation and the Decline of 'Personal

Service' in the Bell System, 1878–1921," *Technology and Culture* 36 (October 1995): 912–49, for the various methods employed by individuals and public institutions to halt dial conversion. For example, on December 4, 1940, the City Council of Superior, Wisconsin, unanimously "adopted a resolution opposing installation of dial telephones." The telephone operators' union had petitioned the council to save the operators' jobs. "Stop Dial Conversion," *Federation Voice* 1 (March 1941): 7.

4   When the workweek was reduced from six days to five and later to three or four days, management called it "sharing the work." Of course, salaries were reduced accordingly.

5   N. R. Danielian, *AT&T: The Story of Industrial Conquest* (New York: Vanguard Press, 1939), p. 211. The 1935–36 FCC investigation found that standardized operating loads had been established in 1911 and were "unnecessarily low" between 1922 and 1929. Loads were increased by 22 percent from 1933 to 1935, according to their estimations. See FCC, *Proposed Report Telephone Investigation* (Washington, D.C.: GPO, 1938), pp. 290–91.

6   FCC, *Investigation of the Telephone Industry in the United States* (Washington, D.C.: GPO, 1939), p. 280.

7   Danielian, p. 208.

8   Ibid., p. 206. Drastic reductions in construction and manufacturing caused the force loss in telephone plant and WECO.

9   Ibid., p. 208.

10   Bell Telephone almost doubled its subscribers from 8,736,000 in 1920 to 15,983,000 in 1930. *Bell System Statistical Manual, 1920–1964*, p. 502.

11   Raymond A. Steelman, "War-Time in the Traffic Departments," *Bell Telephone Magazine* 21 (August 1942): 141.

12   Raymond A. Steelman, "Hiring a Quarter of a Million Women," *Bell Telephone Magazine* 25 (Autumn 1946): 133–34.

13   Long distance was 60 percent dial in 1960. The year 1955 showed a small increase in operators but not enough to offset the effects of dial conversions.

14   J. Joseph Lowenberg, "Effects of Change on Employee Relations in the Telephone Industry," Ph.D. Diss., Harvard University, 1962, p. V-9.

15   Ibid.

16   See Green, "Goodbye Central."

17   W. N. Doak to Walter S. Gifford, August 21, 1931, p. 1, AT&T Archives, Box 67.

18   E. F. Carter to Secretary of Labor W. N. Doak, September 9, 1931, p. 3, AT&T Archives, Box 67.

19   Ibid., pp. 3–4.

20   Ethel L. Best, *The Change from Manual to Dial Operation in the Telephone Industry*, U.S. Department of Labor, Women's Bureau, Bulletin 110 (Washington, D.C.: GPO, 1933), p. 4.

21   It should be kept in mind that the temporary workers were full-time operators who replaced those who had resigned.

22   For the multioffice conversion the reduction in the operating force was even more drastic. Ibid., p. 12.

Before change, November 1929	424
At time of change, May 1930	435
Immediately after May 1930	287
After November 1930	128

23   Danielian claimed the Bell System could have retained 18,000 of the lower-paid workers who lost their jobs if it had reduced the $9.00 dividend by $1.00 during the Depression.

24   Commissioner Paul A. Walker issued a "Proposed Report" on April 1, 1938, which harshly criticized the Bell System. When AT&T managers complained that they had not been granted a fair hearing, they were allowed to submit briefs that were consulted in the preparation of a more conservative final report on June 14, 1939. See FCC, *Investigation of the Telephone Industry in the United States*, pp. 597–602; and FCC, *Proposed Report: Telephone Investigation* (Washington, D.C.: GPO, 1938), pp. 711–13.

25   See FCC, *Proposed Report*, pp. 314–16.

26   Ibid., pp. 286–88. Also see Danielian, pp. 207–9.

27   AT&T, "Comments Submitted to Federal Communications Commission by American Telephone and Telegraph Company on Commission Exhibit 2114," Pamphlet No. 16, "Financial Costs of Rendering License Contract Services" (New York: n.p., 1937), pp. 6–7.

28   "Bell System Public Relations as indicated by conferences of March, 1932," p. 1. Synopsis found in AT&T Archives, Box 1310.

29   Ibid.

30   Ibid., pp. 1–2.

31   Report of the proceedings of the General Publicity Conference, September 1934, p. 5, AT&T Archives, Box 1310.

32   Ibid.

33   Thomas R. Brooks, p. 33.

34   Schacht, pp. 37–38.

35   Norma Naughton, retired chairman, Branch 127, Federation of Long Lines Telephone Workers, NFTW, interviewed by John Schacht, July 12, 1970, p. 1. Interviews conducted by John Schacht are found in CWA-University of Iowa Oral History Project, CWA Archive, University of Iowa. Hereafter OHP.

36   Danielian, p. 186.

37   The Bell System continued to deny that automation caused a reduction in the workforce until August 16, 1949, when it announced that 262 Service Assistants and 229 Junior Service Assistants would be demoted because of "lowered traffic volume, better trained forces, increased productivity and mechanization." "Force Adjustment in Traffic, Off," *Local Leader* (published by Local 1, Long Lines Division 10 CWA-CIO), p. 1; "Mechanization Still," August 1949, vol. 1, no. 9, p. 2.

38   W. H. Harrison, "Technology in the Bell System with Particular Reference to Employment," AT&T, New York, April 17, 1940, pp. 1–2, AT&T Archives, Box 75.

39   Ibid., p. 2.

40   Ibid., p. 13.

41   Clifton W. Phalen, "Automation and the Bell System," statement by the president of the Michigan Bell Telephone Company before the Subcommittee on Economic Stabilization of the Joint Committee on the Economic Report, Washington, D.C., October 27, 1955, p. 1, AT&T Archives, Box 2043.

42   Ibid., p. 6.

43   E. F. Carter, AT&T vice president, sent a letter to all associated company presidents, dated April 11, 1933, in which he included a memorandum, "Some Employee Attitudes and Reactions Indicated in Joint Discussions Under Employee Representation Plans, January, 1933," p. 1, AT&T Archives, Box 58.

44   Ibid., p. 2.

45   Ibid.

46   Schacht argues that the association did provide the foundations for true unionism by establishing a structure through which workers could communicate with each other across departmental and geographical lines, etc.

47   "Phone Girls to Join with F. of L.," Boston Post, August 22, 1933. Found in AT&T Archives, Box 46.

48   Grace Barry to American Bell Telephone & Telegraph Company, August 22, 1933, AT&T Archives, Box 46.

49   U.S. Department of Labor, Bureau of Labor Statistics, Characteristics, quoted in Schacht, p. 38.

50   John Schacht interview with Helen C. Carmody, May 11, 1970, OHP, pp. 15–16. Some "1,500 Dallas CWA operators" struck for one day "over the lack of air conditioning which the union has been fighting for 7 years." The temperature in "the operating room [had] reached . . . 105 degrees even with fans blowing over ice buckets." "7 years with the Wrong Women," Long Lines Local 1150 Newsletter, August 10, 1951, p. 2.

51   John Schacht interview with Nelle Wooding, March 24, 1970, OHP, pp. 6–7.

52   For the complete history of telephone unionism, see Schacht; Curry; Thomas R. Brooks; and Barbash.

53   More than 80,000 members were represented by these delegates sent by seventeen different locals. Barbash, pp. 22–23.

54   Thomas R. Brooks, p. 52. Ninety-five delegates from forty-two independent unions who represented 165,000 workers attended. In the end, only those representing 92,000 actually affiliated with the NFTW (represented by sixty-one men and sixteen women).

55   Barbash, pp. 46–47.

56   Ibid.

57   Ibid., p. 45.

58   At its first meeting, the National Federation of Telephone Workers Executive

Board, "in order to speed the work of bringing the various traffic organizations into the ranks of the Federation," authorized the appointment of a "Traffic Organization Committee." Pansy Harris, a member of the Executive Board, headed the committee. "Minutes of Executive Board Meeting," June 10, 1939, New York, p. 5. The Executive Board was increased to nine members in November 1940. "Minutes of Executive Board Meeting," November 11–15, 1940, Milwaukee, p. 20. Among the issues on the agenda set for the second meeting of the panel, to be held June 4–5, 1942, were wage freezes, equal pay for equal work, job protections, a woman representative on advisory committees of the Federal Manpower Board, pensions, skilled worker classification of operators, a woman representative on the Executive Board, etc. "Traffic Panel to Meet June 4 to 5 in Baltimore," *Telephone Worker*, June 1942, p. 10.

59 Executive board members Pansy M. Harris and Theresa R. Donahey lobbied the board on these issues, and they also recommended that the NFTW support the "woman representation on the Man-Power Board now under consideration in Washington. . . ." See "Minutes of the Executive Board," April 6–10, 1942, Chicago, Exhibit 6, "Report by Miss Harris and Mrs. Donahey to the Executive Board on Traffic Problems," p. 2.

60 Ibid., p. 1.

61 Barbash, pp. 31–32. Also see "Minutes, Executive Board Meeting," Salt Lake City, June 11, 1940, Exhibit "C," "Mr. Adams' Verbal Report of the Wages & Hours Hearing on Learner Operator's Rates." During 1943–44, the NFTW successfully fought to establish a 40-cent minimum hourly wage, and the union also "defeated" another attempt to extend the operator learning period. See "Victory for NFTW in Minimum Wage Fight," *Telephone Worker*, August 1944, p. 4.

62 "Women's 'Equal Pay' Bill is Introduced into U.S. Senate," *Telephone Worker*, October 1945, p. 9; and Barbash, p. 32.

63 "Skilled? Of Course!," *Telephone Worker*, May 1941, pp. 9–10. A point worth noting is that telephone operators wanted an explicit distinction made between them and "hatcheck girls, salad makers, elevator operators and other similar labor." In this sense, telephone operators are claiming a skilled status, not only to increase their wages, but to increase their social status. See Jeannette Reedy, "Traffic's Drive for Skilled Classification Approaches Goal," *Telephone Worker*, April 1944, p. 11.

64 Quoted in "Job Study Findings Released by U.S. Department of Labor," *Telephone Worker*, July 1946, p. 2.

65 Sometimes the union presented the hiring of women at wages lower than men's for the same job as a problem for men rather than as an injustice to women. For example, the Central-Southern Regional passed a motion that resolved "that all member organizations endeavor to protect the present wage schedule of male employees by insisting that their respective managements pay all women assigned jobs usually performed by male employees the same rate of wages as heretofore paid the male employees." See "Official Minutes Central-Southern Regional Conference," Chicago, May 15–16, 1942, p. 5. Even NFTW President Paul E. Griffith expressed this opinion when he stated: "No company is going to pay women a man's wage if they can avoid it.

Furthermore if women receive men's pay, the men will have a better chance of getting their job back at old wages when the war is over." See "Minutes of the Western Regional Conference," April 17–19, 1942, San Francisco, Appendix "A," "Text of President Griffith's Address," p. 7. These statements indicate less than a total commitment to equal pay for equal work.

66   See "Minutes of Executive Board Meeting," June 1941, p. 11. At this meeting, the women members of the Executive Board were charged with the duties "to carry on the work of obtaining a classification as skilled for traffic operators" and to submit to the next board meeting "a suggested program of action for obtaining the desired objective of equal pay for equal work." By the April 1942 meeting, the board "took recognition of the fact that only through the application of this principle could existing wage standards be maintained and women workers properly compensated and the jobs of men protected." "Minutes of Executive Board Meeting," Chicago, April 6–10, 1942, p. 14.

67   "Equal Pay for Equal Work: Labor Board's General Order No. 16 Still in Force," *Telephone Worker*, July 1943, p. 11.

68   Beginners were paid $21 weekly, and, after ten years, operators received $32. Schacht, pp. 136–37; and "That Ohio Strike," *Telephone Worker*, December 1944, pp. 4–6.

69   Henry Mayer, "At Long Last—A Telephone Industry Commission," *FTWP News*, July 1945, p. 4. The U.S. government established the National Telephone Panel on January 1, 1945, but it lacked final decision-making powers. On June 15, 1945, the panel was converted into a commission with real power and telephone worker representation.

70   The National Telephone Commission had been established as a direct result of NFTW pressure on the War Labor Board to provide independent telephone unions with representation in wage and labor disputes brought before the board. At first, the Board was reluctant to grant this request, but a strike by the Dayton, Ohio, telephone operators that could have become nationwide convinced the government to relent.

71   The National Telephone Commission awarded wage increases that sought to eliminate the inequities built into the Bell System's regional wage policy. For telephone operators, it shortened the wage progression schedule by two or three years, which effectively raised operators' wages a greater percentage than it did those of other workers. The panel also barred discrimination against married women. The commission ceased to exist on December 31, 1945. Schacht, pp. 136–41, 242.

72   As a result of the panel's review of pending disputes, telephone workers received $3–5 raises, progression schedules were shortened (i.e., eight to nine years for operators rather than ten to eleven years), and grievance and arbitration procedures were improved. Schacht, p. 140.

73   Thomas R. Brooks, p. 51.

74   Ibid.

75   One IBEW representative stated that young women who did not have to support families were "more strike happy than the plant men." For operators, he said,

"the strike is a kind of change from the dull routine," and "some of [the] girls act like a strike was a parade." Melvin Kline Bers, "Unionism and Collective Bargaining in the Telephone Industry," Ph.D. Diss., University of California at Berkeley, 1956, p. 70.

76   Men were concerned over changes in their work process that would result from the introduction of such new technologies as coaxial cable and new switching systems, but at this time they were more likely to gain jobs rather than lose them.

77   Fagen, p. 613.

78   Only after traffic women threatened to leave the NFTW if they did not receive more representation did they gain an increase from one to two places in 1940. Brooks, p. 63. The women kept fighting. At the 1942 NFTW annual convention in a Traffic Panel session discussion of the number of traffic women who should be on the Executive Board, Mary Gannon, the outspoken leader of the Washington, D.C., traffic local, angrily declared: "Why shouldn't we have three women on the Board if it is necessary? What difference does it make if the President, perhaps, should be a woman? I am afraid I don't see things from the man's point of view alone. I think there are intelligent women in the world." See NFTW Traffic Panel Session Proceedings, June 4–8, 1942, Baltimore, p. 160, NFTW Collection at New York University Tamiment/Wagner Archives, Box 5. Hereafter NFTW.

79   Schacht, pp. 74–75.

80   The major threat from the AFL was the IBEW. The American Communications Association (mainly on the West Coast) and the United Electrical, Radio and Machine Workers (UE) were affiliated with the CIO. These two CIO unions also bore the stigma of alleged "communism."

81   Berth Horth, secretary treasurer, NFTW, "Information Furnished the National Labor Relations Board," February 24, 1941, p. 6, NFTW, Box 1, Folder 3.

82   Ibid.

83   In the "Report of the National Traffic Panel Committee to the Tenth National Assembly of National Federation of Telephone Workers," under the heading of "Technological Changes Within the Telephone Industry," an indication appears that the panel had discussed this topic with the NFTW's lawyer who suggested that this matter "be taken care of by NFTW to see what could be done on a national basis," p. 2.

84   See, for example, Resolution 29, which resolved that "the member unions in the National Federation of Telephone Workers take steps to secure satisfactory agreements with their respective managements regarding separation allowances, possible force reduction and part-timing, and. . . . that the member unions in the National Federation of Telephone Workers obtain agreements from their respective Managements, well in advance of the resumption of dial conversions or the introduction of other technological changes, which will spread such changes over periods of sufficient length as to bring about a minimum of force adjustment among Traffic Employees, and, that the member unions keep each other and the National Traffic Panel informed of the development of this program." See Proceedings of the Tenth National Assembly, June 12, 1944, "Resolution 29, Post War Force Adjustments."

85   Proceedings, Second National Traffic Panel Session of the NFTW, June 4–8, 1942, Baltimore, p. 232, reported by Norma Naughton for the Occupational Classification Committee.

86   "Minutes of Executive Board Meeting," Salt Lake City, June 11, 1940, p. 24. Third meeting.

87   See, for example, "Official Minutes of the Central Region Conference of Telephone Unions," Chicago, September 15–17, 1939, pp. 10–11, 16, 26. Other Central Regional, South Central Regional, Eastern Regional, and Western Regional Minutes (intermittently from 1939 to 1946), NFTW, Box 6, Folders 33–36.

88   "Indiana Co. Shows Wrong Way to Deal with Force Cut in Mechanization," CWA Weekly Newsletter, September 1949, p. 2.

89   "Employment Hard Hit by Dial Conversion in Indiana Town," CWA Weekly Newsletter, December 12, 1949, p. 4.

90   See Resolution of the Ninth Annual Convention of Local Presidents in FTWP News, February 1949, p. 7.

91   "Technological Unemployment," PACT News, April 1944, p. 2.

92   "Those Four Hour Meetings," Telephone Worker, November 1945, p. 4.

93   Ibid., p. 5.

94   "Washington Traffic Holds Eight Day Continuous Meeting Session," Telephone Worker, January 1946, p. 4; and Barbash, p. 58, Thomas R. Brooks, p. 102.

95   Thomas R. Brooks, p. 107.

96   Ibid., p. 108.

97   The complete list of demands: (1) union shop and checkoff of union dues, (2) a general wage increase—$12 a week or more, (3) area wage differentials adjustments, (4) shortening of progression schedules, (5) town reclassifications—upward, (6) job descriptions for service assistants in the traffic department, (7) work jurisdiction changes, (8) longer leaves of absences for union officers, (9) improved vacation practices, and (10) larger pensions. See William Gillmore Curry, "Bell Telephone Labor Economics," Ph.D. Diss., Columbia University, 1952, p. 159. With the exception of workers in Indiana, Virginia, and New England, this strike affected the entire Bell System. Virginia and Indiana workers could not strike because of compulsory arbitration utility laws in their states. New Jersey workers ignored the state seizure of the utility and struck anyway. Ibid., p. 163.

98   Ibid., p. 166. See "A Job for the Rank and File" and "The Facts Behind the Phone Strike," West Coast Telephone News, May–June 1947, pp. 1–2.

99   The emergence of CWA and its affiliation with the CIO marks the decline of the NFTW and the end of efforts by the CIO–Telephone Workers Organizing Committee (formed at the same time as CWA), American Communications Association, and the UE to organize telephone workers. IBEW and other independents (some northeastern unions formed the Alliance of Independent Telephone Unions in 1949) continued to compete with CWA. Lowenberg, pp. I-26–I-31. Sixty percent of Bell System workers belonged to the CWA by 1960, and the union had achieved full recognition as the bargaining agent for those workers.

100   Unions agreed that the major concerns included layoffs, transfers, retraining, seniority rights, rehiring, pensions, and termination pay. Lowenberg, p. IV-6.

101   Ibid.

102   Sylvia G. Gottlieb, "It Can Happen to You," *CWA News,* April 1948, p. 8. According to Gottlieb, the "minimum standards" that each clause should include would be "(1) Adequate notice of at least 90 days to the union by the company when layoffs seem necessary; (2) the union should be permitted the selection of limited part-timing instead of lay-offs"; (3) transfer regulation; (4) strict enforcement of seniority among workers performing similar work; (5) no contracting-out.

103   "Agreement Between Traffic Telephone Workers Federation of New Jersey and New Jersey Bell Telephone Company," effective September 27, 1942, with amendments to and including March 14, 1946, p. 6.

104   "Agreement," CWA, Michigan Division 44, and the Michigan Bell Telephone Company, Traffic Department, December 15, 1948, p. 15. If layoffs were planned as a consequence of dial conversion, then the company had to provide the union with a list of employees affected and their seniority dates "not less than thirty days prior to the scheduled cutover date." If a surplus occurred as a result of other conditions, then the union should be "notified in writing not less than thirty days in advance of any contemplated force adjustment . . .," p. 16.

105   "Agreement" between the Chesapeake & Potomac Telephone Company of West Virginia and the CWA, Charleston, W. Va., 1946, p. 22. Also see "Agreement" between Traffic Telephone Workers Federation of New Jersey and New Jersey Bell Telephone Company, effective September 27, 1942, with amendments to and including March 14, 1946, p. 6, and "Traffic Contract," CWA, CIO, District 8, effective June 3, 1952, pp. 26–27.

106   "Have You a Friend That Needs a Job? Tell Them About This," *Long Lines Local 1150 Newsletter,* June 8, 1951, p. 1.

107   The members of this committee (Anne Benscoter, Mae Mann, Nelle Wooding, Virginia Wigglesworth, Beatrice Smith, and Beatrice Strong) represent the most militant women organizers throughout the period under discussion. One wonders if Beirne appointed the committee to quiet their protests against dial. It seems that the committee received a great deal of publicity in the union newspapers, but no real policy ever developed out of it and, by 1950, hardly any mention of it appears in the union newspapers.

108   The purposes of the committee:

1. To study conditions surrounding Bell System Local and Long Distance Conversion programs.
2. To study the effect of these conversion programs upon the national economy, in general, and upon employment opportunity in the telephone industry specifically, and
3. To develop a recommended joint program to be embraced by all CWA Divisions, wherein the undesirable effects of the threatened lay-offs, transfers and other undesirable results of rapid technological improvement, can be minimized.

"Dial Conversion Committee Meets in Washington," *PACT News* (published by the Northwestern Union of Telephone Workers), March 1948, p. 3.

109 The committee met in Washington, D.C., from January 12–17, 1948, and during the week of February 7, 1949.

110 "Summary of Proceedings of the Third Annual Convention of the Communication Workers of America," held in Chicago, June 13–17, 1949, p. 30.

111 Sylvia B. Gottlieb laments the "End of a Career" in 1948 by proposing that the company inform the workers of their exact plans and stop changing the cutover dates so that the operators could make plans/retrain to meet the possibility of layoffs. Gottlieb, "End of a 'Career,'" *CWA News*, February 1948, p. 8.

112 Mary E. Gannon, chairman, Traffic Panel, "Activities of the Traffic Panel: Report on Past Year's work, Future Objectives Outlined," *Telephone Worker*, May 1944, p. 4. This same point was made in "Technological Unemployment," *Telephone Worker*, March 1944, p. 6. At its June 17, 1944, meeting, the NFTW executive board also adopted a resolution in support of this idea. See "Highlights of Tenth National Assembly, June 12–17, 1944, Denver, Colorado," *Telephone Worker*, July 1944, p. 7. Also see Anne C. Benscoter, "Women in Industry," *Telephone Worker*, November 1944, p. 5.

113 "Official Minutes, National Federation of Telephone Workers, Central Regional Conference, September 27–29, 1946, Milwaukee. Attached "Report of the Effect of the Proposed Technological Improvements on the Status of Employment," pp. 1–3.

114 "Minutes . . .," p. 16.

115 "National Traffic Panel Council Meets in Chicago," *Telephone Worker*, November 1943, p. 12.

116 "Post War Planning Committee Makes Recommendations," *Telephone Worker*, January 1944, p. 6.

117 CWA-CIO, "Background of 1950 Telephone Wage Dispute" (Washington, D.C.: CWA, 1950), p. 9. Booklet found in the Beirne Papers, Box 1, Negotiations Planning 1948–49, CWA Archives, Washington, D.C. This position was held by both AFL and CIO unions with the exception of The Cigar Makers International. See Amy Sue Bix, *Inventing Ourselves Out of Jobs: America's Debate over Technological Employment 1929–1981* (Baltimore: Johns Hopkins University Press, 2000), p. 102.

118 Ibid., p. 8.

119 Joseph A. Beirne, "Why We Welcome Automation," Washington, D.C.: CWA, n.d.). Gail Malmgreen of the Wagner Labor Archives at New York University sent me this booklet.

120 Joseph A. Beirne, *New Horizons for American Labor* (Washington, D.C.: Public Affairs Press, 1962), pp. 48–49.

121 See CWA Executive Board Minutes, April 1951–December 1954, p. 344–45.

122 Beirne quoted in the Executive Board minutes, p. 345, CWA Convention Proceedings, 1952, pp. 439–41.

123 Ibid.

124 Apparently the national leadership paid little heed to recommendations

made by union locals. For instance, Local 1150, one of the oldest, largest, and most militant of the CWA locals, which represented mostly long distance and overseas operators, faced with the layoff of 200 full-time temporary operators, suggested to the company a "speed-up" in "training, and retraining programs," cessation of hiring operators and clerks off the street, promotion of "traffic people to clerical jobs in other departments," and, most importantly, facing "up to the fact that carrying some surplus is a legitimate cost of running a business." "Layoffs," *Long Lines Local 1150 Newsletter*, November 13, 1953, p. 1. According to Bix, rank-and-file union members in other industries often protested the pro-technology position of the union officials and offered suggestions such as dismantling the machines or imposing a technology tax on employers. Union officials wanted to appear "reasonable," so they backed away from any kind of radical action. In the 1930s unions were still weak, with few resources; members wanted to hold on to their jobs "at any cost" and feared that radical tactics would "backfire." See Bix, pp. 108–9.

125   Beirne, "Why We Welcome Automation," p. 11.

126   Ibid.

127   Jeannette Reedy, "Gains of the Traffic Unions," *Telephone Worker*, June 1944, p. 11. The actual time an operator remained on the job was longer than the hours worked. If she received a one-hour lunch and two fifteen-minute breaks, these were added to her tour as unpaid time. Operators who worked forty-four to forty-eight hours six days a week at the start of the Depression worked forty hours five days a week by World War II. In 1960, they worked between thirty-seven and thirty-nine hours a week. Split tricks—weekend, holiday, evening, and night assignments—continued to be required of operators, especially those with little seniority. Sex segregation, manifested in mostly all-female traffic, accounting and commercial departments, and mostly all-male plant departments, did not change, nor was it seriously challenged before the 1960s. A continuance of extreme supervision, high operating loads, and petty regulations kept turnover high throughout most of the dial era.

128   PBX operators worked at the switchboards internal to private businesses. Answering service operators, who took messages for customers unable to answer their phones, performed duties similar to PBX operators. Many still exist, although their numbers have been greatly diminished by automatic answering machines and call-forwarding.

129   K. W. Waterson, "Review of Traffic Results for 1925 and Opportunities for Further Improvement," paper delivered at the Bell System Operating Conference, May 1926, p. 38.

130   Ibid., p. 39.

131   New York State investigators in 1920 called the switch by 334 operators from the New York Telephone Company to private switchboards "a natural advance." They concluded: "The pay of the private switch board operator is higher than in the Telephone Company, the hours are more regular, with Saturday afternoon and Sunday free, and the Telephone Company itself believes that when girls leave the Company to go to private switch boards it increases the efficiency of its own system." State of New

York Department of Labor, "The Telephone Industry," Special Bulletin 100 (Albany: J. B. Lyon, 1920), 1920, p. 43.

132 By 1948, the New York Telephone Company had discontinued training PBX operators, though it retained its placement bureau. "Interesting People 6, 6,000 Jobs a Year," *Telephone Review* 38 (February 1948): 5.

133 Ethel Erickson, *The Woman Telephone Worker*, U.S. Department of Labor, Women's Bureau Bulletin 207 (Washington, D.C.: GPO, 1944), Chart 1.

134 Caroline C. Cherrix, *Women Telephone Workers and Changing Technology*, U.S. Department of Labor, Women's Bureau Bulletin 286 (Washington, D.C.: GPO, 1963), p. 7.

135 Women service representatives who had moved into that job during World War I were able to extend their responsibilities in World War II to become Business Office Supervisors. Dial equipment administrators, a job formerly performed by men in the traffic department, gradually became female-dominated by the early 1960s. Emma W. Condit, "Women in Business Office Supervision," *Bell Telephone Magazine* 30 (Summer 1951): 101–2.

136 Erickson, p. 31. See also Ethel Erickson to Bertha M. Nienburg, July 2, 1944, National Archives, Washington, D.C., Record Group 86, No. 207, Correspondence 1944, Box 644.

137 Excerpts from meeting between the Committee of the National Traffic Panel of the NFTW and representatives of the Women's Bureau, October 12, 1943. National Archives, Women's Bureau, Record Group 86, No. 207, Correspondence 1943, Box 644, p. 5.

138 Ibid.

139 Ibid.

140 David Copus, Lawrence Gartner, Randall Speck, William Wallace, Marjanette Feagan, and Katherine Mazzaferri, "A Unique Competence: A Study of Equal Employment Opportunity in the Bell System." This paper, written in 1971 by the lawyers who participated in the Equal Employment Commission investigation into the employment practices of the Bell System operating companies, summarizes the results of the investigation, p. 46. New England Telephone Company, Ohio Bell, and Michigan Bell were the only operating companies that hired any women as craft workers in 1966. I am extremely grateful and indebted to Anne H. Walden, one of the first African American operators, for bringing this document to my attention.

141 Judith Long Laws, "The Bell Telephone System: A Case Study," in Phyllis A. Wallace, ed., *Equal Employment Opportunity and the AT&T Case* (Cambridge, Mass.: MIT Press, 1976), p. 161.

7. Racial Integration and the Demise of the "White Lady" Image

1 George S. Schuyler, "Negro Labor and Public Utilities," *Messenger*, January 1927, p. 4.

2 Ibid. Sylvan remarked further that he trusted that Schuyler would come to the same conclusion and "arrive at the place where you will feel any considerable atten-

tion given by you in the way of agitation or publication will result in still further increasing any heartburning or disappointment now extant."

3 State of New York, Second Report of the New York State Temporary Commission on the Condition of the Colored Urban Population to the Legislature of the State of New York (Albany: J. B. Lyon, 1939), p. 66.

4 The Mayor's Commission on Conditions in Harlem, "The Negro in Harlem: A Report on Social and Economic Conditions Responsible for the Outbreak of March 19, 1935" (New York: 1936), p. 24.

5 New York State Temporary Commission on the Condition of the Urban Colored Population, Public Hearings, 1937. See, for example, the testimonies of Walter D. Williams, general traffic manager, New York Telephone Company, and Peter D. Lowrie, auditor of the Bronx-Westchester area, New York Telephone Company.

6 Ibid., pp. 1512–15.

7 Ibid., p. 1514.

8 Ibid., p. 1513.

9 Ibid., p. 1522.

10 Clarence M. Mitchell to Msgr. Francis J. Haas and George M. Johnson, conference with Mr. August B. Haneke, vice president and general manager, Chesapeake & Potomac Telephone Company, Baltimore, July 5, 1943, p. 1. Brotherhood of Sleeping Car Porters Papers, Box 24, Folder 1, Chicago Historical Society.

11 Ibid.

12 Quoted in Joseph H. B. Evans, regional director, Region IV, to Eugene Davidson, assistant director of field operations, May 28, 1945, FEPC Headquarters Records, Record Group 228, Entry 39, Box 456, National Archives.

13 Ibid.

14 Francis J. Haas, "Memorandum: Conference with Walter Gifford, President, American Telephone and Telegraph Company, in re: Baltimore, Philadelphia and Louisville Telephone Company Exchanges," August 23, 1943, p. 1. Brotherhood of Sleeping Car Porters Papers, Box 24, Folder 2, Chicago Historical Society.

15 Ibid., p. 2.

16 National Urban League, Department of Industrial Relations, "Number Please?: Employment of Negro Workers in the Telephone Industry in 44 Cities" (New York: 1946), pp. 1–2. The cities, which covered the United States, included Atlanta, Boston, Chicago, Detroit, Little Rock, Memphis, Minneapolis, Newark, New Orleans, New York City, Omaha, Philadelphia, Portland, Oregon, and Seattle.

17 Ibid., 5.

18 Harry H. C. Gibson to Elmer W. Henderson, regional director, Region VI, December 18, 1944, p. 5, FEPC Headquarters Records, Record Group 228, Entry 39, Box 456, National Archives.

19 The FEPC received complaints against Bell System companies including New Jersey Bell Telephone Company (Atlantic City), Pittsburgh Telephone Company, Chesapeake & Potomac (Baltimore), Ohio Bell (Columbus), Southern Bell Telephone

Company (Louisville), the Southwestern Bell Telephone Company (St. Louis, New Orleans), Southern California Telephone (San Diego, Los Angeles), Pacific Telephone and Telegraph Company (San Francisco and Palo Alto), and Spokane.

20   Copus et al., pp. 179–81.

21   These positions were occupied by women in the traffic, accounting, and commercial departments. Black men were usually hired in the plant department "as garage men, clerks, elevator operators, janitors, porters, cleaners, and floor men." Edward Lawson to Will Maslow, director of Field Operations, October 17, 1944, p. 4, Record Group 228, Entry 8, Box 71, National Archives. However, the lifting of the color bar in these low-level positions did not represent a true widening of opportunity to a large number of jobs. Telephone women numbered more than half of the 750,000 Bell System employees in 1944.

22   Ibid., p. 2.

23   Ibid., p. 4.

24   Ibid.

25   Ibid., p. 5. This agreement was allegedly between Stanley Isaacs, Adam Powell, Charles Collier, Benjamin Barnett, and the company. FEPC investigators checked with each man and reported that "all four of these persons vehemently denied that they had given their approval to any such plan."

26   Executive Order 8802 forbade discrimination in industries required to conduct the war. Order 9346 mandated that all government contracts pertaining to the war industries contain an antidiscrimination clause.

27   Harry L. Kingman, regional director, to Clarence Mitchell, associate director of Field Operations, November 28, 1944, p. 3, FEPC Headquarters Records, Record Group 228, Entry 39, Box 456, National Archives.

28   Southern Bell operating companies attributed their rejection of black applicants to "general appearance, . . . overweight, health problems, . . . moral turpitude, arrest records," insufficient education, and poor testing. Even to be allowed to take the test, an interviewer had to determine that the applicant was qualified to take it. Subjective observations provided the foundation for such qualifications. See "Complaint Analysis—Bell System," p. 8, EEOC, Box 37.

29   D. C. Emerson, vice president, AT&T, to Bernard Strassburg, chief, common carrier bureau, FCC, December 9, 1969, p. 4, EEOC, Box 35. Southern Bell became two companies in 1968 after hundreds of discrimination complaints were filed against it. Lawyers for the National Organization of Women believed that this tactic was intended to frustrate the EEOC investigations.

30   See the interviewers' reports in EEOC, Box 35.

31   W. R. Carter, Vice President, South Central Bell, to Vice President (Louisiana), Vice President and General Managers, South Central Bell, May 20, 1970, EEOC, FCC Staff Exhibit 48, Box 16.

32   EEOC, Report, "EEOC Compliance Experience with Southern, Southwestern and Pacific Bell," typescript, n.d., p. 4, EEOC, Box 37.

33 W. R. Carter, Vice President, South Central Bell, to Vice President (Louisiana), Vice President and General Managers, South Central Bell, May 20, 1970, EEOC, FCC Staff Exhibit 48, Box 16.

34 For examples, see the March on Washington press releases and newspaper clippings (*St. Louis American*, May 27, June 17, August 5, September 2, 16, 1943; *Chicago Defender*, June 19, September 25, 1943; *St. Louis Argus*, May 28, June 2, August 6, 1943; *Pittsburgh Courier*, June 5, 26, 1943) in the Brotherhood of Sleeping Car Porters Scrapbook, Chicago Historical Society. Complaints to the FEPC (Record Group 228) and the EEOC (Record Group 403) can be found in the National Archives.

35 See, for example, Henry Winfield Wheeler, "The Spider's Web": "Why demand jobs of the Public Utilities? Because they are corporations granted their franchises by the state and the government and we are citizens. Because 10,000 users of telephones have demanded it; because we are right and we will be heard." Clipping from the *St. Louis American*, May 20, 1943. Brotherhood of Sleeping Car Porters Scrapbook, p. 93, Chicago Historical Society.

36 U.S. Senate. *Investigation of Telephone Companies*, S. Doc. 380, 61st Congress, 2nd sess., 1910, p. 20.

37 "Colored Girls Can Help," *Cleveland Plain Dealer*, November 4, 1918, p. 7, and Greenwald, pp. 41–42.

38 "State Law Strikes at Color Bias," *New York Amsterdam News*, May 3, 1933, p. 10. Male-dominated rail and electric utilities were the "particular" focus of this group, but the exclusion of blacks in the telephone industry did not go unnoticed.

39 New York Urban League, Press Release, November 30, 1944, p. 2, FEPC Record Group 228, Entry 63, Box 71, National Archives.

40 Ibid., p. 3.

41 John Henrike Clarke interviewed by Venus Green, January 23, 1986, New York. The strategy was to tie up operators with requests for nonexistent numbers.

42 A spokesman for the March on Washington Movement affirmed that of the black women who had applied "several" were "graduates of leading American Universities and that all of them have had experience in business which would fully qualify them for most any position the Telephone Company has to fill." "MOWM to Stage March on Bell Telephone Company," *St. Louis American*, May 27, 1943. Brotherhood of Sleeping Car Porters Scrapbook, p. 19, Chicago Historical Society.

43 "March Movement Campaign of Protest Against Telephone Company Discrimination," *St. Louis American*, August 5, 1943. Brotherhood of Sleeping Car Porters Scrapbook, p. 165, Chicago Historical Society.

44 T. D. McNeal, director, March On Washington Committee, "Statement of Facts" (leaflet). Brotherhood of Sleeping Car Porters Scrapbook, p. 108, Chicago Historical Society.

45 "Seek Conference for Better Jobs," *Pittsburgh Courier*, June 26, 1943. Brotherhood of Sleeping Car Porters Scrapbook, p. 143, Chicago Historical Society.

46 "300 Citizens Encircled Bell Telephone Building Saturday," *St. Louis Ameri-*

can, June 12, 1943. Brotherhood of Sleeping Car Porters Scrapbook, p. 116, Chicago Historical Society.

47 Ibid.

48 "Widespread Support for March On Telephone Company," *St. Louis American*, June 10, 1943. Brotherhood of Sleeping Car Porters Scrapbook, p. 108, Chicago Historical Society.

49 Ibid.

50 "Negroes Protest Telephone Discrimination Through Mass Payment of Telephone Bills," press release, March on Washington Movement. Brotherhood of Sleeping Car Porters Scrapbook, p. 247, Chicago Historical Society. Also see clipping "Set Payment to Phone Co. in St. Louis," *Chicago Defender*, September 25, 1943, Scrapbook, p. 172.

51 "Girls Picket Phone Company," *St. Louis American*, July 15, 1943. Brotherhood of Sleeping Car Porters Scrapbook, p. 126, Chicago Historical Society.

52 Muriel Ferris to Joseph H. B. Evans, regional director, Region IV, May 28, 1945, p. 1, FEPC Headquarters Records, Record Group 228, Entry 39, Box 456, National Archives.

53 Roi Ottley and William J. Weatherby, eds. (the Federal Writers Project), "The Depression in Harlem," in Bernard Sternsher, ed., *Hitting Home: The Great Depression in Town and Country* (Chicago: Quadrangle Books, 1970), p. 118.

54 "Telephone Companies Refusal to Hire Colored Is Nation-wide," *Baltimore Afro-American*, November 6, 1943, p. 1. Thanks to Eric Arnesen for bringing this clipping to my attention.

55 G. James Fleming, regional director, to Will Maslow, director of field operations, November 7, 1944, FEPC Headquarters Records, Record Group 228, Entry 39, Box 456, National Archives.

56 NAACP, Group II, Legal Files, Container B.95, Folder "Labor Telephone Companies, 1946–1948," Library of Congress.

57 When the EEOC convinced the FCC to conduct hearings during the early 1970s, it requested cases outstanding from the existent state FEPCS, various state agencies (commissions on human rights and human resources, offices of human rights, and civil rights commissions) and state departments of labor so that they could be taken into consideration with the EEOC case. See Peter C. Robertson, director, State and Community Affairs, EEOC to Executive Directors, State and Local Antidiscrimination Agencies, and Project Directors, EEOC Funded Contracts, January 1972, in EEOC, Box 111.

58 Ibid.

59 " 'Would-Be Minstrels' Amuse Buffalo Toll Party-Goers," *Telephone Review* 30 (January 1939), p. 21.

60 "Sodus Minstrels," *Telephone Review* 46 (September, 1955), p. 17.

61 One does wonder what these representations meant to these women in light of Eric Lott's suggestion that white male minstrels were "inhabiting . . . black bodies

as a way of interracial male-bonding"; or David R. Roediger's notion that "white crowds repeatedly colored *themselves*, replacing excluded Blacks from within their own ranks." Roediger also postulates that "the *content* of blackface performances identifies their particular appeals as expressions of the longings and fears and the hopes and prejudices of the Northern Jacksonian urban working class, especially the artisanate." See Eric Lott, "White Like Me: Racial Cross-Dressing and the Construction of American Whiteness," in Amy Kaplan and Donald E. Pease, eds., *Cultures of United States Imperialism* (Durham, N.C.: Duke University Press, 1993), p. 475; and David R. Roediger, *The Wages of Whiteness: Race and the Making of the American Working Class* (London: Verso, 1991), pp. 104, 115.

62   For example, the Southern Association of Bell Telephone Employees limited their membership to "all white employees." See "The Constitution of the Southern Association of Bell Telephone Employees," effective July 1941, p. 8. This union was eventually declared a company union and replaced by the Southern Federation of Telephone Workers, whose constitution did not have this clause.

63   Koons, quoted in Proceedings of the National Federation of Telephone Workers National Assembly, February 1–6, 1943, p. 57. Koons warned that if the telephone workers forced the issue before the "War Manpower Practices Committee," they would be ruled against.

64   Edward Lawson to Will Maslow, director of field operations, October 17, 1944, p. 4, Record Group 228, Entry 8, Box 71, National Archives.

65   Ibid.

66   Membership qualifications for telephone workers' organizations changed over time. In most cases, company unions explicitly limited membership to whites. After the creation of independent unions and the formation of the National Federation of Telephone Workers (NFTW, 1937–39), local affiliates determined their own membership qualifications. Antidiscrimination clauses were not found in any of their constitutions. When the CWA formed (1946–47), an antidiscrimination clause was in its constitution from the beginning.

67   "Resolution No. 1, Fair Employment Practice Committee," *FTWP News*, February 1945, p. 4.

68   Evelyn N. Cooper to Committee Members, confidential memorandum, March 7, 1945, p. 2, Record Group 228, Entry 25, Box 94, National Archives.

69   George M. Johnson, deputy chairman and acting chief of the Legal Division, to Clarence M. Mitchell, associate director of Field Operations, March 8, 1945, Record Group 228, Entry 25, Box 94, National Archives.

70   See Ulysses S. Wiggins, branch president, NAACP, Camden, N.J., to Thurgood Marshall, special counsel, NAACP, New York, May 12, 1943. NAACP Legal Files, Group II, container 86, Library of Congress.

71   In this period of American hate strikes, white male telephone workers at the Western Electric Point Breeze manufacturing plant outside Baltimore stopped working in December 1943 after the company refused to provide separate toilet facilities for black and white workers. When war production was affected by the strike, the U.S.

Army seized control of the plant, defeated the demand for separate facilities, and ended the strike. John N. Schacht, *The Making of Telephone Unionism, 1920–1947* (New Brunswick, N.J.: Rutgers University Press, 1985), p. 114. Schacht argues that the union was company-dominated and that these types of actions did not occur where "legitimate" unions were in place. He states that despite some "stiff objections from white operators . . . small-scale integration of the traffic departments went smoothly, thanks in part to the cooperation of unions and local management," p. 115. He does not explain why members of a company-dominated union would object to company policies or, more importantly, why they would halt war production that provided enormous profits for the company.

72   Clarence Mitchell to George Johnson, "Complaint of the Point Breeze Association Against the Western Electric Company, Baltimore Maryland," August 26, 1943, p. 1. Brotherhood of Sleeping Car Porters Papers, Box 24, Folder 2, Chicago Historical Society.

73   Ibid.

74   "Minutes, President's Committee on Fair Employment Practice," August 28, 1943, p. 2. Brotherhood of Sleeping Car Porters Papers, Box 24, Folder 2, Chicago Historical Society. Although the company portrayed its actions as a show of eagerness to comply with Executive Order 8802, there is reason to believe that it simply did not want to incur the cost of installing additional plumbing in the four buildings associated with the Point Breeze Plant. See "Memorandum on Point Breeze Case Submitted to Sub-Committee of Committee on Appropriations, U.S. Senate, 78th Congress, by Malcolm Ross, Chairman Fair Employment Practice Committee as found in Hearings on National War Agencies Appropriation Bill 1945, p. 159," found in the B. F. McLaurin Collection, Box 7, the Schomburg Center for Research in Black Culture, New York City.

75   Copus et al., pp. 183–84.

76   Ibid., pp. 184–85.

77   Ibid., p. 185.

78   Bernard E. Anderson, "Equal Opportunity and Black Employment in the Telephone Industry," in Phyllis A. Wallace, *Equal Employment Opportunity and the AT&T Case* (Cambridge, Mass.: MIT Press, 1976), p. 183.

79   Copus et al., p. 195.

80   Ibid., p. 207.

81   Ibid., p. 208.

82   It should be mentioned that operators were not the lowest-paid workers in the Bell System. Low-grade clerks were employed who received a little less than operators. Not surprisingly, these jobs were held by black women who were not operators.

83   Black women hired into the Bell System as operators between 1964 and 1969 temporarily reversed a post-Korean War decline in the total number of operators.

Year	Women Operators
1960	159,946
1961	146,063
1962	140,191

Year	Women Operators
1963	139,345
1964	142,198
1965	148,041
1966	154,583
1967	153,133
1968	153,229
1969	163,498
1970	165,461

84   According to Anderson, more than 54,000 blacks had been hired industry-wide between 1950 and 1960, but the "data show for the Bell System alone an increase in black employment of 53,903 during the years 1965–1971." Anderson, pp. 189–90.

85   Copus et al., p. 200.

86   Ibid., p. 183.

87   Written response by James A. Sheridan, manager, human resources, to government inquiry into employment in the central cities, quoted in Subcommittee on the City of the Committee on Banking, Finance and Urban Affairs, U.S. House of Representatives, *Large Corporations and Urban Employment* (Washington, D.C.: GPO, 1978), pp. 655–56. Bell managers did move middle management, engineering, and other clerical departments to the suburbs where black women city dwellers, for the most part, could not afford to live or commute to. See FCC Field Hearings, FCC Staff Exhibits (New York), 3–10, EEOC, Box 16.

88   Anderson, p. 196.

89   James A. Sheridan, manager, human resources. Written response to government inquiry into employment in the central cities quoted in Subcommittee on the City of the Committee on Banking, Finance and Urban Affairs, *Large Corporations and Urban Employment*, p. 656.

90   Ibid., p. 655.

91   Walter Straley, vice president, AT&T, "Report on Force Loss and the Urban Labor Market," paper delivered at the Bell System Presidents' Conference, October 9, 1969, pp. 38, EEOC, Box 99, Classified Files, 1971–73.

92   Ibid., pp. 38, 50.

93   Anderson, p. 196. "The resignation rates of telephone operators in seventeen Bell operating companies ranged from 8.6 per 100 employees in Indiana to 31.7 per 100 in New York in 1971." Copus et al., p. 17. "A 1969 AT&T report indicated that in 19 major metropolitan areas, turnover among Operators with less than six months' service had increased from 80% in 1964 to 120% in 1968. In fact, in many districts turnover among short-term Operators had reached 200% in 1968."

94   Straley, pp. 21–22.

95   Ten black women (New York Telephone and AT&T included) hired between 1946 and 1971 agreed that when they were hired they had thought their starting

salaries were very good. The former operators interviewed for this study all said that the company only offered them operating jobs during the 1960s. The majority of black women applicants were unaware of other opportunities.

96 Anne H. Walden, interviewed by Venus Green, June 27, 1989, at the Varick Community Center, New York.

97 Harriet Tubman (an assumed name), interviewed by Venus Green, July 25, 1989.

98 G. H. Peterson, "Current Experiments in Person-to-Person DDD," *Bell Laboratories Record* 38 (August 1960): 300, and "TSP + EDDD = A-I Service," *195 Magazine* 38 (November 1965): 23.

99 Peterson, "Current Experiments in Person-to-Person DDD," p. 303.

100 Leonard C. Briggs, "TSP–As New As Tomorrow's Telephone Service!," *Bell Telephone Magazine* 41 (Spring 1962): 48.

101 "Operators: Their Wide New World," *Telephone Review* 54 (August-September 1963), p. 2.

102 Mike Zeaman, "Long Distance Superstar," *Bell Telephone Magazine* 55 (March-April 1976): 4. Various types of computerized electronic switching systems were designed to handle specific types of local traffic. Suburban central offices first used No. 2 ESS in 1970, while No. 3 ESS was designed for rural exchanges and installations begun in 1976. The history of the different electronic machines is not related here since the first one usually had the greatest impact on the operators' jobs.

103 Ibid., p. 5.

104 While this study has focused on local and long distance operators, significant changes occurred in other types of operating and the relevant equipment. For example, information, which later became directory assistance (to remind customers that they were being assisted only with telephone business and not train schedules or baseball scores), experienced several changes in work organization as well as technology. In the early 1960s, the directories used by information operators were replaced by small microfilmed copies. Operators used a computer to perform the basic page search to locate the name; they then used the same card (rectangular plastic tracer) and pencil to find the specific person. This whole process was later computerized so that the operator merely typed in the name and the computer found it. And, most recently, the information operator keys in the number and a computerized voice tells the subscriber the telephone number. Intercept, coin, teletypewriter, overseas, and other types of operators have experienced similar technological change in their work. "Directory Assistance Charging," *Bell Telephone Magazine* 53 (September-October 1974): 14. In 1974, Cincinnati Bell increased its profits by 17 percent when it started charging for directory assistance. In the first eight months of charging, the company reduced its force of directory assistance operators from 312 to 212.

105 "Operators: Their Wide New World," p. 4.

106 R. H. Funck, "Designing the Traffic Service Position Console," *Bell Laboratories Record* 42 (June 1964): 209.

107 Ibid.

108 A former operator at the New York Telephone Company who was interviewed for this study, Evelyn Holton, liked the TSP. Holton preferred it because it was new, prettier, desklike, and spacious compared to the "elbow room" only of the old cord switchboards. Most operators liked these aspects of TSPS, but they did not like the speedup facilitated by it.

109 "Chris Teaches Chris," *Telephone Review* 56 (June 1965): 9.

110 R. D. Kroning and D. H. Gale, "Automatic Training for Operators of 100A TSP," *Bell Laboratories Record* 41 (September 1963): 317.

111 Ibid. and "Chris Teaches Chris," p. 9.

112 See Jane Fleishman, "The Health Hazards of Office Work," Mary Sue Henifin, "The Particular Problems of Video Display Terminals," and Wendy Chavkin, "Closed Office-Building Syndrome," in Wendy Chavkin, M.D., ed., *Double Exposure: Women's Health Hazards on the Job and at Home* (New York: Monthly Review Press, 1984), pp. 57–86.

113 The symptoms include "tingling and numbness in the hands and fingers, sharp pain in the hands and wrists while performing tasks, and throbbing, sleep robbing pain at night from the shoulder on down" believed to be caused by "a constant motion of fingers and wrists while working at improperly designed VDT stations, combined with the elements of high job stress and lack of rest breaks." "Carpal Tunnel Syndrome," *CWA News* 48, no. 4 (1989): 6.

114 Cited in Fleishman, pp. 65, 69.

115 Cited in Henifin, p. 73.

116 Robert Howard, "Strung Out at the Phone Company: How AT&T's Workers Are Drugged, Bugged and Coming Unplugged," *Mother Jones*, August 1981, p. 39.

117 Ibid., p. 44.

118 Deposition of Pernella Wattley, May 11, 1972, EEOC, Box 17.

119 See Delois Brown *vs.* South Central Bell Telephone Company, Birmingham, Civil Action No. CA 70-853, filed in the U.S. District Court for the Northern District of Alabama, Southern Division, November 20, 1970, EEOC, Box 101, p. 4.

120 Lee H. Toole, "Title VII of the Civil Rights Law: Company Confidential," to Burke, Munger, Quigley, Sprout, Treyer, and Irwin, April 13, 1965, pp. 1–2. Marked "do not reproduce." EEOC, Box 35.

121 Ibid., p. 3.

122 See EEOC Summary No. 24, EEOC, Box 38.

123 Testimony of Helen Dunbar before the FCC, EEOC, Box 5, vol. 39, pp. 4624–52.

124 Ibid., pp. 4646–47.

125 Ibid., p. 4633.

126 Ibid., p. 4634. Gabrielle Gemma, Bea Miller, and others recalled how bad the food was and that operators frequently became ill after eating it.

127 See, for example, the New York Telephone Company's rate increase request, which says that operating costs are increased by the need to train new and inexperienced employees who "'increase the likelihood of errors.' 'Petition (including

Request for Temporary Rates),' submitted to State of New York, New York Public Service Commission," p. 12. N.d. (most probably 1971 since it uses information from 1970, and the larger case was settled in 1972), EEOC, Box 57.

128   See "[Customer Service Attitude] Program Administration Guide," March 1972, Exhibit 2, EEOC, Box 113, p. 1.

129   Ibid., pp. 4636–37.

130   David A. Andelman, "(212) 555-1212 Has Moved Out of the City," *New York Times,* August 1, 1973, sec. 2, pp. 1, 79.

131   Ibid., p. 79.

132   See Gay Semel's Testimony in EEOC, Box 4, vol. 36, p. 3831.

133   Ibid., p. 3832.

134   Phone interview June 24, 1998.

135   See Gabrielle Gemma, quoted in Grace Lichtenstein, "AT&T Assailed as a Racist Monopoly," *New York Times,* May 9, 1972, and Gabrielle Gemma's testimony before the FCC. EEOC, Box 4, vol. 35, p. 3629. It was so widely believed that all operators were black that Gemma, a white woman, said that "even" she was called this epithet. Winnifred King, Bea Miller, and others had similar recollections about the use of racially derogatory insults.

136   Affidavit by Dorothy J. Mitchell, October 1968, Natchez, Miss., EEOC, Box 37, pp. 1–4.

8. Black Operators in the Computer Age

1   "Equal Opportunity," *195 Magazine* 38 (February 1965): 14.

2   "This We Believe," *Telephone Review* 54 (April 1963): 11.

3   "Our Commitment to Help," *195 Magazine* 41 (December 1968): 12.

4   Ibid., p. 13.

5   Ibid.

6   See "Concentrated Employment Program memorandum of Understanding Between American Telephone and Telegraph Company, Long Lines Department and Communications Workers of America," January 7, 1970, pp. 1–4. Robert F. Wagner Archives, CWA Local 1150 Collection, Box 16, Folder 22. This agreement regarding the "hardcore" created a new title "special trainee" in which a new hire would work for one year and would not be expected to fully comply with the "normal, established and still existent practice, methods, standards and agreements . . .," for a limited period of time. The union and management were to educate the regular employees about this program and avoid unnecessary "labeling or other identification of 'trainees' and agree that every effort will be made to treat the trainees as regular employees except where such treatment would interfere with the stated objectives of the training program to which they are assigned."

7   Frank Novotny, national director, CWA, Sales Bargaining Unit, interviewed by John Schacht at the St. Moritz Hotel, New York City, July 11, 1970. OHP, p. 11.

8   Union responses to the company's "equal opportunity" hiring practices will be discussed in another context.

9   See "Concentrated Employment Program Memorandum of Understanding Between American Telephone and Telegraph Company Long Line Department [and the]
Communications Workers of America," pp. 2–4.

10   See, for example, Seth Johnson et al. *vs.* Western Electric Company, Inc., et al.,
Case No. YSF I 041, EEOC, Box 37.

11   "Proceedings of the 31st Annual Convention of the Communication Workers
of America, June 1969," Clara Allen, the CWA's New Jersey director, gave a report on a
study conducted by the Job Pressure Committee, pp. 142–44.

12   Eugene Mays, assistant to vice president, District 1. Interviewed by John
Schacht at Mays' office, District 1 Headquarters, New York City, May 15, 1970. OHP,
pp. 8–9.

13   Beatrice Miller, interviewed by Venus Green, July 7, 1989, New York City.

14   "Our Commitment to Help," *195 Magazine* 41 (December 1968): 13. "We
Added 11,700 New Employees; Our Total Force Reached More Than 93,000," *Telephone Review* 61 (January 1970): 21. *Telephone Review* propagandized about the company's "stepped up recruiting efforts" in which use was made of "classified ads,
mobile job vans, 'socials,' . . . special 'hiring days,' and employee referrals to obtain the
necessary 'manpower—and womanpower' that was so 'crucial' to the 'service effort.' "

15   Contracts between the U.S. Department of Labor—Manpower Administration
and various Bell companies can be found in EEOC, Boxes 114 and 115. For example,
contracts were signed with Bell Telephone Company of Western Pennsylvania, Michigan Bell Telephone Company, the Chesapeake & Potomac Company of Maryland, the
Chesapeake & Potomac Company of West Virginia, Northwestern Bell Telephone
Company, Des Moines, Pacific Northwest Bell Telephone Company, Portland, Oregon, New York Telephone Company, etc. These contracts detailed the amount of
money paid directly to employees and the amounts paid to the company for training.

16   Jules Cohn, "Testimony of Jules Cohn" (written testimony submitted to the
EEOC, dated August 1, 1972), EEOC, Box 19, Exhibit 13, p. 17.

17   Ibid., p. 5.

18   Ibid., vol. 52, Box 7, p. 6026.

19   AT&T participated in the National Alliance of Businessmen's Job Opportunities in the Business Sector Program (NAB-JOBS). Businesses hired and trained the
hardcore, but "the extra costs of added training, counseling, remedial education,
prevocational training, health service, and other specialized support were to be met by
funds provided by the U.S. Department of Labor." Bernard E. Anderson, *The Negro in
the Public Utility Industries* (Philadelphia: Industrial Research Unit, Department of
Industry, Wharton School of Finance and Commerce, University of Pennsylvania,
1970), p. 215.

20   AT&T "Annual Report of the Department of Environmental Affairs," n.d., but
after 1970. EEOC, Box 100, Miscellany Folder 4, p. 28.

21   "Petition (including request for Temporary Rates)" submitted to State of New
York, New York Public Service Commission, n.d., p. 12.

22   "Petition for Suspension of Rates, Hearing and Declaration of Unlawfulness,"

before the FCC, Washington, D.C., Revision of Tariff FCC No. 263, AT&T Transmittal No. 10989, January 18, 1971, EEOC, Box 87, Folder 1, p. 2. All of these petitions may be found in this box.

23 Ibid., p. 3.

24 H. I. Romnes, chairman, AT&T, "Statement," December 11, 1970, p. 1, EEOC, Box 102.

25 Ibid., p. 3.

26 William T. Patrick Jr., "To Help Them Help Themselves," *Bell Telephone Magazine* 53 (November–December 1974): 32.

27 Ron Tyree, interviewed by Venus Green, July 27, 1989, in New York City. He remembered hearing supervisors threaten to take away the immigration papers of Caribbean women.

28 Anne Walden, interviewed by Venus Green, June 27, 1989, New York City.

29 Evelyn Holton, interviewed by Venus Green, June 29, 1989, New York City.

30 Harriet Tubman, interviewed by Venus Green, July 25, 1989, New York City.

31 Researchers wrote pamphlets designated "For Bell System Information Only," with titles such as "A Profile of Education in America," "The Black Militant: The Negro Moderates," "Urban Commitment of Other Businesses," "City and State Involvement in Solving Urban Problems," "Ghetto Schools and Ghetto Youth," "A Brief History of the Negro in America," "Other Possible Bell System Action in the City," "Federal Programs [for information and possible Bell System or telephone company use in connection with urban problems]," and "Urban Orientation—Phase I (April 1968)." Except for the last one, these pamphlets were dated November 1967. In "Other Possible Bell System Action in the City," the writers concluded "that it can best help solve the urban crisis by concentrating on attempts to improve urban education and to augment the employability of ghetto residents, there are other effective action that can be taken," p. 1. Among those actions were "(1) Employing Negro Veterans; (2) Purchasing—using black suppliers; (3) Loaning Bell System Expertise to Community Organizations; (4) Inter-Industry Training Center—would be used for training the managerial personnel of ghetto businesses; (5) Demanding Improved Municipal Services for the Ghetto; (6) Financial Support for Negro Organizations; (7) Ghetto Clean-Up Campaigns; (8) Social Service Phone Line "through which people in need could learn of the various programs that could prove helpful to them" (pp. 1–7).

32 AT&T, "The Black Militants/The Negro Moderates." N.d., n.p.; if like the others, however, most likely 1967.

33 "Other Possible Bell System Action in the City" argued: "In order to support the more moderate forces within the Negro community, the companies as well as AT&T could consider broadening their contributions policies to include organizations such as the NAACP Legal Defense and Education Fund, the NAACP Special Contributions Fund, the Southern Christian Leadership Conference's American Foundation for Non-Violent Education, the Voluntary Support Committee of the National Association of State Universities and Land-Grant Colleges, which is seeking support for the nation's predominantly Negro public colleges, as well as the A. Philip Randolph

Institute's Education Fund. Unless they receive adequate support from the white community, the moderate Negro leadership will be obscured by the extremists" (p. 7).

34   Ibid.

35   Ibid.

36   EEOC, Box 54, Summaries for Exhibit 2 (folder numbers refer to pages), Folder 1200–1350—Terms and Conditions of Employment Continued, Supplemental Findings of Fact—Male and Female Job Classifications; Historical Exclusion and Segregation, New Hire Data, p. 1496.

37   All three became leading shop stewards, participated in lawsuits against the Bell System, led strikes and other actions. Evelyn Holton also became a shop steward and was active in strikes during her thirty-year history at New York Telephone Company. See Green, "The Impact of Technology Upon Telephone Women."

38   Donald R. Woodford, managing editor, "The Operators," *Bell Telephone Magazine* 51 (January–February 1972): 24–25.

39   Mays, interviewed by Schacht, p. 8.

40   Phyllis A. Wallace, ed., *Equal Employment Opportunity and the AT&T Case* (Cambridge, Mass.: MIT Press, 1976), p. 1.

41   Ibid. Some $15 million of the $38 million was allocated as back wages to workers who had suffered discrimination, and $23 million was set aside for other compensation.

42   Signed on May 30, 1974, and May 13, 1975.

43   Carol J. Loomis, "AT&T in the Throes of 'Equal Opportunity,'" *Fortune*, January 15, 1979, p. 50.

44   Ibid.

45   Herbert R. Northrup and John A. Larson, *The Impact of the AT&T-EEO Consent Decree* (Philadelphia: University of Pennsylvania Press, 1979), p. 66.

46   Ibid., pp. 45–47, 49–50, 53, 55, 59, 60–61, 64–66; tables III-4, 6, 7, 8, 9, 10, 11, 12, and 13.

47   Ibid., pp. 45, 64.

48   Ibid., pp. 45, 64.

49   Ibid., p. 48.

50   Ibid. Nonwhite inside craft women increased from 1,494 in 1973 to 3,491 in 1979.

51   Ibid.

52   Ibid. African American and other "minority" women increased from 4,645 in 1973 to 8,901 of the officials, managers, and sales workers categories in 1979.

53   Ibid., p. 26. In 1974, the company introduced directory assistance charging, which further accelerated the technological decline of operators.

54   Ibid., pp. 40, 45.

55   Ibid., pp. 27–28.

56   Sally Hacker, "Sex Stratification, Technology, and Organizational Change: A Longitudinal Case Study of AT&T," *Social Problems* 26 (June 1979): 539.

57   Ibid., pp. 549–50.

58   Ibid.

59   Ibid., p. 549.

60   Computerized systems (AMA, DDD, TSPS, and other clerical systems) eliminated operating as well as many lower-level clerical jobs. Consequently, lower-level
managers, mostly women, who supervised these women also lost their jobs. Ibid.,
p. 545.

61   Hacker concluded from statistics of the three-year period that she examined,
"16,300 men gained formerly women's work; only 9,400 women gained formerly
men's work." Ibid., p. 545. Northrup's and Larson's figures derived from their six-year
study show a similar gain but smaller differences. Between 1973 and 1979, male operators and clericals increased approximately 14,015, whereas female inside and outside
craft workers increased approximately 12,406. The male figure could be larger if
administrative and other lower-level management jobs were considered. The increase
in female jobs could also be attributed to a larger female gain in craft work after 1975.

62   Hacker, p. 545.

63   Ibid., p. 550.

64   David M. Newman, "New Technology and the Changing Labor Process in the
Telephone Industry: The Union's Response," unpublished paper, 1982, pp. 4–5.

65   These statements are based on my own experience as a switching equipment
technician working at New York Telephone for more than fifteen years. As a steward, I
have been involved in countless discussions, grievances, and other battles with and on
behalf of many of these women.

66   Complaints against the tests are not limited to biases in the actual tests. Unfair
testing procedures include such practices as giving too little time to complete an
examination, giving more time to whites than blacks, giving inadequate and/or inac-
curate instructions to blacks, and giving pretests and study questions only to whites. I
know from personal experience that African Americans were completely left out of
the network of stolen answers circulated among white craft workers.

67   See Folder: Pacific Telephone vs. Smith, EEOC, Box 101.

68   See Case File No. TN09-0156, July 17, 1968, EEOC, Box 109.

69   For example, Charles F. Fair filed charges against Southern Bell Telephone
and Telegraph Company in Atlanta, October 1, 1966, for violating Title VII of the Civil
Rights Act of 1964 "by maintaining a difference in optional retirement ages based on
sex." Women with twenty years of service could retire at age fifty-five, whereas men
with twenty years of service had to wait until they were sixty. The EEOC decided in his
favor on February 7, 1969. See Charles F. Fair vs. Southern Bell Telephone and
Telegraph Company, EEOC, Box 84, EEOC Charges D-83. Other charges can be found
in D-113. James R. Warnke et al. vs. Southern Bell charged discrimination based on sex
for the following reasons:

1. Respondent follows a policy whereby male employees are counselled after accumulating three absences within a one year period, while no action is taken against female employees until they have accumulated six absences within a one year period.

2. Respondent permits its female operators to make a certain number of toll free telephone calls, while denying this privilege to male employees.

The EEOC settled the absence problems of the four men in several individual ways and required the company to affirm its nondiscriminatory policy in relation to absences. The EEOC found no basis of discrimination based on toll calls. See Boxes 107 and 109.

70 See G.W.G., "Areas in which we may be vulnerable relative to equality of treatment," December 13, 1965, EEOC, Box 99, Folder "Miscellany," EEOC R-1054, p. 1.

71 See Elva L. Rhodes vs. Southwestern Bell Telephone Company, Hot Springs, Ark., Charge No. TN02 03, October 1971, and Donnie J. Keef et al. (six others), March 15, 1972, Charge Nos. TN02 0936-0943, EEOC, Box 107.

72 Phyllis A. Wallace, "The Consent Decrees," in *Equal Employment Opportunity and the AT&T Case*, p. 276. IBEW did participate.

73 Ibid., p. 275.

74 Loomis, p. 54.

75 Ibid., p. 55. In the case of Ohio Bell, the overrides benefited white males who were placed in nontraditional jobs. See unpublished paper by Brent Kramer, "Affirmative Action in the Bell System: The Legacy of the 1973 Consent Decree," 1995, p. 4.

76 For example, see Melvin Jones vs. Communications Workers of America, Local 3412, Houma, La., Case No. YNO 1 440, October 20, 1970, EEOC, Box 107.

77 Joseph A. Beirne, "Foreword," in the Diebold Group, Inc., *Automation: Impact and Implications, Focus on Developments in the Communications Industry* (Washington, D.C.: CWA, AFL-CIO, 1965), p. 7.

78 Ibid.

79 Lavie Bolick, assistant to vice president, District 3, CWA. Interviewed by John Schacht at District 3 Headquarters, Atlanta, February 17, 1970. OHP, p. 34.

80 Martha Moudy, CWA Representative in District 3. Interviewed by John Schacht at District 3 Headquarters, Atlanta, February 17, 1970. OHP, p. 16.

81 Mays, interviewed by Schacht, p. 10.

82 Lessie Sanders, interviewed by Venus Green (telephone), October 14, 1989, in New York City. In 1969 Sanders began working for the New York Telephone Company as an operator. After holding several clerical positions, she has now retired.

83 Ibid.

84 Ibid.

85 Ibid.

86 Mays, interviewed by Schacht, pp. 8–9.

87 New York City craftsmen lost a seven-month strike in 1971, partially as a result of operators working because they were not in the CWA. Ilene Winkler argues that the failure of the national to support the local frightened the operators, which is the reason that they rejected membership in CWA. For a description of the strike issues, see Steven Peter Vallas, *Power in the Workplace: The Politics of Production at AT&T* (Albany: State University of New York Press, 1993), 108–11.

88   Scott Stephens, retired international representative, CWA. Interviewed by John Schacht at Stephens's home in Anna Maria, Florida, February 23, 1970. OHP, p. 16.

89   George Kohl's "Changing Competitive and Technology Environments in Telecommunications," Appendix 1, contains part of Ronnie J. Straw's testimony, in Donald Kennedy, Charles Craypo, and Mary Lehman, eds., *Labor and Technology: Union Response to Changing Environments* (University Park: Pennsylvania State University Press, 1985), p. 74.

90   Ibid.; Newman, pp. 22–23.

91   Kennedy et al., p. 73.

92   Ibid., pp. 73–75; Newman, p. 23.

93   Newman, p. 21.

94   Ibid., pp. 23–24.

95   Of course, the objectivity exists only in the language; the eventual administration of the directive showed that the intent had never been to protect black women.

96   New York City, White Plains, N.Y., Denver, Oakland, Pittsburgh, Springfield, Mass., and Jacksonville, Fla. Not all of these operated at the same time.

97   Pat Meckle, interviewed by Venus Green, July 27, 1989, in New York City. Second interview. Local 1150 included AT&T operators and craftsmen working in New York City.

98   Ibid.

99   Ron Tyree, interviewed by Venus Green, July 27, 1989, in New York City.

100   Robert Howard, "Strung Out at the Phone Company: How AT&T's Workers Are Drugged, Bugged and Coming Unplugged," *Mother Jones*, August 1981, p. 39.

101   Anne H. Walden, "Anne Walden on the I.O.C. Closing," *Local Spirit* (New York: Newsletter of Local 1150, CWA, April 1983), p. 1.

102   Ibid., p. 6.

103   Ibid.

104   Meckle, interviewed by Green.

105   By the early 1980s, telephone companies began moving clerical work out of urban areas to suburbs where higher-level managers lived and where they could employ white women who were considered more acceptable by managers and subscribers.

106   Meckle, interviewed by Green.

107   Tyree, interviewed by Green.

108   Walden, interviewed by Green.

109   Unger, "Double Quorum," *Local Spirit*, p. 1.

110   Chet Macy, a white male, who never worked as an operator, went directly into management after leaving union office.

111   Newman, p. 25.

112   According to Ilene Winkler, a Switching Equipment Technician for twenty-five years, union steward, rank-and-file activist, and editor of the rank-and-file newsletter the *Bell Wringer*, "this happened in spite of the CWA national leadership. They negotiated a low clerical rate for the first trial in Texas. The DC local found out and

raised a fuss. . . . Pressure from DC, NYC and other big city locals forced the national union to change." Personal communication.

113 NOW, "Women's Wages: A Key to Preserving Middle Income Jobs" (Washington, D.C.: NOW, August 1986), updated November 1986, by Judith Gregory, George Kohl, Leslie Loble, Louise Novotny, and Karen Sacks, pp. 18, 23. This study omits weekend and out-of-hours premiums that may be included in their figures.

114 Ibid., p. 24.

115 On January 1, 1984, AT&T, as a result of an antitrust settlement with the federal government, divested itself of its twenty-two operating companies. At that time, the companies reorganized themselves into seven regional companies, while AT&T kept its long distance business and Western Electric and Bell Labs, its manufacturing and research units. Divestiture, technological displacement, and the practice of charging for directory assistance offset the influence of affirmative action on the actual number of employees involved. For the 1975–85 decade, the New York Telephone Company attributed a 32 percent decline in its total workforce "primarily" to its divestiture from AT&T in 1984. It is not entirely clear how or if divestiture caused the operating companies to lose jobs, but it is clear that after the 1982 divestiture announcement the company lost more than twenty thousand of its employees. The decline in the number of women, however, had begun well before 1975. In that year, the company introduced directory assistance charging, which further accelerated the decline in operators.

116 Sometimes government officials even participated in delaying justice. For example, Joseph P. Healy, chairman of the governor of Maryland's Commission on Interracial Cooperation stated in 1943 that the strike at Western Electric (an AT&T affiliate) had created such a difficult situation in Baltimore that Healy believed it would be best to withhold action in the telephone matter for the time being. He added that Haneke had indicated he would prefer to see the move toward employment of Negro telephone operators be made in a more northern area. Muriel Ferris to Joseph H. B. Evans, regional director, Region IV, May 28, 1945, p. 1, FEPC Headquarters Records, Record Group 228, Entry 39, Box 456, National Archives.

117 See, for example, these publications from the U.S. Department of Labor (Washington, D.C.: GPO): Women's Bureau, *The Change from Manual to Dial Operation in the Telephone Industry*, by Ethel L. Best, Bulletin No. 110 (1933); Women's Bureau, *Women Telephone Workers and Changing Technology*, by Caroline Cherrix, Bulletin No. 286 (1963); Bureau of Labor Statistics, *Manpower Planning for Technological Change: Case Studies of Telephone Operators*, Bulletin No. 1574 (1968); Bureau of Labor Statistics, *Improving Productivity: Labor and Management Approaches*, Bulletin 1715 (1971); Bureau of Labor Statistics, *Technology and Labor in Five Industries*, Bulletin No. 2033 (1979).

Epilogue

1 Pat Meckle, Winifred King, Bea Miller, Harriet Tubman, and others have said this in their interviews.

2 Winifred King, interviewed by Venus Green. Since this interview, King has been transferred to a new job where she may be happier.

3 Evelyn Holton, interviewed by Venus Green.

4 Ibid.

5 Holton represents only one example of how women subverted the discipline on the cord boards. Martia Goodson told me that women who wanted to talk with each other would plug into the same line at different positions and talk, or one would go out to the free phone and the operator on the inside would plug in to talk.

6 CWA, "Technological Change: Challenges and Choices," Instructor's Manual, prepared by the CWA, Training Department, Development and Research Department, and the Occupational Safety and Health Program, 1985, p. 102.

7 Ibid., pp. 202–24.

8 Stephen H. Norwood argues that in the few places where operators' unions survived for longer periods of time, it was because of the assistance of strongly connected middle-class women's reform organizations such as the Women's Trade Union League. This may be true, but those same organizations failed to address the major problem that operators faced in the workplace. Referring to operators' unionization and militancy, Norwood disagrees strongly with Tentler's argument that women's work experience reinforced their self-perception of "dependence and insecurity." However, when an analysis of race and craft ideology is applied to women's actions, one would tend to agree with Tentler. Unlike waitresses, for whom "craft logic" had been useful in achieving noneconomic goals, operators derived mostly small pay increases from their experiences with unionization. See Stephen H. Norwood, *Labor's Flaming Youth;* Leslie Woodcock Tentler, *Wage-Earning Women: Industrial Work and Family Life in the United States, 1900–1930* (New York: Oxford University Press, 1979); and Dorothy Sue Cobble, *Dishing It Out: Waitresses and Their Unions in the Twentieth Century* (Urbana: University of Illinois Press, 1991).

9 As this book goes to press, CWA has taken another step in the right direction. The union has just concluded a two-week strike against Verizon Communications (a new baby Bell). Over 87,000 telephone workers from Maine to Virginia (37,000 from the mid-Atlantic states) left their workplaces to address issues directly related to technology. In addition to improved wages, job security protections, benefits, and pensions, these workers struck for the right to organize wireless and data/Internet communications workers (the growth areas in telecommunications), and to reduce work related stress. The union's demands included training and lifelong learning programs, restrictions on subcontracting, limiting newly created jobs to union members and ending "secret monitoring . . . unrealistic performance quotas . . . and excessive overtime." The settlement reduced the amount of mandatory overtime, addressed workers' complaints of last-minute assignments, and most important to operators and service representatives, "calls for customer service employees to receive 30 minutes of off-line time per shift in which workers can be off the phones to process customer orders and requests." Furthermore, "it includes provisions to relieve the intensity of monitoring for both operators and service reps." CWA, the AFL-CIO, and

labor experts across America are calling this a "historic" and precedent setting strike, especially as it addresses problems of technological change in the workplace. Of course, the true value of this settlement will be proven by its administration in the actual workplace. For details on the settlement and the demands, see CWA, "Fighting for Respect at Bell Atlantic," a summary of the bargaining issues, March 17, 2000; "Historic CWA Strike Against Verizon Wins Good Jobs, Union Jobs, Hometown Jobs." *Strike Bulletin,* Settlement Issue, August/September 2000; and "CWA Announces Path-Blazing Settlement Ending Verizon Strike by 37,000 Workers," CWA Press Release, August 23, 2000. Thanks to George Kohl at CWA for sending me most of these documents on short notice.

SELECTED BIBLIOGRAPHY

Primary Sources

AMERICAN TELEPHONE AND TELEGRAPH COMPANY ARCHIVES, NEW YORK CITY

This archive was the major depository for complete sets of AT&T manual reports; Bell System periodicals; minutes of internal meetings; traffic, toll, personnel, accounting, plant, publicity, and other conference reports; presidents' letter books and general managers' letter books for letters up to the 1920s; general management correspondence; training manuals; Bell System statistical manuals, 1920–81; industry directories and other important documents. This archive is now located in Warren, New Jersey.

BELL SYSTEM JOURNALS

Bell Laboratories Record
Bell Telephone Magazine
Bell Telephone Quarterly
Headquarters Bulletin
195 Magazine
The Telephone Review

CHICAGO HISTORICAL SOCIETY, CHICAGO, ILLINOIS

The Brotherhood of Sleeping Car Porters Papers

COMMUNICATIONS WORKERS OF AMERICA ARCHIVES, WASHINGTON, D.C.

Depository for the J. A. Beirne Papers, a complete set of CWA convention proceedings, and other union documents. These archives have been moved to the University of Iowa.

DEPARTMENT OF LABOR LIBRARY, WASHINGTON, D.C.

Contains union newspapers, government publications, and other primary materials relevant to labor history.

LIBRARY OF CONGRESS, WASHINGTON, D.C.

Albert Sidney Burleson Papers
National Association for the Advancement of Colored People Papers

NATIONAL ARCHIVES, WASHINGTON, D.C.

Contain records of the War Labor Policies Board, records of the National War Labor Board (World War I), records of the Post Office Department, records of the Women's Bureau, general records of the Department of Labor, and Equal Employment Opportunity Commission records.

NEW YORK PUBLIC LIBRARY, SCHOMBURG CENTER FOR RESEARCH IN BLACK CULTURE, NEW YORK CITY

Anna Hedgeman papers
Benjamin F. McLaurin Papers
Ernest Thompson Papers
National Negro Congress Papers

NEW YORK TELEPHONE COMPANY HISTORICAL ARCHIVE PROJECT, NEW YORK CITY
Contained documents relevant to the history of the New York Telephone Company.
These materials have now been incorporated into NYNEX/Bell Atlantic Corporate
Archives.

NEW YORK UNIVERSITY, TAMIMENT LIBRARY/ROBERT F. WAGNER ARCHIVES,
NEW YORK CITY
In addition to other pertinent materials, this library has acquired the records of the
Federation of Telephone Workers (NFTW) and Local 1150 of the Communications
Workers of America.

UNION NEWSPAPERS
CWA News (national news organ)
Local Spirit (CWA Local 1150 newsletter)
New York Generator (CWA Local 1101 newsletter)
The Telephone Worker (NFTW national news organ)

Census Reports and Government Documents

Ninth Census: Census Reports Compiled from the Original Returns of the Ninth Census
(June 1, 1870). (Congressional Series: 42nd Cong., 1st sess. House. Misc. docs.
unnumbered.) Vol. I. The Statistics of the Population of the United States. Washington, D.C.: GPO, 1872. xlix, 804 pp.

Tenth Census of the United States, June 1, 1880. (Congressional Series: House. 47th
Cong., 2nd sess. Misc. doc. 42, pts. 1–22). Vol. I. Statistics of the Population of the
United States. Washington, D.C.: GPO, 1883. lxxxix, 961 pp.

Eleventh Census of the United States: 1890. (Congressional Series: 52nd Cong., 1st sess.
House. Misc. doc. 340, pts. 1, 4, 7, 14–15, 17–18, 20–26, 28). Vol. I, pt. I. Report on
the Population of the United States. Washington, D.C.: GPO, 1895. ccxiii, 968 pp.

Thirteenth Census of the United States Taken in the Year 1910. Vol. IV. Population: 1910.
Occupation Statistics. Washington, D.C.: GPO, 1914. (Reprint, April 1915), 615 pp.

Fourteenth Census of the United States Taken in the Year 1920. Vol. IV. Population: 1920.
Occupations. Washington, D.C.: GPO, 1923. 1,309 pp.

Fifteenth Census of the United States: 1930. Population. Vol. V. General Report on Occupations. Washington, D.C.: GPO, 1933. iv, 591 pp.

Sixteenth Census of the United States: 1940. Population. Vol. III. Comparative Occupation
Statistics for the United States, 1870–1940. Washington, D.C.: GPO, 1943. xxii, 206 pp.

Census of Population: 1950. A Report of the Seventeenth Decennial Census of the United
States. Vol. III. Census Tract Statistics. P-E No. 1c. Occupation by Industry. Washington, D.C.: GPO, 1954. 75 pp.

The Eighteenth Decennial Census of the United States, Census of Population: 1960. Final
Reports. Vol. II. Subject Reports. PC(2)-7c. Occupation by Industry. Washington, D.C.:
GPO, 1963. xvii, 146 pp.

1970 Census of Population. Vol. II. Subject Reports. PC(2)-7c. Occupation by Industry.
Washington, D.C.: GPO, 1972. xvi, 504, 12 pp.

Canada. Department of Labour. Report of the Royal Commission on a Dispute Respecting

Hours of Employment Between the Bell Telephone Company of Canada, Ltd. and Operators at Toronto, Ontario. Ottawa: Government Printing Bureau, 1907.

Federal Communications Commission. *Investigation of the Telephone Industry in the United States.* Washington, D.C.: GPO, 1939.

State of New York. Department of Labor. "The Telephone Industry." Special Bulletin 100. Albany: J. B. Lyon, 1920.

U.S. Congress. Senate. *Investigation of Telephone Companies.* S. Doc. 380, 61st Congress, 2nd session. Washington, D.C.: GPO, 1910.

U.S. Commission on Industrial Relations. *Investigation of the Wages and Conditions of Telephone Operating.* By Nelle B. Curry. Washington, D.C.: GPO, 1915.

U.S. Department of Commerce and Labor, Bureau of the Census, *Statistics of Women at Work.* Washington, D.C.: GPO, 1907.

U.S. Department of Labor. Bureau of Labor Statistics. *Manpower Planning for Technological Change: Case Studies of Telephone Operators.* Bulletin No. 1574. Washington, D.C.: GPO, 1968.

U.S. Department of Labor. Bureau of Labor Statistics. *Improving Productivity: Labor and Management Approaches.* Bulletin 1715. Washington, D.C.: GPO, 1971.

U.S. Department of Labor. Bureau of Labor Statistics. *Technology and Labor in Five Industries.* Bulletin No. 2033. Washington, D.C.: GPO, 1979.

U.S. Department of Labor. Women's Bureau. *The Change from Manual to Dial Operation in the Telephone Industry.* By Ethel L. Best. Bulletin No. 110. Washington, D.C.: GPO, 1933.

U.S. Department of Labor. Women's Bureau. *The Woman Telephone Worker.* By Ethel Erickson, Bulletin 207, Washington, D.C.: GPO, 1944.

U.S. Department of Labor, Women's Bureau. *Women Telephone Workers and Changing Technology.* By Caroline Cherrix, Bulletin No. 286. Washington, D.C.: GPO, 1963.

Books

Agassi, Judith Buber. *Comparing the Work Attitudes of Women and Men.* Lexington, Mass.: D.C. Heath, 1982.

Allen, Theodore W. *The Invention of the White Race: Racial Oppression and Social Control,* vol. 1. London: Verso, 1994.

Anderson, Bernard E. *The Negro in the Public Utility Industries.* Philadelphia: Industrial Research Unit, Department of Industry, Wharton School of Finance and Commerce, University of Pennsylvania, 1970.

Baker, Elizabeth Faulkner. *Technology and Woman's Work.* New York: Columbia University Press, 1964.

Barbash, Jack. *Unions and Telephones: The Story of the Communications Workers of America.* New York: Harper and Brothers, 1952.

Baron, Ava Baron, ed. *Work Engendered: Toward a New History of American Labor.* Ithaca, N.Y.: Cornell University Press, 1991.

Baxandall, Rosalyn, Linda Gordon, Susan Reverby, eds. *America's Working Women: A Documentary History—1600 to the Present.* New York: Random House, 1976.

Bederman, Gail. *Manliness and Civilization: A Cultural History of Gender and Race in the United States, 1880–1917.* Chicago: University of Chicago Press, 1995.

Beirne, Joseph A. *New Horizons for American Labor.* Washington, D.C.: Public Affairs Press, 1962.

Benson, Susan Porter. *Counter Cultures: Saleswomen, Managers, and Customers in American Department Stores, 1890–1940.* Urbana: University of Illinois Press, 1986.

Bix, Amy Sue. *Inventing Ourselves Out of Jobs: America's Debate Over Technological Unemployment, 1929–1981.* Baltimore: Johns Hopkins University Press, 2000.

Blaxall, Martha, and Barbara Reagan, eds. *Women and the Workplace, The Implications of Occupational Segregation.* Chicago: University of Chicago Press, 1976.

Blitz, Herbert J., ed. *Labor-management Contracts and Technological Change: Case Studies and Contract Clauses.* New York: Frederick A. Praeger, 1969.

Braverman, Harry. *Labor and Monopoly Capital: The Degradation of Work in the Twentieth Century.* New York: Monthly Review Press, 1974.

Brody, David. *Steelworkers in America: The Nonunion Era.* New York: Harper & Row, 1969 (first published in 1960 by Harvard University Press).

——. *Workers in Industrial America: Essays on the Twentieth-Century Struggle.* New York: Oxford University Press, 1980.

Brooks, John. *Telephone: The First Hundred Years.* New York: Harper & Row, 1975.

Brooks, Thomas R. *Communications Workers of America: The Story of a Union.* New York: Mason/Charter, 1977.

Burawoy, Michael. *Manufacturing Consent: Changes in the Labor Process Under Monopoly Capitalism.* Chicago: University of Chicago Press, 1979.

——. *The Politics of Production: Factory Regimes Under Capitalism and Socialism.* London: Verso, 1985.

Burnell, Barbara S. *Technological Change and Women's Work Experience: Alternative Methodological Perspectives.* Westport, Conn.: Bergin & Garvey, 1993.

Butler, Elizabeth Beardsley. *Women and the Trades: Pittsburgh, 1907–1908.* New York: Charities Publication Committee, 1909.

Chandler, Alfred D. *The Visible Hand: The Managerial Revolution in American Business.* Cambridge, Mass.: Harvard University Press, 1977.

Chapuis, Robert J. *100 Years of Telephone Switching (1878–1978), Part 1: Manual and Electromechanical Switching (1878–1960s).* Vol. 1. New York: North-Holland, 1982.

Chavkin, Wendy, M.D., ed. *Double Exposure: Women's Health Hazards on the Job and at Home.* New York: Monthly Review Press, 1984.

Cobble, Dorothy Sue. *Dishing It Out: Waitresses and Their Unions in the Twentieth Century.* Urbana: University of Illinois Press, 1991.

Cockburn, Cynthia. *Brothers: Male Dominance and Technological Change.* London: Pluto Press, 1983.

Cohen, Lizabeth. *Making a New Deal: Industrial Workers in Chicago, 1919–1939.* New York: Cambridge University Press, 1990.

Coon, Horace. *American Tel & Tel: The Story of a Great Monopoly.* New York: Longmans, Green, 1939.

Cooper, Patricia A. *Once a Cigar Maker: Men, Women, and Work Culture in American Cigar Factories, 1900–1919*. Urbana: University of Illinois Press, 1987.

Cowan, Ruth Schwartz. *More Work for Mother: The Ironies of Household Technology from the Open Hearth to the Microwave*. New York: Basic Books, 1983.

Danielian, N. R. *AT&T: The Story of Industrial Conquest*. New York: Vanguard Press, 1939.

Davies, Margery W. *Woman's Place Is at the Typewriter: Office Work and Office Workers, 1870–1930*. Philadelphia: Temple University Press, 1982.

Dodge, Grace, et al. *What Can Women Earn?*. New York: Frederick A. Stokes, 1898.

Dye, Nancy Schrom. *As Equals and As Sisters: Feminism, the Labor Movement, and the Women's Trade Union League of New York*. Columbia: University of Missouri Press, 1980.

Edwards, Richard. *Contested Terrain: The Transformation of the Workplace in the Twentieth Century*. New York: Basic Books, 1979.

Edwards, Richard C., Michael Reich, David M. Gordon, eds. *Labor Market Segmentation*. Lexington, Mass.: D. C. Heath, 1975.

Fagen, M. D., ed. *A History of Engineering and Science in the Bell System: The Early Years (1875–1925)*. N.p.: Bell Telephone Laboratories, 1975.

Faue, Elizabeth. *Community of Suffering and Struggle: Women, Men, and the Labor Movement in Minneapolis, 1915–1945*. Chapel Hill: University of North Carolina Press, 1991.

Fink, Gary and Merl E. Reed, eds. *Southern Workers and Their Unions: Selected Papers, the Second Southern Labor History Conference, 1977*. Westport: Greenwood Press, 1981.

Fischer, Claude S. *America Calling: A Social History of the Telephone to 1940*. Berkeley: University of California Press, 1992.

Flexner, Eleanor. *Century of Struggle: The Woman's Rights Movement in the United States*. Cambridge, Mass.: Harvard University Press, 1959. Revised, 1975.

Fredrickson, George. *The Arrogance of Race: Historical Perspectives on Slavery*. Middletown, Conn.: Wesleyan University Press, 1988.

Gabin, Nancy F. *Feminism in the Labor Movement: Women and United Auto Workers, 1935–1975*. Ithaca, N.Y.: Cornell University Press, 1990.

Gabler, Edwin. *The American Telegrapher: A Social History, 1860–1900*. New Brunswick, N.J.: Rutgers University Press, 1988.

Garnet, Robert W. *The Telephone Enterprise: The Evolution of the Bell System's Horizontal Structure, 1876–1909*. Baltimore: Johns Hopkins University Press, 1985.

Gartman, David. *Auto Slavery: The Labor Process in the American Automobile Industry, 1897–1950*. New Brunswick, N.J.: Rutgers University Press, 1986.

Goldin, Claudia. *Understanding the Gender Gap: An Economic History of American Women*. New York: Oxford University Press, 1990.

Goldmark, Josephine. *Fatigue and Efficiency*. New York: Charities Publication Committee, 1912.

Gordon, David M., Richard Edwards, and Michael Reich. *Segmented Work, Divided*

Workers: The Historical Transformation of Labor in the United States. New York: Cambridge University Press, 1982.

Goulden, Joseph C. *Monopoly.* New York: G. P. Putnam's Sons, 1968.

Greenwald, Maurine Weiner. *Women, War, and Work: The Impact of World War I on Women Workers in the United States.* Westport, Conn.: Greenwood Press, 1980.

Hacker, Sally L. *"Doing It the Hard Way: Investigations of Gender and Technology,"* Dorothy E. Smith and Susan M. Turner, eds. Winchester, Mass.: Unwin Hyman, 1990.

Harris, Howell John. *The Right to Manage: Industrial Relations Policies of American Business in the 1940s.* Madison: University of Wisconsin Press, 1982.

Hartmann, Heidi I., ed. *Computer Chips and Paper Clips: Technology and Women's Employment.* Vol. 2. Washington, D.C.: National Academy Press, 1987.

Hartmann, Heidi I., Robert E. Kraut, and Louise A. Tilly, eds. *Computer Chips and Paper Clips: Technology and Women's Employment.* Vol. 1. Washington, D.C.: National Academy Press, 1986.

Hill, Herbert, *Black Labor and the American Legal System: Race, Work, and the Law.* Madison: University of Wisconsin Press, 1985.

Hirschhorn, Larry. *Beyond Mechanization.* Cambridge, Mass.: MIT Press, 1984.

Hoffman, W. Michael, and Thomas J. Wyly. *The Work Ethic in Business.* Cambridge, Mass.: Oelgeschlager, Gunn & Hain, 1981.

Homans, James E. *ABC of the Telephone.* New York: Theo Audel, 1901.

Hughes, Thomas P. *American Genesis: A Century of Invention and Technological Enthusiasm, 1870–1970.* New York: Viking, 1989.

Ignatiev, Noel. *How the Irish Became White.* Boston, Mass.: Routledge, 1995.

Joekes, Susan P. *Women in the World Economy.* New York: Oxford University Press, 1987.

Juravich, Tom, William F. Hartford, and James R. Green. *Commonwealth of Toil: Chapters in the History of Massachusetts Workers and Their Unions.* Amherst: University of Massachusetts Press, 1996.

Kaligo, Al, Lou Baumbach, and Joe Garzinsky. *Telecommunications Management: A Practical Approach.* New York: American Management Association, Membership Publications Division, 1984.

Kessler-Harris, Alice. *Out to Work: A History of Wage-Earning Women in the United States.* New York: Oxford University Press, 1982.

Kingsbury, J. E. *The Telephone and Telephone Exchanges: Their Invention and Development.* London: Longmans, Green, 1915.

Kusterer, Ken C. *Know-How on the Job: The Important Working Knowledge of "Unskilled" Workers.* Boulder, Colo.: Westview Press, 1978.

Landsberger, Henry A. *Hawthorne Revisited.* Ithaca, N.Y.: Cornell University Press, 1958.

Lipartito, Kenneth. *The Bell System and Regional Business: The Telephone in the South, 1877–1920.* Baltimore: Johns Hopkins University Press, 1989.

Livernash, Robert E., ed. *Comparable Worth: Issues and Alternatives.* Washington, D.C.: Equal Employment Advisory Council, 1980.

Martin, Michèle. *Hello Central? Gender, Technology, and Culture in the Formation of Telephone Systems.* Montreal: McGill-Queen's University Press, 1991.

Marvin, Carolyn. *When Old Technologies Were New: Thinking About Electric Communication in the Late Nineteenth Century.* New York: Oxford University Press, 1988.

Matthaei, Julie. *An Economic History of Women in America: Women's Work, the Sexual Division of Labor and the Development of Capitalism.* New York: Schocken Books, 1982.

Milkman, Ruth. *Gender at Work: The Dynamics of Job Segregation by Sex During World War II.* Urbana: University of Illinois Press, 1987.

——, ed. *Women, Work, and Protest: A Century of U.S. Women's Labor History.* Boston, Mass.: Routledge & Kegan Paul, 1985.

Mohun, Arwen P. *Steam Laundries: Gender, Technology, and Work in the United States and Great Britain, 1880–1940.* Baltimore: Johns Hopkins University Press, 1999.

Montgomery, David. *Workers' Control in America: Studies in the History of Work, Technology, and Labor Struggles.* New York: Cambridge University Press, 1979.

——. *The Fall of the House of Labor: The Workplace, the State, and American Labor Activism, 1865–1925.* Cambridge: Cambridge University Press, 1987.

Mulcaire, Michael A. *The International Brotherhood of Electrical Workers.* Washington, D.C.: Catholic University Press, 1923.

Nielsen, Georgia Panter. *From Sky Girl to Flight Attendant, Women and the Making of a Union.* Ithaca, N.Y.: ILR Press, 1982.

Noble, David F. *America by Design: Science, Technology, and the Rise of Corporate Capitalism.* New York: Oxford University Press, 1977.

——. *Forces of Production: A Social History of Industrial Automation.* New York: Knopf, 1984.

Northrup, Herbert R., and John A. Larson. *The Impact of the AT&T–EEO Consent Decree.* Philadelphia: University of Pennsylvania Press, 1979.

Norwood, Stephen H. *Labor's Flaming Youth: Telephone Operators and Worker Militancy, 1878–1923.* Urbana: University of Illinois Press, 1990.

Novarra, Virginia. *Women's Work, Men's Work: The Ambivalence of Equality.* Salem, N.H.: Marion Boyars, 1980.

O'Neill, William L. *Women at Work.* New York: Quadrangle/New York Times Books, 1972.

Page, Arthur W. *The Bell System.* New York: Harper and Brothers, 1941.

Pool, Ithiel de Sola, ed. *The Social Impact of the Telephone.* Cambridge, Mass.: MIT Press, 1977.

Probert, Belinda, and Bruce W. Wilson. *Pink Collar Blues: Work, Gender, and Technology.* Melbourne: Melbourne University Press, 1993.

Rakow, Lana F. *Gender on the Line: Women, the Telephone, and Community Life.* Urbana: University of Illinois Press, 1992.

Reskin, Barbara F., ed. *Sex Segregation in the Workplace: Trends, Explanations, Remedies.* Washington, D.C.: National Academy Press, 1984.

Reskin, Barbara F., and Patricia A. Roos. *Job Queues, Gender Queues: Explaining Women's Inroads into Male Occupations.* Philadelphia: Temple University Press, 1990.

Rhodes, Frederick Leland. *Beginnings of Telephony.* New York: Harper Bros., 1929.

Roediger, David R. *The Wages of Whiteness: Race and the Making of the American Working Class.* London: Verso, 1991.

———. *Towards the Abolition of Whiteness: Essays on Race, Politics, and Working Class History.* New York: Verso, 1994.

Rotella, Elyce J. *From Home to Office: U.S. Women at Work, 1870–1930.* Ann Arbor, Mich.: UMI Research Press, 1977.

Rothschild, Joan, ed. *Machina Ex Dea: A Feminist Perspective on Technology.* New York: Pergamon Press, 1983.

Sabel, Charles F. *Work and Politics: The Division of Labor in Industry.* Cambridge: Cambridge University Press, 1982.

Sacks, Karen Brodkin, and Dorothy Remy, eds. *My Troubles Are Going to Have Trouble With Me: Everyday Trials and Triumphs of Women Workers.* New Brunswick, N.J.: Rutgers University Press, 1984.

Saxton, Alexander. *The Indispensable Enemy: Labor and the Anti-Chinese Movement in California.* Berkeley: University of California Press, 1971.

Schacht, John N. *The Making of Telephone Unionism, 1920–1947.* New Brunswick, N.J.: Rutgers University Press, 1985.

Scharf, Lois. *To Work and to Wed: Female Employment, Feminism, and the Great Depression.* Westport, Conn.: Greenwood Press, 1980.

Schatz, Ronald W. *The Electrical Workers: A History of Labor at General Electric and Westinghouse, 1923–1960.* Urbana: University of Illinois Press, 1983.

Shaiken, Harley. *Work Transformed: Automation and Labor in the Computer Age.* Lexington, Mass.: D. C. Heath, 1986.

Smith, George David. *The Anatomy of a Business Strategy: Bell, Western Electric, and the Origins of the American Telephone Industry.* Baltimore: Johns Hopkins University Press, 1985.

Smuts, Robert W. *Women and Work in America.* New York: Schocken Books, 1974 (first published by Columbia University Press, 1959).

Stehman, J. Warren. *The Financial History of the American Telephone and Telegraph Company.* Boston: Houghton Mifflin, 1925.

Strom, Sharon Hartman. *Beyond the Typewriter: Gender, Class, and the Origins of Modern American Office Work, 1900–1930.* Urbana: University of Illinois Press, 1992.

Tentler, Leslie Woodcock. *Wage-Earning Women: Industrial Work and Family Life in the United States, 1900–1930.* New York: Oxford University Press, 1979.

Thompson, Paul. *The Nature of Work: An Introduction to Debates on the Labour Process.* London: Macmillan Press, 1983.

Treiman, Donald J., and Heidi I. Hartmann, eds. *Women, Work, and Wages: Equal Pay for Jobs of Equal Value.* Washington, D.C.: National Academy Press, 1981.

Vallas, Steven Peter. *Power in the Workplace: The Politics of Production at AT&T.* Albany: State University of New York Press, 1993.

Wallace, Phyllis A., ed. *Equal Employment Opportunity and the AT&T Case.* Cambridge, Mass.: MIT Press, 1976.

Walsh, Leigh J. *Connecticut Pioneers in Telephony.* New Haven, Conn.: Telephone Pioneers of America, 1950.

Ware, Susan. *Holding Their Own: American Women in the 1930s.* Boston: Twayne, 1982.

Wasserman, Neil H. *From Invention to Innovation: Long Distance Telephone Transmission at the Turn of the Century.* Baltimore: Johns Hopkins University Press, 1985.

Webster, Juliet. *Shaping Women's Work: Gender, Employment, and Information Technology.* New York: Addison Wesley Longman, 1996.

Wertheimer, Barbara Mayer. *We Were There: The Story of Working Women in America.* New York: Random House, 1977.

Wright, Barbara Drygulski, ed. *Women, Work, and Technology: Transformations.* Ann Arbor: University of Michigan Press, 1987.

Zimbalist, Andrew, ed. *Case Studies on the Labor Process.* New York: Monthly Review Press, 1979.

Zuboff, Shoshana. *In the Age of the Smart Machine: The Future of Work and Power.* New York: Basic Books, 1988.

Articles and Dissertations

Abbott, Arthur Vaughn. "The Evolution of the Telephone Switchboard." *Electrical Engineering* 4 (September 1884): 112–13.

Arnesen, Eric. " 'Like Banquo's Ghost, It will Not Down': The Race Question and the American Railroad Brotherhoods, 1880–1920." *American Historical Review* 99 (December 1994): 1601–33.

Atwood, Alden. "Telephony and Its Cultural Meanings in Southeastern Iowa." Ph.D. Diss. University of Iowa, 1984.

Bers, Melvin Kline. "Unionism and Collective Bargaining in the Telephone Industry." Ph.D. Diss. University of California at Berkeley, 1956.

Brand, Horst. "Productivity in Telephone Communications." *Monthly Labor Review* (November 1973): 3–9.

Cowan, Ruth Schwartz. "From Virginia Dare to Virginia Slims: Women and Technology in American Life." *Technology and Culture* 20 (January 1979): 51–63.

Curry, William Gilmore. "Bell Telephone Labor Economics." Ph.D. diss., Columbia University, 1952.

Dymmel, Michael D. "Technology in Telecommunications: Its Effect on Labor and Skills." *Monthly Labor Review,* January 1979: 13–19.

———. "Technological Trends and Their Implications for Jobs and Employment in the

Bell System." Paper written for the Communication Workers of America, November 19, 1979.

Fields, Barbara. "Ideology and Race in American History," in J. Morgan Kousser and James M. McPherson, eds., *Region, Race, and Reconstruction: Essays in Honor of C. Vann Woodward*. New York: Oxford University Press, 1982, 143–177.

Fields, Barbara Jeanne. "Slavery, Race and Ideology in the United States of America." *New Left Review* 181 (May/June 1990): 95–118.

Fischer, Claude S. " 'Touch Someone': The Telephone Industry Discovers Sociability." *Technology and Culture* 29 (1988): 32–61.

Gabel, Richard. "The Early Competitive Era in Telephone Communication, 1893–1920." *Law and Contemporary Problems*, Spring 1969, pp. 3890–3909.

Green, Venus. " 'Goodbye Central': Automation and the Decline of 'Personal Service' in the Bell System, 1878–1921." *Technology and Culture* 36 (October 1995): 912–49.

———. "The Impact of Technology Upon Women's Work in the Telephone Industry, 1880–1980." Ph.D. Diss. Columbia University, 1990.

———. "The 'Lady' Telephone Operator: Gendering Whiteness in the Bell System, 1900–1970," in Peter Alexander and Rick Halpern, eds., *Racializing Class, Classifying Race: Labour and Difference in Britain, the USA, and Africa*. London: Macmillan, 1999.

———. "Race Meets Technology: African American Women in the Bell System, 1940–1980." *Technology and Culture* 36 (April 1995): S101–43.

Hacker, Sally L. "Sex Stratification, Technology and Organizational Change: A Longitudinal Case Study of AT&T." *Social Problems* 26 (June 1979): 539–70.

Hall, Jacquelyn Dowd. "Disorderly Women: Gender and Labor Militancy in the Appalachian South." *Journal of American History* 73 (September 1986): 354–82.

Harris, Cheryl I. "Whiteness as Property." *Harvard Law Review* 106 (June 1993): 1707–91.

Hill, Herbert. "Myth-Making as Labor History: Herbert Gutman and the United Mine Workers of America." *International Journal of Politics, Culture, and Society* 2 (Winter 1988): 132–200.

Howard, Robert. "Brave New Workplace." *Working Papers for a New Society*, November-December 1980, pp. 21–31.

———. "Strung Out at the Phone Company: How AT&T's Workers Are Drugged, Bugged, and Coming Unplugged." *Mother Jones*, August 1981, pp. 39–45, 54–59.

Keller, Evelyn Fox. "Feminism and Science," *Signs* 7 (Spring 1982): 589–602.

Klaczynska, Barbara Mary. "Working Women in Philadelphia—1900–1930." Ph.D. Diss. Temple University, 1975.

Kohl, George. "Changing Competitive and Technology Environments in Telecommunications," in Donald Kennedy, Charles Craypo, and Mary Lehman, *Labor and Technology: Union Response to Changing Environments*. University Park: Pennsylvania State University Press, 1985.

———. "Silent Witness." Unpublished paper in author's possession.

——. "Technological Change in Telecommunications: Its Impact on Work and the Workers." Unpublished draft in author's possession.

Kulik, Gary. "Black Workers and Technological Change in the Birmingham Iron Industry, 1881–1931," in Gary Fink and Merl E. Reed, eds., *Southern Workers and Their Unions: Selected Papers, the Second Southern Labor History Conference, 1977.* Westport, Conn.: Greenwood Press, 1981.

Lerman, Nina E., Arwen Palmer Mohun, and Ruth Oldenziel. "The Shoulders We Stand On and the View from Here: Historiography and Directions for Research." *Technology and Culture* 38 (January 1997): 9–30.

Lipartito, Kenneth James. "The Telephone in the South: A Comparative Analysis, 1877–1920." Ph.D. Diss. Johns Hopkins University, 1986.

——. "When Women Were Switches: Technology, Work, and Gender in the Telephone Industry, 1890–1920." *American Historical Review* 99 (October 1994): 1075–1111.

Lipsitz, George. "The Possessive Investment in Whiteness: Racialized Social Democracy and the 'White' Problem in American Studies." *American Quarterly* 47 (September 1995): 369–87.

Loomis, Carol J. "AT&T in the Throes of 'Equal Opportunity.' " *Fortune,* January 15, 1979, pp. 45–70.

Lott, Eric. "White Like Me: Racial Cross-Dressing and the Construction of American Whiteness," in Amy Kaplan and Donald E. Pease, eds., *Cultures of United States Imperialism.* Durham, N.C.: Duke University Press, 1993.

Lowenberg, Joseph J. "Effects of Change on Employee Relations in the Telephone Industry." Ph.D. Diss. Harvard University, 1962.

Maddox, Brenda. "Women and the Switchboard," in Ithiel de Sola Pool, *The Social Impact of the Telephone.* Cambridge, Mass.: MIT Press, 1977.

McGaw, Judith A. "Women and the History of American Technology." *Signs* 7 (Summer 1982): 798–828.

Mueller, Milton. "The Switchboard Problem: Scale, Signaling, and Organization in Manual Telephone Switching, 1877–1897." *Technology and Culture* 30 (1989): 534–60.

The National Organization of Women. "Women's Wages: A Key to Preserving Middle Income Jobs." By Judith Gregory, George Kohl, Leslie Loble, and Louise Novotny. August 1986, updated November 1986.

Newman, David M. "New Technology and the Changing Labor Process in the Telephone Industry: The Union's Response." Unpublished paper in author's possession.

Norwood, Stephan Harlan. "The Making of the Trade Union Woman: Work Culture and Organization of Telephone Operators, 1900–1923." Ph.D. Diss. Columbia University, 1984.

Ottley, Roi, and William J. Weatherby, eds. (Federal Writers Project). "The Depression in Harlem," in Bernard Sternsher, ed., *Hitting Home: The Great Depression in Town and Country.* Chicago: Quadrangle Books, 1970.

Phillips, Anne, and Barbara Taylor. "Sex and Skill: Notes Toward a Feminist Economics." *Feminist Review* 6 (October 1980): 79–88.

Roediger, David. "Race and the Working-Class Past in the United States: Multiple Identities and the Future of Labor History." *International Review of Social History* 38, supp. (1993): 127–43.

Sacks, Karen Brodkin. "How Did Jews Become White Folks?" in Steven Gregory and Roger Sanjek, eds., *Race*. New Brunswick, N.J.: Rutgers University Press, 1994.

Schmitt, Katherine M. "I Was Your Old 'Hello' Girl." *Saturday Evening Post,* July 12, 1930.

Scott, Joan Wallach. "The Mechanization of Women Work." *Scientific American* 247 (September 1982): 166–87.

Shulman, Steven. "Racism and the Making of the American Working Class." *International Journal of Politics, Culture and Society* 2 (Spring 1989): 361–66.

Sims, Calvin. "Calling Collect? A Computer Is at Your Service." *New York Times,* June 12, 1989, sec. 1, p. 1.

Straw, Ronnie J., and Lorel E. Foged. "Final Report: CWA/AT&T Conference on New Technology and Work Innovations." Submitted to the German Marshall Fund of the United States, November 15, 1984.

Vallas, Steven P. "White-Collar Proletarians? The Structure of Clerical Work and Levels of Class Consciousness." *Sociological Quarterly* 28 (Winter 1987): 523–40.

Waldinger, Roger. "Another Look at the International Ladies' Garment Workers' Union: Women, Industry Structure, and Collective Action," in Ruth Milkman, ed., *Women, Work, and Protest*. Boston: Routledge & Kegan Paul, 1985.

Walker, Laura J., and Joy Anne Grune. "Pay Equity and New Technology Jobs for the Future." Paper developed for the CWA Second National Women's Conference, the Coalition of Labor Union Women, Center for Education and Research, Washington, D.C., 1984.

Aberdeen (Washington), 100

Abernethy, Charles L., 159

Absence control, 72–73, 98, 151–52, 157, 222, 243, 259–60, 287n. 70, 333n. 69

Accents. *See* Telephone operators: language used by

Affirmative action programs (of Bell System), 226–29, 237–48, 256, 257, 336n. 115

AFL. *See* American Federation of Labor

African American men, 210, 211, 247, 284n. 31, 321n. 21

African American women: Bell System's public relations about hiring of, 227–34; blaming of, for poor telephone service, 223–25; as clerical workers, for Bell System, xi, 198, 199, 209, 213; as crafts workers, 239–42, 244, 256, 259; demeaning depictions of, by white operators, 134, 135, 206; as domestics, 88, 291n. 114; dominance of, as telephone operators, 211–12, 220–36, 250, 329n. 6; entry of, into Bell System, 7, 195–226; exclusion of, from telephone industry, 2, 3, 53, 55, 87, 126, 139, 195–201, 320n. 16; fight of, against discrimination, 201–4; as "hardcore," 220, 224, 229–33, 235, 236, 329n. 6; labor unions' discrimination against, 195, 206–9, 228, 245–46, 324nn. 62, 66, and 71; particular image of, sought by Bell System, 234–35; as supervisors, 198, 235. *See also* Caribbean women

Age: as Bell System hiring criterion, 65–66, 72, 81, 154, 258; of telephone operators in the 1920s, 156; and union activity, 94, 313n. 75

Alliance of Independent Telephone Unions, 315n. 99

American Bell Telephone Company (ABT), 13, 14, 93, 118

American Civil Liberties Union (ACLU), 233

American Communications Association (ACA), 183, 314n. 80, 315n. 99

American Federation of Labor (AFL), 102, 104, 111, 173, 178, 179, 296n. 87, 314n. 80

American Telephone and Telegraph Company (AT&T): as long distance provider, 13, 14; as monopoly, 14; opening of male-dominated work to women by, ix–x; as parent Bell System company, 276n. 93. *See also* AT&T Long Lines; Bell System

Anderson, Bernard E., 211

Anderson, E. J., 134–35

Area codes, 130

Arkansas, 211, 295n. 54, 305n. 22, 320n. 16

Atlanta (Georgia), 101, 102, 245–46, 320n. 16

AT&T Long Lines (Bell System Long Lines), 38, 131, 139, 142, 149–50, 199, 210, 276n. 93, 336n. 115. *See also* American Telephone and Telegraph Company; Bell System; Long distance

Automatic call distribution, 128–29

Automatic Electric Company, 120, 123, 299n. 11

Automatic Message Accounting (AMA), 132, 133

Automatic Number Identification (ANI), 133

Automatic Telephone and Electric Company of Illinois, 120

Automation (of switchboards): Bell System's public relations about, 125, 159, 166–69; as deterrent to unionism, 115–16, 183; development of, 116–29; early features of, 86; effects of, on workers, 5,

Automation (of switchboards) (*cont.*)
6, 112, 159–69, 178–86; for long distance, 129–33, 160, 183, 214–18, 250–54; and operators' "servant" image, 4; operators' views of, 90, 111; as progress, 179, 186–91; semiautomatic, 122; as strike neutralizer, 183; subscribers' objections to, 159, 164; transition from, to computerization, 214–18; unions' lack of resistance to, 245. *See also* Computerization; Dial era; Switchman; Technology

Babylon (Long Island), 223, 224
Bailey, Clarence W., Jr., 243
Baltimore (Maryland), 93, 203–4, 209, 234
Baltimore Afro-American, 204
Barnett, Benjamin, 321n. 25
Barrett, R. T., 55, 58
Barry, Grace, 171
Barton, E. M., 46, 298n. 5
Beach, F. G., 93
Beahm, Mildred, 182
Beirne, Joseph A., 178, 182, 185, 187–88, 190, 245
Bell, Alexander Graham, 11, 12
Bell Laboratories, 132, 271n. 21, 336n. 115. *See also* Engineers
Bell Patent Association, 12
Bell System (AT&T and associated companies): and bargaining on national level, 179, 183; consent decrees of, 7, 237–42, 255–57; definition of, 11; discrimination by, 2, 3, 53, 55, 62, 65, 87, 126, 134–36, 139, 157, 195–211, 221–24, 226–28, 233, 236, 237, 250–51, 257, 265n. 3; divestiture of, 1, 11, 255, 336n. 115; domination of telephone industry by, 5, 13–16, 116; expansion of jobs in, after automation, 188–89; experiments of, with automation, 121–24; as "family," 137–38, 143–44, 151–54; hierarchy in, 48, 50, 52, 55; history of, 11–52; indepen-

dent telephone companies' competition with, 5, 11–16, 46, 51, 58, 67, 116, 120, 284n. 30; as leader in technological development, xi–xii, 1, 5, 11–12, 14, 36; managerial uses of race and gender by, 3, 53, 55, 64–67, 196–201, 220, 225–26, 228–33, 236, 240–42, 249–52, 262; standardization in, 15, 38–41, 47–52, 55, 67, 73, 75–77, 86–87, 89. *See also* Automation; Clerical workers; Company unions; Craft workers; Discipline policies; Dividend payments; Engineers; Hiring policies; Hours of work; Independent telephone companies; Job benefits; Managers; Paternalism; Public relations; Supervisors; Technology; Telephone operators; Training; "Upgrade and Transfer Program"; Welfare programs; Work processes
Bell System Long Lines Department. *See* AT&T Long Lines
Bell System Technical Conference, 125
Bell Telephone Company, 12
Bell Telephone Company of Canada, Ltd., 80
Bell Telephone Company of Pittsburgh, 205
Bell Telephone Magazine, 215, 233
Benefits. *See* Job benefits
Benscoter, Anne, 316n. 107
Best, Ethel L., 164
Bethell, F. H., 137
"Big city problem" (diseconomies of scale), 26, 117–18, 122–24
Bishop automatic system, 298n. 6
Bix, Amy Sue, 318n. 124
Black, Vernal, 155
"The Black Militants/The Negro Moderates" (Bell System pamphlet), 235–36
Blake, Francis, 270n. 7
Blake transmitter, 12, 17, 22
Blauvelt, W. G., 124
Boggs, R. H., 196

Bolick, Lavie, 245–46
Boston (Massachusetts), 234, 320n. 16; automation in, 123; Bell System's first woman operator in, 16, 60; medical plans for operators in, 73; operator activism in, 99–100, 103, 126, 170; switchboards in, 286n. 57; telephone operators in, 16, 44, 60, 108–9; turnover among operators in, 94; unions in, 96, 103. See also *specific companies and unions in*
Boston Globe, 87
Boston Post, 87
Boston Telephone Operators' Union (IBEW), 90, 94, 99, 109, 134
Boycotts, 110, 201, 202
Boys' work. *See* Men's work
Branch Terminal switchboards, 31, 34, 280n. 145
Braverman, Harry, 267n. 8, 268n. 10
Brooklyn (New York), 70–71, 130
Brunswick (Georgia), 101
Bryn Mawr summer school for workers, 90
Buffalo (New York), 206, 285n. 42
Bugniazet, Gustave, 110
Burleson, Albert S., 14, 101–2, 115
"Busy signal," 123, 124
"Busy" test, 29–30, 43–44, 47
Butler, Elizabeth Beardsley, 80–81, 87
Butte (Montana), 96, 97, 99, 111, 126, 295n. 75

California Rural Legal Assistance, 233
Camden (New Jersey), 209
Canada, 12, 13, 80, 138, 286n. 57, 290n. 97
Canvassing, 64, 284n. 30
Caribbean women, 234, 258
Carmichael, Stokely, 236
Carmody, Helen C., 171–72
Carter, E. F., 164
Carty, John J., 29, 40, 44–45, 56, 122, 126
Catholics, 208, 258
Centralized Automatic Message Accounting (CAMA), 132–33

Central New York Telephone and Telegraph Company, 50–51
Central Union Telephone Company (Chicago), 30, 47, 48–49, 93
Chesapeake & Potomac Telephone Company (C&P), 73, 93, 159, 198, 204, 320n. 19
Chicago, 78, 81, 88, 92, 100, 140–41, 210, 320n. 16; automation in, 123, 130; switchboards in, 286n. 57. See also *specific telephone companies in*
Chicago Federation of Labor, 102
Chicago Telephone Company, 60, 100, 284n. 30
Chief operators: duties of, 48, 50, 51; men as, 49, 57, 66, 107, 287n. 61; possibility of electing, 105–6; resistance to, 93, 225; women as, 60, 61, 281n. 154. *See also* Monitor operators; Supervisors
Chinnock switchboards, 272n. 41, 286nn. 57 and 59
Church Federation of St. Louis, 203
Cigarmakers, 111, 297n. 100, 317n. 117
Cincinnati Bell, 327n. 104
CIO. *See* Congress of Industrial Organizations
Cities: automation for, 121–22, 125; bonuses paid to operators in, 99; computerized switching stations in, 4; diseconomies of scale in, 26, 117–18, 122–24; inefficiency of telephone service in, 26, 273n. 49, 276n. 85; racial demographics of, 195, 212–13, 223–24, 250; working conditions for operators in, 69–70. See also *specific cities and companies*
City and Suburban Bell Telephone Association (Cincinnati), 72, 92
City-Wide Citizens' Committee on Harlem, 202
Civil Rights Act of 1964, 211, 221, 227, 242, 244
Civil rights movement, 195, 202, 211–12, 235–36

Clarke, John Henrike, 202

Class. *See* African American women: as "hardcore"; African American women: particular image of, sought by Bell System; Status; "White lady" image; Working-class solidarity

Clerical workers (in telephone industry), ix–xi, 60, 87, 157, 188–90, 209, 251–52, 261; African American, xi, 198, 199, 209, 213, 239, 240–41, 258–60, 284n. 31; decline in, 240; men as, 238–39, 284n. 31; in suburbs, 335n. 105; wages of, 287n. 66, 325n. 82

Cleveland (Ohio), 92, 102, 131, 132, 182

Closed shops, 95, 96–97, 106

Coalition of Labor Union Women, 255

Cohn, Jules, 232

Collier, Charles, 321n. 25

Colorado Telephone Company Benefit Association, 108

Columbia (South Carolina), 101, 102

Columbia University (New York City), xi

Combined Line and Recording method (CLR), 41–43, 150, 279n. 123

Commercial Department (of Bell System), 15

Committee on Equity (CWA), 253, 255

Common Battery switchboards, 31, 34, 36, 280n. 145

Communications Workers of America (CWA), 178, 183, 184–91, 230, 231, 263; antidiscrimination policy of, 324n. 66; attacks on affirmative action by, 244–48; emergence of, 315n. 99; Local 1150 of, 250, 253, 317n. 124; Local 4350 of, 187; membership of, 315n. 99; and technology displacement, 248–53

Company unions: discrimination by, 324n. 62; managers' use of, 6–7, 115, 127, 137–58, 169–70, 265n. 1; resistance to, 138

"Comparable worth," 255. *See also* "Equal pay for equal work"; Wages

Computerization: to control workers, 7; ef-

fects of, on men's work, 295n. 72; impact of, on work processes, 5, 217–18, 258; and racial composition of workforce, 4, 7, 227. *See also specific computerized equipment*

Condell, Jennie R., 93

Conference calling, 189

Conference of European Telegraph and Telephone Administration Technicians, 122

Congress of Industrial Organizations (CIO), 178, 179, 183, 207; and CWA, 315n. 99; NFTW's refusal to affiliate with, 173, 314n. 80

Connecticut Union of Telephone Workers, 219

Connolly, M. D., 116

Connolly, T. A., 116

Considine, Ellen, 19, 271n. 25

Control: Bell System's use of new technology as means of, over workers, 3, 6, 7, 11–12, 25–26, 29, 45–47, 73–78, 82–83, 128–29, 218–19, 224, 226, 227, 241, 261–62; of managers over work processes, 6, 29–31, 45–52, 55, 73–79, 82–83, 86–87, 128–29, 142, 218, 226, 241, 261. *See also* Absence control; Chief Operators; Discipline policies; Managers; Productivity; Supervisors; Telephone operators

Control Switching Points (CSP), 131

Cooper, Evelyn N., 205, 209

Coordinating Committee for Employment, 202

Courtesy (toward subscribers): as requirement for operators, 51, 53, 55–58, 67–69, 79, 182, 223. *See also* Telephone operators: language used by

Coy, George W., 20–21

Coy switchboards, 20–22

Cozad, W. F., 146–47

C&P. *See* Chesapeake & Potomac Telephone Company

Craft workers (in telephone industry), x–
xi, 190, 261; deskilling of, 241–42; discrimination in hiring of, 211, 237; ideology associated with unions for, 6,
90–91, 103–6, 110, 179–81, 184–86,
245, 262, 296n. 87; labor unions for,
104, 140, 283n. 21; nonwhite women
as, 239–42, 244, 256, 259; skills associated with, x, 19, 180–81; unfair treatment of, 254; white men as, 5, 211, 254,
318n. 127; white women as, 237–38,
256, 319n. 140. See also Linemen;
Switchman

Crossbar switches, 130–32, 217, 254,
302n. 56

Curry, Nellie B., 79, 81

Cutler, Charles, 51

CWA. See Communications Workers of
America

Dallas (Texas), 95

Danielian, N. R., 310n. 23

Davies, Margery W., 266n. 6

Davis, Joseph P., 78

Dayton (Ohio), 177

Delaware and Atlantic Telegraph and Telephone Company, 47–49

Des Moines (Iowa), 96–97, 105–6, 293n.
30, 296n. 75

Detroit (Michigan), 71, 132, 177, 182, 210,
320n. 16

Dial conversion. See Automation

Dial Conversion Committee (of CWA), 185–
86, 316n. 107

Dial era, 6–7, 127–33, 159–91

Dial phones, 118

Dial Service "A" boards (DSA), 128

Dial tone, 123

Direct Distance Dialing (DDD), 133, 214–18,
250

Directory assistance, 235, 246, 327n. 104;
charging for, 227, 239, 327n. 104, 336n.
115; working conditions of operators in,

218, 223, 224, 261, 327n. 104. See also
Information

Disability. See Illnesses

Discipline policies (of Bell System), 6, 16,
48–51, 56, 67, 79, 105, 219; penalties associated with, 78–79, 108, 231, 251

Divided boards. See No. 1 Relay switchboards

Dividend payments (by Bell System), 165–
68, 170. See also Stock (for employees)

"Division of labor" method of relaying
calls, 25–26, 51

Dixon, A. F., 125–26

Doak, W. N., 164

Donahey, Theresa R., 312n. 59

Dorsey, V. L., 209

Dress codes, 222, 235

Duluth Telephone Company, 293n. 30

Dunbar, Helen, 222–23

Durant, George F., 287n. 62

Dwyer, Robert, 289n. 93

Edison, Thomas, 12

Edwards, Richard, 268n. 10

EEOC. See Equal Employment Opportunity
Commission

Eldridge, H. E., 141

Elevated Streetcar Workers, 109

Ellsworth, J. D., 98, 290n. 97

Emnia, Loreta E., 182

Employee associations. See Company
unions

Engineers: and automation, 116–27, 132–
33, 214, 300n. 22; on CLR, 42–43; and
computerization, 217–18; role of, in Bell
System, 15; role of, in standardizing
work processes, 16, 45–47, 75–79, 285n.
51; and speed-ups, 150, 217; switchboards designed by, 6, 20, 31, 34; white
males as, 4–5, 271n. 21; on women, 146,
154. See also Bell Laboratories; specific
engineers

Englewood (New York), 132

Equal Employment Opportunity Commission (EEOC), 204, 244, 266n. 3; appeal of, that FCC investigate discrimination charges, 233, 237, 323n. 57; consent decrees of, 7, 237–39, 242, 255–57; discrimination complaints filed with, 226, 231, 237, 320n. 29; establishment of, 205; investigations of telephone industry by, 201, 211, 221, 232, 319n. 140; opening of male-dominated work in telephone industry to women by, ix–x; white males' fears of, 243, 244

Equal Pay Act of 1945, 176

"Equal pay for equal work," 3, 176, 177, 190. See also "Comparable worth"; Wages

Equipment (telephone): inefficiency of early, 20–29, 36; leasing of, 12, 13; as more important than workers, 86, 172; standardization of, 15, 36; unreliability of early, 19, 29, 35, 37, 53, 58, 59, 67, 121; worn by telephone operators, 45, 79–80, 280n. 136. See also Exchange systems; Switchboards; Technology; Work processes

Ergonomics, 43–45, 218

Erickson, Ethel, 177

Escorts (for telephone workers), 221, 243

Evansville (Indiana), 247

Exchange systems, 16, 20, 26; buildings for, 59, 86; distance of early, 35; male managers as responsible for, 48; size of, and operators' working conditions, 69–70; and telephone numbers, 124, 130. See also Private Branch Exchanges

Executive Order 8802, 200, 202, 204, 207, 209

Executive Order 9346, 200

Expanded Direct Distance Dialing, 217

Factory workers, 53, 79, 87, 213–14, 283n. 24, 287n. 66

Fair, Charles F., 333n. 69

Fair Employment Practices Committee (FEPC), 195, 198–200, 204–5, 207–10, 256

Farnham, W. E., 127–28, 307n. 50

Farnsworth, J. E., 95–96

Fatigue and Efficiency (Goldmark), 81

Faue, Elizabeth, 295n. 58

FCC. See Federal Communications Commission

Federal Communications Commission (FCC), 165, 222, 224, 233, 237, 323n. 57

FEPC. See Fair Employment Practices Committee

Fish, Frederick P., 78, 96–97, 288n. 72

"Floor walkers," 48

Florida, 100–103, 210

Forbes, William H., 73

Fort Smith (Arkansas), 295n. 54

Fort Worth (Texas), 95

Frame attendants, xi

Galveston (Texas), 95

Gannon, Mary E., 182, 190, 314n. 78

Gartman, David, 267n. 7

Gemma, Gabrielle, 225

Gender: companies' interest in dividing workers by, 3, 53, 55, 100; discrimination on basis of, 200–201, 237, 262, 333n. 69; division of labor based on, x, xi, 2–3, 60, 104, 237, 239–42, 257, 262, 269n. 13, 318n. 127; as factor in technology displacement, 178–80, 240, 245, 250–54, 262, 269n. 13; impact of new technology on, 4–5; and race used to prevent working-class solidarity, 3, 226, 243, 262; skill defined in terms of, 2, 6, 18, 53, 262. See also African American men; African American women; Men's work; White men; White women; Women's work

General Health Course for Women, 152

General Order No. 16 (National War Labor Board), 177

General Toll Switching Plan, 130
Gherardi, Bancroft, 123, 125, 126, 139
Gifford, Walter, 198–99
Gillespie, Mabel, 108
Gilliland switchboards, 272n. 41, 286nn. 57 and 59
Gilmore, R. E., 205
Glass, Carter, 159
Glass Bottle Blowers' Association, 297n. 100
Goldmark, Josephine, 81
Goldmark, Pauline, 306n. 35
Gompers, Samuel, 111
Goodson, Martia, 337n. 5
Gordon, David, 268n. 10
Gottlieb, Sylvia B., 176, 184, 317n. 111
Government: control of telephone industry by, in World War I, 98, 100–103, 115; dependence of, on Bell System, 257; funding of training by, for minorities, 228, 231–32, 256, 330n. 19; intervention in telephone industry by, 7, 100, 237–48, 255–57; investigations of telephone industry by, 80–81, 86, 93, 164–68, 176–77, 198–200, 204–5, 211, 222, 319n. 140; possibility of telephone industry ownership by, 14; regulation of telephone industry by, 14, 165, 270n. 16. See also *specific government agencies and departments*
Gray, Elisha, 12
Great Depression, 157–58, 160–61, 163–76, 195–97, 202, 205
"Greenies," 219
Grievances, 139, 188, 260
Griffith, Paul E., 312n. 65

Hacker, Sally L., 239–40
Hall, E. K., 138, 142–43, 145, 147–49, 151, 157–58, 166
Hall, Edward J., 43–44
Handy, Dorothy, 182
Haneke, August B., 198

Harlem Employment Agency, 134
Harlem Riot (1935), 204
Harris, Pansy, 312nn. 58, 59
Harrison, W. H., 168–69
Hayes, Hammond V., 31, 280n. 145
Healy, Joseph P., 335n. 116
Herlihy, Ann, 173, 176
Hibbard, A. S., 37–38, 45
Hierarchy (in Bell System), 48, 50, 52, 55
Hill, Herbert, 224
Hiring policies (of Bell System), 6, 86, 105, 201–4; age as factor in, 65–66, 72, 81, 154, 258, 313n. 75; changes in, xii, 210–14, 223–24, 227–36; government investigations of, 319n. 140; regarding African Americans, xii, 2, 3, 53, 62, 65, 87, 126, 134–36, 157, 195–211, 223–24, 226, 227–28, 233, 235–37, 250–51, 257, 265n. 3; regarding homosexuals, 265n. 3; regarding immigrants, 55, 62, 65, 87, 157; regarding Jews, 62, 65; regarding male operators, 221–22; regarding married women, 156, 170, 205, 313n. 71; regarding "militants," 236, 250–51; regarding white women, 53, 57–67, 94–95, 139; resistance to, 201–4; standards for, 229–30, 236. See also Affirmative action programs; Promotions; Recruitment; Training
Holton, Evelyn, 234, 259, 327n. 108, 332n. 37
Homosexuals, 265n. 3
Hours of work, 69–70, 78–81, 156; emphasis on, in male craft union ideology, 95, 99, 103–5, 111, 112, 179–80, 185, 186; during Great Depression, 171, 172; operators' criticism of, 90, 91, 108, 109–10; strikes regarding, 95, 99. See also "Split tricks"
Housewives Cooperative League, 204
Houston (Texas), 95
Hudson, John E., 51, 118
Hunter College, ix

IBEW. *See* International Brotherhood of
Electrical Workers

Illegitimacy. *See* Single parenthood

Illery, Alma, 204–5

Illinois Bell Telephone Company, 199, 222

Illnesses (associated with telephone operators), 77–81, 108, 151–52, 219–20, 226,
251, 265n. 1. *See also* Absence control

Immigrant women, 55, 62, 65, 87, 157, 206

Independent telephone companies, 265n.
1; automation by, 119–20, 122–23; Bell's
acquisition of, 122; Bell System's competition with, 5, 11–16, 46, 51, 58, 67, 116,
120, 284n. 30; hiring of African Americans by, 284n. 34; long distance service
not provided by, 119; sympathy strikes by
workers in, 96, 106; union contracts
with, 97

Independent unions. *See* Labor unions

Indianapolis (Indiana), 93

Indians, 56–57, 265n. 3

Industrial psychology, 137

Information: end of, provided by operators,
100, 124, 327n. 104; provided by telephone operators, 49, 60, 62, 82–83,
100, 128, 271n. 27. *See also* Directory
assistance

Instruction books. *See* Rule and instruction
books

Intermediate Distributing Frame (IDF), 46,
51, 73, 77, 83, 111

International Brotherhood of Electrical
Workers (IBEW), 244, 314n. 80, 315n.
99; as craft union, 104, 140; labor organizing by, 100, 101–2; Local No. 66, 95;
sympathy strikes of, 106; women organized into separate department in, 103,
108–10, 178. *See also* Boston Telephone
Operators' Union

International Direct Distance Dialing
(IDDD), 250

International Operating Center (IOC-New
York City), 250–54

International Service Position Systems
(ISPS), 250

Interstate Commerce Commission (ICC),
14

Iowa Federation of Labor, 106

Iowa Telephone Company, 96, 105–6,
273n. 49, 293n. 30

Isaacs, Stanley, 321n. 25

Jacksonville (Florida), 100–103

Jersey City (New Jersey), 19, 132

Jews, 62, 65

Job benefits, 86–87, 98–99, 137, 156–57,
222, 287n. 70; managers' discretion in
allotting of, 72, 86, 99, 223, 251–52,
260. *See also* Mutual Benefit Plans; Welfare programs

Job loss: government investigations of, in
telephone industry, 164–68; for minorities, 227, 234, 239–42, 245, 250–54; as
result of directory assistance charges,
327n. 104; as result of new technologies,
2, 4, 6, 119, 159–61, 164–70, 176, 178–
87, 239–42, 245, 248–54, 262, 269n. 13

Johnson, George M., 209

Johnson, Lyndon B., 228

Jones, Matt, 138

Jones, Merenthia, 235

Kalamazoo Experiment, 77–78

Kansas, 210

Kansas City (Missouri), 48

Kennedy, Mary, 19

Kessler-Harris, Alice, 266n. 6, 296n. 87

Key pulsing equipment, 302n. 58

King, Martin Luther, Jr., 226, 235

King, Winifred, 258–59, 329n. 135, 336n. 1

Kingsbury, N. C., 300n. 39

Kingsbury Commitment, 15

Korean War, 160, 162

Labor unions (independent), 6–7, 138, 140,
160, 169–79, 205–9, 305n. 22; boy op-

erators not interested in, 61; company spies in, 96, 97; craft ideology of, 6, 90–91, 103–6, 110, 179–81, 184–86, 245, 262, 296n. 87; deterrence of, 115, 137–58; discrimination against African Americans by, 195, 206–9, 228, 245–46, 324nn. 62, 66, 71; failure of, to address new technology, 104, 110, 111, 179–91, 245, 248–50, 260, 262, 295n. 72; government opposition to, in World War I, 101–2; importance of involvement of, in conceptualizing new technology, 263; leadership of, as failing to represent membership, 246–48, 258, 260, 318n. 124; male, as operators' allies, 6, 90–91, 93, 104–5; newspapers of, 89–90; objections of, to consent decrees and affirmative action, 7, 237, 242–48; organizing of telephone workers into, 4, 95–112, 126–27, 134, 157–58, 160, 171–79; recognition of, 91, 96–97, 99, 100, 102–6, 110, 134, 177; white men's domination of, x, xi, 4, 6, 100, 105–6, 109–11, 178–79, 245. *See also* Company unions; *specific unions*
La Guardia, Fiorello H., 308n. 2
La Porte (Indiana), 118
Larson, John A., 238, 239, 333n. 61
Law switchboards, 70, 272n. 41, 286n. 57
League for Democracy, 135
Lexington (Massachusetts), 31
Life insurance benefits, 98
Lillie, Nathaniel W., 58, 284n. 29
Lincoln (Nebraska), 183
Linemen, 103, 106, 109, 283n. 21, 287n. 65, 293n. 30
Little Rock (Arkansas), 320n. 16
Local telephone service: automation of, 35, 160; development of, 20–35, 39; engineers' guidelines for, 75
Lockouts, 101
Lockwood, Thomas D., 20, 26, 43, 44, 91, 117–20, 28in. 154

Long distance: and African American operators, 199, 210; AT&T's monopoly over, 14, 119; automating of, 129–33, 160, 183, 214–18, 250–54; company unions organized for operators of, 139, 150; development of, 13, 15; engineers' guidelines for, 75; increase in, during World War II, 162, 183; increase in rates for, 233; operators of, in union activities, 182, 318n. 124; operators' skills in, 37–38; switchboards for, 35–37, 127. *See also* AT&T Long Lines; Overseas telephone service
Los Angeles (California), 78, 81, 210
Lott, Eric, 323n. 61
Louisville (Kentucky), 101, 204
Lowrie, Peter D., 320n. 5
Lynch, Margaret J., 19–20

Macey, Chester L. ("Chet"), 253–54
MacKenzie, Cecil, 61, 282n. 2, 285n. 42
Main Distributing Frame (MDF), 45–46
Managers: African Americans hired as, 237; attitudes of, toward African American operators, 222–23; control over work processes by, 6, 29–31, 46–52, 55, 73–79, 82–83, 86–87, 128–29, 142, 218; discretion of, in allotting benefits, 72, 86, 99, 223, 251–52, 260; discrimination in hiring of, 211, 237; duties of, 47–52, 139, 225; goals of, 51, 57, 82; male trade unionists' views of prerogatives of, 104, 106, 111, 112, 184–86, 260, 295n. 72; men as, 47–48, 55, 28in. 154; new technology developed as means of helping, to control workforce, 3, 6, 7, 11–12, 25–26, 29, 45–47, 73–78, 83, 224, 226, 227, 241, 261–62; operators' resistance to, 91–92; use of company unions by, 6–7, 115, 127, 137–58, 169–70, 265n. 1; use of race and gender by, 3, 53, 55, 64–67, 196–201, 220, 225–26, 228–33, 236, 240–42, 249–52, 262; wages for, 287n. 65; women as, 59, 63, 64, 190,

Managers (*cont.*)
237–38, 255–56, 28ın. 154. *See also*
Chief Operators; Supervisors
Mann, Mae, 247, 316n. 107
Manual exchanges. *See* Switchboards
(manual)
March on Washington Movement
(MOWM), 202, 203
Marriage, 93–94, 154; and Bell System hir-
ing practices, 156, 170, 205, 313n. 71. *See
also* Single parenthood
Maryland Commission on Interracial Co-
operation, 335n. 116
Massachusetts, 12–14, 31, 73, 250. *See also*
Boston
Massachusetts General Hospital, 73
Matrons, 60, 73, 221
Maynard, George C., 72–73
Mayor's Commission on Conditions in
Harlem, 196, 204
Mays, Eugene, 231, 236, 247
McBride, H. D., 45, 65, 66, 77–78
McClure, D., 200, 207
McGath, Evelyn R., 306n. 35
McIntosh, Eugene, 134
McNeal, T. D., 203
McTighe, Thomas J., 116
Mechanization (of telephone switch-
boards). *See* Switchboards (manual)
Mechanized Loop Testers (MLTS), 241,
254
Meckle, Pat, 250, 252–53, 336n. 1
Media (Pennsylvania), 132
Memphis (Tennessee), 320n. 16
Men's work: Chief Operator as originally,
49, 57; contrasted to women's work, 104,
178; equipment maintenance as, 20,
190; expansion of, through technology,
5, 169, 178, 180, 187, 240; feminization
of, ix–xi, 3, 5, 19, 53–88, 190, 240, 254;
management as, 47–48; supervision as,
128; telephone operators as, ix, 19, 55–
59, 71–72, 221–22; wages for, 149. *See*

also African American men; Linemen;
Switchman; Wages; White men
Mental health (of operators), 219–20. *See
also* Illnesses
Mercer, Bill, 229, 231–32
Meridian (Mississippi), 101
Merit raises, 148
Messenger, 196
Metropolitan Telephone and Telegraph
Company (New York City), 51, 70, 274n.
55
Mexican Americans, 265n. 3
Mexico, 13
Michigan Bell Telephone Company, 169,
184, 319n. 140
Miles, Frances E., 155
Milkman, Ruth, 266n. 6
Miller, Bea, 213–14, 225, 231, 235, 236,
336n. 1
Milwaukee (Wisconsin), 93
Minimum wage, 176
Minneapolis (Minnesota), 101, 320n. 16
Minstrel shows, 135, 206, 323n. 61
Mitchell, Clarence, 209
Mitchell, Dorothy J., 225–26
Mix, Jessie, 82
Monitor operators, 46, 48–50
Montgomery, David, 268n. 10
Morning tests, 83
Morristown (New Jersey), 132
Morse down call, 277n. 107
Mortgages, 157, 214
Multiple switchboards, 29–31, 34–36, 83,
274n. 55, 279n. 131, 280n. 145
Mutual Benefit Plans, 107–8
Mutual Telephone Company (Des Moines),
97, 106, 293n. 30

Nash, Kenneth E., 265n. 3
Nashville (Tennessee), 101
Natchez (Mississippi), 225–26
National Alliance of Businessmen (NAB),
229, 330n. 19

National Assembly of Telephone Workers, 173

National Association for the Advancement of Colored People (NAACP), 202, 204, 233

National Bell Telephone Company, 12

National Federation of Telephone Workers (NFTW), 173–79, 181–84, 186, 187, 207, 208, 324n. 66; in Pennsylvania, 208

National Industrial Recovery Act (NIRA), 170, 171

National Institute for Occupational Safety and Health (NIOSH), 219

National Labor Relations Board (NLRB), 182

National Negro Congress, 202

National Organization for Women (NOW), 233, 321n. 29

National Telephone Commission, 313n. 71

National Telephone Exchange Association (NTEA), 31, 70, 71

National Telephone Panel (later, Commission), 177–78, 180

National Traffic Panel Committee, 180, 185, 186

National War Labor Board, 102, 177–78

Native Americans, 56–57, 265n. 3

Naughton, Norma, 168, 180–81

Newark (New Jersey), 123, 132, 246, 320n. 16

New England Telephone and Telegraph Company, 87, 109, 111, 138, 305n. 22, 319n. 140

New Haven (Connecticut), 20

New Jersey Bell Telephone Company, 184, 209, 243, 266n. 3, 320n. 19

New Jersey Division Against Discrimination, 205

Newman, Dave, 241, 249, 254

New Orleans (Louisiana), 210, 243, 320n. 16

Newspapers (company and union), 89–90. See also *specific titles*

New York and New Jersey Telephone Company, 49

New York City: antidiscrimination efforts against Bell System in, 201–2, 205, 320n. 16; attempts by African Americans to become operators in, 209–10; automation in, 123, 130, 132; first long distance calls from, 40; first office exclusively for long distance service in, 36; first Traffic Service Position office in, 217; first woman operator in, 19; Harlem Riot in, 204; inefficiency of calls in, 273n. 49; IOC's closing in, 250–54; labor unions for operators in, 246–47; operators' wages in, 70; PBX in, 189; switchboards in, 286n. 55; turnover among operators in, 94. See also *specific telephone companies in*

New York Operator's School, 61, 67

New York Public Utilities Commission, 256

New York state civil rights laws, 202, 256

New York State Commission Against Discrimination, 205

New York State Public Service Commission, 202

New York State Temporary Commission on the Condition of the Urban Colored Population, 197–98

New York Telephone Company: African Americans discriminated against by, 134–36, 196–202, 205, 207–8, 255–56; African Americans hired by, ix–xi, 210, 211, 213–14, 229–33, 235, 333n. 65; author's experience with, ix–xi, 333n. 65; automation in, 127, 303n. 66; bonus plan of, 99; decline in workforce of, 335n. 112; deskilling at, 241; employee rules of, 50; federal funds for, 231–32; labor organizing in, 134; number of operators at, 125–26; as "one big family," 137; operators' resistance to policies of, 258; pioneer telephone operators at, 60–61;

New York Telephone Company (*cont.*)
rate increase justifications of, 233; tech-
nology displacement in, 251–52; transfer
by operators from, to private switch-
boards, 318n. 131; turnover at, 99; work-
ing conditions at, 222–23
New York Times, 223–24
New York Tribune, 93
NFTW. *See* National Federation of Tele-
phone Workers
Noble, David, 268n. 10
Norfolk (Virginia), 102, 123
Northrup, Herbert R., 238, 239, 333n. 61
Northwestern Bell Telephone Company,
146
Norwood, Stephen H., 107, 295n. 75, 337n.
8
Novotny, Frank, 230
NTEA. *See* National Telephone Exchange
Association
No. 1 Crossbar switchboards, 133
No. 1 Electronic Switching System (No. 1
ESS), 217
No. 1 Relay switchboards, 34–35, 51, 73, 83,
86, 92
No. 1 Toll switchboards, 36
No. 3 Toll switchboards, 36
No. 4A Toll switchboards, 130–31
No. 4 Toll switchboards, 130
No. 5 switchboards, 130, 132
Nutrition courses, 152–54
Nutt, Emma M., 16–17, 60, 62

Oakland (California), 131, 250
Occupational Job Evaluation Committee,
248, 249, 255
O'Connor, Julia, 109, 110–11
Ohio Bell, 236, 319n. 140, 320n. 19
Oklahoma, 211
Omaha (Nebraska), 78, 127, 320n. 16
Opportunities Industrialization Center
(OIC), 233–34
Orton, Maud, 80

Overseas telephone service, 160, 189, 214,
217, 250, 318n. 124
Overtime, 170

Pacific Bell Telephone Company, 100, 221–
22
Pacific Telephone and Telegraph Company,
77, 107, 200, 320n. 19
Panel switching systems, 122–23, 130, 132,
133, 217, 302n. 45
Part-time workers, 167–68
Patents (for telephone technology), 11, 12,
15, 116–19, 284n. 30
Paternalism (of Bell System), 65–67, 72–
73, 86, 90, 98–99, 136, 156–58, 229,
236, 262. *See also* Welfare programs
Paterson (New Jersey), 71
Patriarchy, 2–4, 138
Patrick, William T., Jr., 233
Pay equity. *See* "Comparable worth"; "Equal
pay for equal work"
Peg counts, 45–46, 51, 128
Penalties. *See* Discipline
Pensions, 72, 98–99, 157
Perry, Marian Wynn, 205
Personal service (by telephone operators):
to attract subscribers, 4, 5, 18–19, 25,
29–30, 39, 53, 55–62, 116, 118, 120–21,
221; decreases in, 49, 55, 81–86, 115,
124–25, 159. *See also* Information
Pettingill, H. J., 96
Phalen, Clifton W., 169, 186, 229
Philadelphia (Pennsylvania), 71, 123, 130,
182, 210, 320n. 16
"Pilot" lights (on switchboards), 46, 83, 92
Pink Ticket Plan, 144, 154
Pittsburgh (Pennsylvania), 80–81, 87, 132,
205
Pittsburgh Survey, 80
Pittsburgh Telephone Company, 320n. 19
Plant Department (of Bell System), 15,
318n. 127, 321n. 21
Point Breeze Association (union), 209

Pope, Henry W., 60
Portland (Oregon), 97, 320n. 16
Post switchboards, 272n. 41, 286nn. 57 and 59
Poughkeepsie (New York), 214
Powell, Adam, 321n. 25
Powell, Adam Clayton, Jr., 202, 235
"Primary markets," 268n. 10
Private Branch Exchanges (PBX), 188, 284n. 34
Productivity: not addressed by labor unions, 110–12; not applicable to men's work, 104; Bell managers on, 169; early technology introduced without regard for, 25–26, 51; increases in, 29, 45–47, 142, 150–51, 160–65, 170, 217, 218–19, 222, 226, 258, 261, 280n. 145; later emphasis on, 29–30, 77–78, 82, 83, 133; measurement of, 45–47, 73–78, 83, 128–29, 218, 219, 226, 241, 261; operators' resistance to, 91–92. See also Engineers
Progressives, 80
Promotions: discrimination in, 72, 213, 227, 242, 256; in telephone industry, 87, 153, 157, 190, 237–38, 240, 242
Proposed Report (Walker), 165–66
Prostitution, 290n. 100
Public relations (Bell System's): about automation, 125, 159, 166–69; goals of, regarding company unions, 144–46; about hiring of African Americans, 227–34; operators' participation in, 154–56, 166
Public utilities: discrimination forbidden in, 196, 202, 256; standards expected of, 165, 203; telephone service as, 147, 270n. 16
Puerto Ricans, 265n. 3

Race: division of labor based on, xi, 4, 198, 211, 227, 237–42, 257, 262; as factor in technology displacement, 227, 234, 239–42, 245, 250–54; and gender used

to prevent working-class solidarity, 3, 226, 243, 262; managerial uses of, 3, 62, 65–67, 196–201, 220, 225–26, 228–33, 236, 240–42, 249–52, 262; as modifier of workplace-related issues, 2; skill defined in terms of, 2, 6, 53, 55; white, as requirement for early Bell System's hiring, 53, 57–62, 65–67, 139; white women's insistence of exclusivity of, 3, 53, 55, 87–88, 134–36, 157, 195–96, 198, 199, 205–10, 225–26, 291n. 114. See also African American men; African American women; Hiring policies; White men; White women
Racial division of labor, xi, 4, 198, 211, 227, 237–42, 257, 262
Racism. See Bell System: discrimination by; Race: managerial uses of; "White lady" image (of telephone operators); White women: racial exclusiveness of
Rates. See Telephone rates
Reassignment Pay Protection Plan (RPPP), 248, 249, 251–52, 254
Recruitment (of telephone operators), 64–67, 213–14, 223–24, 229–35
Reich, Michael, 268n. 10
Representative associations. See Company unions
Restrooms, 209–10, 324n. 71
"Retiring" rooms, 73, 86
Reuse, Mary T., 306n. 35
Robinson, G. P., 97
Rocky Mountain Bell Company, 97, 288n. 72
Roediger, David R., 291n. 114, 323n. 61
Romaine-Callender Automatic Exchange, 118, 298n. 6
Romnes, H. I., 228, 233
Roosevelt, Franklin D., 202, 204
Rotary switching systems, 122
Rozzelle, Frank, 60
Rule and instruction books (of Bell System), 47–52, 75. See also Training

Rural exchanges, 13; automation of, 117, 121; efficiency of, 26, 273n. 49, 276n. 85; operators' importance in, 121; working conditions in, 69–70. *See also specific towns and companies*

Sacha (CWA delegate), 187
St. Louis (Missouri), 71, 100, 102, 202–3, 234, 283n. 21
St. Paul (Minnesota), 101
San Antonio (Texas), 95
Sanders, Lessie, 246–47
San Francisco (California), 70, 106–7, 132
Schacht, John N., 230, 311n. 46, 324n. 71
Schmitt, Katherine M.: on boy operators, 56–58; as pioneer telephone operator, 60–61, 82, 91–92; training school run by, 61, 67, 73
Schuyler, George S., 196
Scientific management, 51, 76–78, 82, 267n. 8
Seattle (Washington), 320n. 16
Secondary markets, 268n. 10
Segregation: of restrooms, 209–10, 324n. 71. *See also* Racial division of labor; Sexual division of labor
Semel, Gay, 224–25
Semi-mechanical systems, 122–23
Service Inspectors, 47
Sexism. *See* Gender: discrimination on basis of
Sexual division of labor, x, xi, 2–3, 60, 104, 237, 239–42, 257, 262, 269n. 13, 318n. 127. *See also* Men's work; Women's work
Shaiken, Harley, 268n. 10
Shawnee (Oklahoma), 102
Sherman Anti-Trust law, 14
Sick leave. *See* Absence control
Single parenthood, 200–201, 242
Skills: changes in, due to new technology, 15, 20–35, 125, 127, 131, 133–36, 241, 262; defined as race and gender, 2, 6, 19, 53, 55, 262; degradation of, 7, 49, 52, 55,

73, 75–77, 79, 89, 112, 125, 131, 217–18, 226, 241–42, 261, 267n. 8; of long distance operators, 37–38, 43, 133; of nineteenth-century operators, 6, 59; physical vs. social, in dial era, 133–36; physical vs. social, in early telephony, 5, 17–20, 29–30, 34, 37–39, 52, 53, 60–62, 81; physical vs. social, in long distance service, 37–39; and wages, 176–77, 180–81, 312n. 63. *See also* Work processes
Smith, Beatrice, 316n. 107
Smith, Charles L., 284n. 31
Smith, Charles R., 293n. 24
Smith, E. B., 96, 97, 105–6
Smith, L. M., 152–53, 306n. 35
Smith-Vassar automatic system, 298n. 6
South: Bell System's preference for black women from, 258; discrimination against African Americans in, 200–201, 210–11, 221, 324n. 62; relations between black and white operators in, 225–26; union organizing in, 100–103, 138, 245–46. *See also specific southern states, cities, and companies*
South Carolina, 210
South Central Bell, 200–201, 221
Southern Association of Bell Telephone Employees, 324n. 62
Southern Bell Telephone and Telegraph Company, 100, 200–201, 210, 243, 305n. 22, 320n. 19, 321n. 29, 333n. 69
Southern California Telephone Company, 320n. 19
Southern Federation of Telephone Workers, 324n. 62
Southern New England Telephone Company, 120–21, 148, 219–20
South Sioux City (Nebraska), 133
Southwestern Bell Telephone Company, 94–96, 101, 202–3, 210, 320n. 19
Southwestern Telephone and Telegraph Company, 95–96

Speed-up. *See* Productivity

"Split tricks," 109, 110, 112, 172, 318n. 127

Spokane (Washington), 320n. 19

"Spread the work" programs, 167, 170

Springfield (Massachusetts), 250

Stanbery, J. N., 199

Standard switchboards, 23–26, 29, 30, 83, 280n. 145

Stannard, A. C., 144, 146

Status (associated with telephone operators), 60, 79, 87–88, 91, 134, 147, 157, 195, 205–6, 213, 218, 220–36, 287n. 66, 312n. 63

Steiss, A. J., 97

Step-by-step switching systems, 122–23, 130, 132, 133, 302nn. 45, 56

Stephens, J. Edward, 202

Stephens, Scott, 247

Stock (for employees), 99, 157, 168, 222. *See also* Dividend payments

Stone, George N., 92

Straley, Walter, 212–13

Straw, Ronnie J., 248

Stress. *See* Illnesses

Strikebreakers, 87, 95–97, 100, 103, 106, 107, 138, 305n. 22

Strikes, 87, 88, 90, 91–93, 138, 283n. 21; from 1900–1920, 80, 95–97, 99–100, 102, 103, 105–7, 127, 293n. 30, 295n. 54, 305n. 22; CWA's positions on, 187–88, 255, 260; fear of, against hiring of African Americans as telephone operators, 206, 208, 209; hate, 324n. 71; ineffectiveness of future, 261; police sympathy for, 97–98; sympathy, for telephone operators, 95, 96, 103, 106, 109, 296n. 83; wildcat, 246, 251; during World War II, 177, 182–83. *See also* Strikebreakers

Strong, Beatrice, 316n. 107

Strowger, Almon B., 118

Strowger Automatic Telephone Exchange, 118, 119, 121, 122–23, 298n. 6

Subscribers: abuse of African American operators by, 195, 224–25; courtesy toward, an operator's requirement, 51, 53, 55–58, 67–69, 79, 182, 223; equipment needed in homes of, 21; objections of, to automation, 159, 164; operators' benefits paid for by, 98; operators forbidden to converse with, 49, 81–83, 86, 116; "personal attention" from telephone operators used to attract, 5, 18–19, 25, 29–30, 39, 119, 120–21, 221; responsibility of early, for wires, 16; role of, in automated service, 117–18, 121–23, 125, 133, 159; role of, in computerized service, 217; use of, in strikes, 96; as white men, 53, 59, 82, 116

Substance abuse, 219–20, 258, 260

Suburbs, 4, 223, 224, 326n. 87, 335n. 105

Sullivan, Teresa, 94, 134, 135

Sunny, B. E., 58, 71, 100

Superior (Wisconsin), 309n. 3

Supervisors (of telephone operators), 46, 48, 49, 72, 79, 82, 91, 105–6, 172, 222, 225–26; African American women as, 198, 235; increase in number of, 128–29, 133; men as, 128, 241; white women as, 241. *See also* Chief Operators; Control; Discipline policies; Managers; Productivity

Supplemental Income Protection Plan (SIPP), 248, 249, 252, 254

Switchboard Committee meetings, 31, 43–44

Switchboard Conference of 1887, 26, 31, 45, 59

Switchboards (manual): African American women hired to work, 227; alleged demands for rearrangement of, 107; continued use of, for long distance, 127; description of early local service, 16–17, 20–35; description of long distance, 35–37; impact of, 3–6, 82, 83, 86; installation and maintenance of, 15, 16, 20; lack of uniformity in early, 20, 70; numbers

Switchboards (manual) (*cont.*)
of operators needed for, compared to automated, 164–65; operators' physical compatibility with, 43–45, 218; "pilot" lights on, 46, 83, 92
Switchman: African American women's attempts to become, 195; author as, ix–x, 333n. 65; deskilling of, 241; duties of, xi, 16–17; retraining of, 254
Sylvan, T. P., 196

Technology (new): Bell System as leader in, xi–xii, 1, 5, 11–12, 14, 36; Bell System's use of, as means of control, 3, 6, 7, 11–12, 25–26, 29, 45–47, 73–78, 82–83, 128–29, 218–19, 224, 226, 227, 241, 261–62; and company unions, 142; cwa's training program regarding, 260–61, 263; displacement due to, affecting minorities more than whites, 227, 234, 239–42, 245, 250–54; displacement due to, affecting women more than men, 178–80, 240, 245, 250–54, 262, 269n. 13; displacement due to, as progress, 168–69, 179, 239–40, 317n. 117; displacement due to, monetary allowances for, 176, 248–49, 252, 254; and efficiency, 280n. 145; expansion of men's work through, 5, 169, 178, 180, 187, 240; importance of labor unions' involvement in conceptualizing, 263; labor unions' failure to address, 104, 110, 111, 179–91, 245, 248–50, 260, 262, 296n. 72; notion that cheap labor inhibits development of, 126; operators' inability to resist, 1–5, 90; in other industries, 297n. 100; possible challenges to, 107; and skill degradation, xi, 7, 57, 91, 261; use of, to maintain services in large cities, 212; women reformers' failure to address, 108–9. *See also* Automation; Computerization; Equipment; Job loss; Skills; Switchboards; Working

conditions; Work processes; *specific kinds of technology*
Technology Change Committees, 248–49
Telephone Employees' Association, 208
Telephone numbers, 123–24, 129–30
Telephone operators: accountability of, 26, 30, 31, 92; African American women as, 7, 195–96, 199–200, 210–36, 250, 329n. 6; compared to servants and factory workers, 4, 53, 79, 87, 213–14, 283n. 24, 287n. 66; courtesy required of, 51, 53, 55–58, 67–69, 79, 182, 223; as dead-end job for women, 72, 153, 213, 227, 234, 240; illnesses associated with, 77–81, 108, 151–52, 219–20, 226, 251, 265n. 1; job loss by, 2, 4–6, 119, 120, 122, 124, 126, 128, 149, 159–70, 179–87; labor pool for, 116, 125–26, 134, 199–202, 210, 212–13, 223–24, 227–32, 288n. 72; language used by, 49, 50, 61, 68, 69, 200, 205, 224–25, 234; as majority of Bell System employees, 15–16; men as, xi, 19, 55–59, 71–72, 237, 240, 243, 250, 256; moral standard for; numbers of, 4–5, 7, 162, 183, 217, 227, 239, 254, 256, 261; "personal attention" by, de-emphasized, 49, 55, 81–86, 115, 124–25, 159; "personal attention" by, emphasized, 4, 5, 18–19, 25, 29–30, 39, 53, 55–62, 116, 119, 120–21, 221; predominance of African American women as, 211–12, 220–33, 250; resistance by, 4, 6, 77–78, 99–112, 115, 116, 126–27, 137–38, 258–60; resistance by, executives' response to, 137–58, 236, 250–51; status associated with, 60, 79, 87–88, 91, 134, 147, 157, 205–6, 213, 218, 287n. 66, 312n. 63; status associated with, decline of, 195, 220–36; "white lady" image of, 2, 3, 5, 53, 57, 57–62, 65–66, 87–91, 103, 104, 133–36, 138, 146–47, 195–96, 200–201, 205–6, 220–26; as young, 65–66, 72, 81, 154, 258, 313n. 75. *See also* Chief Op-

erators; Discipline policies; Hiring; Labor unions; Productivity; Recruitment; Skills; Supervisors; Training; Turnover; Wages; Working conditions; Work processes

Telephone rates, 13, 119, 228, 231, 233, 237, 256; early operators' knowledge of, 17; government investigation of, 165; for long distance, 35, 39–40, 132; low, in early days, 26, 29; operators' benefits paid for through increased, 98

Telephone Review, 206

Telephones: leasing of, 12, 13

Telephone service: as defense industry, 202, 204, 257; first commercial, 20–21; fully automated, 116, 123–33, 298n. 3; growth in, 160–61, 210; improvements in, as primary goal of managers, 51, 57, 82; overseas, 160, 189, 214, 217, 250, 318n. 124; as public utility, 147, 270n. 16. *See also* Local telephone service; Long distance; Technology; Telephone operators; *specific telephone companies*

Telephone Traffic Union (TTU), 182, 246–47

Telephone Worker, 173, 176, 182

Teletypewriters (TWX), 160, 189

Temple (Texas), 95

Temporary National Economic Committee, 168

Temporary workers, 164–65, 185, 309n. 21

Tentler, Leslie Woodcock, 337n. 7

Texas, 95–96

Thayer, H. B., 99, 101

Thompson, Edna, 156

Toll calls. *See* Long distance

Toll switching systems, 217

Towns. *See* Rural exchanges; *specific towns and companies*

Trades and Labor Assembly (Des Moines), 106

Trades and Labor Council of Denver, 102

Traffic Department (of Bell System), 15; statistics of, 45, 140. *See also* Engineers

Traffic Service Position (TSP), 215–21, 227, 258

Trafford, B., 92

Training (for Bell System), 6, 60, 62, 65–69, 73, 86, 87; author's experience of, x; automatic, 218; by CWA on new technology, 260–61, 263; expenses of, 99, 233; federal funds for, of minorities, 228, 231–32, 256, 330n. 19; of "hardcore" employees, 231, 329n. 6; for inefficient operators, 78; length of period for, 180–81, 231; of men in new technology, 180; schools for, 61, 67, 279n. 123; whites' refusal of, for African Americans, 198. *See also* Rule and instruction books

Trunking: defined, 273n. 46; of local calls in cities, 70, 122; of long distance calls, 41, 120, 124, 130, 150

Tubman, Harriet, 213, 234–36, 336n. 1

Tucker, Geneva, 214, 258

Turner, J. L., 68

Turnover (among telephone operators), 93–95, 99, 154, 156–57, 161, 210, 213, 307n. 62, 318n. 127, 326n. 93; benefits of, for Bell System, 94, 99

Tyree, Ron, 214, 250–51, 253

Union for Democratic Action, 204

Union Telephone Operator, 90, 135

United Electrical Radio and Machine Workers (UE), 314n. 80, 315n. 99

U.S. Commission on Industrial Relations, 81

U.S. Constitution, 244

U.S. Department of Labor: funding for training of minorities by, 228, 231–32, 256, 330n. 19; Women's Bureau of, 164, 176–77, 181, 189, 190

U.S. House Subcommittee on Science, Research, and Technology, 248

U.S. Independent Telephone Association, 176

U.S. Patent Office, 11, 12. *See also* Patents

U.S. Post Office, 14, 100–103, 214

U.S. Senate, 81, 93

U.S. Steel, 198

U.S. Supreme Court, 171, 244

United Telephone Operators of America, 170, 171

Universal switchboards, 21

"Unpaid circuit time," 277n. 105

"Upgrade and Transfer Program" (UTP) (of Bell System), 237, 240, 242, 251–52

Urban exchanges. *See* Cities

Urban League, 199, 202, 204, 229

Vail, Theodore N., 14, 100, 123, 137, 138, 270n. 7

Van Meter, J. L. R., 142, 147, 149

Video display terminals (VDTS), 219

Waco (Texas), 95

Wages: adjustments in, due to consent decree, 237; of African American urban telephone operators, 212–14, 227, 256; of clerical workers, 287n. 66, 325n. 82; and company unions, 142, 147–49; of female telephone workers, ix–xi, 3, 58–59, 70–72, 79–81, 87, 96, 97, 110, 116, 125–26, 134, 142, 147–49, 156, 158, 227, 242, 254–55, 287n. 66, 312nn. 63 and 65, 325n. 82; during Great Depression, 164–73; and male craft union ideology, 103–5; of male telephone workers, 3, 71–72, 149, 156, 287nn. 61 and 65, 312n. 65; and merit raises, 148; minimum, 176; operators' criticism of, 90–93; penalties affecting, 78; strikes regarding, 95, 99–103, 182; turnover as means of keeping down, 94; during World War II, 176–79, 313n. 71. *See also* "Equal pay for equal work"

Wagner Act, 171, 173, 208

Walden, Anne H., 213, 234–36, 251–53, 319n. 140

Walker, Paul A., 165–66

Wallace, George Y., 97–98, 288n. 72

War Production Board, 209

Washington, D.C., 73, 132, 177, 182

Waterson, K. W., 124–25, 150

Wattley, Pernella, 221

Waycross (Georgia), 101

Welfare Council, 202

Welfare programs (for telephone workers), 60, 73, 86–87, 90, 98–99, 136, 137, 151–53, 155, 205, 221, 243, 288n. 72

Westcott, W. R., 92

Western Electric Company (WECO): AT&T as holding company for, 14, 336n. 115; as manufacturer of Bell System equipment, 13; products of, 122, 302n. 45; strikes at, 183, 209, 324n. 71, 336n. 116; work of, 15, 271n. 21, 298n. 5

Western Electric Manufacturing Company, 13, 23

Western Union Telegraph Company, 12, 14

"What I Did Today Plan," 144, 154–56

Wheeler, Henry Winfield, 322n. 35

"White lady" image (of telephone operators), 2, 3, 5, 53, 55, 57–62, 65–66, 87–91, 104, 133–36, 138, 146–47, 200–201, 205–6; decline of, 2, 3, 5, 195–96, 220–26; expansion of, 103

White men: in clerical work, 238–39; as craft workers, 5, 211, 254, 318n. 127; domination of telephone workers' unions by, x, xi, 4, 6, 100, 105–6, 109–11, 178–79, 245; fear of female majority in telephone unions of, 178, 296n. 83; fears of, about EEOC, 243, 244; on hiring of African Americans, 228; as less strike happy than young women, 313n. 75; promotions for, in telephone industry, 153; as supervisors, 241; as telephone engineers, 4–5; turnover among, 94–95. *See also* Craft workers; Managers; Men's

work; Race: managerial uses of; Sexual division of labor
White women: acceptance of men's definitions of, 88, 107, 109; characterizations of, by white men, 3, 145–47, 151, 153–54; as consent decree beneficiaries, 237–39, 256; decline in number of, as telephone operator, 211–13; demands of, contrasted with white men's, 103–12; employment possibilities for, 1, 3, 60, 210, 213; expansion of jobs for, after automation, 188–90; hiring of, by Bell System, 1–2, 53, 57–62, 65; managerial assumptions about, 3, 5, 53, 57, 58–65; as outnumbering men in telephone work, 103, 104, 178; privileges of, 221; racial exclusiveness of, 3, 53, 55, 87–88, 134–36, 157, 195–96, 198, 199, 205–10, 225–26, 291n. 114; as supervisors, 241; use of, by union to block other women's progress, 244. See also Race: managerial uses of; Sexual division of labor; "White lady" image (of telephone operators); Women reformers; Women's work
Wichita (Kansas), 97, 101
Wiencek, Ruth, 173
Wigglesworth, Virginia, 316n. 107
Williams, Walter D., 197–98, 204
Williams switchboards, 272n. 41, 286nn. 57 and 59
Wilmington (Delaware), 123, 234
Wilmington (North Carolina), 101
Wilson, C. H., 30, 31
Wilson, Woodrow, 102
Winkler, Ilene, 335n. 112
Women reformers: as operators' allies, 6, 90–91, 93, 104–5, 108–10, 290n. 100, 337n. 8. See also Women's Trade Union League; *specific reform organizations*
Women's Bureau. See U.S. Department of Labor: Women's Bureau of
Women's Trade Union League (WTUL), 100, 108–10, 296n. 87, 337n. 8

Women's work: changes in, due to technology, 1–5, 15–16; Chief Operators as, 48; elements associated with concept of, 2, 53; wages for, 149. See also Labor unions; Skills; Telephone operators; Temporary workers; Wages
Wooding, Nelle, 172–73, 305n. 22, 316n. 107
Work culture (of telephone operators), 89–90
Workday/workweek. See Hours of work
Workers' control, 3–4, 52, 105–6
Workforce reduction. See Job loss
Working-class solidarity: race and gender used to prevent, 3, 226, 243, 262
Working conditions, 5–6; changes in, due to technology changes, 16, 55; decline in, 221, 222–23, 241; for directory assistance operators, 218, 223, 224, 261, 327n. 104; of early telephone operators, 60, 69–73, 76–80, 111; as improved by technology, 169; and labor unions, xi, 103–12; managers' attention to, 43–45; operators' responses to, 4, 88–112, 182; of telephone operators in the 1920s, 156–58; of telephone operators in the 1930s, 160–79; of telephone operators now, 261. See also Job benefits; Productivity; Strikes; Work processes
Working Conditions and Service Quality Improvement Committee, 248, 249
Work loads. See Productivity
Work processes: from 1876–1878, 16–20; from 1878–1900, 20–52; changes in, due to technology, 1, 43, 124–25, 127–29; distribution of, 45–46, 128–29; labor unions' involvement with control of, xi; managers' control over, 6, 29–31, 45–52, 55, 73–79, 82–83, 86–87, 128–29, 142, 218, 226, 241, 261; standardization of, 6. See also Automation; Computerization; Productivity; Skills; Switchboards
World War I: African American women's attempts to be hired as operators during,

World War I (*cont.*)
201–2; telephone industry during, 6,
100–103, 115, 124–25, 178
World War II, 160, 161–63, 176–86, 199–
202, 204, 210; racial integration of Bell
System during, 195, 256; telephone as
defense industry in, 202, 204, 257

Young Men's Christian Association
(YMCA), 202
Young Women's Christian Association
(YWCA), 202

Zenith Telephone Company, 293n. 30

Venus Green is Assistant Professor of History at
the City College of the City University of New York.

Library of Congress Cataloging-in-Publication Data
Green, Venus.
Race on the line : gender, labor, and technology
in the Bell System, 1880–1980 / Venus Green.
p. cm.   Includes bibliographical references and index.
ISBN 0-8223-2554-3 (cloth : alk. paper)
ISBN 0-8223-2573-x (pbk. : alk. paper)
1. AT & T—Employees—History.   2. Telephone
operators—United States—History.
3. Afro-American women—Employment—
United States—History.   I. Title.
HE8846.A55 G64 2001
331.4'813846'08996073—dc21
00-061747